GRASS ROOTS

A Commonsense Action Agenda
for America

SCOTT HENNEN
WITH JIM DENNEY

THRESHOLD EDITIONS
NEW YORK   LONDON   SYDNEY   TORONTO

Threshold Editions
A Division of Simon & Schuster, Inc.
1230 Avenue of the Americas
New York, NY 10020

First Threshold Editions hardcover edition July 2011

For information about special discounts for bulk purchases,
please contact Simon & Schuster Special Sales at
1-866-506-1949 or business@simonandschuster.com.

The Simon & Schuster Speakers Bureau can bring authors to your live event.
For more information or to book an event contact the Simon & Schuster Speakers
Bureau at 1-866-248-3049 or visit our website at www.simonspeakers.com.

Designed by Ruth Lee-Mui

Manufactured in the United States of America

1   3   5   7   9   10   8   6   4   2

ISBN 978-1-4516-0886-1

To the Father, Son, and Holy Spirit
to whom I owe everything;

To my wife, Maria, the love of my life,
and to three of the best kids on the planet:
Alex, Hannah, and Haley;

And to the faithful members of
The Common Sense Club, my listeners,
who put me on this incredible journey

CONTENTS

Real conversation that is transcribed verbatim is often ungrammatical and difficult to follow. Some dialogue from on-air conversations with guests and callers has been edited or restructured for clarity, grammar, and ease of reading. In every case the intent of the speaker has been respected and preserved.

FOREWORD

Upon taking office in 2009, President Barack Obama ushered in a period of profligate spending, an explosion in deficits and our national debt, and an unprecedented increase in the power and reach of the federal government. These threaten not only America's prosperity but also our commitment to limited government and personal freedom.

But thankfully, for every action there is an equal and opposite reaction. Which brings us to the tea party, a powerful new movement with a rich, familiar history. That movement and its history are at the heart of Scott Hennen's excellent and much-needed book, *Grass Roots*.

The tea party movement has drawn a tremendous amount of attention in the last few years—some of it unfavorable, some favorable, but often much of it shallow and cursory. Scott Hennen's volume is different. It provides the keen insights of someone who has an intimate understanding of his subject, someone who has been a part of this grassroots movement from the beginning.

Scott Hennen, a burly and plainspoken radio voice from America's northern plains, explains the spirit and philosophy that gave rise to this movement's passion and energy. He does a marvelous job of capturing its essential nature, including the fact that there is no single organization, no lone leader, and no one plan of action guiding the tea party movement.

Still, there is a single, powerful idea that animates the tea party: America is the greatest nation in history because its government is accountable to the people, not the other way around. In America, the people rule. Our Constitution places confidence in the citizenry by limiting the powers of the state, by defusing its power, by putting checks and balances in place, and by guaranteeing essential liberties.

Yet federal spending's dramatic expansion in the last two years, the current administration's widespread interference in our private economy, and a radical experiment in turning one-sixth of our economy over to government by "reforming health care" could undermine cherished freedoms and accelerate and deepen America's fiscal crisis.

Grass Roots shows how ordinary Americans, many of whom have never before been seriously involved in politics, reacted to this onslaught by speaking out, stepping up, and becoming civically engaged. They organized thousands of local groups, showed up at town hall meetings and rallies, and found creative and powerful ways to make their voices heard in the ballot booth, in America's statehouses, and at both ends of Pennsylvania Avenue.

Hennen chronicles the movement's growth with verve and insight by using the stories of some of its members. He explains their motivations and offers a spirited defense of the tea party against its liberal critics, some of whom defamed the movement and its members.

It's true that some in the tea party movement see themselves as an adjunct of the Republican Party, principally concerned with affecting who gets nominated to carry the GOP banner in elections.

But it's my sense (and Scott's) that most in the tea party don't want it to become simply a GOP auxiliary. Instead, they want to be part of a movement of persuasion, one that educates Americans about the fiscal challenges we face and then holds politicians in both parties accountable. They want the tea party to be like the civil rights, pro-life, and Second Amendment rights movements that have had such a powerful impact on public opinion and our nation.

The tea party movement is changing our country politically, economically, and culturally. In the 2010 election, for example, the tea party helped draw to the polls a higher percentage of the voter-eligible population than in any other midterm contest since 1982. It also helped move a huge swath of independent voters into the GOP column in 2010: independents voted for Republican candidates by a 59 percent to 38 percent margin, a 24-point swing away from the Democrats just two years ago and a staggering 36-point swing to the GOP from four years ago.

Economically, the tea party is not only putting pressure on lawmakers to cut spending and re-limit government; it is also inspiring many Americans to reconsider their own individual circumstances and even spurring them to put their own fiscal houses in order. They're paying down debt, saving more, and developing more responsible plans for their families' needs and their own retirements.

But perhaps the biggest influence the tea party is having is in the realm of our culture, inspiring a recommitment to personal responsibility, self-reliance, and the age-old American belief that we owe future generations a nation that is stronger and better than the one we inherited. Much of that has been lost in the last few years. The tea party is a movement that is trying to reclaim these things. It believes a return to first principles is the best way forward. So does Scott Hennen.

Grass Roots is not simply a marvelous account of a remarkable political movement. It is also an effort by a man who loves America to tell the story of a movement that is trying to reclaim the best of America.

—Karl Rove

DINNER-TABLE DEMOCRACY

I was born into a radio family in Montevideo, Minnesota. My parents, Jerry and Jeanette Hennen, were both in the radio business. They gave me opportunities to work part-time in radio from when I was twelve years old. The people in and around Montevideo could tune in to Radio KDMA on Sunday mornings and hear my voice change right on the air. I grew up loving the broadcast business; it was all I knew.

In those days, standard radio fare consisted of music, news, and farm reports. Talk radio, as we know it today, didn't exist. Oh, sure, there were talk shows of a sort going all the way back to the 1950s, with rude, abrasive hosts like Joe Pyne or oddball hosts like Long John Nebel. But *conservative* talk radio—talk with a passion for American values of faith, freedom, justice, and equality—still waited to be invented.

Though Mom and Dad got me into the radio game, I got into *talk* radio because of a fellow named Ronald Wilson Reagan. I was in high school when Reagan was president of the United States. I didn't fully understand what was happening in the wide world of politics and global events, but I knew this much: Ronald Reagan was inaugurated during a time of crisis, when the inflation rate was 11.8 percent, unemployment was at 7.5 percent,[1] our military was in disrepair, and America was retreating in the face of Soviet expansionism. But when

Ronald Reagan took charge, *he took charge*. Within the first few years of his presidency, he had revived the U.S. economy, restored our military, and had begun to turn the tables on the Soviet Union. Whenever I heard this man speak of his love for America, I thought, "What a leader! I'd follow this man off a cliff!"

I have always felt a special affinity for Ronald Reagan, in part because he began his professional career in the radio business, broadcasting at Radio WOC in Davenport, Iowa, and at Radio WHO in Des Moines. I could imagine nothing better than sitting behind a radio microphone and talking about the same values and ideals that Reagan presented in his speeches. I had never heard of anyone doing that on the radio—but I was sure that if I had the chance, I could make the format work. So my love of country, love of politics, and love of radio all intersected at once, and I started my first talk show in 1986—the first of its kind in North Dakota.

That was two years before Rush Limbaugh started his New York–based national show, which has become the template for conservative talk radio at the local and national level. Rush, of course, is a genius without peer, and the ultimate role model for all of us in conservative talk radio. But in those pre-Rush days, I was inventing and re-inventing my own format from day to day. I called my first show *Valley Talk,* and that show evolved into *Hot Talk,* which evolved into *The Common Sense Club,* the show I host today. My talk show platform has given me the opportunity to interview thousands of newsmakers, including Presidents Jimmy Carter, George H. W. Bush, Bill Clinton, and George W. Bush. Vice President Dick Cheney has been a frequent guest on my show, and I have been honored to accept several invitations to the White House and the Oval Office.

I never got to meet Ronald Reagan personally—though I came very close. When my dad was a salesman for the radio station where I worked, he was invited to a White House press event with President Reagan. Dad was going to take me with him, but my boss heard about the invitation and pulled rank on us. He went to the White House instead, and took his daughter—so I didn't get to go.

On two occasions as a radio reporter, I got to cover President Reagan. In October 1986, the president came to Grand Forks, North Dakota, to speak at a campaign event for Senator Mark Andrews. I covered the event and was awed by the opportunity to see the Great Communicator in person.

Then, in February 1988, President Reagan went to Mazatlan, Mexico, for a summit with Mexican president Miguel de la Madrid Hurtado. By coincidence, I was going to be in Mexico on radio station business at the same time, so I obtained press credentials and covered his trip. I took with me a life-size cardboard cutout of the president that we used for promotions at the radio studio. When I wasn't covering the summit, I took the cutout to the beach at Mazatlan and made a small fortune from people who wanted to get their picture taken with "President Reagan."

Ronald Reagan was, without a doubt, the greatest president of the twentieth century. The moment he placed his hand on the Bible and took the oath of office, America began to change. We were all inspired by the Gipper's sunny optimism, his love of freedom, and his vision of America as a "shining city on a hill." To this day, I get misty-eyed when I remember his speeches about our country and his passionate love for the principles on which this nation was founded.

I've never gotten a case of the warm fuzzies while watching President Obama bow and scrape before foreign dictators and apologize for America. I know MSNBC commentator Chris Matthews claims he gets a thrill down his leg listening to our Apologizer-in-Chief, but I haven't had the pleasure of experiencing that thrill myself. Oh, it definitely feels like somebody's doing *something* on my leg when Obama talks—and then he tells me it's raining.

It's certainly a contrast to what I grew up with. President Reagan inspired me in my youth, and he continues to inspire me daily. For example, in his farewell address to the nation on January 11, 1989, he said, "All great change in America begins at the dinner table. So, tomorrow night in the kitchen, I hope the talking begins. And children, if your parents haven't been teaching you what it means to be an American, let 'em know and nail 'em on it. That would be a very American thing to do."[2]

This is profound thinking: All the truly meaningful changes in

America begin in the American home, within the American family—
at the grassroots level. The truly great social shifts in American culture
aren't instigated by a president or senator or a Supreme Court justice.
All great change begins as grassroots citizens see their duty to their
country and to future generations, then lay aside their own pursuits
and ambitions, and get involved in the fight to preserve this idea we
call America.

But it's getting harder and harder to keep food on that dinner table
Reagan was talking about, isn't it? That's because *61.34 percent of
your family income* is consumed by the government (including taxation and the cost of government regulation, according to Americans
for Tax Reform Foundation and Center for Fiscal Accountability).
This means that you, as an American wage earner, are forced to work
from January 1 to August 12 each year just to pay the government,
before you start paying yourself.[3] We are tax slaves, staggering under
a crushing burden of out-of-control spending and federal debt. And
the people we sent to Washington to defend our freedom are the very
ones who have sold us into this slavery . . . the ones who have stolen
the food from our dinner tables.

That's why grassroots Americans are angry. That's why we are saying, "Enough! No more! We are taking our country back!" *That* is
the great change that begins at home—grassroots, dinner-table democracy, exactly what Ronald Reagan urged us to do.

Reagan also told us, "Concentrated power has always been the
enemy of liberty."[4] And that is why liberty has been on the ropes in
recent years. It was concentrated power, governing against the will
of the people, that gave us hundreds of billions of dollars' worth of
bailouts and "stimulus" spending. It was concentrated power that
gave us Obamacare, a federal usurpation of one-sixth of the American economy. It was concentrated power that gave us the so-called
"Dodd-Frank Wall Street Reform and Consumer Protection Act,"
one of the greatest legislative outrages in American history—brazenly
authored by and named for two of the worst villains in the financial
meltdown of 2008, Senator Christopher Dodd and Representative
Barney Frank. Again and again, since the inauguration of Barack

Obama as president, we have seen our liberties stripped away by the concentrated power in Washington, D.C.

The good news is that grassroots Americans see what is happening to their country, and they are taking the power of the people into the town hall meetings and tea party rallies and right to the steps of the Capitol in Washington. Grassroots Americans are speaking truth to power, and "the powers that be" will soon become "the powers that were."

It's my privilege to be the chairman of the Common Sense Club, this town hall meeting of the airwaves where grassroots Americans from across the heartland gather to share information and encourage each other to fight the good fight. A listener once told me, "You keep the airwaves crackling"—but the truth is that you and all the other grassroots Common Sense Club members truly make the airwaves crackle. And it's you, visiting my website at scotthennen.com, who truly make the Internet crackle as well. You are not just a spectator to these momentous events in our time—you choose to be involved, to add your voice to the growing chorus of voices calling for smaller, more responsive, more responsible government. You choose to *make change happen*.

You and I, working together at the grassroots level, are making dinner-table democracy a reality. In homes across the nation, and at the tea party rallies in city parks and parking lots and backyards around the country, the talking has begun, and great change is beginning.

The media and politicians of both parties like to portray us as radicals and extremists—but there's nothing radical or extreme about the change we are calling for. We are simply telling our leaders: "Obey the Constitution. Don't spend more money than the government takes in. Defend liberty. Support our troops and their mission. Let us raise our kids and worship our God freely, as we see fit." That's it. That's all we're asking. And for that, the ruling class and the chattering class call us "radical" and "extreme"?

This agenda is just plain old common sense.

The founding fathers believed in the importance of common sense.

They wrote about it in the Declaration of Independence when they said, "We hold these truths to be self-evident. . . ." What does that phrase mean? It means: "It's just common sense. Anyone can see the truth of the matter. It's as plain as the nose on your face."

What are the obvious, commonsense truths we hold to be self-evident? "That all men are created equal, that they are endowed by their Creator with certain unalienable Rights, that among these are Life, Liberty and the pursuit of Happiness." And you can't argue with that logic.

But now our government leaders, who are bereft of common sense, are taxing and spending at an insane rate, depriving us of our way of Life, threatening our Liberty, and road-blocking our pursuit of Happiness. They are turning working Americans into tax slaves, and trapping nonworking Americans in a cycle of dependency on government checks. I hold these truths to be self-evident, that America can't go on this way, that our economy and our society are headed for collapse, that something must be done.

And since our leaders in Washington won't do it, it's up to you and me. It's up to grassroots Americans. We have to band together and help restore America to sanity. And we can do it. Grassroots Americans built this country, and grassroots Americans can save it.

In the coming pages, I'm going to reveal to you a commonsense agenda for transforming America at the grassroots level—real dinner-table democracy. I'm going to show you what grassroots Americans are already doing to bring about great change in America—making a difference, defending freedom, and saving America for future generations. And I'm going to show you, step-by-step, what *you* can do, right where you are, to make a meaningful difference in the destiny of your country. Throughout this book, we'll explore such questions as:

- What is the tea party movement? How do I get involved?
- Why is the tea party movement always under attack in the media?
- What can one person do to help make government smaller and more responsive to the people?
- What can I do to support our military and help fight terrorism?

- How can I sort out the claims and counterclaims about energy and the environment? What can I do to help secure America's energy future?
- With the news media so full of biased and dishonest reporting, what can one person do to hold media accountable for the truth?
- What can I do to help restore the economy and put people back to work?
- How can I get involved in the fight to defend human life against the onslaught of abortion, health care rationing, and "death panels"?
- How can I defend my First Amendment right to boldly live out my faith and speak up for my beliefs in the public square?

These are the questions I'll answer in the coming chapters. Each chapter is followed by what I call "The Commonsense Action Agenda"—a step-by-step list of grassroots actions you, your family, and your neighbors can take to make a difference for America. This is your handbook for getting effectively, patriotically involved right now.

History is about to be made, my friend. You and I have a part to play.

Let's get started.

1

GRASSROOTS PEOPLE JUST LIKE YOU

In September 2008, as America prepared to choose its next leader, all economic hell broke loose. The biggest financial companies in the nation staggered toward collapse—Goldman Sachs, Lehman Brothers, Merrill Lynch, Fannie Mae, Freddie Mac, and insurance giant AIG. Global investment giant Bear Stearns and mortgage lender IndyMac had already failed earlier in the year. On September 15, Lehman Brothers filed for Chapter 11, the largest bankruptcy filing in American history.

Into this atmosphere of panic stepped Treasury secretary Hank Paulson. According to Senator James Inhofe of Oklahoma, Paulson made a conference call to members of Congress on September 19. He told legislators they needed to meet in emergency session and give him the authority to buy up so-called "toxic debt" held by financially troubled institutions—to the tune of hundreds of billions of dollars. If Congress failed to do so, Paulson claimed, the nation faced economic disaster "far worse than the Great Depression." The result, he said, would be civil disorder and martial law.

Congress believed Paulson's dire warnings. Both Democratic candidate Barack Obama and Republican senator John McCain supported Paulson's call for a Wall Street bailout. McCain even suspended his campaign and flew to Washington to help shove the plan through Congress. The American people smelled a rat, and opposed the bailout by a margin of three to one (in some polls, four to one). But legislators listened to Secretary Paulson, not the American people, and they gave him $700 billion and czarlike authority under a program called TARP (Troubled Asset Relief Program).

But did Paulson buy up "toxic debts" as he had promised? No! Inhofe says that Paulson abandoned his plan "the day after he got the money."[1] Instead of purchasing troubled assets, Paulson (the former CEO of Goldman Sachs) injected the money directly into several companies, including $85 billion for AIG—and AIG used those taxpayer dollars to repay a $13 billion debt to Goldman Sachs, Paulson's former employer.[2] Inhofe now says that Paulson employed a classic bait-and-switch technique, using dire predictions of economic and social calamity to stampede the Congress into coughing up hundreds of billions of taxpayer dollars to provide welfare for Wall Street.[3]

On September 26, 2008, as Congress heatedly debated Paulson's bailout proposal, I had former Speaker of the House Newt Gingrich on my radio show. "I think for most Americans," he said, "it should be very discouraging to watch their government ask them to give $700 billion away to people who tried to get rich and failed, and who believed in capitalism as long as they were winning, and now would like to have socialism to bail them out."

I asked Newt if he could see any free market alternatives to the TARP bailouts.

"There are a lot of steps you could take," he replied. "For example, you could open a window at Treasury and say, 'We will loan money at the cost of Treasury lending plus two percent to anyone who wants to come in. We will give you five years to work this out, but you're going to have to work it out.' Now, I could accept a workout. But I'm against a bailout."

"What would happen to the economy if there were no bailouts?" I asked.

"Ultimately," Newt said, "these financial institutions would go to bankruptcy court and the bankruptcy court would sell them. And somebody like Warren Buffett would show up and buy them. And you would have a shakeout. We've done this historically many times.

We did it in 1907, in 1919, in 1929. We did it for real estate in 1974. We did it for the savings and loan institutions in the 1980s."

But we did not let the free market take its course in 2008. Instead, the Congress gave us the TARP bailouts, the nationalization of banks and car companies, stimulus, "Cash for Clunkers," and trillions in new debt.

The TARP boondoggle was a wake-up call to a vast segment of the American people, especially in the heartland of America. In call after call from my radio listeners, I heard America's frustration mounting and its blood pressure rising. People wanted to know why leaders of both parties were meeting in secret, cutting backroom deals, saying one thing and doing another, while arrogantly asserting the right to give our hard-earned tax money to Wall Street "wizards" who took home million-dollar bonuses after bankrupting their companies. The American people didn't want bailouts for Wall Street, but the "ruling class" in Washington (weren't they supposed to be our *servants?*) wouldn't listen.

Barack Obama's campaign slogan of "hope and change" connected with voters, especially those who shortsightedly assumed, "I might as well vote for change—Obama can't be any worse than Bush!" The American people would soon discover that it could, in fact, get worse. A lot worse.

In February 2009, soon after Barack Obama's inauguration, the Democrat-controlled Congress passed a $787 billion "stimulus" bill and President Obama signed it into law. It was largely a gift to public-sector employee unions at taxpayer expense. President Obama and the Democrats would eventually spend hundreds of billions more to nationalize General Motors, to bail out Chrysler, to run the "Cash for Clunkers" car buyback scheme, and ultimately to nationalize the entire health care system—one-sixth of the entire U.S. economy.

On February 19, 2009, after the Obama administration announced a $75 billion program to subsidize mortgages for delinquent homeowners, CNBC business reporter Rick Santelli led an on-air revolt from the floor of the CME Group in Chicago. "The government is promoting bad behavior," Santelli ranted on camera. "This is

America! How many of you people want to pay for your neighbor's mortgage? . . . Raise your hands!" When others on the floor shouted their agreement, Santelli added, "President Obama, are you listening? We're going to have a Chicago Tea Party!"[4]

Eight days after the Santelli rant, I was in Washington, D.C., doing my show from CPAC (Conservative Political Action Conference) 2009. There, I interviewed many of the movers and shakers in the conservative movement, including Grover Norquist, president of Americans for Tax Reform. We were just one month into the Obama administration, and it was already clear that President Obama intended to spend us all into oblivion. So I asked, "How do we as conservatives stop this Obama juggernaut?"

"We need to bring all of the outside groups together," Grover said. "Whether you care about the Second Amendment or traditional values or taxes, everybody is threatened by this administration." The "outside groups" that Grover Norquist spoke about sound remarkably like the groups we now know as "tea parties."

After the show, I handed Grover that day's *Wall Street Journal* with an article by the paper's Congress reporter, Naftali Bendavid. The piece reported that Obama and the Democrat-controlled Congress proposed providing an *additional* $250 billion for troubled banks (on top of the already-passed TARP bailout) while reducing the tax benefits of charitable giving for large-income donors (which would devastate private charities). Democrats, wrote Bendavid, "were generally enthusiastic about Mr. Obama's first budget, and said they plan to move it quickly through Congress."[5]

It was infuriating to see the liberals in Washington steering America to the far left, driving the nation toward ruinous spending while killing incentives for charitable giving. I said, "Grover, what we need are massive protests—call them 'tea parties' after the Boston Tea Party—a huge national uprising to tell the government, 'No more taxing. No more spending. No more deficits. Stop taking away our freedoms, stop piling debt onto our children.' We need to make a stand and symbolically dump the tea in the harbor."

Even though the video of Rick Santelli's CNBC rant was just starting to go viral on the Internet at that point, I had not heard about it. But the American people were reeling from the shock of the federal spending spree—from the TARP bailouts to the Obama stimulus plan (passed on February 17) to all the spending that President Obama and the Democrats had proposed. Americans were furious at the sight of the government spending their money like it was trash. It was inevitable that people would invoke the image of the Boston Tea Party to express their rage.

I came back from CPAC and began talking to grassroots conservatives in Fargo-Moorhead and Grand Forks about organizing a "Tax Day Tea Party." Planning had scarcely begun before the Red River started rising and we saw that we were in for the flood fight of our lives. So we had to put off our tea party plans until August.

The idea of a tea party tax revolt, modeled after the Boston Tea Party of 1773, was like a spark falling on dry grass. It caught fire across the nation. The American people were already in a revolutionary mood, angered and frustrated because their leaders were not listening. There's no single leader, no one group or organization behind this movement. It sprang into existence by spontaneous combustion. As Michael Reagan once said, the tea party movement "is as grassroots as your front lawn."

The most phenomenal feature of the tea party movement was that it was made up of ordinary folks—"salt of the earth" people who have spent their lives earning a living, raising their families, going to church, paying their taxes. These are people who have never carried a protest sign or shouted a slogan in their lives. But they had seen their government turn a dangerous corner. The arrogant ruling class in Washington, D.C., was piling up debt and redistributing wealth at an alarming rate, then handing the bill for all this extravagance to future generations.

Here in the heartland and across America, the people understood something our so-called leaders were too dense and corrupt to understand: Government is too big. Taxes are too high. Inept government policies had produced a near 10 percent unemployment rate, a $15 trillion national debt (growing at $3.9 billion per day), and more than $100 trillion in unfunded entitlement liabilities. Meanwhile, government printing presses were churning out worthless currency, dooming the nation to a future of runaway inflation.

The 2008 economic crisis didn't "just happen," like a change in the weather. It wasn't a failure of the free market system. *Government made it happen*. Every one of these crises, without exception, was triggered by inept and arrogant government—by people *we* elected, but who are openly contemptuous of the will of the people. We the People have had it. We are rising up and cleaning house and restoring common sense to our government.

A SLEEPING GIANT HAS AWAKENED

Grassroots Americans made plans to hold their first tea party rallies on Tax Day: April 15, 2009. Propelled by passion and patriotism, they used new and traditional media—blogs, Facebook, Twitter, and talk radio—to spread the word. The Tax Day protests were held in small towns and big cities across America, drawing hundreds of thousands of people; North Dakotans held a huge Tax Day tea party in Bismarck, though I was unable to attend, due to the floods. More tea party events followed in May and June, with a huge coast-to-coast tea party rally on July 4. The first tea party I attended was in Bismarck on July 2, after the floodwaters subsided. Thousands turned out in Fargo and Grand Forks—and those protests were really the beginning of the end for our own Senators Byron Dorgan and Kent Conrad and Representative Earl Pomeroy.

Then came the Taxpayer March on Washington on September 12, which drew a crowd estimated (by FreedomWorks, one of the event organizers) at 600,000 to 800,000 people. One of my listeners, Becky Skogen from Canby, Minnesota, was there. She told me, "When we got up to the front lawn of the Capitol and turned around, we could look in every direction and not see the end of the crowd."

In early November, on the eve of the House health care vote, Congresswoman Michele Bachmann (R-Minnesota) called my show and asked my listeners to drop everything and come to D.C. to "pay a house call on Nancy Pelosi." My listeners responded in droves, trekking by plane, car, RV, or chartered bus to the nation's capital. One of my listeners, Julie Sorensen, a mom from Moorhead, Minnesota, boarded a bus with her two teenagers. She couldn't afford to go, but other listeners donated funds to make her trip possible. All along the way, she emailed progress reports: "We're on the bus and ready to roll! . . . Hearing rumors that legislators will try to keep us away. . . . We're in D.C.! Hey, Congress, can you hear us now? Kill the bill! Kill the bill!"

Those who were there that day knew they had just witnessed a new and unprecedented phenomenon in America—a vocal-yet-peaceful protest, a quiet riot of everyday Americans who wanted to save their nation and preserve its blessings for future generations.

And that phenomenon is still going on. The tea parties, town halls, marches, and protests have just begun. The movement is gathering steam and gaining momentum. The people are going to have their say, and the government will have to listen.

A sleeping giant has awakened.

In the early days of those tea party gatherings, I always asked for a show of hands from people who are protesting for the very first time. Invariably, hands went up from 80 percent or more of the crowd. Tea partiers are not rabble-rousers or malcontents by nature. They are not (as Nancy Pelosi has called them) "Astroturf"—meaning, fake grass roots that have been ginned up by the Republican Party or in some other centralized strategy. These are ordinary Americans—the authentic voice of this country.

They have sprung up spontaneously, and are discovering they are not alone in their love of country and their fear of where America is headed. They are showing up at town hall meetings of their elected representatives and lecturing these so-called public servants on their constitutional duties. This leaderless movement is leading the so-called leaders.

The tea party activists are speaking truth to power—and the people in power don't like it one bit.

MAKING THE POWERFUL SQUIRM

Michael and Julie Liffrig love their country and they're doing everything they can to save America for the next generation. They have a lot invested in America's future, because they are raising nine children on a five-hundred-acre ranch west of the North Dakota capital city of Bismarck. Mike is an attorney, mediator, jury consultant, and owner of First Court in Bismarck. In 2004, he ran unsuccessfully as a Republican candidate for United States Senate against longtime Democrat incumbent Byron Dorgan. Julie has a degree in elementary education and a master's in public health, and together she and Mike homeschool their children.

During our national health care debate in late 2009, Julie called my show with a report on Senator Kent Conrad's town hall meeting in Center, North Dakota, about forty miles northwest of Bismarck. "There were about a hundred people at Senator Conrad's event—and I'm afraid he had to lecture all of us again and again for our lack of manners."

"Are you telling me that you and the good people of Center, North Dakota, were *rude* to Senator Conrad?"

"I'm afraid we were, Scott. He said we kept interrupting him."

I laughed. "Tell me what happened."

"Well, there was a young man, about twenty-two years old, who spoke very articulately. He had read the Obamacare bill, he knew what was in it, and he asked Senator Conrad some very pointed and specific questions. Senator Conrad was very defensive. When this young man asked why the health care bill permits taxpayer-funded abortions, the senator said, 'I've been very clear about that. I told you, I support the Hyde Amendment, which does not allow federal funding for abortions.' "

"He wanted you to shut up and accept his answer."

"Exactly. But when you read the actual provisions of the bill, you find that the Hyde Amendment doesn't apply. The Hyde Amendment has to be reauthorized year by year—and you can't depend on a Democratic president and a Democratic Congress to vote that way. So the problem of taxpayer-funded abortions is very real. When this young man tried to point out that Senator Conrad was not addressing the issue, the senator accused him of interrupting and he lectured us all about our 'bad manners.' "

"Julie," I inquired, "did anyone ask Senator Conrad if he'd be willing to support language in the bill that explicitly states, in no uncertain terms, that taxpayer funds will not be spent for abortions under the Obamacare plan? He needs to know that people won't accept wiggle room and deceptive language from these politicians."

"The young man asked Senator Conrad how he planned to ensure that taxpayer dollars would not be used for abortions. But the senator simply repeated, over and over, 'I support the Hyde Amendment,' as if that answered the question. Another young person, a fifteen-year-old girl, also pressed him on that point. But the senator seemed impatient and frustrated, and he just repeated, 'I support the Hyde Amendment.' "

"What did the other folks in the meeting think?"

"I interviewed about a half a dozen people who had gone to the meeting. The people of Center were disappointed. They thought of it as *their* town meeting, and they felt Senator Conrad was supposed to listen to *them*. But the senator kept referring to it as *his* meeting. 'This is how I'm going to run *my* meeting,' he said. Scott, I don't think these politicians realize how condescending they look. I feel especially bad for the young people who attend. Is this what Senator Conrad wants to present to the next generation—the image of a government that refuses to listen? A government that says 'Shut up and quit interrupting while I tell you how the government will run your life'?"

"Keep holding his feet to the fire, Julie," I said.

And the tea party movement did hold Senator Conrad's feet to the fire. The result: in January 2011, he announced his decision to retire rather than run for reelection in 2012.

Senator Conrad's announcement came exactly one year after North Dakota's other Democratic senator, Byron Dorgan, surprised voters by announcing his retirement. That announcement effectively ended a forty-year career in elected office. Senator Dorgan's only explanation was that he was leaving politics to pursue other interests.

But you and I know the real reason. The tea parties and town hall meetings and people like Julie Liffrig proved to Conrad and Dorgan that they could no longer survive as blue senators in a red state. They could no longer pretend to represent the people of North Dakota while representing the special interests in Washington, D.C.

Thanks to the new media, and especially the interactive dimension of talk radio, the people were on to them. They were asking all the right questions. They were speaking truth to power—and they were making the powerful squirm.

WHY WE ARE ANGRY

Another North Dakota elected official who hid from tea party supporters was Congressman Earl Pomeroy—North Dakota's only at-large representative for the entire state over nine terms. After seeing the tough questioning that Senators Conrad and Dorgan faced at town hall meetings, Pomeroy resorted to what he called a "tele-townhall meeting." He refused to hold a single face-to-face meeting with the people who elected him. Instead, he held a tightly controlled teleconference event stacked with political allies.[6]

When I spoke at tea party events in North Dakota, I called him out. "Hey, Earl," I said, "what's a 'tele-townhall meeting'? What are we, the great unwashed? Are you afraid to walk among your constituents, for crying out loud? Earl, come on my radio show! We'll let the people ask you their questions, and you can give an answer that *everyone* can hear! Of course, you might have to talk to someone who disagrees—but isn't that what you're paid to do?"

Needless to say, not a peep from Congressman Pomeroy. And that's why, on November 2, 2010, his constituents voted him out of office.

Don't get me wrong. I'm not saying Earl Pomeroy is a bad guy. Though he and I are at loggerheads politically, I consider him a friend—the kind of friend you find yourself jousting with again and again. We have actually fought a number of battles as allies. For example, Earl and I worked closely together during the flood of 1997, and I gave him high marks for his hard work on behalf of the people of North Dakota during the flood fight.

Earl and I also forged a bond of friendship in the early days of the War on Terror, when the 142nd Engineering Battalion of the North Dakota National Guard was deployed to Iraq. Earl's support for our Guard soldiers in Iraq could not be faulted.

I often talked to members of the 142nd on the air. On one occasion, the soldiers of our Guard unit told the story of an Iraqi citizen called "Mr. M." This man had been imprisoned by Saddam Hussein's regime, and he was so grateful to the Americans for the liberation of Iraq that he provided valuable help to our troops. On several occasions, he pointed out terrorist bomb-making sites where IEDs (improvised explosive devices, such as roadside bombs) were assembled.

When the terrorists found out that Mr. M was helping the Americans, they murdered him in front of his teenage son. From then on, Mr. M's widow and seven children feared for their lives. So our soldiers turned to our government for help in getting the family out of Iraq. Congressman Earl Pomeroy went to Iraq, met with the soldiers, and took this family on as his personal cause. He was instrumental in cutting through red tape and getting them to the United States.

My wife, Maria, and I welcomed Mr. M's widow and children to North Dakota and helped them get settled in their apartment. When I think of how hard Earl worked to get them to safety, I'm truly grateful. So while I'm at odds with Earl Pomeroy politically, while I'm critical of the way he ducked his constituents in 2010, I see him as a friend, and I'll never forget the good things he's done. I'm convinced he'd be in office today if he had voted with his constituents instead of voting with Nancy Pelosi during the Obamacare debate. And holding a few town hall meetings around the state would have helped a lot.

I get a kick out of the media fascination with the tea parties and town hall meetings. I hear the pundits say, "Did you see what happened at that town hall meeting? Those people actually raised their voices! They really sounded angry!" But you know what? There's *nothing wrong* with being angry! In fact, if you see your country being systematically dismantled and driven into a black hole of debt by your elected leaders, you *ought* to be angry. There's something seriously wrong with anyone who is *not* angry!

Politicians should not be afraid to face the anger of their constituents. Even if the people raise their voices and wave their signs, they're good folks who love their country. They just want to be heard. The political careers of Pomeroy, Conrad, and Dorgan ended because they chose to ignore the people. (Pomeroy was defeated in the November 2010 election, and Conrad and Dorgan both announced their retirements rather than face defeat at the hands of an angry electorate.) Yet there's something in this state that we call "North Dakota nice." The people of North Dakota disagreed with what their elected leaders were doing, yet these politicians could have scored a lot of points if they had simply taken the time to listen and understand the concerns of the people.

When people feel no one is listening, what do they do? They shout! They bang on the table and shake their fists in the air! The anger of the tea party movement offended the delicate sensibilities of liberal journalists, entertainers, and politicians. *Newsweek* called the thousands of tea party activists protesting Obamacare at the Capitol steps "just a few hundred people who are angry at the government."[7] Bill Clinton compared the anger of the tea party movement to the Oklahoma City bomber, saying, "When you get mad, sometimes you end up producing the exact opposite result of what you say you are for."[8] President Obama said of the tea party movement, "Their anger is misdirected."[9] Singer Sheryl Crow said the tea partiers were "not sure what they're angry about."[10] And Harry Smith of CBS News asked, "Can anger govern?"[11]

Anger doesn't come naturally to the grass roots. Here in the heartland, people are generally friendly, trusting, and peace-loving. It takes a lot to get us riled. But we know when we are being lied to, when our vote is taken for granted, and when our children's future is being stolen. And that's when we get angry.

In the red state of North Dakota, conservative people voted time after time for Senators Conrad and Dorgan and Congressman Pomeroy, liberal Democrats all. North Dakotans believed them when they came home to the state masquerading as "moderates" or "blue dog Democrats," wearing flannel shirts and talking in a down-home accent, telling us, "I'm fighting for you in Washington!" Yet these same politicians couldn't wait to get back to their Georgetown cocktail parties and those marble halls, where they voted 99 percent of the time with Harry Reid and Nancy Pelosi. It took Barack Obama and his big-government agenda to wake us up and make us realize that we had been hoodwinked all these years.

I call Congresswoman Michele Bachmann of Minnesota "the chairperson of the Common Sense Club Caucus" in the United States House of Representatives. She credits me with giving her the idea for the tea party caucus in the House. When she began the tea party caucus, the mainstream media hyperventilated and said it was crazy to give the tea party movement a voice in the legislative branch. But Michele calmly responded, "We are not going to be the mouthpiece of the tea party. . . . We are here to listen."[12]

During one of her appearances on my show, we talked about the anger of grassroots Americans toward their elected representatives. Michele said, "How else should the American people respond? When President Barack Obama and the United States Congress continue to thwart the will of the American people and spend money that we don't have and put a government bureaucracy in charge of the entire health care system, what else would they expect the American people to do? The anger we see and hear all around us is a revival of the Spirit of 1776. The people are saying, 'We are Americans! We won't allow you to shove your European-style socialism down our throats! We will vote, we will march, we will take our country back!' "

She's right. Freedom is under attack. Democracy is in peril because of a runaway federal government—and *that's* why we're angry. It's not an out-of-control rage. It's called *righteous indignation*—and it's the same kind of positive, constructive anger that founded America. As Michele says, it's "the Spirit of 1776."

It's important to understand that our grassroots anger is not a partisan emotion. We in the tea party movement are just as angry with arrogant, ruling-class Republicans as we are with arrogant, ruling-class Democrats. What many in the media don't seem to understand is that there is a sharp divide between tea party Republicans like Michele Bachmann and what I call "cocktail party Republicans" who are almost indistinguishable from the Democrats.

Grassroots Americans won't stand for one more assault on our values. We are not going to accept any more TARPs or stimulus plans or Cash for Clunkers schemes or record deficits or soaring debt. We have drawn a line in the sand, and any politician, Republican or Democrat, who crosses that line does so at the risk of his or her career.

SANDBAGGING THE WASHINGTON ELITISTS

The Red River of the North forms the border between North Dakota and Minnesota. The Fargo-Moorhead metro area, where my broadcast studio is located, straddles the banks of the Red River. The river is prone to flooding the prairie lands every spring because its waters flow northward and tend to pile up and overflow the banks when it hits unmelted ice farther north. The area is especially in peril if the spring thaw is sudden and dumps too much snowmelt into the river at once. One major flood along the Red River occurred in 1997, devastating the city of Grand Forks. During that flood, the river at Fargo-Moorhead reached a level of 39.6 feet—and many experts thought it was the flood of the century.

But in the early spring of 2009, the Red River once again threatened to overflow its banks. By March 27, the river at Fargo-Moorhead reached nearly forty-one feet—yet did not overflow. What was different this time around? Answer: volunteers.

People of every color, creed, and political persuasion—men and women, young and old—streamed out of the surrounding communities and gathered at the river, piling up sandbags and reinforcing the levees. The banks of the Red River became ground zero for community involvement, and our flood fighters became an example to the nation of human solidarity in a time of crisis.

Volunteerism is in our DNA out here in the heartland. We look out for each other, we trust in God, and we don't want the bureaucrats from D.C. poking their noses into our lives and telling us what to do. When problems come our way, we find a way to solve those problems at the local level. And we are always ready to serve our communities without regard to political calculation or pursuit of an agenda.

For some reason, however, the elites in Washington, D.C., didn't think a bunch of North Dakota clod-kickers were up to the challenge of fighting the flood. The Department of Homeland Security, at the behest of President Obama, urged massive evacuations. The unspoken message was, "You can't handle this problem. Let the federal government save you." At the same time, the federal government had just passed TARP and the stimulus, and Washington was drowning under a self-inflicted flood of debt. "No, thanks, Uncle Sam," we said, "we'll handle this ourselves."

The irony of this situation is that the flood of 2009 coincided with Barack Obama's push for "stimulus" spending. He said he wanted to find "shovel-ready" projects across the United States and fund those projects with "stimulus" money. Yet here was a project that was truly "shovel-ready." Cities on both sides of the Red River needed flood protection, whether in the form of diversion or dikes or flood walls. Fargo-Moorhead and Grand Forks had spent millions on temporary solutions over the years. Yet the federal government could have saved all of that money by building a permanent infrastructure to protect those cities from natural disaster.

As I said on the radio at the time, "President Obama, if you really want to throw money at a project that will do some good, and if you want to spend that money in a way that's consistent with the Constitution, then come to North Dakota and bring a golden shovel."

Obama later told the *New York Times Magazine* that he realized too late that "there's no such thing as shovel-ready projects" when it comes to public works.[13] That's a shocking admission of incompetence. As Fox News commentator Charles Krauthammer observed, "It's not actually surprising that he doesn't know a shovel-ready project didn't exist, because having never worked in the private sector he wouldn't be sure what a project is and there isn't a lot of shoveling at Harvard Law School."[14]

If President Obama had ever actually held a shovel in his hands, he might have realized that the flooding in North Dakota *is* a shovel-ready project if there ever was one. But since President Obama wouldn't know a "shovel-ready" project if he fell into one, all of us here in the heartland will set an example of self-reliance, community spirit, and neighbor helping neighbor. We'll show the elites in our nation's capital how grassroots Americans solve their problems.

It's interesting to contrast the Red River flood crisis of 2009 with the chaos of Hurricane Katrina in New Orleans in 2005. Clearly, Katrina was a bigger disaster by several orders of magnitude—and the devastation was made worse by the failed response of government at every level, especially the local and state level.

But the images of Katrina that are burned into our minds are images of lost souls stranded on rooftops and flood-encircled freeway overpasses, of criminals looting abandoned buildings, of thirty-five thousand people huddled in the Louisiana Superdome without water, power, or sanitation—*and all of the victims waited for the federal government to rescue them.* They had been conditioned for decades to think of themselves as wards of the state, as being incapable of helping themselves and one another.

Here in the heartland, generations of Americans have been raised to rely on themselves and on each other—not the federal government. The Red River flood fight of 2009 was a nail-biter, but by the grace of God and the hard work of thousands of volunteers, we got through it. I was a firsthand witness to the effort, spending many hours with my microphone at the riverbank, broadcasting reports and interviews with the volunteers. The waters rose, but the sandbags rose even higher, and the city was spared.

The following year, in the spring of 2010, the river rose again. It was a challenging time, because while North Dakotans were again fighting a flood, back in Washington, a very different fight was going on—the fight to stop Obamacare. Here in the heartland, we were in full-fledged battle mode, fighting two wars at the same time. Once again, we had flood fighters on the front lines, sandbagging the Red River—yet we were also sending busloads of volunteers to Washington, D.C., hoping to block the federal usurpation of the greatest health care system in the world.

(Did America's health care system have some huge problems? Absolutely—but most of those problems were directly traceable to federal intrusion via the Medicare bureaucracy. And nearly all of those problems could have been fixed without a government takeover, by implementing free market solutions. Here are just a few examples of free market solutions: Republicans have been proposing *Health Savings Accounts* (HSAs) since the 1980s; HSAs would give consumers an incentive to contain costs and eliminate fraud and waste. *Risk pools* could be established by the states to provide coverage on a sliding scale for people with preexisting conditions. Allowing Americans to *buy insurance across state lines* would increase competition and drive down costs. *Tort reform*—capping "pain and suffering" and punitive damages at, say, $500,000 each—would dramatically reduce health care costs.)

Many North Dakotans were forced to fight the rising river while also making time to call or write Congressman Pomeroy and Senators Dorgan and Conrad, trying to convince them to vote the interests of their constituents instead of the ideology of Nancy Pelosi and Harry Reid. Fighting a two-front war took a physical and emotional toll on North Dakotans. We won the battle against the river. We lost the battle against our own government.

But grassroots Americans don't accept defeat. We'll keep on fighting the river for as long as it takes. And we'll keep fighting to repeal and replace Obamacare.

The very fact that we have to fight the river year after year is a testament to the failure of the federal government. Our lives are annually disrupted because the federal government has failed to deliver on a promise made decades ago by career politicians and bureaucrats to provide permanent flood protection in this region.

This failure is all the more amazing when you realize that the federal government wastes more so-called stimulus money in any given hour than it would take to build a permanent flood protection system across this plain. The Red River region has been "shovel-ready" for years, but the corrupt Democratic Party agenda wants to spend "stimulus" money only where it can benefit political allies and union bosses. What the feds call "stimulus" is really all about politics—using *your* hard-earned tax dollars to enlarge the government and empower the Democratic Party.

That's why we're not holding our breath, waiting for the federal government to come to our rescue. Since the 1960s, the federal government has been promising to complete the Garrison Diversion—a vast system of reservoirs, irrigation canals, and flood control systems. Former Republican senator Mark Andrews (who was defeated by Kent Conrad in 1986) said on my show that he was very close to getting the Garrison project completed before he left office. Today, more than a quarter century later, the project remains uncompleted. The phrase "Garrison Diversion" symbolizes government incompetence at its worst. The project is yet another casualty of single-party (i.e., Democratic Party) rule.

But the fight goes on. And the people leading this fight are the volunteers of the tea party movement. We will fight the rise of big government the same way we fight the rising floodwaters. We will sandbag the Washington elitists with grassroots determination and perseverance. They may have the power of the federal government on their side, but we have the power of the people.

"THE SHOT HEARD ROUND THE WORLD"

America was founded by this same spirit of grassroots volunteerism. The tea party activists of today are, in a civic sense, the direct descendants of the original Boston Tea Party activists of 1773. Many people today talk about the "Tea Party" (with a capital *T* and capital *P*) as if it were a political party, like the Republican Party or the Democratic Party. But the tea party is nothing of the kind. There is no one "Tea Party"—all are local expressions of a nationwide grassroots movement.

It's true that there are several national organizations—the Tea Party Express, Tea Party Patriots, Tea Party Nation—but no single group speaks for the tea party movement. There is no one founder of the movement, no national leader. The tea party group that meets in Fargo, North Dakota, has no official connection with the tea party in Amarillo, Texas, or Jaffrey, New Hampshire, or Issaquah, Washington.

But what do these various tea parties have in common? They are united in their opposition to big government and runaway spending and insane federal debt. They are united in a belief in citizen government, less regulation, and lower taxes as a means of private-sector job creation. They are united in their love of country, love of freedom, respect for the Constitution, and support for the American soldier and the American veteran.

In short, all of these various, disconnected entities called "tea parties" are united by principles and values and patriotism. The tea partiers I've met come in all shades, from white to mocha to black. They are disaffected Republicans, Democrats, Libertarians, and Independents who share one conviction: *Government is too big and out of control.*

Many people today are surprised to learn that the original Boston Tea Party was not a protest against high taxes on tea. In reality, John Hancock and his fellow Tea Partiers dumped the tea into the harbor to protest a tax *decrease.* The Brits had actually *cut* the tax on a pound of tea by three pence (three-hundredths of a pound sterling) in order to prop up the British East India Company—a corporation that the British Crown had decided was "too big to fail." Americans had stopped buying tea from the East India Company, and were buying cheaper, untaxed tea from smugglers. The East India Company's lobbyists had bought off members of the corrupt Parliament, convincing them to cut the tea tax so that American colonists would start buying tea again.

On the night of December 16, 1773, a group of patriots called the Sons of Liberty, led by John Hancock, gathered at Boston's South Meeting House, disguised themselves as Mohawk Indians, then went to Griffin's Wharf and boarded three British ships, the *Dartmouth,* the *Eleanor,* and the *Beaver.* As a crowd of spectators cheered, the Sons of Liberty hauled up chests of tea from the holds, smashed them open, and dumped the tea into the harbor.

Like the tea party movement today, the Boston Tea Party was a revolt against big-government corruption, corporate bailouts, and government interference in the free economy. Above all, the Boston Tea Party was an act of grassroots activism, designed to send a statement of righteous indignation to a tyrannical big-government oppressor. The original Boston Tea Party is the role model for all tea party activists today.

Most of us know the names of the founding fathers, the wise men who wrote and signed the Declaration of Independence, the Constitution, and the Federalist Papers—men like George Washington, Benjamin Franklin, John Adams, Thomas Jefferson, John Jay, James Madison, and Alexander Hamilton. But the American Revolution was not the sole achievement of a few famous men. It was truly a *grassroots rebellion* intended to seize political power from the privileged and powerful few, and transfer that power where it right-

fully belonged—into the hands of We the People. This new nation, the United States of America, was built by the sweat and blood
of everyday Americans whose names are no longer remembered
today.

The Boston Tea Party was followed by the Worcester Revolution
of 1774, in which thousands of farmers, shopkeepers, and craftsmen
of Worcester County, Massachusetts, rebelled against British rule
and tossed every Crown-appointed official out of office—*without firing a shot*. Angered by the Massachusetts Government Act (one of
the Intolerable Acts, which Britain imposed to punish the colonists
for the Boston Tea Party), and fearing that the Brits would confis-
cate their property and livestock, the Worcester patriots formed a
militia of nearly five thousand men and forced every British official
in thirty-seven Worcester County towns to resign and leave town
in disgrace. The Worcester revolutionaries conducted themselves
democratically—every decision was made by a vote of the entire
grassroots rank and file.

Most of the displaced British officials took refuge in Boston. There,
the commander of British forces in the colonies, General Thomas
Gage, reported to the Crown that "the flames of sedition" were
spreading throughout the colonies. Meanwhile, the democratic patriots of Worcester County governed themselves peacefully and unchal-
lenged for seven months.[15]

The peace was shattered in April 1775, when the British launched
attacks on Lexington and Concord to put down the grassroots rebellion in those villages. General Gage sent Lieutenant Colonel Francis Smith and His Majesty's Tenth Regiment of Foot to disarm the
colonists and capture two colonial leaders, John Hancock and Samuel
Adams. As the British troops moved noisily through the countryside,
inquiring about the location of Hancock and Adams, patriot leaders
summoned the grassroots militias.[16]

Two of those leaders were Paul Revere and William Dawes. On
the night of April 18, 1775, they kept watch on the steeple of Boston's
Old North Church. Up in the steeple, Revere's friend John Pulling
spied on the British troops below. If the Brits departed by the land

route, Pulling would shine a single lantern from the steeple. But if the Brits set off in boats across the Back Bay, John Pulling would shine two lanterns, signaling a more immediate attack on Lexington and Concord. As Revere and Dawes watched, they saw the light of two lanterns appear in the steeple—and they set off at a hard gallop to warn the militias in Lexington, Concord, and surrounding villages.

Revere and Dawes split up and took different routes, so that if the British captured one, the other might get through. As they rode and spread the alarm, other riders—about forty in all—leaped onto their horses and took the message throughout the Massachusetts countryside, summoning the militia. Most of those riders were anonymous patriots—grassroots Americans whose names are forever lost to history.[17]

At around midnight, Paul Revere reached the village of Lexington and went to the house of Parson Jonas Clark, pastor of the Lexington Congregation. Revere pounded on the door of the parsonage, waking Parson Clark and his two guests—John Hancock and Samuel Adams, the very men the British sought. Clark was a firebrand preacher who hated British oppression and loved the words of St. Paul, ". . . where the Spirit of the Lord is, there is freedom."[18] When one of the men asked Parson Clark if his parishioners would stand and fight the British, the preacher said, "I have trained them for this very hour. They would fight and, if need be, die too under the shadow of the house of God."[19]

At sunrise on April 19, 1775, an advance guard of British soldiers, commanded by Major John Pitcairn, entered the village of Lexington. They were met at Lexington Green by about eighty Lexington militiamen and scores of villagers who watched from the edge of the green. Captain John Parker, the Lexington militia commander, ordered his men to hold their fire. British Major Pitcairn also gave the hold-fire order—

But someone fired anyway. To this day, no one knows who fired the first shot in the American Revolutionary War. But years later, poet Ralph Waldo Emerson, whose grandfather fought at Lexington and Concord, commemorated those battles with these words:

By the rude bridge that arched the flood,
Their flag to April's breeze unfurled,
Here once the embattled farmers stood,
And fired the shot heard round the world.[20]

Parson Clark had promised that his parishioners "would fight and, if need be, die" for the cause of freedom—and that morning, he saw it happen. As the smoke of the musket fire cleared and the British soldiers continued marching through Lexington on their way to Concord, several members of Parson Clark's congregation lay dead or dying on Lexington Green. Through tears, Parson Clark said, "From this day will be dated the Liberty of the World."[21]

In Concord, the king's troops met a superior force of about five hundred grassroots militiamen. After a fierce battle, the British retreated and didn't stop to regroup until they had run all the way to Boston. The combined militias of the surrounding villages laid siege to the city of Boston. And so the Revolutionary War began.

GRASSROOTS PATRIOTS JUST LIKE YOU

Most of the true heroes of that war are unknown to us today. They were not generals who commanded armies. They were not the signers of the Declaration of Independence, nor were they the framers of the Constitution. There are no monuments or statues in their honor. They were just grassroots patriots who saw what needed to be done, and they did it. We do know a few of their names, a few of their deeds.

Dr. Thomas Young was a leading organizer of the *original* Boston Tea Party. Though his name is never mentioned in the same breath with Washington or Jefferson, it was Dr. Thomas Young who first suggested dumping the East India Company tea into Boston Harbor. If not for Dr. Young, there would have been no Boston Tea Party.[22]

And there was a sixteen-year-old farm girl named Sybil Ludington of Putnam County, New York. She has sometimes been compared to Paul Revere. On the night of April 26, 1777, when a messenger came with news of the approaching British army, she rode her horse named Star on a thirty-mile circuit, summoning the patriot militia to her father's farm to assemble for battle. Her ride would be considered a feat of incredible endurance in the daylight—yet Sybil Ludington rode by night and, at one point, had to fend off a robber with her father's musket. Her courage enabled a patriot victory over the British at the Battle of Ridgefield, Connecticut.[23]

Blacksmith Timothy Bigelow took part in the Worcester Revolution of 1774, when the farmers and tradesmen of Worcester County, Massachusetts, drove every British official out of office without firing a shot. After hearing about the Battle of Lexington and Concord, he joined the patriot forces and fought in the Saratoga campaign, assisting in the capture of British general John Burgoyne. He also fought under General Washington at Valley Forge, West Point, Monmouth, and Yorktown.[24]

Mercy Otis Warren was a poet and playwright who taught herself how to read by eavesdropping on her brothers' lessons (young ladies were often denied a formal education in colonial times). Her husband, James Warren, was a passionate revolutionary activist, and she herself was a close friend of John Adams (who would later serve as the second president of the United States) and his wife, Abigail. Though Mercy Otis Warren had never seen a play performed onstage (such performances were banned in Puritan Boston), she wrote three satirical plays, *The Adulateur, The Defeat,* and *The Group,* which were published and widely distributed in the colonies—the first plays by an American female writer. Her plays attacked British rule and promoted the revolutionary cause. After America achieved independence, Mercy wrote a pamphlet, *Observations on the New Constitution* (1788), which helped shape the Bill of Rights.[25]

Two centuries before Joe the Plumber there was Joseph Plumb Martin. At age fourteen, Joseph heard about the battle at Lexington and Concord and begged his grandfather, who was also his guardian, to let him go to war. In June 1776, after Joseph turned fifteen, his grandfather gave him permission to enlist in the Connecticut militia. Before the end of that year, he had fought in the Battle of Brooklyn, the Battle of Kip's Bay, and the Battle of White Plains. At age sixteen, he enlisted in the 8th Connecticut division of the Continental Army, commanded by General George Washington. He spent the rest of his teenage years and early twenties serving under General Washington, experiencing all the hardships and privation of a common foot soldier. He refused to accept being discharged until the end of the war in 1783. Throughout the war, he kept a journal that has served as a valuable resource for historians.[26]

A doctor, a sixteen-year-old farm girl, a blacksmith, a playwright, and a teenage soldier were just a few of the grassroots activists of the American Revolutionary era. These were the average people who loved their country. They stepped up. They got involved. They took a risk. They sacrificed. They were people just like you.

The time has come for you and me to add our names to the list of grassroots people who are willing to bet everything we have on the future of America. The time has come to get involved and make a difference. That's why I'm telling you these stories—the stories of people just like you, people who are doing whatever they can to save America. They are doing their part.

Now it's time for you and me to do ours.

THE COMMONSENSE ACTION AGENDA

Here are some grassroots actions you can take, starting today:

✓ Read and study the Declaration of Independence and the United States Constitution. Memorize the Preamble to the Constitution.
✓ Know the Bill of Rights—especially the First Amendment: "Congress shall make no law respecting an establishment of religion, or prohibiting the free exercise thereof; or abridging the freedom of speech, or of the press; or the right of the people peaceably to assemble; and to petition the Government for a redress of grievances." Be ready to recite the Five Freedoms of the First Amendment at a moment's notice: Freedom of Religion, Freedom of Speech, Freedom of the Press, Freedom of Assembly, and Freedom to Petition the Government.
✓ Take a class in the Constitution or U.S. history.
✓ Start a book club with neighbors or people from your church. Study and discuss books about American history, the Constitution, the founding fathers, or grassroots activism. (The book you hold in your hands would be a great place to start!)
✓ Find a piece of legislation you are passionate about. Whether you want that legislation passed or defeated, study it carefully and become an expert on that bill. Then attend a town hall meeting and challenge your elected leader. Tell your friends and neighbors about that bill and what it means to everyone's future. Get involved in your government.
✓ Keep writing letters and making phone calls to your elected representatives. Be courteous but insistent. To contact the president or vice president, go to www.whitehouse.gov/contact/. Get contact information for your congressperson at writerep.house.gov/writerep/welcome.shtml and your senator at www.senate.gov/general/contact_information/senators_cfm.cfm.

2

GUARDING THE SPIRIT OF FREEDOM

My pal Ross Ueckert, a fifty-five-year-old army veteran, is a living, breathing celebration of the Declaration of Independence. In the summer of 2009, Ross picked up an American flag and started out from Medora, North Dakota, headed for the Lincoln Memorial in Washington, D.C.—a journey of 1,600 miles, traveling by shoe leather all the way.

Flag in hand, walking from town to town, he spoke at tea parties and veterans' groups, waved to the people who honked at him, and chatted with folks along the way. He spent nights in the homes of supporters or camped out in his truck to show support for the troops. From time to time, Ross would call *The Common Sense Club* and I would put him on the air to give my listeners a progress report. After hearing Ross on the radio, people would seek him out on the road to say "We're proud of you," or "God bless you," or "May I carry the flag for a while?"

Ross's sister, Myrna, would drive ahead of him in a pickup truck, park a couple of miles down the road, and wait for him to catch up. There were banners on both sides of the truck. One read "We the People" and the other "We the People—Veterans." Wherever people stopped to talk to Ross, he had them sign the banners. Ross had planned to take those banners to Washington and deliver them to members of Congress. "But we had a heck of a windstorm in Illinois," he recalled, "and it ripped both of them to shreds. We still have the signed portions, but we had to take them off the truck."

Why did Ross Ueckert walk all the way to the nation's capital? "We've just got to show our elected officials the power of the people," he told me at the start of his journey. "They've never seen the power of the people. I've been watching politics for a lot of years, and nothing changes. The politicians are just working for themselves. I'm going to ask some questions, and I just want to hear a straight answer. I want to tell the politicians that the American spirit is alive and well, but we want the government out of our way."

As Ross walked from state to state, he was amazed at all the citizens who would stop and talk or pray with him beside the road. "I had absolutely no clue that was going to happen," Ross told me. "It was such a journey of growth, such a journey of blessings."

Once, as Ross carried his flag outside Bismarck, a young woman pulled her car over, rolled down the window, and said, "Why are you walking with that flag?"

"I'm walking against the corruption in Washington, D.C.," he said, "and I'm walking for the American veteran."

The young woman instantly began to cry. She opened the door, jumped out, and gave Ross a big hug. There by the road, he talked to the young woman for about fifteen minutes. As they talked, she took a bracelet off her wrist and held it up.

"I haven't taken this bracelet off since I got it," she said. "Take it, and when you get to Washington, I want you to remember my brother, John. That's his name on the bracelet."

Ross saw that the bracelet bore the name of Army Pfc. John D. Amos II, C Company, 1st Battalion, 21st Infantry Regiment, 25th Infantry Division. At age twenty-two, on April 4, 2004, Private Amos was killed when an improvised explosive device blew up his vehicle in Kirkuk, Iraq. The woman pressed the bracelet into Ross's hand, and the two of them wept together beside the road.

"When I first started walking," Ross recalled, "I was angry and frustrated." But the moment the young woman gave him that bracelet, all his anger and frustration melted away. "It was no longer about my anger toward our leaders," Ross told me. "It was all about America, and how proud I am of the people in this country. It was all about the American veterans, and about those who sacrificed everything for this country."

Since then, Ross has continued his trek with a new attitude. "I've had so many people stop and talk to me about God, our country, and our veterans. I have shed more tears along these roads than ever in my life. People kept saying I was inspiring them, but they were giving me far more than I could ever give them. It humbles me to meet these people, because it tells me that the pride and patriotism of the American people is still alive. We can no longer let these professional politicians take our freedoms away. We have to stand up for what we believe. That's why I'm going to Washington.

"I was so elated every step of the way, and especially by the number of people who stopped and talked to us. My sister and I were camped by the road one morning, and we had hardly woken up and this fellow stopped and talked to us. He had driven past and saw our We the People banner on the back of our pickup, and he pulled off and looked up our website on his laptop computer. Then he came back to talk to us and sign the banner. He said, 'Keep doing what you're doing. God bless you.' People like that kept me going.

"Our government has been bought and sold by lobbyists and big money. Why do our representatives pass legislation without reading it? Why do they push thousand-page bills through Congress in the middle of the night? We have to step forward and say, 'Enough is enough.' Our leaders in Washington have never seen the power of the people. We've got to show them who's boss.

"Some people have criticized me and criticized the tea party movement, saying we're wrapping ourselves in the flag. Well, that flag I carried symbolizes the principles and values of the founding fathers. I'm proud to wrap myself in that flag. And I'm proud to wrap myself in the Constitution. People ought to try wrapping themselves in the flag for a change. If they would come out here and walk these roads, their view of this country would never be the same.

"There's a prayer I said every day of my walk, and I say it today, too: 'God, put my feet on the path you want me to take. Put the words in my mouth that you want me to speak. And give me the wisdom to speak to the people you put in front of me.' God answered that prayer every day. In fact, there were four times during my walk when he physically redirected my path. I was going one way, but God sent me a different way.

"A good example is when I was leaving Fargo and going into Minnesota. I started walking on I-94, heading to Minneapolis. I hadn't even gotten a half mile into Minnesota when a Minnesota state trooper stopped me and told me I couldn't walk on I-94. So I took Highway 10, and it was a much better route to walk because I met a lot more people on the way. That was God's way of telling me, 'I've got a better path for you.' "

On Sunday, October 3, 2010, Ross, his sister Myrna, and his son Conner (who had joined him along the way) came to within thirty-five miles of Washington, D.C. "I wanted to walk all the way to the Lincoln Memorial," Ross told me. "So we got into the pickup and drove into D.C. to check the roads out. Well, it was clear that I wouldn't be able to walk into the city. There is too much traffic and no place to walk alongside the road."

Leaving his flag in the truck, Ross went to the Washington Monument. The day before, some four hundred leftist groups had gathered on the National Mall for a rally they called One Nation Working Together. The groups included environmentalists, antiwar activists, civil rights activists, and organizers from unions like the Service Employees International Union. Ross recalled, "I walked along the Mall and there was trash everywhere, even floating in the reflecting pool. Those people called themselves environmentalists, yet they just dumped their trash anywhere. We visited the World War II Memorial, and it was littered with bottles and things. How people can be so disrespectful is beyond me. It almost made me sick. We picked up some of it and saved it, SEIU and Code Pink signs, just to show what these people stand for."

Unable to walk into the city, Ross had a few extra days to drive around D.C. with Myrna and Conner and visit the Holocaust Museum, the National Air and Space Museum, Mount Vernon, and other sites. On Columbus Day, October 12, Ross took the flag and walked from the Washington Monument, past the World War II Memorial, and up the steps of the Lincoln Memorial. At the top of the steps, he did as he had promised to the woman who gave him the bracelet. He read the inscription in memory of Army Pfc. John D. Amos II, and he paused to think about this young man's life and sacrifice. And he prayed.

Later that day, he took the flag to Senator Byron Dorgan's office. Senator Dorgan met with Ross for about twenty minutes, and they had their pictures taken together. The senator later had the flag flown above the Capitol building, then shipped back to Ross with a certificate. Despite my many differences with Senator Dorgan, I salute him for reaching out to Ross and flying Ross's flag above the Capitol. Ross plans to carry that flag from the Washington Monument to the Lincoln Memorial every October 12 from now on.

Ross Ueckert is a one-man walking tea party.

THE TEA PARTY UNDER ATTACK

The tea party movement had scarcely been born when it came under an obscene attack. It began on Rachel Maddow's show on MSNBC, April 9, 2009, when she and guest Ana Marie Cox (of the now-defunct radio network Air America) exchanged potshots at this brand-new cultural phenomenon called tea parties. They giggled and smirked as they traded remarks about "tea bagging" and seemed to be enjoying some inside joke.[1]

From the Maddow show, the snickering quickly spread to other cable anchors. When CNN political analyst David Gergen remarked that Republicans were "searching for their voice," CNN anchor Anderson Cooper countered, "It's hard to talk when you're tea bagging." And back at MSNBC, David Shuster, sitting in for *Countdown* host Keith Olbermann, launched into a leering, mugging shtick filled with a dozen or so "tea bagging" references, all of which seem to involve some sort of sexual innuendo.[2]

The use of the "tea bagger" epithet went all the way to the top. *Newsweek* reporter Jonathan Alter, in his book about President Obama's first year in office, reports that Mr. Obama himself said that the $787 billion stimulus bill, which he signed into law in February 2009, "helped to create the tea-baggers and empowered that whole wing of the Republican Party."[3] Nice, Mr. President. Very presidential.

The attacks on the tea party had just begun—and they were about to get much worse than obscene innuendos. One of the leaders of the Democratic Party tried to marginalize the movement by suggesting that the tea parties weren't a true grassroots movement at all. The millions of tea party protesters who sprang up nationwide weren't really sincere or spontaneous. They had somehow been ginned up, she claimed, by the Republican Party. Interviewed on April 15, 2009, by KTVU News in San Francisco, House Speaker Nancy Pelosi said that the tea party movement "is funded by the high end—we call it 'Astroturf,' it's not really a grassroots movement. It's Astroturf by some of the wealthiest people in America to keep the focus on tax cuts for the rich."[4] Pelosi also tried to link the tea party movement to Nazism, claiming that supporters of the movement were "carrying swastikas and symbols like that."[5]

Around that time, MSNBC's Keith Olbermann and his guest Janeane Garofalo decided to go as low as you can go, and smear the tea party movement with the most vile accusation of all. On Thursday, April 16, 2009, following a nationwide display of Tax Day tea party patriotism, Olbermann sneered, "Well, the tea bagging is all over, except for the cleanup. And that will be my last intentional double entendre on this one at least until the end of this segment. . . . On a more serious note, we're now joined by actor-activist Janeane Garofalo."

Garofalo, who had never been to a tea party, proceeded to explain with absolute authority what is inside the soul of the "tea bagging rednecks" (her words) at these rallies. "Let's be very honest about what this is about," she said. "It's not about bashing Democrats, it's not about taxes, they have no idea what the Boston Tea Party was about, they don't know their history at all. This is about hating a black man in the White House. This is racism, straight up."[6]

And there it was. The race card.

Garofalo offered no evidence for her accusation, of course. In the world of liberal hit jobs, no evidence is needed. It didn't take long for the racism charge to be picked up and seriously advanced by a Democratic Party heavyweight—former president Jimmy Carter. On the morning of September 16, 2009, as tea party opposition was ramping up against President Obama's health care plan, Carter told NBC's Brian Williams, "I think an overwhelming portion of the intensely demonstrated animosity toward President Barack Obama is based on the fact that he is a black man, that he's African-American." Carter didn't say that racism might motivate a few people at the fringes—he said that "an overwhelming portion" of tea partiers are racists.

A short time later, Mr. Carter stood before a student audience at Emory University in Atlanta and repeated the charge, claiming that tea partiers "have been influenced to a major degree by a belief that he should not be president because he happens to be African-American. It's a racist attitude."[7] Carter proceeded to poison the minds of those students against an entire segment of patriotic Americans who were simply exercising their First Amendment right to free speech, to peaceably assemble, and to petition the government for a redress of grievances. The charge of racism is extremely serious—and irresponsible in the absence of evidence.

Are there a few racists hanging around the fringes of the tea party movement? All I can tell you is that I have attended nearly a hundred tea party rallies and town hall meetings, and I have never seen one racist sign, and have never spoken to a single person who expressed a racist idea. Here's my challenge to you: Go to my website at scotthennen.com and click on the "media" link. You'll find video and photos of a number of tea parties around North Dakota. There are shots that pan the crowd, and you can see dozens of tea party signs. I will pay a thousand dollars to the first person who finds even one racist sign in any of the videos on my website.

Is it racism to oppose wasteful "stimulus" spending, the soaring national debt, the government takeover of the auto industry and the financial sector and the health care industry? Does Jimmy Carter truly believe that tea partiers would *approve* of trillion-dollar deficits if he or John Kerry or George W. Bush were president? Does Carter think for a moment that the tea party movement would be *opposed* to a president named Herman Cain, Clarence Thomas, Condoleezza

Rice, J. C. Watts, Walter Williams, Allen West, or Thomas Sowell? I would vote for any one of those great Americans in a heartbeat. So would you. So would any true member of the tea party movement.

The same day Jimmy Carter leveled the racism charge, Mike Motschenbacher was a guest on my show. Mike was the organizer of the Rally in the Valley, a big tea party event at the Scheels Hardware parking lot in Fargo. When asked about the former president's remarks, Mike said, "Once the liberals play the race card, you know they're getting scared, because the race card comes from the very bottom of their bucket of tricks. For them to call us racists is insane. We are concerned citizens of the United States. Jimmy Carter should know better. If the liberals want to disagree with us on policy, fine, bring it on. But to accuse us of racism without any proof, just to smear the opposition, that's a low blow. It's despicable."

Becky Skogen of Canby, Minnesota, said of the racism charge, "As an American citizen, I resent even having to bring this up. Those of us in the conservative movement have made it clear that we don't care about people's race. At every tea party I've been to, there have been African-Americans in the crowd and there have been African-Americans on the platform talking about their love for this country. Black tea partiers are just as sick and tired of this phony 'racism' charge as the rest of us. The tea party movement is a diverse and inclusive movement, and it reflects the best of America."

Who are these tea partiers? Who are these people who are so maligned by the media and even by many of our own government leaders?

Dustin Gawrylow is the director of the North Dakota Taxpayers Association. "The folks who are showing up at these tea parties," he told me, "are just concerned citizens. They're people who are not normally involved in politics. In fact, most of them are totally turned off by organized politics, which is more about power and greed than it is about service to the country. The tea parties give average people a chance for their voices to be heard and their bodies to be counted."

We say we want people to get involved in their government. We say we want people to care about their country, look out for their neighbors, and volunteer time for the sake of the next generation. So thousands of grassroots Americans do exactly that—and what happens? They are viciously *attacked* in the media.

There's nothing random about these attacks. It's part of a concerted strategy by the liberal establishment in this country. My friend Ed Schafer, the former governor of North Dakota and former agriculture secretary under George W. Bush, explained it this way on my show: "The leftist media, the White House, Nancy Pelosi and Harry Reid, they all try to dismiss the tea party movement by calling them kooks and Astroturf in an effort to scare people away. They think that if they can give the tea party movement a bad image, then people will think twice about attending the next tea party rally. If they can make the tea party movement look like some sort of fringe movement, filled with kooks and racists, then people will stop joining and stop attending the rallies. That's the strategy.

"Fortunately, it's not working. Instead of keeping people away, these attacks are inspiring *more* people to join. People are saying, 'I want to stand up and be counted because I love my country, and I don't want the leftists to get away with slandering my friends and neighbors.' There are thousands and thousands of people out there who are genuinely concerned about the direction of this country. Many of them would join the tea party movement if you invited them. That's how the movement grows."

The tea party movement fought hard against Obamacare in March 2010, yet we lost the Battle of Capitol Hill. We won't win every battle, but we'll win the war against big government.

We know we are winning because even our most bitter opponents are now trying to steal some of our energy and our momentum. In September 2010, a year after stating that "an overwhelming portion" of tea partiers are racists, Jimmy Carter wrote in *USA Today*, "In some ways my successful campaign for the presidency in 1976 resembled the tea party movement of today."[8]

And Nancy Pelosi? After calling our movement "Astroturf" and comparing us to Nazis, she now wants to hog some tea party glory for herself. In a February 2010 interview with ABC's Elizabeth Vargas, she said, "We share some of the views of the tea partiers in terms of the role of special interests in Washington, D.C."[9]

Whoa, Jimmy! Easy there, Nancy! You'll give yourselves a bad case of whiplash with all that spin!

"THE TEA PARTY MADE ME DO IT"

On January 8, 2011, twenty-two-year-old Jared Lee Loughner went to an open meeting at the La Toscana Village mall in Tucson, Arizona. At 10:10 A.M., Loughner drew a 9mm Glock semiautomatic pistol and shot Congresswoman Gabrielle Giffords in the head. He then shot randomly into the crowd until he was taken down by several bystanders. When the gunsmoke cleared, nineteen people were shot, six fatally. The dead included United States District Court judge John Roll, one of Congresswoman Giffords's staffers, and nine-year-old Christina-Taylor Green.

Less than two hours after the attack, Sheriff Clarence W. Dupnik of Pima County, Arizona, stood before reporters and, without a scintilla of evidence, assigned blame for the massacre to conservative talk radio and the Fox News Channel. He said, "I think the vitriolic rhetoric that we hear day in and day out from people in the radio business and some people in the TV business . . . I think it's time that we do the soul-searching. . . . When you look at unbalanced people, how they respond to the vitriol that comes out of certain mouths, about tearing down the government, the anger, the hatred, the bigotry that goes on in this country is getting to be outrageous. And unfortunately, Arizona, I think, has become . . . the mecca for prejudice and bigotry."[10]

The following day, Sheriff Dupnik was interviewed by Megyn Kelly on Fox News Channel's *America Live*. She asked him if he had any evidence that "vitriolic rhetoric" on the airwaves played a part in the Tucson tragedy. "I don't have that information yet," Dupnik replied. "The investigation is in its very initial phases. But . . . there's no doubt in my mind that when a number of people, night and day, try to inflame the public that there is going to be some consequences from doing that."

Kelly pressed the sheriff. Was he really offering sheer speculation without any facts to support it?

"That's my opinion, period," said the sheriff, and he added that it troubled him whenever "allegedly credible people get up in front of cameras and microphones and say things that are not true and try to inflame the public." Amazingly, he seemed oblivious to the irony of his own words.

Kelly asked Dupnik why he put a political spin on a criminal case.

"Well," he replied, "I think it's more than just political spin. I'm not sure that it really has anything to do with politics. You know, I grew up in a country that was totally different than the country we have today. . . . Politicians from different parties could sit down, forget about their ideology, and work on the country's problems. We don't see that happening today. In fact, we see just the opposite. We see one party trying to block the attempts of another party to make this a better country."[11] Wow, no political spin there!

James Kelly, a former military defense analyst living in Tucson, suggested in his blog, The Cholla Jumps, that the reason Sheriff Dupnik came out swinging against conservatives and talk radio is that he was launching "a preemptive strike." Sheriff Dupnik and his office were well acquainted with Jared Loughner—and they'd had many opportunities over the years to prevent this tragedy. Kelly writes:

> Jared Loughner has been making death threats by phone to many people in Pima County. . . . When Pima County Sheriff's Office was informed, [Dupnik's] deputies assured the victims that [Loughner] was being well managed by the mental health system. It was also suggested that further pressing of charges would be unnecessary and probably cause more problems than it solved as Jared Loughner has a family member that works for Pima County.[12]

Did Sheriff Dupnik really demonize conservatives just to divert attention from the failures of his own office? Whatever the sheriff's motives, it's bizarre and unprecedented for a law enforcement agency to call a press conference less than two hours after a crime, then engage in off-the-wall political spin, unsupported by a shred of evidence.

People were dead. Families were grieving. And what was Sheriff Dupnik doing? He was providing the gunman with a defense! Can't you hear it now? "I'm not responsible for killing those people! Talk radio made me do it! The tea party made me do it! Sarah Palin made me do it! Sheriff Dupnik said so!"

Perhaps if Sheriff Dupnik's office had performed its sworn duty instead of doing favors for Jared's county-connected "family member," Jared Loughner might have had a conviction in his rap sheet. That conviction might have barred him from passing a background check and buying the murder weapon.

The political left and the liberal chattering class were quick to take their cue from Sheriff Dupnik. Within hours, Democrat congressman Raul Grijalva told *Mother Jones* that the tea party movement and Sarah Palin were to blame. "[When] you stoke these flames, and you go to public meetings and you scream at the elected officials, you threaten them—you make us expendable. . . . Some of the extreme right wing has made demonization of elected officials their priority. . . . The Palin express better look at their tone and their tenor." [13]

New York Times columnist Paul Krugman also leaped into the fray, condemning conservatives for creating a "climate of hate," leading to the Tucson rampage. "Where's that toxic rhetoric coming from?" he asked. "Let's not make a false pretense of balance: it's coming, overwhelmingly, from the right. . . . So will the Arizona massacre make our discourse less toxic? It's really up to G.O.P. leaders." [14]

Krugman was also quick to compare the Tucson shooting to the bombing that destroyed the Alfred P. Murrah Federal Building in downtown Oklahoma City on April 19, 1995. In fact, it's interesting that Krugman would raise the specter of the Oklahoma City bombing.

After the November 2010 election, in which Republicans gained sixty-three seats in the House and six seats in the Senate, it was clear to everyone that President Obama had received (to use his term) "a shellacking." Soon after the election, Democratic strategist Mark Penn appeared on Chris Matthews's *Hardball* on MSNBC. The question under discussion: Can President Obama recover from this political setback?

"The president himself has to reconnect with the people," Penn said. "Remember, President Clinton reconnected through Oklahoma." He referred, of course, to the Oklahoma City bombing. At that time, President Clinton was still suffering from a stinging defeat at the hands of Newt Gingrich and his Contract with America. The tragedy in Oklahoma City, six months after the election, enabled Clinton to regain his political momentum and win reelection. Penn added, "Obama needs a similar event. . . . Words will work if he finds that right moment." [15]

This is a shocking statement. A leading Democratic Party strategist is openly proposing that Barack Obama needs a deadly tragedy in order to "reconnect" with voters and regain his lost political momentum. I wish there were some other way to interpret Mark Penn's words, but his meaning is plain for all to see.

Just two months after Penn said those words, the left got its wish— its "Oklahoma City moment." Paul Krugman, in his *New York Times* column, trumped up a connection between Oklahoma City and Tucson. And Krugman's allies in the liberal press proceeded to exploit the tragedy in Tucson for all it was worth.

TURNING CONSERVATIVE OPINION INTO A "THOUGHT CRIME"

In the days following the shooting, the mainstream media oozed with self-righteous hypocrisy and smarmy political correctness. Eleven days after the shooting, CNN's John King issued this on-air apology: "Just a moment ago, my friend Andy Shaw . . . used the term 'in the crosshairs' in talking about the candidates out there. We're trying, we're trying to get away from that language. Andy is a good friend. He's covered politics for a long time, but we're trying to get away from using that kind of language. We won't always be perfect. So, hold us accountable when we don't meet your standards." [16]

You know what's *really* offensive? That apology! "In the crosshairs" is a perfectly good metaphor. The use of that phrase is not

going to send anyone out on a murderous rampage—not even someone as obviously insane as Jared Lee Loughner. Imagine how impoverished our language will become if the political correctness police get
their way. We would lose such phrases as:

Going ballistic. Loose cannon. Taking potshots. Battleground
states. Nuke the opposition. Full metal jacket. Lock and load. War on
poverty. Gun-shy. Keep your powder dry. Battle plan. Hair-trigger.
Praise the Lord and pass the ammunition. Sword of Damocles. He
met his Waterloo (or his Alamo). Launch a salvo. Friendly fire. Character assassination. Right on target. Lock, stock, and barrel. Shoot
from the hip. Suppression fire. From my cold, dead hand. Frontal assault. Targeted tax cut. Going off half-cocked. There's no silver bul-
let. War room.

I frequently appear on Ed Schultz's Rapid-Fire Response panel
on MSNBC. How politically incorrect is that? And while we're at it,
shouldn't CNN apologize for airing a show called *Crossfire*? And remember what candidate Obama said during the 2008 primary campaign in Philadelphia? "If they bring a knife to the fight, we bring a
gun!" Such heated rhetoric!

What is so brilliant about the liberal strategy is that it (pardon the
expression) kills two birds with one stone. It seeks to rob us of our
First Amendment rights and our Second Amendment rights in one
fell swoop.

If these terms are to be banned from public discourse, then what
does that tell us? Should hunters be ashamed of their guns? Should
we be embarrassed by the fact that our country was born from a revolutionary war? Should we disarm our police force? Should our sons
and daughters be ashamed of serving in the armed forces? Should
Target Corporation change its stores' name and logo?

Do you see how silly political correctness is? Do you see how liberalism robs the human mind of common sense? This Orwellian attempt to turn conservative opinion into a "thought crime" seems all
the more ridiculous when we see who Jared Lee Loughner really is.
He's as far as anyone could get from a tea partier or a conservative—
and he is certifiably, straitjacket crazy. Here's a sampling of his Internet postings:

If B.C.E. years are unable to start then A.D.E. years are unable to begin. B.C.E. years are unable to start. Thus, A.D.E. years are unable to begin.

You're a treasurer for a new currency, listener? You create and distribute your new currency, listener? You don't allow the government to control your grammar structure, listener?

All conscience dreaming at this moment is asleep. Jared Loughner is conscience dreaming at this moment. Thus Jared Loughner is asleep.[17]

Ashleigh Banfield interviewed one of Loughner's friends, Zach Osler, asking, "What about the speculation that he may have been fueled by partisan politics and rhetoric in the media?"

Osler replied, "He did not watch TV. He disliked the news. He didn't listen to political radio. He didn't take sides. He wasn't on the left; he wasn't on the right." Osler also said that Loughner abused alcohol, illegal drugs, and a legal hallucinogenic herb called salvia.[18]

What *did* influence the gunman? Osler said, "I really think that this *Zeitgeist* documentary had a profound impact upon Jared Loughner's mindset and how he viewed the world he lives in." [19]

Zeitgeist is a far-left documentary made in 2007 by Peter Joseph. Riddled with paranoid conspiracy theories, it claims that Jesus Christ was a myth invented by a group of first-century conspirators. It also claims that a secret cabal of international bankers plotted the 9/11 attacks, as well as the events that triggered World War I, World War II, and the Vietnam War. *Zeitgeist* comes from the far fringes of the extreme left—not the right.

Lynda Sorenson, a student who took an algebra class with Loughner in the summer of 2010, emailed friends and expressed concern about Loughner's weird behavior. For example, she wrote on June 14 that Loughner "scares the living crap out of me. He is one of those whose picture you see on the news, after he has come into class with an automatic weapon. Everyone interviewed would say, 'Yeah, he was in my math class and he was really weird.' I sit by the door with my purse handy."[20]

Another friend of Loughner, Bryce Tierney, recalls a time in 2007 after Loughner had attended a Gabrielle Giffords town hall meeting. Tierney remembers Loughner being angry and agitated about the meeting. "He told me that she opened up the floor for questions," Tierney recalled, "and he asked . . . 'What is government if words have no meaning?' He said, 'Can you believe it, they wouldn't answer my question.' Ever since that, he thought she was fake, he had something against her. . . . I told him, 'Dude, no one's going to answer that.' "[21]

The only "climate of hate" was inside the tortured, irrational mind of Jared Loughner. He stalked Gabrielle Giffords because she couldn't answer the nonsense question, "What is government if words have no meaning?" The Tucson shooting wasn't a political act. It was a psychotic break.

In September 2010, an environmental activist named James J. Lee took hostages at the Discovery Channel headquarters in Silver Spring, Maryland. Lee (who was shot and killed by police) wrote on his website that he had an "awakening" after viewing Al Gore's movie *An Inconvenient Truth*.[22] Should conservatives blame the environmental left for James Lee's actions? No. Conservatives don't play that game. Why? Because we believe in *personal responsibility*. We believe in blaming the person who pulls the trigger, not other segments of society.

Paul Krugman and the rest of the blithering elite would have us believe that "toxic rhetoric" comes overwhelmingly from conservatives. Is that so? Then why did the leftist Daily Kos have to scrub a posting from its website? On the day of the shooting, Daily Kos erased a January 6, 2010, post about Gabrielle Giffords, written by a Tucson blogger with the headline, "My CongressWOMAN voted against Nancy Pelosi! And is now DEAD to me!" But someone saved a screenshot before Daily Kos could ditch the evidence.[23]

Daily Kos founder Markos Moulitsas also posted some "toxic rhetoric" about Giffords, placing her name on a "target list" of Democrats who had "sold out the Constitution" and failed to be extreme-left enough to suit him. Along with other "blue dog Democrats" on Moulitsas's "target list," Giffords had earned "a bulls eye on [her] district." [24]

Howard Dean, as chairman of the Democratic National Commit-tee, once said, "I hate the Republicans and everything they stand for." An editor of the liberal rag the *New Republic* opened an op-ed piece, "I hate President George W. Bush." Senator John Glenn once referred to Republican campaign ideas as "the old Hitler business." CBS talk show host Craig Kilborn once showed a clip of George W. Bush dur-ing the 2000 campaign with the heading "Snipers Wanted." [25]

At a Common Cause event in Rancho Mirage, California, just three weeks after the Tucson shooting, leftist speakers demonized the hon-est political views of conservatives as hateful and evil. One speaker, former Obama green jobs czar Van Jones, compared conservatives to slave owners engaged in "economic tyranny and economic domina-tion," and declared, "We will not live on a national plantation." [26]

Investigative journalist Christian Hartsock took a video camera to the Common Cause event and interviewed attendees. One woman decried the "devastating influence" of the tea party movement, add-ing that "it makes me feel ashamed to be an American." A number of attendees expressed hatred for conservative black Supreme Court jus-tice Clarence Thomas. One man said, "Put him back in the fields, he's a scumbag!" A woman said of Thomas, "Cut off his toes one by one and feed them to him." Another woman advocated *lynching* Justice Thomas: "String him up—and his wife, too!" And yet another female Common Cause participant challenged talk show host Glenn Beck to a duel. [27]

The shooting in Tucson was an American tragedy. But the nation had scarcely begun to grieve when Sheriff Dupnik, Paul Krugman, and other voices on the left decided to exploit this tragedy for partisan political gain. These voices of division are what is wrong with Amer-ica today. Even so, grassroots conservative Americans are still ready and willing to reach out, to heal these divisions, and to find common ground.

One of the last public acts Congresswoman Gabrielle Giffords performed before she was wounded took place when members of the House of Representatives read the United States Constitution on the House floor. Congresswoman Giffords was assigned to read the First Amendment. I believe that assignment came from the hand of Providence.

The right to free speech is a sovereign right of all people, and we're not going to surrender that right to a crazed gunman—or to the cynical opportunism of the left.

"DON'T TREAD ON ME"

In his book *The New Road to Serfdom*, British conservative politician Daniel Hannan (a member of the European Parliament for South East England) demonstrates an understanding of the tea party movement that most American reporters and Democrat politicians seem to lack. He observes:

> The Tea Party phenomenon is an example of that rare beast, a genuinely spontaneous popular movement. . . .
>
> There are limits, of course, to what such a movement can achieve. It has no legislators and can pass no laws. It has scant financial resources. Indeed, it has so far failed in its two main aims: to defeat the Obama health-care bill, and to reduce the levels of taxation and debt. But legislation takes place against a background of national debate and consensus, and this is what the Tea Partiers have helped to shift. . . .
>
> The Tea Party Movement is nourished by a very American creed, namely that governments don't have the answers, that reform comes from below, that people are wiser than their leaders. By taking their message directly to the streets, the Tea Partiers changed minds in a way that politicians couldn't. They have, in short, created an atmosphere in which candidates opposed to Big Government can win.[28]

Why do the tea partiers put up with the ridicule, scorn, and hatred of the media and government leaders to attend tea party rallies, hold up signs, and protest their government? Why do they charter buses and join together, a million strong, in our nation's capital? What is the source of this patriotic passion that drives them?

Let me introduce you to a great American named Grace Custer from East Grand Forks, North Dakota. I met Grace when I spoke at the Rally in the Valley in Fargo in 2009. I handed her the microphone, and she spoke from the heart and expressed the soul of a grassroots patriot.

"My husband and I have raised four children," she said. "Our youngest sang the national anthem here tonight. This is from my heart. I've had enough of politicians who only seem to care about themselves, their agenda, their unethical sweetheart deals, pleasing their special interest groups, and so on. I have no confidence in leaders who won't talk to us or listen to us. I'm offended by elected officials who want to shove a health care plan down our throats that they don't even want for themselves.

"I don't care what they say about free health care, free stimulus money, or free anything else. All of these 'free giveaways' are just another way of enslaving us and taking away our freedom.

"I'm grieved by the way this administration seems hell-bent on breaking the back of this country by destroying small business and undermining capitalism. As an American citizen, I'm weary of being talked down to and insulted by elected officials who paint people like me as a swastika-emblazoned radical or an idiot just because we happen to believe our leaders should be accountable to us as constituents. I am personally offended to hear a man running for president insult our military and our mission, and then when elected go around apologizing to rogue nations for our country.

"He has made fun of special needs people,[29] and labeled a police officer as acting stupidly, all the while admitting he didn't have all the facts. Well, excuse me, but I am not gullible and I won't be taken in by a suave, cool demeanor. If only President Obama were humble enough to admit that *he* was the one who acted stupidly, and then apologized for himself instead of apologizing for America!

"This is not about politics or one party versus another. Our republic is being led away from the principles upon which it was founded, and without which we will not long survive. We need to get back to the Constitution and we need to get back to the Bible. The answer we need is in 2 Chronicles 7:14: 'If my people, who are called by my name, will humble themselves and pray and seek my face and turn from their wicked ways, then will I hear from heaven and will forgive their sin and will heal their land.' We need healing in this land!

"When common ordinary citizens, like those of us here, band together and finally get the chance to vote these self-serving politicians out of office, then we'll see change and experience hope for America again."

Grace Custer got cheers and applause throughout her talk—and a huge ovation at the end. And as for me, I'll admit that I was more than a little choked up to hear this wife and mother from East Grand Forks take a bold stand for her family, her nation, her values, and her faith on behalf of all the other tea party patriots.

The tea parties catch a lot of flak because of the anger expressed at these events. But anger isn't all that is expressed—in fact, the emotion I see most often at tea party events is *joy,* a sense of *excitement,* a sense of *enthusiasm* among people who are passionate about America. Even while we fight to keep our freedom from slipping away, we're optimistic and hopeful because we're Americans.

As Becky Skogen told me, "There's a sense of *fun* at every tea party event. I especially love the signs. The American people are so creative. My favorite is the one I saw in Washington, D.C.—'If You Think You've Got It Bad, Somewhere Out There Is a *Mister* Pelosi.' "

Becky's right. I just love the signs I see at every tea party event. Yes, we're concerned about the future of our country—but that doesn't keep us from having a laugh-out-loud great time. Here are a few of my favorites:

"Party Like It's 1773!"
"Are You Better Off Now Than You Were $12 Trillion Ago?"
"My Country Sold My Liberty for Hope and Change and All I Got Was This Lousy Tyranny!"
"If You Cap Us, We'll Trade You!"
"I Am Not the Government's ATM"
"Born Free—Taxed to Death!"

"We Pay You to Read the Bill!"
"Just When I Thought It Couldn't Get Any Worse . . . Al Franken!"
"Give Me Liberty, Don't Give Me Debt!"
"If America Socializes Medicine, Where Will Canadians Go?"
"I Can See November from My House!"
"We Work Hard So You Won't Have To"

Ah, don't you love it? Yes sir, tea partiers know how to have fun.

But of all the slogans I see at tea party events, my favorite is not on a sign but on a flag—a golden yellow flag with a coiled rattlesnake and the words "Don't Tread on Me." This iconic symbol, the Gadsden Flag, has endured for over two hundred years, yet many people don't know the story behind it. The Gadsden Flag was designed by General Christopher Gadsden, who led the South Carolina patriot movement during the American Revolution.

The rattlesnake emblem has its origins in the satirical writings of Benjamin Franklin, published in his newspaper, the *Pennsylvania Gazette*. Franklin observed that, since Britain liked to send its convicted prisoners to America, the colonists should return the favor and send rattlesnakes to England. The image captured the imagination of Franklin and his fellow revolutionaries, and they embraced the ready-to-strike rattler as a fitting symbol of the independent American spirit. The rattlesnake, he once observed, "never begins an attack, nor, when once engaged, ever surrenders. . . . She never wounds till she has generously given notice, even to her enemy, and cautioned him against the danger of treading on her."[30]

In 1775, the Second Continental Congress established the United States Navy to intercept ships bringing war supplies to aid British forces in America. Congress also authorized the creation of five companies of United States Marines to serve aboard the navy ships. The Marines carried yellow drums with a coiled rattlesnake and the "Don't Tread on Me" motto painted on the drumheads. Gadsden was a member of the Marine Committee, and to this day, no one knows if Gadsden influenced the design of the Marines' drums, or if the drums inspired the design of the Gadsden Flag.

Since the beginning of the tea party movement in early 2009, the

Gadsden Flag has symbolized its vigilant, patriotic spirit. The tea partiers didn't start this fight. They were living quietly, working at their jobs, and raising their families, when their irresponsible leaders began spending America into oblivion. These grassroots Americans had given generous notice. They had petitioned their government. They tried to reason with their elected leaders.

But the government refused to listen. Our leaders insisted on treading over the rights, the wisdom, the freedom, and the clearly expressed will of the American people. If a man deliberately ignores the warning sound of the serpents' rattle, who is responsible for what happens next—the serpent or the man?

As Becky Skogen said on my show, "If I were a member of Congress I would be terrified right now." Becky's right—every other November, the rattlesnake has its day.

GRASSROOTS AMERICANA

My pal Rob Port of SayAnythingBlog.com is an important North Dakota grassroots tea party voice. He told me, "The tea party movement is really diverse. There's no one model, because it's not led from the top down. It's a totally bottom-up, grassroots movement, essentially leaderless, without any central coordination. Every tea party event is its own experience.

"I think every movement needs leaders. But there is so much spontaneous energy behind the tea party movement that it needs very little leadership energy. We're all so focused on the cause that we move together toward the goal without a strong leader telling us where to go. If someone says, 'Let's meet in Grand Forks on Saturday night,' count on it, we'll show up.

"There's a lot of real genius in this movement. There are a lot of ideas for ways to limit government. If the leaders in Washington would implement just half of those ideas, we could turn this country around."

I've had the opportunity to speak at a number of tea party rallies. But as Rob said, the tea party movement isn't about what some guy on the platform has to say, but about what grassroots people have to say. These rallies bring us all together, so that we can get acquainted with other like-minded people and see that we are not alone. And here in North Dakota and Minnesota, we really listen to the people. Many politicians have forgotten the fine art of listening—and that's why they lose touch with the people. So instead of having a lot of speakers and a program at our tea party events, we like to go into the crowd and let people talk. They always have great things to say.

Every tea party event, whether in California or Ohio or Florida, is an expression of grassroots patriotism—but I don't think the grass roots grow any greener than they do here in the heartland. We pass the microphone around the crowd and let everyone speak in a democratic (with a small *d*) way. You might ask, "But how can you let just *anybody* take the microphone and say what they think? What if someone says something completely off-the-wall?" Well, it happens once in a great while—but when it does, the crowd does an amazingly good job of policing itself. If we were to screen everyone who gets to speak, if you had to have certain qualifications to take the mike, it wouldn't be a tea party, would it? And it wouldn't be grassroots.

When folks take the mike, there's always a bit of hesitation because they've never done anything like this before. They're not polished public speakers. But when they talk from the heart, you get a lump in your throat and a tingle down your spine, because they are saying exactly what's on your own mind. They're not comfortable protesting the government. But when the *government* of America stops living up to the *ideals* of America, they have to speak out.

At the tea parties in North Dakota and Minnesota, I've seen hundreds of grassroots Americans speaking out for the first time in their lives. I remember Kevin, a father whose two little girls stood nearby. "I'll admit that I'm scared about America's future," he said, "and I'm also teed off because we're being lied to by Washington. We're being lied to by the media. Our president tells us that we can keep our private health care plan if we want it—but then we read page sixteen of the bill and it proves he's not telling the truth. It's not just the health care bill—it's TARP and cap and trade and stimulus and on and on. So I brought my little girls here so they can see all of your faces and know that we're not alone."

As he said that, someone in the crowd shouted, "You don't have to apologize for being an American here!"

Kevin grinned, choking with emotion, and said, "It's good to know that I can ask you all to keep praying—and I know it won't fall on deaf ears."

And I remember a man in a white golf shirt, who took the mike eagerly and with a look of infectious excitement in his eyes said, "Listen, North Dakota may be small, but we're mighty! We are *mighty*! And the very powers are in God's hands and it's time that the politicians listen to the people. Because the Bible says, 'God puts one down and sets up another,'[31] and I think there are going to be some replacements coming!"

A mother said, "I don't see this current administration placing our youth at the top of their priorities. Across the country, you'll see in the media that teen pregnancy rates are rising, STD rates are rising. But you know what's happening in North Dakota? Teen pregnancy and STD rates are *falling*! And you know what? North Dakota has spent a lot of money on abstinence education, and it's *working*! Don't let anybody tell you that abstinence education doesn't work. It *is* working!"

A man in a blue shirt stood up and said, "Many of you have been in the military, and you've taken an oath, the same oath that the president and the Congress have taken—an oath to preserve, protect, and defend the Constitution of the United States. And I think you and I take that oath a lot more seriously than they do.

"We are facing a fiscal train wreck. What solution has Congress proposed? They want to give us *more* bureaucratic entitlement programs, *more* gasoline on the flames, even though these programs are proven not to work. So they are spending more and borrowing more, and that train is coming faster and faster. Are these elected leaders that stupid—or are they bankrupting this nation with deliberate intent? Either way, it's unacceptable to you and to me.

"Where in the Constitution does it give the government permission to be in the insurance business? Or the banking business? Or the communications industry? Or the car-manufacturing business?

"This nation was founded on popular sovereignty. We're the boss, they are the servants, they work for us. We all wish there was a Balanced Budget Amendment to the Constitution, but we can enforce a balanced budget even without an amendment. Congress comes up for election every two years and you can let your representatives know that you're not going to vote for anyone who votes to raise the national debt by even one nickel.

"This is a defining moment. Now is the time, patriots. Act now. Soon it will be too late. I pray that the God of the universe will bless America again. Preserve, protect, and defend!"

Leon Francis, an African-American tea partier, took the microphone at one tea party event and said, "We already have Obama Motors, Obama Energy, Obama Banking, and more czars than I can count. Beware, people, beware. We're Americans! As Ronald Reagan said, the nine most terrifying words in the English language are, 'I'm from the government and I'm here to help.' "

A woman from Minnesota, Eloise from Dilworth, stepped up to the microphone and said, "I know what many of you have been thinking: 'What can I do to save my country? I'm just one person!' Well, there are a lot of things you can do. Being here tonight is a good start. But we need to keep informed about what's going on in the government—and listening to Scott Hennen's radio show is a good start.

"Next, get involved. Help the candidates who are committed to smaller government and more freedom. Volunteer to stuff envelopes and knock on doors. And don't be taken in by politicians who talk out of both sides of their mouths. Make them keep their promises! Hold their feet to the fire!

"Above all, pray to the Almighty. We've got to fall on our knees and ask God to help our country. If we do that, He will answer."

I'll never forget a boy, about thirteen years old, who took the microphone and said, "I had a conversation on Facebook with someone from my own town. And he called us idiots for opposing the national health care plan. That is just rude!" It did my heart good to see the next generation standing up for constitutional values, and speaking to his peers straight from his heart—even at the cost of being called an "idiot."

And there was another young man, about twenty years old, from Herman, Minnesota. His name was Lucas and he looked and talked like a distance runner. "We all came here to blow off some steam in protest," he said. "But remember, this is not the end of this kinetic energy. This is the starting block for this marathon, and our finish line is election day. We have to run through that tape and keep our government honest."

A man named Lee from Kindred, North Dakota, told us about attending one of Senator Dorgan's town hall meetings at a farmstead five miles west of Colfax. "The place was hard to find, hard to get to," Lee said. "Even so, tons of people showed up. Senator Dorgan has been saying that this bill is not government health care. I brought a printout of a section of the bill which clearly shows that it is. It says so right in the bill, pages thirty, thirty-one, and forty. And after I showed it to him in black and white, the senator looked me in the eye and said, 'It's not in the bill.' Now, the reason he held a town hall meeting on a farmstead, way out of town, is because he and everybody else in D.C. are scared of people like you who are here tonight. So keep it up. Call your representatives, call your senators, not just once, but every single day."

We heard from Maury, a former Los Angeles police lieutenant who had retired to Grand Forks. "The other day," he said, "I was listening to Scott on the radio. He was talking about our troops protecting us in Iraq and Afghanistan. And I got to thinking that we have a responsibility right here in the United States to preserve our country so that when our troops come back, they have a free country to come back to."

Sue Ann from Wheatland, North Dakota, took the mike and held up her cell phone. "Could I see a show of hands," she said, "of everyone who has one of these in your pocket? That's right, it's a cell phone. I urge you to put the numbers of your representative and your senators in your cell phone. Whenever you want to let your representatives know what you think, hit that speed dial and give them a call. If we all did that every day, think of the difference we would make!"

An older gentleman took the microphone and said, "I want to remind you of a word from the Bible: 'Great peace have they that love thy law, and nothing shall offend them.'[32] So don't be offended by the attacks and the things that are going on in the world. Your enemy wants you to feel offended and terrorized. Get it out of your head. Focus on God's peace."

And stay-at-home mom Renae Mitchell of Fargo, who has organized a number of patriotic events in our area, took the microphone and held up a currency note. "How many of you," she said, "have ever seen a one-hundred-trillion-dollar bill? Anybody? This is a very real bill. This is a genuine one-hundred-trillion-dollar bill. They are printing these in the nation of Zimbabwe. What does this one-hundred-trillion-dollar bill buy you? A pack of gum. This is called hyperinflation. It has destroyed the economy of Zimbabwe, and the monetary policy of Zimbabwe is exactly the policy our country is following today. And if we think we are somehow so special that we can defy the laws of economics then we are sadly mistaken.

"Let me leave you with a quote from one of my favorite tax-protesting, rabble-rousing patriots, Sam Adams. 'It does not require a majority to prevail, but rather an irate, tireless minority keen to set brush fires in people's minds.' And I don't know about you, but I'm irate, and I'm tireless, and I'm ready to win this! We have to win for the sake of our children's future, and we can and we will!"

Wow! What a cross-section of grassroots Americana!

No political party could manufacture this kind of passion for America. These everyday Americans speak simply yet more eloquently than any politician or talk show host. They have infinitely more wisdom and insight than any media pundit. When grassroots Americans talk about their hopes and fears and love for America, I am absolutely riveted.

Who is guarding the spirit of freedom in America today? Not the ruling class in Washington. Not the chattering class in the media. It's you and me—We the People.

The grass roots of America.

THE COMMONSENSE ACTION AGENDA

Here are some grassroots actions you can take, starting today:

✓ Ross Ueckert, the "one-man walking tea party," walked from North Dakota to Washington, D.C., to honor veterans and bring attention to government corruption. He came up with a creative way to make a patriotic statement to America. Does his example inspire you? What creative action could you take to make your patriotic voice heard in a creative new way?

✓ Every day, Ross Ueckert prayed, "God, put my feet on the path you want me to take. Put the words in my mouth that you want me to speak. And give me the wisdom to speak to the people you put in front of me." How might your life change if you said that prayer every day? Consider making a commitment to praying that prayer on a daily basis for the next thirty days.

✓ If there are no tea party events planned in your area, get together with other commonsense conservatives and plan one. Talk to people in neighboring communities who have held tea parties. Ask for advice in planning and publicizing a tea party—but don't feel you have to follow anyone else's format exactly. There is no "one-size-fits-all" format for grassroots activism. Feel free to experiment and try out new ideas.

✓ You might want to focus on a specific theme for each tea party event. Put up signs and banners underscoring that theme. Here are a few ideas: On April 15, focus on taxes and out-of-control spending. On July 4, focus on themes of liberty. On September 17, Constitution Day, focus on themes of limited constitutional government.

✓ Have a sign-up sheet at every tea party so you can collect email addresses and contact information and keep people informed of future events.

✓ Assign someone to take photos and video to illustrate the size, enthusiasm, and patriotic spirit of your tea party event. Make them available to the local news media and post them to Facebook, Twitter, and other social media.

✓ Expect attacks from liberals and the media. Don't let other people goad you into name-calling or losing your temper. Always keep your cool and remember that you have the truth on your side.

✓ When the news media covers your event fairly, compliment and thank them. They just might make a habit of it.

3

PROMOTING SMALLER, SMARTER GOVERNMENT

D o you find it hard to remember the difference between $1 million, $1 billion, and $1 trillion? Well, so do our elected representatives. But Renae Mitchell of Fargo knows how to explain the difference so even a senator can understand it.

"Instead of dollars, think of seconds," she told the crowd at one tea party rally. "One million seconds equals 11.6 days. One billion seconds equals roughly 32 years. One trillion seconds equals 32,000 years. Now, our government is more than $14 trillion in debt, and heading toward $15 trillion—so if the government started paying off that debt today at a rate of a dollar per second, it would take nearly a half million years to pay it off. And that doesn't even take into account the interest on the debt, nor the unfunded liabilities for Social Security, Medicare, and Medicaid and prescription drug benefits, which are estimated at more than $100 trillion. Our government is spending us into oblivion and saddling our children with an unsustainable debt. How will we ever dig ourselves out of this hole?"

Renae Mitchell is not afraid of powerful people and doesn't hesitate to speak her mind. In August 2009, Senator Byron Dorgan (D-North Dakota) held a town hall meeting at the firehouse in Casselton. Renae got up in front of that crowd, looked Senator Dorgan in the eye, and said, "I'm a stay-at-home mom from Fargo. My husband and I worked hard, lived within our means, and made the right choices. I worked full-time for six years before we had kids. My husband and I paid down our mortgage, saved our money, and did all the right things. At the same time, a lot of our friends were buying houses and cars they couldn't afford while we stayed in our little house for twelve years. That's called being responsible. We worked hard in those years so that I could stay home and take care of my kids.

"So here's what I want to know from you, Senator: While the federal government is making it harder and harder for me to stay home and take care of my kids, how can you and your fellow Democrats and Republicans vote for all of those big-spending programs that are not paid for, then look me in the eye and tell me that I have to pay for people who made the wrong choices?"

The meeting erupted in cheers and applause. It was a long time before Senator Dorgan could restore order and attempt to answer Renae Mitchell's question.

I wish we had 535 commonsense moms like Renae Mitchell in the United States Congress. Grassroots citizens like Renae know not only the value of a dollar, but the value of a *trillion* dollars. A Congress full of grassroots moms would stop the insanity, put our government on a sensible budget, and clean house in Washington, D.C.

THE VICIOUS BIG-GOVERNMENT SPIRAL

"Conservatism favors the restraint of government," humorist P. J. O'Rourke wrote in *Parliament of Whores*. "A little government and a little luck are necessary in life, but only a fool trusts either of them. Also, conservatism is, at least in its American form, a philosophy that relies upon personal responsibility and promotes private liberty. . . . I have only one firm belief about the American political system, and that is this: God is a Republican and Santa Claus is a Democrat."[1]

When the founding fathers crafted our Constitution, they established a government with restricted powers and restrained responsibilities. You find the scope of our government outlined in Article I, Section 8: taxation, coinage, national defense, the court system, post offices, roads, and the repayment of debts. There's nothing in Article I,

Section 8, about government getting into the banking or automobile manufacturing business, or getting into the health insurance business, or controlling all the nation's schools from Washington, D.C., or subsidizing various industries or the arts or public broadcasting.

Our fourth president, James Madison, was the principal author of the United States Constitution and has rightly been called its father. Madison wrote over a third of the Federalist Papers, the most authoritative commentary on the Constitution and the last word on the original intent of the framers of the Constitution. In *The Federalist* No. 45, published January 26, 1788, Madison wrote, "The powers delegated by the proposed Constitution to the federal government, are few and defined."[2] In other words, the original intent of the framers of the Constitution was that the role of government should be severely limited to a few, well-defined powers and responsibilities. Any functions not specifically defined by the Constitution are reserved to the states and to the people. Any laws that are written or spending that is authorized by Congress that goes beyond that limited scope are plainly unconstitutional. So what we have today is a government that is operating well beyond the boundaries of its constitutional limits.

That is why government is too big and too expensive. By allowing government to grow beyond those limits, we have created a government that is destined to collapse of its own immense weight—*unless we act now* to restore common sense and constitutional limits to our government.

As government grows, so does the number of government workers, which means U.S. taxpayers have to pay more for government salaries—and government pensions. Today, fewer than 10 percent of U.S. workers are employed in the manufacturing sector (versus roughly 25 percent in the early 1970s).[3] By contrast, government employees account for 18 percent of U.S. workers and 51.5 percent of all union membership.[4] We have almost twice as many government employees as manufacturing employees, yet government does not produce anything, does not contribute to the economy, and does not create wealth. There is something terribly wrong with this picture.

The growth of government has produced the growth of government unions, such as the Service Employees International Union

(SEIU) and the American Federation of State, County, and Municipal Employees (AFSCME). I'm not opposed to unionization in principle—I have a tremendous respect for the American worker, and in times past, trade unions have prevented workers from being exploited and mistreated. There is no better worker in the world than right here. The question is: are American workers well served by their union leadership? Today, many union bosses exploit workers for power and wealth in much the same way that corporate bosses did a few generations ago. I don't see how unions today are helping the cause of the American worker.

In the private sector, there are free market checks and balances that prevent unions from gaining more power than they should. If a union extracts too many concessions from a private company during contract negotiations, the company can't remain competitive; it will go bankrupt. If there are no checks and balances on union demands, the union will eventually kill the company, like a parasite consuming its host—and the union jobs will disappear. So there is a free market incentive for unions to moderate their demands in the private sector.

But this free market incentive doesn't exist in the public sector. Government doesn't have to be competitive, and government unions do not worry that their demands could bankrupt the government. Unlike private companies, government doesn't have to worry about the bottom line. There is no bottom line. When government wants more money, it simply raises taxes or it borrows another trillion dollars from China.

So as government grows bigger, it hires more workers, who join government unions. This gives union lobbyists more money to slosh around the halls of Congress to buy billions of dollars' worth of favors and concessions. Government payrolls grow fatter and more expensive, government unions grow more powerful, and We the People get stuck with the bill. Conn Carroll of the Heritage Foundation explains:

> Generous contracts paid for by your tax dollars have become the main source of union growth. While private-sector unions lost 834,000 members in 2009, public-sector unions actually gained 64,000 members. Not only has the federal government been adding

new union members, but the government is also paying them more than their services are worth in the private sector. Depending on the methodology employed, the average federal employee receives as much as 40 percent more in total compensation than an equally skilled private-sector worker would receive. Including both wages and benefits, overpaying federal workers costs taxpayers approximately $40–50 billion per year. Government unions then take your tax dollars, turn right around, and use them to lobby for even bigger government.[5]

What's worse, while private sector workers get laid off by the millions in a recession, government jobs are recession-proof. In fact, government payrolls continue to expand even as the economy and the tax base shrink. From 2007 through 2010, the private sector shed approximately 12 million jobs while the government added 188,000 public sector workers to its payroll.[6]

According to the Department of Labor's Bureau of Labor Statistics (BLS), private sector workers earn an average of $27.49 per hour ($19.45 in wages, $8.05 in benefits) while government workers average $39.83 per hour ($26.24 in wages, $13.60 in benefits). The average salaried federal worker earns $71,206 per year versus $40,331 for the average salaried worker in the private sector.

And the disparity is growing. The BLS reports that, from December 2006 to December 2009, private sector compensation increased by 6.9 percent versus 9.8 percent for government workers. Government pay packages are becoming surprisingly fat. From December 2007 to June 2009, the number of federal government workers making at least $150,000 *more than doubled* from about 30,000 to more than 66,000—and this took place *during a recession*, while the private sector was shedding millions of jobs. And *USA Today* observes that when the 2007–2008 recession began, "the Transportation Department had only one person earning a salary of $170,000 or more. Eighteen months later, 1,690 employees had salaries above $170,000." Economist Mark J. Perry points out that this represents *an increase of 168,900 percent*, again during a recession, as unemployment devastated the private sector.[7]

Meanwhile, the political class continues to generate new programs and spend wealth that hasn't even been created yet, producing a whole host of budget-busting big-government programs: the American Recovery and Reinvestment Act of 2009 (President Obama's failed $787 billion stimulus program), unemployment extension ($83 billion), the Children's Health Insurance Program ($73 billion), the Dodd-Frank Wall Street Reform Bill ($10 billion), foreclosure relief ($11.3 billion), the Serve America Act ($6 billion), and on and on.[8] So we have a vicious spiral in which tax-and-spend politicians and government unions drive a perpetual and out-of-control expansion of big government.

Liberal-progressives love big government. Ruling-class politicians love big government because it gives them enormous power. They become rich and influential by dispensing political favors at taxpayer expense. The bigger government grows, the more power they wield. They top the guest list of every Washington party, they hobnob with other powerful elites, the media clamors for their opinions and pronouncements on the news of the day. For the ruling class, the government spells *power*.

But let's give rank-and-file liberals—the Democratic Party's grass roots—credit for good intentions. I think most grassroots liberals believe that big government is the way to improve people's lives, especially the lives of the poor. They really believe that poor people would wither and die if the government welfare state weren't there to write them a check every month to pay their rent and buy their groceries. Your average Democratic voter may not fully understand how the welfare state perpetuates a cycle of dependency, generation by generation, or how the welfare state traps people in poverty and enslavement to a government check.

Star Parker has been a guest on my show. She's the founder of CURE (Coalition for Urban Renewal and Education) and a recent Republican candidate for Congress from California's 37th District (Long Beach and Compton). An African-American conservative, she tells her own story of welfare dependency in her book *Uncle Sam's Plantation: How Big Government Enslaves America's Poor and What You Can Do About It*. She began collecting welfare in 1976 after moving to

California. She found that she could live recklessly, get pregnant multiple times, spend her days smoking pot and roller-skating at Venice Beach, spend her nights at clubs, and the government (that is, the taxpayers) would pick up the tab for everything.

She discovered that she could get free grant money by taking a couple of classes at the city college. She could collect extra welfare money by getting pregnant, then have a Medicaid-funded abortion a couple of months later. When she contracted a sexually transmitted disease, she was treated at the "free" clinic. Her welfare caseworker advised her, "Do not open a bank account and do not get married." Parker recalled that the caseworker "did not want to spend her time seeing me. She instructed me on how to fill out the monthly CA-7 form to ensure that I would receive my checks without having to come back to her office. She sent me away with food stamps, free healthcare, and a voucher for a deposit on my new apartment. . . . Just like that I was hooked. Welfare became my source of sustenance, and I became dependent on the government."

Star Parker did not begin to break free of the big-government welfare trap until, one Sunday morning "after almost four years of bellying up to the government trough," she sat in church and a black minister thundered from the pulpit, "God is your source, not the government!" It was as if the minister was speaking only to her.

Until she heard those words, it was as if she had been living in a big-government-induced stupor. For four years, she had been trapped in a belief system that the welfare state had systematically drummed into her brain. She explained her mind-set this way: "Provision was made to ensure that it would not be necessary for me to take responsibility for my actions and lifestyle. . . . I believed I was entitled to receive government welfare anytime I wanted it and viewed it as an unlimited resource. This belief was intrinsic to my worldview. I didn't realize my belief system had trapped me in spiritual and economic poverty. What else could I believe considering my life experience?"[9]

Grassroots liberals believe that by supporting big-government programs, they are showing compassion to people like Star Parker. But she will tell you that big government was destroying her life, destroying her initiative, and enabling her to completely waste her human potential for several years. The welfare state funded her four abortions—a destruction of four innocent lives that she deeply regrets today.

In early 2010, when Star Parker announced her campaign for Congress, she wrote a column explaining why she was running, saying that she was determined to send a message to the American people and the American government: The big-government welfare state is killing the American Dream for America's chronically poor. "As a young woman," she says, "I was on welfare myself. I saw from inside the perverse and destructive culture it created. A dehumanized culture of dependence and irresponsibility that encourages behavior exactly the opposite of what a successful life demands." She adds, "The result speaks for itself. Fifty years and a trillion plus dollars in spending after President Johnson announced the War on Poverty, poverty rates are unchanged." [10]

I believe that you and I, as grassroots conservatives, can reach out to our friends and neighbors, our coworkers and family members, who are grassroots liberals. We can engage them in conversation at the water cooler and over the back fence. Part of loving your neighbor is opening a dialogue and talking about real-life issues. We can talk to them about the destruction that the big-government welfare state produces in human lives. We *can* influence those well-intentioned (but misinformed) grassroots liberals who think that a government check from a bureaucrat equals compassion.

We conservatives know that big government is not the solution—it's the problem. We know that as government expands, liberty shrinks. As government shrinks, liberty expands. Big government usually takes one of two forms: (1) the welfare state, which promises to give you everything you want; and (2) the totalitarian state, which takes away everything you have. Whether you live under either one, you lose your freedom.

Liberal-progressives often accuse conservatives of being "antigovernment," which I find absurd. Conservatives don't believe in anarchy. We firmly believe in the United States Constitution, and the Constitution is nothing more or less than a blueprint for sound government. But constitutional government is *limited* government. The founding fathers designed the United States government to provide a commonsense balance between governance and freedom—and they designed the Constitution to push the needle toward less government and more freedom. So while we conservatives do believe in government, we also subscribe to the old Latin maxim meaning, "He governs best who governs least."[11]

Another accusation liberals often level at conservatives and the tea party movement is that we don't really care about the federal debt and deficits and runaway spending. They say, "Where was the outrage among tea partiers when George W. Bush was busting the budget and running up debt? Tea partiers got mad at big government only when a black man was in the Oval Office." I must emphasize that (a) tea partiers are not racists, and (b) George W. Bush was not the budget-busting big spender the left claims him to be.

Here are the facts about federal spending during the Bush era:

Average federal spending under Bush was less, in terms of share of gross domestic product, than it was under Bill Clinton, George H. W. Bush, and even Ronald Reagan. Of those four presidents, the deficits under Bill Clinton were the smallest, as a percentage of the overall economy, because of two factors: the dot-com boom of the 1990s and the fiscal restraint imposed by the Newt Gingrich–led Republican Congress. The second-smallest deficits of those four presidents took place under George W. Bush. The Bush budget deficit averaged 2 percent of gross domestic product, which ranks below the fifty-year average of 3 percent.

These statistics from Bush's book *Decision Points* put Bush-era spending into perspective:

		SPENDING TO GDP	TAXES TO GDP	DEFICIT TO GDP	DEBT TO GDP
Reagan	1981–1988	22.4%	18.2%	4.2%	34.9%
Bush 41	1989–1992	21.9%	17.9%	4.0%	44.0%
Clinton	1993–2000	19.8%	19.0%	0.8%	44.9%
Bush 43	2001–2008	19.6%	17.6%	2.0%	36.0%

Clearly, George W. Bush presided over a smaller government—in terms of spending as a percentage of GDP—than his three predecessors, including Ronald Reagan. Measured against historic standards, the Bush deficits were modest and responsible.[12]

Of course, as conservatives, we want our government to stop running deficits and start running surpluses. The only way we will ever pay down the national debt is by operating year by year in the black. As Admiral Mike Mullen, the chairman of the Joint Chiefs of Staff, has bluntly observed, "The most significant threat to our national security is our debt."[13] Admiral Mullen adds that taxpayers will pay approximately $600 billion in 2012 *just on the interest* on the national debt—an amount equal to the entire defense budget.[14] The debt not only limits defense-spending options, but hamstrings our policy decisions. For example, if we ever need China to apply pressure to the ill-behaved North Korean regime, how much influence will we have when we are indebted to China for nearly a trillion dollars?

That's why the tea partiers are up in arms over the national debt. It's concern for the future of America that ignites tea party passions—not the color of Barack Obama's skin. When liberals play the race card, they are trying to change the subject. The tea partiers are angry because Barack Obama has *more than tripled* the Bush deficits with his pork- and earmark-riddled budgets, the 2009 stimulus bill, Cash for Clunkers, and more—the biggest government spending spree in human history. Grassroots Americans know that the unprecedented Obama debt load threatens the future of their children and grandchildren.

Was George W. Bush a perfect president from a conservative point of view? Did I always agree with him? No. But President Bush was an able and dedicated wartime president *and* a president who managed the economy well. The wisdom of George W. Bush is borne out by the fact that there was never another attack on U.S. soil during the Bush presidency—and it is borne out by the economic numbers.

During his presidency, America experienced *fifty-two months of uninterrupted job growth*. Worker productivity—the key long-term indicator of a nation's economic health and competitiveness—rose at a 2.6 average annual rate during the Bush presidency, outperforming both Bill Clinton (2.0 percent) and Ronald Reagan (1.6 percent). The 2003 Bush tax cuts produced an enormous economic surge, prompting the

World Economic Forum to call the U.S. economy the most competitive economy in the world. The Bush tax policies produced such a vibrant economy that by 2007 the deficit had shrunk to only 1 percent of GDP.[15]

I believe that in years to come, George W. Bush will be ranked among the five best presidents this country has ever had. He'll be revered alongside George Washington, Thomas Jefferson, Abraham Lincoln, and Ronald Reagan. George W. Bush was president when we suffered the worst attack from a foreign enemy on American soil. The coordinated attack on 9/11 killed more Americans than the attack on Pearl Harbor in 1941. Nearly three thousand people died, the vast majority of them civilians. The attacks horrified the nation and shook our national confidence. Many experts believed that the destruction of the World Trade Center in New York City would plunge the entire nation into an economic calamity.

But George W. Bush responded forcefully. He skillfully managed the economy and kept America from sliding into panic or recession. He launched the War on Terror and kept Al Qaeda off balance and on the run. Without concern for his own political future, he persevered in fighting the war in Iraq to a successful conclusion, even after the war had become politically unpopular.

Though the government grew under George W. Bush, it *exploded* under Barack Obama. During his first three months in office, Obama signed both the $787 billion stimulus bill and the $410 billion omnibus spending bill, which included 8,500 earmarks worth $7.7 billion. He wasted no time in breaking his campaign pledge from the first presidential debate: "We need earmark reform. And when I'm president, I will go line by line to make sure that we are not spending money unwisely."[16] Around the same time, the Obama administration announced a budget projection that would produce $9 trillion in deficits over the coming decade, sending the national debt skyrocketing to $23 trillion (nearly 75 percent of GDP) by 2019.[17]

And that was only the beginning. In his State of the Union address in January 2010, President Obama promised trillions of dollars in new big-government spending—Obamacare, a cap-and-trade energy bill, more "stimulus" spending (disguised as a "jobs bill"), and more. President Obama proposed these new programs fully aware that the Social Security and Medicare entitlement costs are scheduled to balloon like a—well, like a balloon. Over the next few years, 78 million baby boomers are going to retire and flood the entitlement system with demands for taxpayer dollars—a whopping $106.4 trillion in unfunded liabilities. Those are benefits the federal government has promised to pay out to baby boomers over the coming years, over and above the annual budget and payments to reduce the national debt—*and there are no projected revenues to cover those payouts*. America's GDP for one year is about $14 trillion, so the entitlement liability equals almost eight years of *the entire economic productivity of the United States* or roughly *twice the annual GDP of the entire world*.[18]

President Obama and the Democrats are intelligent, well-informed people. They know about the fiscal iceberg that's directly ahead of our ship of state—yet they not only refuse to change course, but are determined to steer straight for that iceberg, full steam ahead. What part of "certain disaster" do they not understand? I can't believe that my fellow Americans, even the liberal-progressive Americans of the Democratic Party, have set out to deliberately collapse the American economy and dismantle American society . . . but they couldn't do a more devastating job than by spending us into oblivion.

And that is not a figure of speech.

REAGANOMICS WORKS; OBAMANOMICS FAILS

Robert L. Borosage is the president of the Institute for America's Future, a far-left think tank, and has worked closely with such leftist leaders as Jesse Jackson, the late Paul Wellstone, Barbara Boxer, and Carol Moseley Braun. Soon after passage of President Obama's so-called stimulus bill, Borosage wrote a column advocating even *more* irresponsible deficit spending. "The real danger," he wrote, "isn't that Obama is spending too much, but too little. . . . Most likely, Obama will have to come back for another stimulus and more money for restructuring the banks. . . . The president has repudiated the failed conservative policies of the past and called on the country to change course. He has put forth a budget that calls for sweeping change. He has raised the stakes. This will be a transformational presidency if he succeeds. We dare not let him fail." [19]

Failed conservative policies? When have truly conservative policies been implemented in America's recent past? Authentic, unadulterated conservatism has never been the governing principle in America during my lifetime. For as long as I can remember, our government has been *at most* a kind of constant chess game between limited-government conservatives and big-government liberals.

When Ronald Reagan rescued America from the incompetent clutches of Jimmy Carter, he was able to achieve a dramatic transformation of our economy and our standing in the world. He defeated the Soviet Union without firing a shot. But while Reagan was able to put many conservative reforms into effect during his two terms, he faced opposition from a Democrat-controlled big-government Congress throughout his time in office.

One of Reagan's campaign pledges in 1980 was that he was going to abolish the cabinet-level Department of Education, which Jimmy Carter had created as a favor to the teachers' unions. The Department of Education has never educated even one child—it adds a layer of bureaucracy and intrusive regulation to the process of educating children, and it violates Article I, Section 8, of the U.S. Constitution, which makes no mention of education as a federal function. The framers of the Constitution intended that education should be left to the states and local districts. And the wisdom of the framers is reflected in the fact that standardized student test scores have declined steadily ever since the creation of the Department of Education.

So again, I ask you: when has genuine, 100 percent conservatism ever been tried? Even though Ronald Reagan spent eight years in office battling big-government liberals in the Congress and the bureaucracy, and even though he was never able to shrink the size of government but only slow its growth, he achieved miracles.

Ronald Reagan's program for restoring America was simple but profound: Cut tax rates. Cut domestic spending. Cut oppressive regulations on business. His problem: how to get his conservative agenda through the Democrat-controlled House and Senate. Every budget

Ronald Reagan sent to Congress, Speaker Tip O'Neill declared dead on arrival. So Reagan was never able to achieve the far-reaching reforms and drastic budget cuts he wanted. Even so, he was able to prod Congress into slowing the rate of government spending from 5 percent per year under Carter to a more modest 3.7 percent per year.

He was also able to overhaul the U.S. tax system, beginning with the Economic Recovery and Tax Act of 1981. By 1986, Reagan had slashed individual tax rates across the board (the top marginal rate went from 70 percent to 28 percent), while providing businesses with expanded investment tax credits and depreciation deductions. These tax rate cuts became the dynamo that powered the resurgence of the once-gasping American economy.

Liberals often claim—either ignorantly or dishonestly—that Ronald Reagan's tax cuts produced huge deficits. Well, there were big deficits during the Reagan years, but they were not caused by the Reagan tax cuts. In order for the tax cuts to have caused the deficits, revenue would have to shrink. Instead, tax revenue *nearly doubled* during the Reagan years, from $599 billion in 1981 to $991 billion in 1989. Adjusted for inflation, tax revenue increased (in constant 1987 dollars) from $767 billion in 1981 to $916 billion in 1989, a 20 percent increase.

If revenues increased so dramatically, why did the federal government run deficits throughout the Reagan years? I'm sure you know the answer: Federal spending *exploded* during the 1980s, from $590.9 billion in 1980 to $1.25 trillion in 1990. Adjusted for inflation, that represents a 33.4 percent jump in spending at the same time revenue increased 20 percent.[20] So, did the Reagan tax cuts bust the budget? No. It was spending by the Democrat-controlled Congress that deserves the blame. Then as now, our problem is not that we aren't taxed enough, but that big-government politicians *spend too much*.

Ronald Reagan took over an economy that had been devastated by Jimmy Carter's big-government policies, and he liberated that economy by slashing taxes, domestic spending, and oppressive regulation. The result, according to the National Bureau of Economic Research: the economy came roaring back, expanding month after month, quarter after quarter, producing almost two decades of near-continuous growth. This period of economic expansion lasted from

November 1982 through March 2001, with only a brief nine-month downturn from July 1990 to March 1991. According to the Department of Labor, the Reagan expansion created an astounding 41.6 million jobs.

Now, contrast Ronald Reagan's record of limited government and big economic growth with Barack Obama's record of big government and economic decline. Barack Obama promised that his gargantuan $787 billion "stimulus" package would create jobs and keep unemployment from rising above 8 percent. And if stimulus spending actually worked the way liberals think it does, throwing $787 billion at the economy should have done the trick. But Obama lost 4 million jobs in his first year in office, and unemployment reached 10 percent. According to former White House political director Jeffrey Lord, "Obama has now produced the worst one-year record of job creation by a presidential program since the end of World War II—which is to say in 70 years."[21]

Any fair-minded observer would have to admit that big-government policies, such as massive deficit-ballooning "stimulus" schemes, are doomed to fail. They didn't work during the Great Depression. They didn't work during the Carter years. And they didn't work for Barack Obama. What does work? Limited-government policies that free the taxpayers, free the business sector, and reduce the scope and intrusiveness of the government.

In short, Reaganomics works; Obamanomics fails.

Not only did the Reagan tax cuts produce a boom in economic activity and employment, but they also produced a boom in charitable giving. Liberals like to disparage the 1980s as the "Me Decade," an era of selfishness and greed. In reality, as Dinesh D'Souza points out, "the 1980s saw the greatest outpouring of private generosity in history. Americans who contributed about $65 billion (as measured in 1990 dollars) in charity in 1980 gave more than $100 billion annually by the end of the decade, a real increase of 57%. The average American who gave $377 to charity in 1980 raised his or her contribution to $493 in 1990." This amazing increase in charitable donations during the Reagan years was "greater than at any other time in the postwar era," wrote D'Souza—and Americans didn't just write charitable checks.

They truly got into the *spirit* of giving, volunteering more time to civic, social, and religious causes than ever before.[22]

Now, imagine what would happen if we could elect true limited-government conservatives who would scale the government back to its constitutional limits and slash programs that fail to meet the test of Article I, Section 8, of the Constitution. Imagine if we had a truly conservative president and a truly conservative Congress who would dismantle programs, cut taxes, and truly set the free market system *free*. Imagine if we replaced the welfare state with incentives for people to donate generously to private charities and religious agencies that meet social needs *far* more effectively and compassionately than any government bureaucrat could.

A low tax rate would put America back to work again. Businesses and industries would create new wealth hand over fist, producing full employment and a truly astonishing standard of living. There would be so much surplus wealth that charitable agencies would be flush with money to meet every social and human need.

A government run 100 percent by the conservative principles of Friedrich Hayek, Ludwig von Mises, and Milton Friedman would be the utopia that humanity has dreamed of for thousands of years. We know this is true because every time America returns to those free market conservative principles—even partially and incompletely, as we did during the Reagan years—economic miracles take place.

With the 2010 election, the GOP now has the chance to prove it is still the Party of Reagan, that it can deliver on its promises to scale government back, and that it can halt America's headlong plunge into bankruptcy. And if, in 2012, we elect a president who will turn bold conservative ideas into action, we could witness a new American renaissance.

THE BIG-GOVERNMENT BLAME GAME

One of the big lies the Democrats often level at Republicans is this: "Republicans hate old people! Republicans want to take away Social Security! Republicans want to cut Medicare!" Election after election, the Democrats trot out this lie and try to scare old people to death. But what is truly amazing is that *the Democrats themselves actually cut*

Medicare by a half trillion dollars in order to fund Obamacare.[23] The hypocrisy is absolutely breathtaking.

I've seen liberal pundits ridicule a sign at a tea party rally that read, "Keep your government hands off my Medicare!" They are amused at the poor tea party protester who doesn't seem to understand that Medicare is a big-government program, so the idea that government shouldn't be interfering with Medicare is an oxymoron. The fact is that over the decades our government has taught the American people to rely on these government programs. Now, Medicare is failing the people who depend on it—and the Democrats are undermining Medicare even further by defunding the program in order to fund an even bigger health care boondoggle called Obamacare.

Columnist Ross Douthat observes in the *New York Times* that tea partiers "say they're for small government, but they don't want anyone to touch their Social Security and Medicare. This is by far the most persuasive liberal storyline. Poll after poll suggests that Tea Partiers are ambivalent about trimming entitlements, even though that's the spending that will ultimately send either deficits or taxes through the roof."[24]

Well, he does have a point. Social Security and Medicare are big-government programs, and the unfunded liabilities of these programs will bankrupt the United States government in a few years if we don't take action now. But we are where we are. We can't go back to the 1930s and undo the New Deal. We can't go back to the 1960s and undo the Great Society. For decades, millions of people, including retirees, have made long-term decisions and organized their lives around government programs such as Social Security and Medicare. There is no conservative, no Republican, who suggests that we should pull the rug out from under these people who have relied upon these government promises.

But there are a lot of ideas for keeping these programs solvent, and all of these ideas should be on the table. Should we raise payroll taxes? No—tax hikes kill the economy, and we need a strong economy to bring revenue into the system. Raise the age for receiving the full retirement benefit? Means-test and trim benefits for higher-income recipients? Offer incentives to younger workers to divert funds to private accounts and accept lower benefits? Eliminate other government programs and apply the savings to these "entitlement" programs? These and other ideas should be explored. But we have to protect those who are vested in the Social Security and Medicare systems at the same time we protect these systems from a catastrophic collapse.

The best plan I've seen for solving America's long-term fiscal crisis is Congressman Paul Ryan's "Roadmap for America's Future." It's an ambitious, all-inclusive plan based on conservative, free market principles—principles that have already been proven to work. As Congressman Ryan explains, "The purpose of the Roadmap is to get spending in line with revenue—not the other way around."[25] The key to the Roadmap is a workable plan for reforming Social Security and Medicare to make them sustainable over the long run. The plan would also overhaul the income tax system (creating a simplified two-rate tax code that would fit on a postcard); eliminate the alternative minimum tax; eliminate taxes on saving and investing; eliminate the estate tax; replace the corporate income tax with an 8.5 percent business consumption tax; freeze nondefense discretionary spending for ten years; cap the growth rate of spending; and more.

It's a bold plan that exemplifies Paul Ryan's political courage. He once said of the Roadmap, "If I lose my job over this, then so be it. In that case, I can be doing more productive things. If you're given the opportunity to serve, you'd better serve like it's your last term every term. It's just the way I look at it. I sleep well at night."[26]

It's unfortunate there aren't a few hundred more Paul Ryans in Congress—and I think it's a disgrace that only fifteen Republican challengers signed on to the Roadmap prior to the 2010 midterm election. The Roadmap should have been our platform as conservatives, and the fact that it was largely ignored by the GOP is a troubling sign. Even North Dakota's own Rick Berg, a solid conservative who defeated nine-term Democratic congressman Earl Pomeroy, didn't sign on to the Roadmap.

I think many Republicans feared the demagoguery of the Democrats and the media who dishonestly smear the Roadmap's entitlement reforms as "cutting Social Security and Medicare." This timidity on the part of many Republicans shows that they have not caught up with grassroots Americans on these issues. Many GOP politicians are still stuck in the old mind-set that says that Social Security and Medicare are the "third rail of politics"—touch them and you'll face political electrocution. But grassroots Americans understand that if we don't reform entitlements, the system will collapse. If that happens, there will be *no* Social Security and *no* Medicare for *anyone*. These programs are dying right now—and the American people know it. They're waiting for the politicians—and especially the Republicans— to catch up to that realization and do what needs to be done to save the system.

The Democrats love the blame game. They create the crisis, then blame it on George W. Bush, the Republicans, and conservative principles. The mortgage crisis and the financial meltdown of 2008 can be traced to a number of causes, beginning with the Community Reinvestment Act (CRA) of 1977. Signed into law by President Jimmy Carter, the CRA was intended to make housing more affordable for the poor. In practice, however, it led directly to the subprime mortgage mess. During the 1990s, President Clinton ordered regulators to revise CRA rules to give people in "distressed" inner-city and rural areas more access to credit—even though these changes would force banks to make loans to people who were less likely to repay them. The federal government effectively forced banks to absorb losses in order to perform a supposed "service" to the community and help people to buy homes they couldn't afford.[27]

Fannie Mae and Freddie Mac, two government-sponsored mortgage companies, got into the act. The Clinton administration pressured Fannie Mae and Freddie Mac to extend more credit to low-income borrowers by expanding their loan portfolios in economically distressed areas, to comply with the Community Reinvestment Act. Fannie and Freddie carried out the Clinton directive by securitizing mortgages through mortgage-backed securities. This way, banks that made so-called subprime loans—that is, loans to the riskiest of borrowers—could unload those loans (and the risk) to Fannie and Freddie, quasi-private companies backed by the taxpayers.[28]

One of the biggest players in the subprime market was Countrywide Financial Corporation,[29] whose CEO, Angelo Mozilo, was handing out favors to Democratic Party leaders like Halloween treats. Countrywide was lending money like there was no tomorrow, packaging worthless subprime paper, and selling it off to Fannie and Freddie. At the same time, Mozilo was buying off Democratic Party politicians with so-called FOAs or Friend of Angelo mortgages. Powerful Democrat politicians who could keep the federal government off Angelo's back got mortgages with no origination fees, below-market rates, and other nice perks.

The list of Angelo's friends includes Senator Chris Dodd, former Clinton cabinet member Donna Shalala, former UN ambassador the late Richard Holbrooke, former Fannie Mae CEOs James Johnson and Franklin Raines, former HUD director Henry Cisneros, former Clinton aide Paul Begala, and Senate Budget Committee chairman Kent Conrad (who got a favorable mortgage for his beach house in Delaware and specially arranged financing for his investment property in Bismarck; a federal investigation ensued).[30] In fact, Mozilo and Countrywide made a $1 million below-market-rate loan to Conrad, who then voted for TARP, which in turn bailed out Countrywide with billions of dollars in taxpayer funds.[31] Not coincidentally, Senator Conrad announced in January 2011 that he would not seek reelection.

As the mortgage bubble grew toward an inevitable bursting point, Fannie and Freddie contributed heavily to the Democratic Party, and especially to the presidential campaigns of John Kerry, Hillary Clinton, and Barack Obama. Fannie Mae CEO Franklin Raines was a former Clinton administration budget director and later a consultant to the Obama campaign. In 2003, when the Bush administration tried to impose tighter financial oversight of Fannie and Freddie, it was blocked in the House by Democratic congressman Barney Frank of Massachusetts.[32] Congressman Steve King (R-Iowa) came on my show and said, "We brought an amendment to the floor on October 26, 2005, that would have moved Fannie and Freddie toward higher standards for capitalization and regulation and consistency with other lending institutions. Barney Frank came to the floor and emphatically and furiously opposed that amendment, and the amendment was defeated."

There are many villains in the story of the financial collapse of 2008. But if any one politician deserves the lion's share of blame, it is the man who blocked every attempt by the Bush administration to reform the system: Congressman Barney Frank. Bill Sammon notes that, as far back as 1991, "the *Boston Globe* reported that Frank pushed the agency [Fannie Mae] to loosen regulations on mortgages for two- and three-family homes, even though they were defaulting at twice and five times the rate of single homes, respectively."[33]

In 2003, as the Bush administration was trying to rein in the excesses of Fannie Mae and Freddie Mac, Barney Frank fought tooth and nail to preserve the unsustainable status quo. "These two entities—Fannie Mae and Freddie Mac—are not facing any kind of financial crisis," Frank insisted. "The more people exaggerate these problems, the more pressure there is on these companies, the less we will see in terms of affordable housing."[34]

That same year, Frank also said, "I want to roll the dice a little bit more in this situation towards subsidized housing."[35] Of course, Frank denied that he was rolling the dice with taxpayer money, saying, "There is no [taxpayer] guarantee, there is no explicit guarantee, there is no implicit guarantee, there is no wink-and-nod guarantee."[36] While it's true that there were no *formal* guarantees that the taxpayer would be on the hook for Fannie and Freddie's bad loans, it was clear that the taxpayer would be the ultimate backstop in case they failed—which is exactly what happened.

Even as late as mid-2009, a year after the financial collapse, Barney Frank and New York congressman Anthony Weiner continued to put pressure on Fannie Mae and Freddie Mac to drop their lending standards.[37] But who did Frank blame for the meltdown he helped cause? In an interview with CNBC financial analyst Maria Bartiromo, he predictably blamed it all on "right-wing Republicans."

Bartiromo replied, "With all due respect, Congressman, I saw videotapes of you saying in the past: 'Oh, let's open up the lending. The housing market is fine.' "

Said Barney Frank, "No, you didn't see any such tapes."

"I did," Bartiromo insisted. "I saw them on TV."[38]

But Barney Frank insisted that Maria Bartiromo did not see what she saw, did not hear what she heard—and he didn't say what he said. How does a man like Barney Frank sleep at night, knowing that he played a big part in toppling the world economy and putting millions of people out of work? And where does he get the nerve to ask for another term in office?

THE OBAMA FACTOR

And then there was Barack Obama.

His role in the financial meltdown began in 1994, when he was just out of Harvard Law School. He joined two other attorneys in filing a landmark lawsuit, *Selma S. Buycks-Roberson v. Citibank Federal Savings Bank.* The plaintiff, Ms. Buycks-Roberson, had been turned down for a loan because of bad credit, for which she suffered "embarrassment, humiliation, and emotional distress." Obama & Company upped the ante, turning the case into a class-action lawsuit alleging racial discrimination. In the end, Citibank settled, and the plaintiffs collected a total of $60,000—and the attorneys collected legal fees totaling $950,000. *Buycks-Roberson v. Citibank* was one of the first of many cases arising out of the Community Reinvestment Act in which banks were accused of racism and forced to make bad loans.[39]

During the 1990s, Barack Obama was closely involved with the pressure group ACORN, helping to train ACORN community organizers in shakedown techniques for use against Chicago-area banks. These intimidation tactics were a major factor in the subprime mortgage mess and the 2008 financial collapse.[40]

Barack Obama was also a leading recipient of political donations from the mortgage industry. He was the number-one recipient of contributions from Countrywide Financial ($22,900); Senator Christopher Dodd was second ($20,000).[41] And the top recipients of campaign contributions from Fannie Mae and Freddie Mac from 1989 through 2008 were Christopher Dodd ($133,900), John Kerry ($111,000), Barack Obama ($105,849), and Hillary Clinton ($75,550). A little further down on that list were North Dakota senators Kent Conrad ($64,491) and Byron Dorgan ($38,750).[42]

You have to wonder why quasi-governmental agencies like Fannie and Freddie are allowed to donate to the lawmakers who are supposed to oversee them. Perhaps those contributions explain why Senator Dodd, as chairman of the Senate Banking Committee, was still hailing Fannie and Freddie as "fundamentally strong" just weeks before the government stepped in and bailed out both agencies with taxpayer dough.[43]

Bottom line: the Democratic Party, led by Jimmy Carter, Bill Clinton, Christopher Dodd, Barney Frank, and yes, Barack Obama, created the conditions that led to the mortgage crisis and the financial meltdown of 2008. When the Bush administration tried to intervene to rein in Fannie and Freddie, the Democrats blocked the effort. When the house of cards inevitably collapsed near the end of the second Bush term, the Democrats blamed George W. Bush for everything. Then, once Barack Obama was in office, Christopher Dodd and Barney Frank wrote the most ironically named piece of legislation ever written, the Dodd-Frank Wall Street Reform and Consumer Protection Act. The words *reform* and *consumer protection* ought to be in quotes. The bill makes no mention whatsoever of Fannie Mae and Freddie Mac, nor does it solve any of the underlying problems created by the Community Reinvestment Act. Most of the conditions that produced the meltdown of 2008 are still in place today—and the next meltdown will probably be far worse.

Barack Obama loves to take potshots at "the previous eight years" or "the past decade" or the problems he supposedly "inherited" from the Bush administration. In July 2010, President Obama gave a speech on the economy at the University of Nevada, Las Vegas, and he talked about the economic conditions of today being "the consequence of a decade of misguided economic policies—a decade of stagnant wages, a decade of declining incomes, a decade of spiraling deficits." But as former White House economist Keith Hennessey points out, there was no "decade of spiraling deficits." The Bush administration ran comparatively modest deficits that averaged about 2 percent of GDP until the final year, when the market collapsed and the economy tipped into a deep recession. Prior to the crash, Hennessey observed, "President Bush's budget deficits were 0.6 percentage points smaller than the historic average. Deficits did not 'spiral' during the Bush presidency or the decade. They bumped around the historic average, then spiked up in the last year."[44]

But even more to the point, if Barack Obama wants us to believe he simply inherited today's economic problems because of the deficits of the Bush years, he has a huge credibility problem. Barack Obama served in the United States Senate from January 2005 through November 2008. During that time, many spending bills came before the United States Senate—*and Senator Barack Obama did not vote against any of those spending bills except one.* The only time he ever voted against spending was on September 20, 2007, when he voted "yes" on a Feingold amendment to cut off funding for the troops in Iraq. He can't blame Bush for the deficits of the Bush years without also blaming himself.[45]

The meltdown of 2008 was caused by government. Of course, there was plenty of corporate greed on Wall Street, but it took big-government interference, beginning with the Community Reinvestment Act, to create the massive distortions in the marketplace that made all of these insane subprime mortgages not merely possible, but *federally mandated.* Had the market been allowed to operate under commonsense free market rules, no banker in his right mind would have lent money to people who couldn't repay—and no banker would have ever been intimidated by an upstart ACORN attorney and community organizer named Barack Obama.

HOW BIG-GOVERNMENT PROGRAMS HARM THE ECONOMY

Big government uses the complex and intimidating tax code and regulatory code to manipulate behavior in the marketplace. Big-government politicians and bureaucrats use taxpayer dollars to reward, bribe, and bail out their cronies. Big-government policies cause perfectly healthy businesses to fail and prevent new businesses from starting up.

A prime example of how big-government programs distort the market and harm the business community is Barack Obama's Car Allowance Rebate System (CARS), better known as "Cash for Clunkers." This was Obama's plan to provide taxpayer-funded cash incentives to induce people to buy more-fuel-efficient new cars while turning in their older, less-fuel-efficient cars for scrap. On the surface, it sounds like a good idea: the program supposedly helps the environment, taking gas-guzzling "clunkers" off the road while stimulating sales of new cars at a time when automakers are hurting. But big-government attempts to manipulate the marketplace *always* run up against the Law of Unintended Consequences. Cash for Clunkers distorted the market and harmed the public in several important ways.

First, Cash for Clunkers took thousands of perfectly drivable vehicles out of the used-car market, driving up the price of used cars. This hurt thousands of students and financially strapped families who typically can't afford to buy new cars. Here we see another example of how the "green" agenda crushes the working person. Junk science resulted in junked cars, distorting the marketplace and depriving people of transportation for going to work or to school.

Second, Cash for Clunkers hurt those who make their living by selling and servicing older cars. Mike, a caller on my show, put it this way: "I talked to my mechanic this morning here in Grand Forks, and I asked him, 'How's business?' He said, 'It's terrible. If something doesn't pick up soon, I'm out of business.' I said, 'What's going on?' He said, 'It's Cash for Clunkers. They destroyed a thousand or more cars in the Grand Forks area alone. All of the mechanics and part shops are hurting because there aren't enough cars to work on. And you know what the worst of it is? I have to pay income taxes to the federal government, and the government is taking my money and using it to put me out of business.' "

Third, Cash for Clunkers actually hurt the economy. A September 2010 study by researchers Amir Sufi (University of Chicago) and Atif Mian (University of California at Berkeley) showed that the program produced a bump in sales during its two-month term—an additional 360,000 cars sold. But in the seven months following the end of Cash for Clunkers, car sales slumped by 360,000 cars. The result: a net wash. The $3 billion big-government program didn't increase car sales—it simply motivated people who would have bought a car anyway to buy sooner.[46]

The only way to get out of the economic mess we are in is to create new wealth. But as libertarian blogger Adam Maji of Tucson observes, Cash for Clunkers "destroys wealth by not letting these vehicles be used up over their useful life. It destroys wealth by routing scarce resources into activities—in this case, auto construction—that would not otherwise take place, denying other industries access to those resources. It destroys wealth by taking on liabilities, through borrowing, that have to be paid back later by the taxpayers (reducing their purchasing power in the future) or by taxing them immediately (reducing their purchasing power today)." Moreover, Cash for Clunkers thwarts its own goal of reducing energy use because the energy spent building a new car exceeds the energy saved by that car's fuel efficiency over several years.[47] So what did we as taxpayers get for our $3 billion? Harm to the economy and harm to the environment. This is a case study in the colossal failure of big government.

Peter Schiff, president of Euro Pacific Capital, Inc., put the Cash for Clunkers program in perspective in a YouTube video. "The country is in trouble," he said. "We've borrowed all this money, and we are basically broke, right? We've got to get out of this hole. And they say: 'What should we do? Let's destroy some cars! . . . Let's try to find a way to encourage people who have cars that work, and they have no loans, and let's see if we can get them to go deep into debt to buy a brand-new car they didn't need so they can have a car payment.' Stroke of genius! So we spent I don't know how many billions of dollars to buy up cars and pour battery acid on the engines. These are cars that already worked. I mean, why not at least give them to poor people? Why destroy them and make them so nobody can drive them?"[48]

As Steven Moore of the *Wall Street Journal* once said, "We fought a war against big government and you know what? Big government won."[49]

THE MAGIC OF THE MARKETPLACE

Gerald Ford used to say, "A government big enough to give you everything you want is big enough to take away everything you have."[50] It's true. The bigger your government, the smaller your freedom.

When the economy melted down in 2008, we didn't need "stimulus," and we didn't need Obamanomics. We needed the wisdom of

Ronald Reagan. At a campaign rally in 1984, he said, "Now, we need government, of course. But when you go from government to *big* government—to government as the neighborhood bully—it's time for a change, and change we made. We started putting our house in order. . . . We did it together, and we did it for everybody."[51] And in 1986, Reagan contrasted the economy he inherited with the economy his policies produced:

> Back in 1980 . . . the American economy was the worst mess since the Great Depression. Government was everywhere: running up taxes, causing inflation, raising interest rates, and taking bigger and bigger shares of your earnings. To get big government off your backs and out of your pockets, we slowed government growth, slashed needless regulations, and enacted an across-the-board personal income tax cut of nearly 25 percent. Then we indexed taxes, making it impossible for inflation to push you into higher and higher tax brackets ever again. . . .
>
> Critics dubbed our plan "Reaganomics" and predicted economic ruin. Let's look at what's happened instead. Inflation has fallen from more than 12 percent to less than 2 percent. Interest rates are down. Mortgage rates are down and housing starts are up, helping industries like timber. And just listen to this: During these nearly 4 years of economic growth, we've seen the creation of more than 11½ million jobs in the United States. . . . I could tell our economic program was working when they *stopped* calling it "Reaganomics"![52]

Doesn't that sound like *exactly* the prescription we need today? Wouldn't you give anything to have Ronald Reagan running this country today instead of Barack Obama? I know I would. Instead, this country is led by people whose brains are steeped in Marxist and Keynesian theories that have never worked in practice. They are so much in love with big government that they undoubtedly think of ruling America as a stepping-stone to the socialist dream of "global governance." Witness the adolescent crush these people have on big-government programs.

Vice President Joe Biden said it this way: "Every single great idea that has marked the 21st century, the 20th century and the 19th century has required government vision and government incentive."[53] *Every* great idea, Joe? You mean, you've never heard of Thomas Edison, Henry Ford, the Wright Brothers, Walt Disney, Sam Walton, Bill Gates, Steve Jobs, or Howard Schultz? The genius of America is in the *free enterprise system*, not big government.

And President Obama, while promoting his $787 billion "stimulus" package in February 2009, said, "Do you just want government to do nothing, or do you want it to do something? . . . With the private sector so weakened by this recession, the federal government is the only entity left with the resources to jolt our economy back to life."[54] Then he proceeded to spend us trillions of dollars further into debt in his effort to "jolt" the economy. The more he spent, the more jobs were lost. Now we have trillions more dollars of debt and nothing to show for it.

Reagan knew. If you want to revive an ailing economy, the best thing government can do is get out of the way. Cut taxes. Cut spending. Cut regulation. Set the free market free to do what it does best—innovate, invest, and create jobs. Barack Obama is dead wrong. The federal government doesn't have *any* resources to jolt the economy. The federal government cannot create wealth—all wealth creation takes place in the private sector. All lasting and meaningful job creation takes place in the private sector. All economic activity takes place in the private sector. Big government is absolutely incapable of "jolting" the economy back to life—the utter failure of Obamanomics has proven that for all time.

Again, Ronald Reagan has the final word on what really works when you want to rescue and revive a troubled economy. Speaking to a gathering of eleven thousand bankers and financiers in October 1981, he said, "The societies that have achieved the most spectacular, broad-based economic progress in the shortest period of time are not the most tightly controlled nor necessarily the biggest in size nor the wealthiest in natural resources. No, what unites them is their willingness to believe in the magic of the marketplace."[55]

FRAN TARKENTON FOR PRESIDENT!

I remember December 28, 1975, like it was yesterday. I was in my uncle Luverne Thielges's living room in Canby, Minnesota, watching television with my cousins. On TV, Fran Tarkenton and the Minnesota Vikings led Roger Staubach and the Dallas Cowboys in the divisional playoff game at Met Stadium in Bloomington, Minnesota. It had been a hard-fought war in the trenches between two great quarterbacks and two of the most dominant defenses in the NFL.

With less than two minutes left to play in the fourth quarter, the Cowboys had the ball, but I was sure that Tarkenton and the Vikings had this one in the bag and were on their way to their fourth Super Bowl. The Cowboys started on their own 15, and put together a nine-play drive to midfield. At that point, there were thirty-two seconds left on the clock. No way could Staubach get into the end zone with so little time.

Staubach lined up in the shotgun, took the snap—and the Purple People Eaters came at him like a stampede. Staubach pump-faked left, then looked right and threw a long desperation pass. Downfield, Cowboys wide receiver Drew Pearson pushed off on Vikings cornerback Nate Wright, knocking him to the ground—a clear case of offensive pass interference, as every unbiased Vikings fan could clearly see. Pearson made the catch (he actually trapped the ball between his elbow in his hip) and loped into the end zone for the (alleged) touchdown. With that, Fran Tarkenton and an entire legion of Vikings fans were robbed of a trip to the Super Bowl.

After the game, Staubach told reporters he closed his eyes and said a Hail Mary as he threw that pass. "It was just a Hail Mary pass—a very, very lucky play." Ever since then, a desperation throw to the end zone has been known by that name.

Of course, I have many happy memories of watching Fran Tarkenton and the Vikings during his eighteen-season NFL career, and I grew up absolutely revering this man. So it was an extraordinary honor to have Fran Tarkenton as a guest on *The Common Sense Club* in the summer of 2010. He's not only a Hall of Fame quarterback, but a highly successful entrepreneur, the founder of several companies including Tarkenton Software, GoSmallBiz.com, and Tarkenton Financial. He's also the author of several self-help books, including *What Losing Taught Me About Winning*. I asked Fran about his work in the business community, and he told me about his products for helping entrepreneurs succeed in this troubled economy.

"We have to get the truth out there to the silent majority, the American taxpayers," he said. "If we don't create a sense of desperation, change never happens. But the silent majority has started to sense the desperation in our economy. So we see this movement and the tea parties, because people see that this country is led by a president and an administration that are inept. This president has no background for leadership, no background in decision making. He has run nothing in his life. You don't learn how to make decisions in Harvard Law School. You learn how to make decisions and solve problems by running businesses every day.

"He's been getting a free pass. He's an attractive guy. He's a great speaker. We wanted him to succeed, but he hasn't. He has people around him who come from the progressive side of the Democratic Party, which means they think that they're smart and that we're dumb."

I said, "If I could arrange a meeting between Fran Tarkenton and President Obama behind the closed doors of the Oval Office, what do you say to him?"

Fran replied, "I would tell him that he needs to involve business-people in his inner circle—people who actually know what it means to make a payroll. He needs to cut tax rates. He needs to promote entrepreneurship by removing the regulatory barriers that have made it increasingly difficult for small business people to succeed today. We have regulations upon regulations upon regulations!

"But at the end of the day, our problem is really this: If you talk to anybody on the inside of Washington, Democrat or Republican, they will tell you that this president is a big-government socialist. He is left of left. He does not believe in what we are and what has built this country. He is never going to be a promoter of business. He wants to redistribute the wealth."

I interjected, "But if you said all that to President Obama, he'd say,

'Wait a minute, Fran, I'm pro-business!' Because that's his talking point. What would you say then?"

"I'd say," Fran replied, "you are what you do, not what you say. Your words ring hollow because what you're doing is not pro-business, it's not pro–job growth. It is bigger government. And big government harms people and harms the economy as we spend our-selves into oblivion. This uncontrolled government spending is going to put us in the same condition that Greece and Spain are in today. Big government has never worked."

I said, "I saw you on Neil Cavuto's show the other day, and you were followed by a buddy of mine, Steven Moore from the *Wall Street Journal*. He said, 'Fran Tarkenton for president!' And I totally agree. Are you up for that?"

Tarkenton laughed. "No, I am not up for that, but I tell you what, the strength of our country has always been in the people and now the people have to get out and be heard. Those of us in the business community understand something that the president does not: You cannot get away with spending more than you make. It ultimately catches up to you. Businesspeople have already adapted. We are be-coming more efficient in how we spend our money. We do more with less, because that is ingrained into the American culture. The Ameri-can people understand that you can't spend money you don't have. But the politicians don't get it. That's why the state of California is bankrupt, Minnesota and Wisconsin are going broke, and America is going broke. It's time for all of us to say, 'Enough!' "

I would certainly sleep better at night if I knew that a real leader like Fran Tarkenton was in the White House. He understands what I understand, what every business owner knows who has ever lain awake at night, thinking about the employees and their families who depend on the success of his business. Fran Tarkenton understands that the biggest challenge any businessperson faces in America is big government. If we could get big government out of our way, there is no limit to the wealth, the jobs, and the compassionate charity this economy would produce!

As Fran Tarkenton says, it's up to us, the American people, this great sleeping giant, to rise up and say, "Enough!"

THE COMMONSENSE ACTION AGENDA

Here are some grassroots actions you can take, starting today:

✓ Do you know anyone like young Star Parker—someone who feels entitled to live irresponsibly at taxpayer expense without a second thought? Could you influence that young person to become more like the mature and responsible Star Parker? Are there people within your sphere of influence for whom you could become a mentor and a role model? Consider helping young people develop character, a sense of responsibility, and a willingness to break free of the big-government welfare trap.

✓ When you hear people denigrating George W. Bush as a "budget buster," speak up! Point out the facts about the Bush economic record—the fact that President Bush presided over a strong economy (fifty-two months of uninterrupted job growth) and a smaller government, in terms of spending as a percentage of GDP, than his three predecessors, including Reagan and Clinton. Become a one-person truth squad for conservative values and principles.

✓ Download Congressman Paul Ryan's "Roadmap for America's Future" at www .roadmap.republicans.budget.house.gov. Study it, forward the link to friends and family members, and spread the word about this plan to restore America's greatness through conservative, free market principles.

✓ Be bold! Hard-core liberals aren't shy about spouting their opinions—and they never worry about offending conservatives. You don't have to be rude or abrasive, but you can say, "You know, there's another point of view on that subject. . . ." Then state your beliefs and back them up with facts. You'll be amazed at the people you persuade to the conservative point of view!

4

SECURING OUR ENERGY FUTURE

They call Harold Hamm the "blue-collar billionaire."

Harold is the founder and chairman of Continental Resources, Inc., an independent oil and gas exploration and production company based in Enid, Oklahoma. He is also number 44 on the Forbes 400 list of richest Americans. I once interviewed him on my radio show, and we had a great conversation about what his company was doing to secure America's energy future. Mere minutes after the interview, Brian Engel, the vice president of public affairs for Continental Resources, called me and said, "Mr. Hamm feels that you and he are kindred spirits, and he'd like to invite you down to Oklahoma to see the operation."

So in March 2010, I flew to Enid, where Harold took me to his headquarters and introduced me to his executive team. From Harold on down, these were all "hard-hat executives," guys who were equally comfortable on a drilling rig or in a mahogany-paneled boardroom. Jeff Hume, the president of the company, remarked, "Scott, did you know that twenty-five percent of the GDP America lost in the 2008 meltdown came from the energy sector?"

"You've got to be kidding me," I replied.

"Absolutely true," Jeff said.

"I'm just a guy on the radio," I said, "but it seems to me that if twenty-five percent of our economy came out of energy, then energy would be the quickest way to put it back."

"That's right."

"In that case," I said, "we've got to figure out a way to do that, don't we?"

"Good idea."

"Then let's go make the case for energy. Let's get busy securing this country's economy and energy future—and let's start in North Dakota."

And that's exactly what Harold Hamm and his team are doing.

EXPLORING FOR ANCIENT WEALTH

Harold Hamm was born in Lexington, Oklahoma, the son of a share-crop farmer, the youngest of thirteen children. "We grew up poor," he recalled. "We grew up working for somebody else and we never owned land. I'm not saying we were born in a log cabin. We did buy one, though, once we came into some money."

When Harold was a boy, the Hamm family moved to Enid, which was experiencing an oil boom at the time. "I'd never been around that kind of people," he said, "you know, people in the oil patch. They were different from the people I grew up around. They were excited about what they were doing." What they were doing was pulling wealth out of the ground to power the engine of industry.

That excitement got into Harold's blood. "It fired a passion," he recalled. "It grasped my young mind. I thought, 'If I discover ancient wealth and do a little better than the competition, I could make a strike and have a find. There are no limits to the possibilities.'" Harold's heroes were Oklahoma oilmen like George Getty and his son, J. Paul Getty, mule skinner–turned-oilman Bill Skelly, and Robert S. Kerr, who also served as governor of Oklahoma.

"I graduated from high school," Harold said, "but I couldn't go on to college because I didn't have two nickels to rub together. So I went into the oil patch. I wouldn't recommend this to anybody. I did everything a little bit backward. I started by cleaning oil sludge out of tanker trucks and learning the business from the bottom up. I found that the people in the oil patch are generous. When I asked questions, they took time and taught me. So I learned the business by working for other people, then I got a truck of my own. I established this little company in 1967 and I built it up from there."

Harold started out as a "wildcatter"—oil patch slang for someone who drills risky wells in unmapped geological formations, hoping to strike oil. He borrowed money to sink the well—and sure enough, he struck oil. "If we hadn't struck oil," he told me, "I wouldn't be on any *Forbes* list today. I'd still be paying that dude off. As it turned out, that little field had six million barrels of oil in it. We got a good start from there. It's kind of like what Robert S. Kerr once said—'I'm just like you, except I struck oil.'"

Once he had made some money, Harold could afford college. Even though he had been out of high school for a decade, he decided to go to Phillips University in Enid and learn the skills he needed to build his company, both the geologic skills and the business administration skills. He took that knowledge into the oil patch and built Continental into one of the largest independent oil producers in America. He also married, raised a family of five children, and is a grandfather of ten today.

Harold looks at the oil business through the lens of his farmboy upbringing. "When I grew up on a farm, I knew the names of all the cattle, every cow. Well, today I know the names of all my wells and what they're like. Each well has its own unique characteristics, its own personality. When you're in this business long enough, you get to know each well as an individual."

In recent years, Harold and Continental came to North Dakota to develop the resources of the Bakken shale formation in the subsurface of the great Williston Basin, covering parts of North Dakota, Montana, and Saskatchewan. Following the oil bust of the 1980s, oil exploration in North Dakota had come to a standstill. But Harold studied the geology of the area and believed that there was potentially a giant oil field—400 million barrels or more—in North Dakota.

It wasn't just oil that drew Harold Hamm to North Dakota—it was also the business and regulatory climate. When Harold met with the then governor of North Dakota, Ed Schafer, he found a man who understood what business needs in order to thrive, provide jobs, and create wealth. Ed had earned a master's in business administration from the University of Denver, and had served as president of the Gold Seal Company from 1978 to 1985. After two terms as governor, presiding over the economic renaissance of our state, Ed served in the George W. Bush cabinet as secretary of agriculture. The prosperity that North Dakota enjoys today goes back to the early 1990s and the vision, leadership, and business prowess of Ed Schafer.

Governor Schafer opened a lot of doors for Harold Hamm. "I was impressed," Harold told me, "with the business-friendly atmosphere in North Dakota. I was especially impressed when Ed Schafer went with me to committee meetings in the legislature and testified along with me about the need for incentives. The legislature gave us incentives for horizontal drilling, so that we could develop those resources. The regulatory climate has been good in North Dakota. A rational regulatory environment makes things happen."

Harold Hamm was also drawn to the people and culture of our state. "I found I had a great affinity for the people of North Dakota," he said. "I came off an old farm and these farm people in North Dakota were just like me. They're hardworking, tenacious, and they work till everything is done. That's how my family was when I was growing up, when we picked cotton. We never quit working until it was all in. Sometimes that meant my brothers and I picked cotton until December. When we got all the cotton pulled, then we could go to school. I saw how hard the people of North Dakota worked and how they dealt with hardship, and I knew that these were my kind of people.

"I also saw the pioneering spirit of North Dakota. That's what Teddy Roosevelt found when he came to North Dakota to hunt bison. He ended up putting down roots in the Badlands as a cattle rancher. He recognized the vast resources of North Dakota, and he felt that same exhilaration I felt, looking out at a land that is full of untapped potential. Land like that brings out the best qualities in people."

One way Harold demonstrated his pioneering spirit was through his early adoption of new technologies for discovering and extracting oil. Continental Resources invented and trademarked the ECO-Pad, a stable base for positioning oil wells. As many as eight separate wells can pump oil to a single ECO-Pad. Instead of cluttering the countryside with oil wells and pipelines, there is just one earth-friendly ECO-Pad aboveground. Everything else is below the surface.

Harold was also one of the first to use seismic exploration and 3-D imaging. This technology works on the principle that sound waves move differently through different densities of material. Just as a sonogram can peer inside the human body, a seismic 3-D image can reveal the faults in the earth's crust, the shape and density of underground formations, the different layers and formations, and the exact location of oil and natural gas deposits.

The miracle of 3-D imaging, combined with computerized mapping, makes it possible to use new drilling technologies, such as horizontal drilling. "This is one of the biggest revolutions in technology," Harold said. "Horizontal drilling has opened up the Bakken. We go down to ten thousand feet, then turn right and go horizontally another nine thousand or ten thousand feet. Then we use fracture stimulation, or 'fracking,' to break up the rock within particular zones. As you fracture the rock, you release the oil and gas. When you open up that zone, you might have a half-a-billion-barrel oil well.

"The Bakken shale has turned out to be the largest accumulation of oil in the Lower Forty-Eight. In fact, our geologists think the oil shale formations in North Dakota and Montana hold about twenty billion barrels of recoverable crude—about five times what the U.S. Geological Survey estimated in 2008. These formations also contain the natural gas equivalent of four billion barrels of oil. A few years ago, those resources would not have been recoverable. But a number of factors have come together—the regulatory environment, the imaging technology, the frack technology—to put these resources within reach. There would have been no way to exploit the Bakken with the old technology. Fracking enables you to turn an uneconomical strata into one of the world's largest oil fields. It took a partnership of the industry, the public, the legislature, and the regulatory environment to make it happen."

Starting with one truck, Harold Hamm built his company into a $9 billion publicly traded corporation—and Harold himself owns more than 80 percent of the stock. And here's the amazing thing about Harold Hamm and Continental Resources, Inc.: he operates this incredibly profitable company with just 440 employees. That makes him the greatest entrepreneur I have ever met.

Harold Hamm is not only a great businessman, but a great human being and humanitarian. He donated $1.8 million to help finance the expansion of the North Dakota Heritage Center, a museum on the grounds of the state capitol in Bismarck.

He has also adopted the cause of diabetes research by founding the Harold Hamm Oklahoma Diabetes Center at the University of Oklahoma. He endowed the center with a $10 million gift plus more than $40 million in research grants, focused primarily on the treatment of diabetic retinopathy (a leading cause of blindness). Harold has also led the charge to eliminate sugary soft drinks from school vending machines in Oklahoma.

Harold's wife, Sue Ann Hamm, is one of the wisest, most perceptive people I've ever met. She once told me, "Harold has something more valuable to give than his money—his time." Considering how wealthy he is, that's an extraordinary statement. But it's absolutely true. Because when Harold gives you the gift of his time, he also gives you the gift of his wisdom, knowledge, and experience.

I love to act as a catalyst, bringing people together and causing a chemical reaction. One of the great privileges of my life was to bring Harold Hamm and Ron Offutt together—the oil baron and the agribusiness baron. When you bring oil and ag together, anything is possible.

Today, Harold sits on the board of the Ron Offutt School of Business Leadership at Concordia College. There, these two great entrepreneurial leaders, Ron and Harold, join forces to help train a new generation of business leaders for America.

My good friend Gene Nicholas (one of North Dakota's great business and political minds) owns hunting land near Regent, North Dakota. So Gene offered to let us hunt on his land during pheasant season. It was a weekend to remember. We assembled a gathering of titans, including Harold Hamm, Ron Offutt, our soon-to-be-governor Jack Dalrymple, venture capitalist Michael Tokarz, my friend and banker Dan Carey, another oil business buddy, Mike Cantrell, and a few other notables. Harold and Gene told me, "Be sure to bring your

son, Alex, and anyone who'd like to come with him." So we included
Alex and our nephew, Brad Mackowick.

We had three fantastic days tramping around the ranch, talking
about everything imaginable, from the best way to cook a pheasant to
billion-dollar business deals. I was glad Alex and Brad could be a part
of that experience. I think it widened their horizons just to be there,
taking it all in.

At the end of the hunt, Harold Hamm made a special point of seeking out Alex and Brad, shaking their hands, putting his arms around
them, and saying, "It was great to be out there hunting with you boys."
It choked me up to see him reaching out to those two boys and making
them feel special. That's the kind of man Harold Hamm is.

Meanwhile, Harold stays focused on the goal of securing America's
energy future. "The people of North Dakota," he said, "deserve a lot
of credit for creating an inspirational environment here so that the
energy industry can grow. America is turning itself around. A lot of
people don't realize that we are actually *increasing crude oil supplies* in
America today."

Wait, did Harold Hamm actually say that America is already becoming more energy independent? What about that big advertising
blitz by T. Boone Pickens? In his so-called Pickens Plan, Pickens said
that America imports more than 65 percent of its oil, much of it from
the Middle East—and that the percentage is *growing*. "Oil is getting
more expensive to produce [and] harder to find," Pickens said, "and
there just isn't enough of it to keep up with demand."[1]

"It's not true," Harold counters. "A lot of people try to diminish our industry, but let's look at the facts. We import about
fifty-three percent of our oil from outside of this country, not sixty-
five percent—and that percentage is *shrinking*, not growing. We only
get about six percent of our oil from the Middle East. The rest comes
mostly from Canada, Mexico, Venezuela, and Africa. And I believe
that within the next five years, if we continue on this course, we could
break that fifty-percent threshold and begin producing more than we
import. So the Bakken is a very important play for American energy
independence."

I asked Harold what could derail our progress toward that goal.

"Only one thing I can think of," he said. "If Washington places a lot of punitive legislation upon us, they can stop our progress. It has happened before, and it could happen again.

"Right now, America is the third-largest crude oil producer in the world—just a tad behind the leaders. Everybody thinks Saudi Arabia is first, but actually Russia is the top oil producer in the world, with about 10 million barrels a day of production. The Saudis are at 9.9 million barrels a day. The United States is at 9.3 million barrels. Iran is a distant fourth at 4 million barrels a day. If we want to maintain our leadership in the world, we need to have an industry-friendly regulatory environment."

HYDROCARBONS ARE HERE TO STAY

One of the biggest threats to our energy future is something called "happy talk." I picked up this term from Robert Bryce, author of *Power Hungry: The Myths of "Green" Energy and the Real Fuels of the Future*. He writes:

> Over the past few years, Americans have been inundated with energy happy talk. And it has come from personalities ranging from Dallas billionaire T. Boone Pickens and former Vice President Al Gore to *New York Times* columnist Thomas Friedman. . . . For Pickens, the bogeyman to be slain is foreign oil. For Gore, the villain is carbon dioxide. And while the sin to be cured varies with the preacher, the message of deliverance is largely the same: Repent. Give up those evil hydrocarbons and embrace the virtues of renewable energy before you face the eternal damnations of foreign oil, global warming, and a carbon footprint that's bigger than Boone Pickens' ego.[2]

The environmental left would have us believe that we can solve all our energy problems and meet all of our energy needs without fossil fuels. We can do without coal, we can do without oil, we can do without gas—all we need is wind turbines and solar panels and lots and lots of conservation. Well, that's nothing but leftist happy talk. And the only cure for that is common sense and straight talk.

I invited Robert Bryce on my show to give my listeners some of his high-octane straight talk on energy. He began by telling me how his research on energy issues had transformed his views. "I come from the liberal left," he said. "A few years ago, I was fully convinced that wind and solar were the ways forward, and that nuclear energy was bad." His credentials as a onetime leftist are solid—he had previously written a scathing attack on the Bush family oil connections called *Cronies*, as well as an Enron exposé entitled *Pipe Dreams*. His views changed while he was researching another book called *Gusher of Lies*.

"I focused on the interdependence of the global energy economy, and I looked closely at corn ethanol and the biofuels issues. In the course of my research, I realized I didn't understand enough about the scale of our energy consumption. So I wrote *Power Hungry,* in part, to educate myself—but I also wrote it to show people that our energy and power delivery systems are not determined by political correctness or carbon content. They are determined by physics and math.

"President Obama gave a speech and said that Americans have an addiction to fossil fuels. I thought, 'Man, this makes me long for the days of George W. Bush when he just said that we're addicted to oil.' Because Obama is saying we're addicted to *all* fossil fuels, including coal and natural gas.

"Actually, we're not addicted to fossil fuels, we're addicted to *prosperity*. And that's the point. This is what gets lost amid all the happy talk: 'Oh, we'll just quit using fossil fuels and we'll live in unobtainium-powered homes and drive unicorn-powered cars'—and there is simply no understanding of the scale of energy consumption in the U.S. or around the world. People have no conception of how long it takes to transition an economy from one energy source to another.

"Here are the numbers: The U.S., on an average day, uses about 46 million barrels of oil-equivalent from all forms of energy—that's nuclear, hydro, coal, oil, natural gas, solar, wind, and everything else. Of that 46 million barrels of oil-equivalent per day, 40 million barrels of oil-equivalent come in the form of hydrocarbons.[3] That's equal to the output of five Saudi Arabias' worth of oil. Where are we going to find five Saudi Arabias' worth of oil-equivalent and have it all be carbon-free—*and* have it all be available in the next decade or two or three? It's not going to happen.

"I want a politician to stand up and tell the truth: 'Look, hydrocarbons are here to stay. Love 'em, hate 'em, they are here to stay because nothing else comes close when it to comes to energy density, power density, cost, and scale.' "

I asked Bryce to tell my listeners about a visit he had made to a coal mine.

"That was the Cardinal Coal Mine in western Kentucky. It produces high-sulfur coal for electric utilities. Before we went underground, the mine manager ran the numbers for me. The Cardinal Mine produces about fifteen thousand tons of coal a day. I asked him the BTU content, then I did a simple conversion of tons and BTUs, and it came out to about sixty-six thousand barrels of oil-equivalent per day from that one mine. I was flabbergasted. I thought, 'That's an *incredible* amount of productivity!' And they had only three hundred or four hundred people on their payroll, running two shifts, six days a week. I thought, 'Man, that is why we use coal! The productivity of that one mine is astounding—yet it's only the thirty-fifth-largest mine in America!' "

I said, "That brings us to the four imperatives that you say guide the energy business: power density, energy density, cost, and scale. Coal obviously ranks high in each of those criteria, right?"

"Absolutely," he said. "Power density is the factor I primarily focus on in *Power Hungry*. Power density refers to the energy flow that can be harnessed from a given area, volume, or mass. This sounds technical at first, but it's really very simple. Power density enables you to compare coal, wind, nuclear, and other energy sources in a way that makes sense. Let me give you a simple example to show you how to understand power density.

"I live in Austin, Texas. The South Texas Project is a big nuclear plant located southeast of Austin. It produces 2,700 megawatts of power and occupies an area of 18.75 square miles—slightly smaller than the area of Manhattan. It produces about 56 watts per square meter of area.

"Now, if you wanted to produce the same 2,700 megawatts of

power using wind turbines, you'd need an area of about nine hundred square miles—about the size of Rhode Island. If you wanted to produce an equivalent amount of power with corn ethanol, you'd need an area nearly the size of West Virginia.

"Power density numbers force you to recognize the advantages of certain energy sources versus the limitations of others. If you want to replace a high-power-density system like nuclear or coal with a low-power-density system like wind or corn ethanol, you are going to run up against problems of cost and scale. That's why I said earlier that our energy and power delivery systems are determined by physics and math.

"That's a rather long explanation, but to me power density is the key metric. It proves conclusively that hydrocarbons are here to stay. Regardless of any arguments you might make about peak oil or depletion or global warming, it's clear that hydrocarbons are necessary to our future. One hydrocarbon source, natural gas, is available in abundance in the U.S., thanks to the shale gas revolution—the ability of natural gas companies to fracture the shale beds and produce large quantities of natural gas.

"And we need to make use of nuclear power, which provides the kind of energy productivity we demand at a cost we can afford, and in the scale we need. So natural gas and nuclear are the fuels of the future—they are clean, abundant, and they can provide electricity, which is an essential ingredient in maintaining our modern civilization."

"What about transportation?" I asked. "What do physics and math tell us about the future of gasoline-powered cars versus electric cars?"

"The key metric when it comes to transportation is energy density, which is the amount of heat energy contained in a given area or volume or mass. So you compare gasoline with batteries and you find that gasoline has eighty times the energy density of the best lithium ion batteries by weight. That's why electric cars are not competitive with gasoline-powered cars. They're getting huge government subsidies right now, but electric cars have serious drawbacks—limited range, long recharge times, and high costs—compared to gasoline-powered cars.

"The reason we continue to use gasoline in our cars and jet fuel in our jets is the incredible energy density of the fuel. When you're in an airplane at thirty thousand feet, you want fuels that are very energy-dense. That's what refined petroleum products provide."

That's straight talk, not happy talk—and that's the energy discussion we need to have in America today.

COAL—THE FUEL OF THE FUTURE?

My state is leading an energy revolution. North Dakota is setting an example of what the United States of America *should* be doing to restore its broken economy and its damaged leadership role in the world. Here in the heartland, we have rejected the liberal mind-set that says America has to accept decline and scarcity as a way of life.

Here we have a commonsense regulatory environment. It's not "anything goes." There are rules and environmental standards that must be met if you want to do business in our state. But the rules are rational and reasonable. We don't allow the green movement, with its hidden socialist agenda, to run roughshod over our industries.

I recently had former vice president Dick Cheney as a guest on my show, talking about the economy and energy. I told him that, while forty-nine states had lost jobs since the Obama "stimulus" plan went into action, *one* state in the nation had actually produced *more* jobs.

With understandable home-state pride, he said, "Wyoming."

"Actually, the state that has been adding jobs is the great state of North Dakota. Why? It has nothing to do with the 'stimulus' bill. Stimulus didn't create jobs. Energy created jobs. North Dakota has been following *your* energy strategy, Mr. Vice President."

And I proceeded to remind Dick Cheney of the National Energy Policy Development Group (aka the Cheney Energy Task Force) of early 2001. The left ginned up a controversy, claiming the task force relied too much on advice from the energy industry, lacked representation from groups like Greenpeace and the Sierra Club, and operated with too much secrecy. In the end, the task force produced a policy report in May 2001 promoting the idea of an "all of the above" approach to solving our energy problems. Whereas the environmental left wanted to put America on a starvation diet of wind and solar energy, the Cheney group recommended pursuing every energy source including nuclear, coal, natural gas, hydro—*and* the environmentalist favorites, wind and solar.

"Mr. Vice President," I said, "a lot of us here in the heartland remember how the media tried to portray you as a bad guy because you had people from the energy industry sitting around the conference table. But we think it actually makes sense to have people who are *experts* on energy sitting at that table, giving the benefit of their experience. The critics forgot that your report recommended we do all of the above, everything from nuclear and coal to wind and solar, and yes, conservation, too. You've told us we've got to do it all, Mr. Vice President, and that is what we are doing here in North Dakota."

"Scott," he said, "thank you for remembering."

People sometimes accuse me of shilling for oil. I don't have a problem with that. I love big oil, because I know what big oil has done for North Dakota, and for America. I proudly shill for oil, and for every other form of energy. If it powers a car, lights up a lightbulb, or lifts a jet plane off the ground, I support it. I'm the biggest booster you'll ever find for an all-of-the-above approach to powering this great nation. But you can't power a car with windmills, and you can't lift a plane off the ground with natural gas. Anyone who thinks we can meet all of our energy needs without fossil fuels is living in a dream world.

Here in North Dakota, we are showing America some creative ways to produce the energy America needs. You can drive out to the town of Beulah and see the only place in North America that produces synthetic natural gas on a large scale. There the Dakota Gasification Company uses lignite coal to make synthetic natural gas, which is piped to homes and businesses in the eastern United States. On an average day, the synfuels plant converts about eighteen thousand tons of coal into 145 million cubic feet of natural gas for consumer use or electricity generation. Beulah, North Dakota, is showing America how to produce energy that is economical, efficient, and environmentally responsible.

I was born in Minnesota, and I love that state—but let's face it: the Land of Ten Thousand Lakes is a blue state. It's the land of Al Franken, Walter Mondale, and Hubert Humphrey. A lot of Minnesota voters—especially around the Twin Cities—are as far left as any you might find in Berkeley, California, or Madison, Wisconsin. And my message to such folks is: You'd better wake up! When you flip that light switch, where do you think the power comes from? It may well come from coal that was removed responsibly from a surface mine in North Dakota. If Barack Obama and the Democrats have their way, the electricity at your fingertips is going to cost you a lot more. They see coal as a *curse*, not the God-given, beneficial resource it truly is.

On January 17, 2008, candidate Barack Obama sat down with the editorial board of the *San Francisco Chronicle* and explained his views on the cap-and-trade system he wants to put in place. He summed up his plan by saying, "If somebody wants to build a coal-fired plant, they can. It's just that it will bankrupt them because they are going to be charged a huge sum for all that greenhouse gas that's being emitted."[4] Led by President Barack Obama, the liberal-progressive movement wants to shut down the coal industry. If they get their way, the cost of everything, including electricity, will skyrocket.

I recently spoke with Mike Carey, executive director of the American Council for Affordable and Reliable Energy. He told me, "Barack Obama and the Democrats know how important coal is to this country. That's why they wanted to enact cap-and-trade legislation—because they know that what's being traded is *tax revenue*. They are eyeing the tax money that would come from the coal industry—money they can use to move their agenda forward. So cap and trade would hurt America, it would hurt your state, and it would hurt your family."

"You flip on a switch," I said, "and it's going to cost you more."

"There's no doubt about that," Mike said. "The issue was presented to the public as: 'We will cap the amount of carbon emissions from certain facilities.' In reality, the agenda was: 'The power industry won't be able to build new facilities, they'll have to shut down older facilities, and the public will have to buy power from other sources at higher prices, because they'll be taxed for the carbon emissions.' "

I told Mike about a power project called Big Stone II, which was to be located in Grant County, South Dakota. A five-utility consortium had planned to spend $1.6 billion to build one of the cleanest, most advanced coal-fired power plants in the nation. It would generate 600 megawatts of power and create hundreds of new jobs in North Dakota, South Dakota, and Minnesota. Between the Obama administration and the extremist environmental groups, the project's opponents managed to slow-walk the project until the consortium saw the handwriting on the wall: building Big Stone II could put them out of business.

The Minnesota North Star Chapter of the Sierra Club posted a "fact sheet" about the plant on its website, suggesting that the power output of Big Stone II could be replaced by a bunch of windmills. The area that Big Stone II served "is one of the planet's most fertile grounds for developing wind energy."[5] But, as Robert Bryce just showed us, the power density of wind power is very low. To replace the amount of energy Big Stone II would have produced, you'd have to cover most of Grant County with windmills.

"Mike," I concluded, "the day Big Stone II would have opened, it would have been cleaner than any other coal-burning plant in the nation. But the environmentalists shut it down and killed all of those jobs."

"It makes no sense," Mike said. "If we want to end our dependence on foreign energy resources, we've got to look domestically. And coal is one of the best domestic resources we have.

"There are many ways to extract energy from coal, and one use that was talked about before the Obama administration came into office is converting coal into diesel. It's not a new technology. The South African energy company Sasol has been doing this for the past forty years and the Germans did it in World War II. You can convert coal into diesel fuel, then power airplanes with it. But the Obama administration says no to any project which is fossil-fuels based."

"Mike," I said, "many in the energy industry act as if the train has left the station in terms of global warming and climate change. Why not fight it? Instead, energy companies like Xcel and British Petroleum are actually climbing in bed with the environmentalists and lobbying for cap and trade."

"They've figured out ways to make money by selling carbon offsets and credits. It's like the story of the emperor's new clothes. Carbon offsets and credits are 'invisible clothes,' and the people who sell them make a fortune without creating anything."

"It's a great scam," I said. "I wish I'd thought of it. Mike, the whole global warming agenda is based on junk science and left-wing politics. When I go to tea parties, I say, 'Global warming is a fraud!' And the crowd roars, because people know it's a fraud. But the energy industry has decided to go along to get along. That just makes me crazy!"

"I agree," Mike said. "I recently saw a documentary on Antarctica that showed scientists boring through the ice cap and pulling up core samples that showed that Antarctica was once a hot swamp. The earth goes through natural warming and cooling cycles, and the idea that we, as humans, can change the climate is not based on good science. We need to continue that debate, because the climate change agenda is more about political science than geophysical science. We've got to fight cap and trade and all the other environmental wackiness coming out of Washington, D.C."

"To do that," I said, "we've got to change Washington. Some years ago, the Washington Coal Club gave Senator Byron Dorgan its 'Mr. Coal Award.' I saw that award as an act of political cowardice on the part of the Coal Club. They hoped that by giving Senator Dorgan an award, he'd go a little easier on the coal industry. But Senator Dorgan was no friend of coal in any way, shape, or form. He did little but browbeat the industry and say, 'You'd better get behind cap and tax or else.' "

"I went before Barbara Boxer's committee," Mike went on to say, "and you can imagine the kind of 'fair shake' the coal industry got there. And I went before Congressman Ed Markey's Select Committee on Energy Independence and Global Warming.

"I testified about the new technologies for burning coal more cleanly, and the fact that coal has a role to play in the new energy age. When I pointed out that the Obama administration and the EPA are waging an assault on coal, Democratic congressman Jay Inslee of Washington said, 'If there's an assault being waged here, it's by your industry against my grandchildren!' Those people had their minds made up."

GETTING THE GOVERNMENT OUT OF THE WAY

Congressman Paul Ryan of Wisconsin has emerged as one of the most thoughtful Republican leaders in the House of Representatives. He's the author of HR 6110, the Roadmap for America's Future bill, a commonsense attempt to deal with the looming problem of runaway entitlements. On June 11, 2010, I had Congressman Ryan on my show, and we talked about the regulatory insanity that endangers America's energy future.

"I visited a fracking rig," he told me, "just to understand how this stuff works. It's amazing technology. Fracking is an environmentally safe method of extracting natural gas and oil from the shale fields. The environmentalists claim fracking is dangerous to the water table, but that's nonsense. Fracking takes place far below the water table. It doesn't even affect the water table.

"We have centuries' worth of natural gas right under our own soil in states like Oklahoma, Pennsylvania, North Dakota, and Louisiana. But they have bills in both the House and Senate to regulate or ban fracking. They want to put these resources off-limits, and there's no scientific reason for doing so. That's where this Congress is headed and where this president wants to take us. And it's a future in which we have a lower standard of living, less control of our own destiny, and a shrinking economy. That's why, in the district I represent— which went for Dukakis, Clinton, Gore, and Obama—people are outraged. They want to see a commonsense energy policy."

Harold Hamm is also concerned about the creeping federal regulations that threaten our energy future. "It's one of our biggest concerns. On the EPA side, the regulatory side, it just continues to get worse. And in Congress, they're talking about increasing the per-barrel tax paid to the Oil Spill Liability Trust Fund from eight cents a barrel to as much as forty-nine cents a barrel. Our company has never caused any cleanups, but they're going to tax us anyway. From the EPA side, it's just a slow creep as they continue to be more involved in your business every day. We don't see it getting any better."

One of the worst threats to North Dakota's economy and energy future comes from our own senator Kent Conrad. As a member of

President Obama's deficit commission, Conrad supports a plan to hike taxes on the oil industry by dropping the deduction for intangible drilling costs. Senator Conrad says we all have to sacrifice to bring down the deficit, yet he's oblivious to the fact that North Dakota's oil boom was the *only* reason our state escaped the recession that began in 2008. The only "sacrifice" Kent Conrad understands is a tax hike; sacrificially cutting *spending* is a foreign concept to him.

Harold Hamm calls the deficit commission's proposed changes "a tremendous blow to the domestic oil and gas industry." He told me, "The oil industry is an investment-intensive industry. It takes years of exploration and preparation to bring an oil well into production. The loss of this deduction will reduce our ability to invest in new drilling by around one-third. That means one-third less capital investment in the state and one-third fewer oil industry jobs."

Liberals like Kent Conrad don't seem to understand that when you raise taxes, you diminish the very activity you are taxing. Result: higher tax rates bring in *less* tax revenue, not more—and everyone suffers. If we truly want to solve the deficit problem, we have to cut government spending, not raise taxes on those who create the wealth.

We have to stop killing the goose that lays our golden eggs. The oil boom benefits everyone in our state—yet government is trying to kill the boom! Oil brings in almost a third of our state tax revenue. Revenue from oil has created scores of millionaires, provided property tax relief for homeowners, funded education, funded flood protection, and much more. Along with former governor Ed Schafer, I'm engaged in an effort to lower state taxes on the oil industry in North Dakota, because our taxes on oil production are higher than tax rates in Oklahoma, Texas, and Montana—and I don't want to chase oil production to those other states. We want to keep this boom going. (For more information, visit www.FixTheTax.com.)

Calvin Coolidge—the president who wisely kept taxes low and government small during the economic good times of the Roaring Twenties—is often quoted as saying, "The business of America is business." In fact, his exact words were, "The chief business of the American people is business. . . . The chief ideal of the American people is idealism." For Coolidge, the pursuit of financial success is sacred, improving the life of *every* American. That is why he once wrote, "The man who builds a factory, builds a temple. The man who works there, worships there."[6]

Today, it seems that the business of our government is to obstruct business. The obstructionists of the environmental left complain that coal is a "dirty" fuel. But here in North Dakota we have fifteen coal-fired power-generating units operating at nine power plants. Seven of those plants are clustered together in the west-central part of the state, near Bismarck; the other two are near the eastern border with Minnesota. If you were hiking or fishing anywhere near those power plants, you'd never even know they were there. The air is as clear as crystal. Today's clean coal-burning technology makes coal one of the cleanest, safest sources of energy in the world—and the state of North Dakota has an *eight-hundred-year supply* of economically recoverable coal.

If only we had more leaders like Calvin Coolidge, leaders who understand how America became great. Our greatness didn't come from our ability to impose taxes and rules and regulations on American business—it comes from the freedom of American entrepreneurs to take bold risks, to work hard, to combine a good idea with sweat and ingenuity, and to reap the rewards of success.

The energy business is good for America. The left may demonize Big Oil and Big Coal, but here in the heartland, common sense reigns supreme. We don't spend our time dreaming up ways to impede commerce and industry. We believe in the pursuit of happiness, the pursuit of success, and yes, the pursuit of wealth.

Yes, the energy boom puts more stress on the roads, housing, and workforce accommodations in the western counties of the state—but isn't that a problem a rational state government should *want* to have? The tax revenues generated by the new boom in oil and gas are shared with the counties, and everyone benefits. Moreover, the energy companies work closely with state and local governments, building roads at their own expense, promoting safety, and lending expertise to the counties.

Though North Dakota is leading the way in commonsense energy policy, we could do so much more. Not long ago, I was talking to Dave Roberts, an executive with Marathon Oil, one of the largest oil companies in the world. He told me, "Of all the places in North America where we extract oil and gas, we get our best return on investment in North Dakota."

I said, "How much do you invest in North Dakota?"

"A billion and a half over two years."

"Is that all?" I said. "That's not a lot of capital for a company like yours. You decide where every pin goes in the map, and you know you get the best return right here in North Dakota. Why don't you double that? Why don't you sink *three* billion into this state? I mean, I'm just a radio guy, and you know more about your business than I do, but it seems to me that you should focus on the things that give you the biggest return."

"You won't like the answer, Scott. It's because your state can't handle it. It takes a lot of infrastructure to support all that drilling. And it's not just the roads and pipelines. The more drilling you do, the more people come into the region. So you need housing, schools, hospitals, and so forth to serve all of that human capital. North Dakota just isn't ready for us to double our investment. You can't handle it."

"You've issued quite a challenge," I said. "You're saying that if we could deliver the infrastructure you need, you'd double your investment."

"Of course. But that would take a long time. Maybe fifty years."

"Well, I know people in government, people in business—and if I could put you together with them, they might change your mind. You'd be amazed at what the good people of North Dakota can handle."

Not long after my talk with Dave Roberts, I spoke at a tea party rally in Fargo. After my speech, I was talking to some folks, and a man came up and introduced himself. "I'm Bruce Engkjer," he said, "and I live here in the Fargo area. I sell steel structures all around the world. My brother and I own Mastercraft-Liberty Steel Buildings."

"Have I seen any of your buildings around Fargo?" I asked.

"No," he said. "We don't sell many of our products in North Dakota. But we're building an entire town in Madagascar."

"Madagascar?! You've got to be kidding me!"

"You should come to my office one of these days, and I'll show you some pictures of the buildings we're putting up. They have diamond mines in Madagascar and they need a lot of infrastructure for the miners. So we provide the steel buildings for the mining towns. They're not palatial, but they're comfortable and big enough for families."

As he talked, it occurred to me that these steel houses might be the answer to the problem of building infrastructure to support the oil boom in North Dakota. Steel houses go up quickly, they're durable, and they provide a place where people can put a pillow down and care for their families. I said, "You know what? You ought to be selling this in North Dakota."

"I don't think there's a market for my product here."

"Not around Fargo. But in the western part of the state, where there's a lot of oil drilling going on, they really need your product."

And within a few days, I was introducing Bruce Engkjer to some friends in the oil industry. These are grassroots connections that could one day play a big part in helping America become energy independent—and they came about because a stranger introduced himself at a tea party and became a friend.

I'm passionate about America's energy future. And I'm passionate about all that *could* happen in America if we could just get government out of the way, and get business, community, and state leaders talking together. I'm passionate about finding ways to make America work once more.

So here's a memo to all the Democrats, socialists, Sierra Clubbers, and assorted tree huggers: You say you love clean air? I do, too. I know your heart is in the right place. I believe you when you say you want green energy. Well, one nuclear plant, situated on a modest patch of ground, can supply more energy than *thousands* of acres of solar panels or windmills.

I've often wondered, "Why don't we have a nuclear plant in North Dakota?" There are parts of the state where you can drive for hours and never see another human being. In some parts of the country, if you mention nuclear energy, people say, "Not in my backyard!" Well, North Dakota has plenty of backyard. We'll be happy to get a nuclear plant, plus all the wealth and jobs that go with it.

Some people hear the word *nuclear* and immediately respond,

"What about Three Mile Island in 1979? What about Chernobyl in 1986? What about Fukushima Dai-ichi in 2011?"

Well, let's think about that for a moment.

The Chernobyl accident in the Soviet Union was caused by an ill-advised test of an inferior and unsafe reactor design. As a result, thirty-one people died in the first three months, and hundreds more were sickened by radiation. The Soviet plant did not even have a containment structure, and it used flammable graphite instead of water to control neutron radiation. When the graphite caught fire, the Chernobyl plant burned for four days, releasing far more radioactive material than the atomic bomb that destroyed Hiroshima.

Fast-forward almost twenty-five years. On March 11, 2011, Japan was struck by the 9.0 Sendai earthquake and killer tsunami. The Fukushima Dai-ichi nuclear power plant near Okuma was crippled by what experts call a "planetary magnitude" disaster. The quake was so violent it shifted the Japanese main island, Honshu, about eight feet to the east, knocked the earth's axis askew by as much as ten inches, and shortened the earth's twenty-four-hour day by 1.8 millionths of a second. It also caused nearly $200 billion in damage and took an estimated twenty-seven thousand lives.

The Japanese power plant suffered a "station blackout," a complete loss of most of the multiple-redundant safety features designed to cool down the reactor in an emergency. Even so, the plant's well-built light-water reactors (designed by General Electric and commissioned in the 1970s) shut down the moment the quake hit. Though the reactor vessels remained intact, fuel in the plant underwent at least partial meltdown, and radiocative material was released into the atmosphere. Workers who struggled valiantly to bring the stricken nuclear plant under control were exposed to high levels of radiation.

The Japanese crisis is clearly a setback for the global nuclear industry, which was just beginning to recover from its post-Chernobyl paralysis. Just as the world was on the verge of a "nuclear renaissance," it now appears that we are headed for the nuclear dark ages once more.

Emotion tends to trump reason in the public discussion of nuclear energy. Instead of hiding our heads in the sand, we need to take a

clear-eyed, rational look at the lessons of the Fukushima Dai-ichi accident. We need to make decisions based on evidence and reason, not
panic. What are the lessons of Fukushima?

First, technological redundancy can fail in a catastrophe. Even
though Fukushima had layered safety backup systems, an event of
this magnitude can knock out *all* of those systems at once. We should
not put all of our faith in redundancy alone.

Second, while the Fukushima facility employed the best technology
of the 1970s, we have even better technology today. Ian Hore-Lacy of
the World Nuclear Association notes that today's reactors "are one or
two orders of magnitude safer than older models," in large part due
to passive cooling systems that would have prevented the partial meltdown at Fukushima.[7]

Third, we do not live in a risk-free world. Even conventional energy entails risk. In 2010 alone, we saw a number of energy-related
disasters—the Upper Big Branch Mine disaster in West Virginia that
killed twenty-nine coal miners, the British Petroleum Deepwater
Horizon oil rig blowout that killed eleven and fouled the coastlines
around the Gulf of Mexico, and the Pacific Gas & Electric gas pipeline
explosion in San Bruno, California, that killed eight people in their
homes. A technologically advanced society runs on energy, and energy entails risk. We have to accept a certain amount of risk while
doing everything possible to minimize that risk.

Fourth, if you want to make nuclear energy as safe as possible,
keep nuclear plants away from earthquake faults. Two California
nuclear facilities—the Diablo Canyon and San Onofre nuclear power
plants—are (like Fukushima Dai-ichi) located in coastal earthquake
zones. Wouldn't it make more sense to build nuclear plants in geolog-
ically stable regions where the ground doesn't shake—for example, in
North Dakota?

The real lesson of the Fukushima Dai-ichi accident is that we *can*
build and operate safe nuclear power plants. Even this four-decade-
old nuclear facility proved to be remarkably sturdy in the face of one
of the worst natural disasters in human history.

Nuclear power is the most concentrated form of energy we know.

One kilogram of nuclear fuel yields about twenty thousand times as much energy as an equivalent amount of coal—and it leaves no carbon footprint.[8] Today, the world produces roughly 14 percent of its electrical power from nuclear plants. In fact, the fifty-nine nuclear plants in France produce *78 percent* of that country's electrical output, enabling France to export some of its nuclear-generated electricity to neighboring countries.

Nuclear energy is already one of the safest, cleanest forms of energy available—and we can make it even safer. So let's follow Dick Cheney's sensible plan, and let's split a few atoms. Let's dig up some coal. Let's drill for oil and gas. Let's brew up some biofuels and spin a few windmills. Let's do it all. And yes, let's be wise and conserve our resources, and let nothing go to waste. That was part of Dick Cheney's plan, too.

Grassroots Americans like you are the key to making the "all of the above" approach a reality. For example, the tea party movement helped bring about a Republican takeover of both houses of the Minnesota legislature. One of the first acts of the new legislature in early 2011 was a vote in both chambers to repeal the 1994 moratorium on nuclear power plant construction. Though Governor Mark Dayton, a Democrat, appears poised to veto the bill, Minnesota voters have taken a significant step toward securing their energy future.

Here in the heartland, business leaders and grassroots Americans are doing the job the federal government has failed to do. North Dakota has become the fourth-largest oil-producing state in America, and the Bakken shale formation is estimated to contain at least 11 billion barrels of oil (Harold Hamm told me he believes there is easily *twice* that much retrievable oil in the shale). It is all extractable with current technology. North Dakota currently pumps 350,000 barrels of crude oil per day, and production is expected to double within the next few years.[9]

North Dakota has more energy resources than Saudi Arabia has oil. As someone once said, "Lead, follow, or get out of the way." Here in the heartland, we choose to lead—and it's time for the federal government to get out of our way.

THE GREEN MENACE

One of the biggest threats to energy independence, prosperity, and human life itself is today's radical environmental movement. That's right—radical environmentalism *kills*.

The environmental movement wasn't always composed of extremists with a socialist agenda. One of the first conservationists was Theodore Roosevelt, who came from New York to North Dakota as a young man. While ranching in the Badlands, near Medora, he developed a deep love of nature, which defined him for the rest of his life. As president, he oversaw the creation of 150 national forests, eighteen national monuments, and five national parks. Teddy Roosevelt was one of a number of commonsense conservationists including John J. Audubon, George Bird Grinnell, and John Muir.

But the wheels began coming off the conservation movement in the 1960s. In 1962, Rachel Carson published her bestselling book, *Silent Spring,* a scathing critique of chemical pesticides. The book was hailed as a brilliant exposé of that evil substance, DDT (dichlorodiphenyltrichloroethane). Only recently have scientists begun to reexamine Carson's claims.

DDT is a pesticide developed by Swiss chemist Paul Hermann Müller in 1939. In 1948 he received the Nobel Prize in Medicine because of the success of DDT in reducing the incidence of disease throughout the world. The vast majority of deadly infections—malaria, yellow fever, bubonic plague, dengue, sleeping sickness, and typhus—are transmitted by insect bites. DDT saves lives by killing the carrier insects.

Paul Müller's own tests showed that DDT was effective and deadly to insects, such as mosquitoes, but had little or no effect on human beings and other animals. It was inexpensive to produce, costing only pennies per pound. The World Health Organization reported in 1967 that DDT had eliminated malaria from ten nations, which had previously experienced millions of malarial deaths annually.

Because the use of DDT was so widespread, the publication of *Silent Spring* set off a media firestorm. The book claimed that DDT was harmful to fish and birds, and was a potential carcinogen among humans—and Carson's claims were supposedly backed by studies showing that DDT caused liver tumors in mice and decimated bird populations. In 1970, Richard Nixon formed the Environmental Protection Agency—partly in response to public emotions generated by *Silent Spring*. In 1972, EPA head William Ruckelshaus banned the production of DDT.

Decades later, scientists rechecked the studies cited in *Silent Spring* and found them to be flawed. For example, it turned out that liver tumors in the mice were caused not by DDT, but by aflatoxin, a carcinogen in the food fed to the mice. But by then, the damage had been done. Deprived of DDT, many impoverished countries saw the rate of deaths from malaria skyrocket. Ceylon (Sri Lanka), which had seen its annual malaria death rate drop from 2.8 million to just seventeen cases in 1963, saw the death rate climb back to 2.5 million per year after spraying stopped.

A few clear-thinking scientists realized that the DDT ban was driven by emotion, not science. For example, entomologist Gordon Edwards, who taught biology at San Jose State University in California, used to swallow teaspoons full of DDT in front of his students to demonstrate its safety. DDT obviously did him no harm. Always in robust health, he died of a heart attack at age eighty-four while hiking up Divide Mountain in Glacier National Park. Edwards called the DDT ban "an abject capitulation to environmental extremists and a tremendous defeat for science and mankind."

A few years ago the Congress of Racial Equality shocked the environmental movement by staging a demonstration against Greenpeace. Black activists carried signs that read "DDT Saves African Lives" and "Well-Fed Greens—Starving Africans." It's true: radical environmentalism has killed tens of millions of people, most of them mothers, infants, and children in Africa and Asia. When millions die because of political correctness and environmental hysteria, let's call it what it really is: green genocide.[10]

Today, the radical environmentalists are killing our way of life and working to impose their socialist agenda on the world. And they are succeeding. There are many green organizations we could examine, but let's take a look at just one: the Apollo Alliance. This organization, which has close ties to the Obama administration, presents itself as "a coalition of labor, business, environmental, and community leaders working to catalyze a clean energy revolution that will put millions of Americans to work in a new generation of high-quality, green-collar jobs."[11] Senate majority leader Harry Reid credited the Apollo Alliance with having written much of the stimulus bill (the American Recovery and Reinvestment Act of 2009), which Congress passed without reading.[12] Self-described Marxist and former green jobs czar Van Jones has served on the board of Apollo Alliance.[13]

But as my friend Phil Kerpen points out, there is an even more dangerous Jones at Apollo Alliance. Jeff Jones is a onetime domestic terrorist and co-founder (with Mark Rudd and Bill Ayers) of the radical Weather Underground. He was a fugitive from justice for more than a decade until the FBI arrested him in 1981 for his involvement in antigovernment bomb attacks. Today, says Kerpen, Jeff Jones directs the Apollo Alliance New York affiliate and is a consultant with the national organization. In that capacity, he helped write grant proposals for federal stimulus funds, which transfer taxpayer dollars into the coffers of Apollo's political and environmental allies.[14]

"The Apollo Alliance," Phil said, "is an umbrella organization that has solved one of the last major problems facing the liberal-progressive agenda. That problem was the huge clash between organized labor and the environmentalists. Organized labor tries to protect union jobs in order to generate union dues. The environmentalists are antigrowth and antiprosperity, so they want to shut down industry and kill jobs. The Apollo Alliance did what no one was able to do before: it got the union guys and the environmentalists on the same page, working together toward the same goals.

"Apollo also pulled in social justice folks, such as the community organizers. So it unified the three core constituencies of the left under the banner of green jobs. Of course, green jobs are not economically viable jobs. They don't make economic sense in the free market. So green jobs can exist only because of big-government intervention. They are really political jobs that do more harm than good to the economy.

"So from the perspective of environmentalists who want to deindustrialize the United States, green jobs are attractive because they are expensive and they redirect economic resources. Green jobs are a drag on economic growth, but the union guys find them attractive because they can put requirements into these jobs to make every green job a union job. That's what Apollo Alliance did in writing the stimulus bill, and they plan to take it even further in proposed cap-and-trade legislation.

"Apollo Alliance has gotten warring constituencies to work together, all pushing for green jobs, all seeking huge federal appropriations to fund the green agenda. And the Apollo Alliance is the clearinghouse for this effort. John Podesta from the Center for American Progress, chairman of the Obama transition team, is on the board. The president of the Apollo Alliance is Phil Angelides, the former treasurer of the state of California. Leo Gerard from the United Steelworkers, who got the Obama administration to put tariffs on Chinese tires, is on the board. They've got other heavy hitters from the SEIU and Sierra Club. So you have the big boys from the labor movement and the environmental movement working together and writing the legislation that spends your tax dollars. That money is going to political payoffs, feather-nesting, corruption, skimming, and so on."

In August 2008, candidate Barack Obama asked an audience in Lansing, Michigan, "Will America watch as the clean-energy jobs and industries of the future flourish in countries like Spain, Japan, or Germany? Or will we create them here, in the greatest country on earth, with the most talented, productive workers in the world?"[15] And as president he claimed, "Spain generates almost 30 percent of its power by harnessing the wind, while we manage less than one percent."[16]

Is the green revolution truly creating jobs and expanding the economy in Spain? I called upon an expert, Dr. Gabriel Alvarez, professor of economics at Madrid's King Juan Carlos University, and author of the myth-shattering paper "Study of the Effects on Employment of Public Aid to Renewable Energy Resources." Dr. Alvarez explained his conclusions:

"The study found that the whole green jobs scheme was expensive for Spanish taxpayers," he said. "In fact, we have devoted thirty billion euros to the green jobs experiment, and after eight years, we have seen 60,000 jobs created. This works out to about $750,000 per job. In our research, we tried to determine how many jobs had been destroyed by shifting these financial resources out of the private marketplace. We found that we would have created 2.2 jobs for every green job that has been created. So the green jobs program was destroying twice as many jobs as it created."

Dr. Alvarez went on to explain that one out of ten green jobs are actually maintenance and operation jobs at a functioning energy facility. Nine out of ten are *construction* jobs. They are the jobs of those who build the windmills and install the solar panels. So here's the catch-22: If you don't continue that pace of new construction, if you don't keep feeding the beast, 90 percent of those jobs have to be terminated. Green jobs are not self-sustainable; they require continuous government subsidies. So the green jobs agenda boils down to a fraudulent pyramid scheme.

When Dr. Alvarez's study was published, the U.S. green lobby pounced on it. I asked Alvarez how the study was greeted in Spain. "The Spanish government did note that the study was not good for the Spanish image in the outside world," he replied. "Yet on April 30, 2010, the Spanish government issued a decree that said that this whole green jobs scheme—and I quote—'is deeply harming the system and puts at risk not only the financial situation of the electric sector companies, but also the sustainability of the system itself.' So the government has affirmed the conclusions of our study."

What's more, *Investor's Business Daily* reported in May 2010 that Chris Horner, a senior fellow at the Competitive Enterprise Institute and a frequent guest on my show, had obtained a copy of the Spanish government report, and said that the socialist government of Spanish prime minister José Luis Rodríguez Zapatero "now acknowledges the ruinous effects of green economic policy" and acknowledged that "the 'green economy' stunt must be abandoned, lest the experiment risk Spain becoming Greece." In fact, said Horner, "the figures published in the government document indicate they arrived at a job-loss number even worse than the 2.2 figure" from the Alvarez study.

Investor's Business Daily adds that a study of the green jobs program in Italy reached an even more devastating conclusion. Researchers Carlo Stagnaro and Luciano Lavecchia of the Italian think tank Istituto Bruno Leoni "found that in Italy, the losses were worse than they were in Spain: Each green job cost 6.9 jobs in the industrial sector and 4.8 jobs across the entire economy." Stagnaro and Lavecchia concluded, "To the extent that the 'green deal' is aimed at creating employment or purported as anti-crisis or stimulus policy, it is a wrong policy choice."[17]

Our leaders have thrown in the towel and said, "We'll install the technology to capture carbon dioxide, even if it raises the cost of every product we produce, even if it shuts down our economy and impoverishes our people, even if we are the only nation engaging in this charade." Are China, India, or Brazil pursuing the green agenda? No. The United States of America is expected to hobble its economy and carry the economic burden for eliminating so-called greenhouse gases for the entire planet.

The president of the Czech Republic, Václav Klaus, is an economist who grew up under Soviet-style communism. During an official visit to Great Britain in 2007, Klaus gave a speech in London in which he warned:

Environmentalism . . . is becoming a new dominant ideology, if not a religion. Its main weapon is raising the alarm and predicting the human life-endangering climate change based on man-made global warming. The recent awarding of [the] Nobel Prize to the main apostle of this hypothesis [Al Gore] was the last straw because by this these ideas were elevated to the pedestal of "holy and sacred" uncriticisable truths. . . .

The climate change debate is basically not about science; it is about ideology. It is not about global temperature; it is about the concept of human society. It is not about scientific ecology; it is about environmentalism, which is a new anti-individualistic, pseudo-collectivistic ideology based on putting nature and environment and their supposed protection and preservation before and above freedom. . . .

The irrationality with which the current world has embraced

the climate change (or global warming) [is] a real danger to the future of mankind.[18]

The Obama administration is determined to kill the fossil fuels industry and replace coal, oil, and natural gas with wind and solar energy. This is a destructive course, because the physics and the math don't lie. Wind and solar cannot supply a reasonable fraction of America's energy needs within the next few decades—if ever.

The left tries to sell the green agenda by "sweetening" the deal with economic inducements. This is one of the oldest tricks in the liberal-progressive playbook: "If we pass the stimulus bill, it will create or save millions of jobs. If we pass Obamacare, it will bring down costs and reduce the debt. If we pass cap and trade, it will create countless green jobs and fix the economy." But it's all a scam.

The notion of "green jobs" is a fantasy. These phony green jobs will destroy *real* jobs that provide *real* energy in the *real* economy. Just as Rachel Carson's *Silent Spring* inflicted death on millions of people around the world, the green jobs agenda is death to the American energy industry and the American economy. And the entire "green jobs" movement is based on a lie that so-called anthropogenic (human-caused) global warming is even taking place. The UN's Intergovernmental Panel on Climate Change may claim that there is a "scientific consensus" that global warming is occurring—but the evidence, and growing dissent among scientists, prove otherwise.

A recent article by Willie Soon of the Harvard-Smithsonian Center for Astrophysics, Robert Carter of the International Climate Science Coalition, and David Legates, hydroclimatologist at the University of Delaware, takes a clear-eyed look at the claims of the radical environmentalists. The authors point out that carbon dioxide (CO_2), which the environmentalists demonize as a "pollutant," is actually "the gas of life." People and animals exhale CO_2, and plants breathe it in. The leaves, stalk, and root system of a plant benefit and grow faster in the presence of higher concentrations of CO_2, and the plant metabolizes water and nutrients more efficiently. The more CO_2 plants take in, the more oxygen they give off.

Higher levels of CO_2 have produced greater diversity of bird species in China by enriching the plant-based food supply of birds. The authors write, "By insisting that no human CO_2 should be emitted, they [the radical environmentalists] are promoting continued suboptimal growth of food plant species in the face of impending global food shortages—and poorer functioning and less diversity in the global ecosystem."

Does human-caused carbon dioxide lead to dangerous global warming? No, say the authors. "If rising atmospheric CO_2 levels drive global temperatures upward . . . why is Earth not suffering from the dangerous 'fever' that Al Gore predicted? Instead, after mild warming at the end of the twentieth century, global temperatures have leveled off for the past decade, amid steadily rising carbon dioxide levels. . . . The scientific reality is that even the United Nations Intergovernmental Panel on Climate Change has been unable to demonstrate a cause-and-effect scientific connection between rising human CO_2 emissions and dangerous warming."[19]

Global warming alarmists will tell you that temperatures have been steadily rising in recent years, according to the Global Historical Climatology Network (GHCN). But researchers such as Dr. Ross McKitrick (of the University of Guelph and the Global Warming Policy Foundation) warn that the GHCN data are contaminated by "urban heat island" effects—that is, by man-made heat sources. In recent years, GHCN temperature-monitoring equipment has been increasingly placed near airports. Currently, roughly half of all temperature measurements come from airports. This means that temperature measurements have likely been affected by "traffic, pavement, buildings and waste heat, all of which are difficult to remove from the temperature record."[20]

Another researcher, S. Fred Singer of the Science and Environmental Policy Project, examined temperatures recorded at 107 sites around the state of California from 1909 to 1994. He found that stations located near high population centers consistently registered higher temperatures than those in less populated areas. In other words, the temperatures these instruments recorded weren't the result of global warming. They were "urban heat island" effects from cars, airplanes, air conditioners, and so forth.[21] The so-called global warming data are hopelessly contaminated by artificial heat sources.

While carbon dioxide levels have been rising, the best data shows that global temperatures have remained fairly flat. Why is that? The answer is simple: Carbon dioxide does not produce global warming.

Joseph D'Aleo, executive director of the International Climate and Environmental Change Assessment Project (ICECAP), has analyzed the most reliable data from the United States Historical Climatology Network. Using data covering a 113-year period from 1895 through 2007 he looked at three environmental factors and measured their correlation to global warming. Those factors were carbon dioxide, irradiance from the sun, and the temperature of the oceans. In other words, if carbon dioxide causes global warming, then the earth's temperature should be higher when CO_2 levels are high, and lower when CO_2 levels are low.

D'Aleo found that, for the years 1895 through 2007, there is a relatively weak correlation between solar irradiance levels and temperature levels (57 percent). There is an even weaker correlation between CO_2 levels and temperature levels (43 percent). And if you look at a recent decade, 1998 to 2007, the correlation between CO_2 levels and temperature levels becomes practically nonexistent (2 percent). There is only one factor that strongly correlates to atmospheric temperature levels, and that is the temperature of the oceans. D'Aleo combined ocean warming data from the Atlantic and Pacific oceans over the past 108 years, and he found a statistically strong correlation of 85 percent.

So the evidence shows that whether the earth's atmosphere is warming or cooling, the temperature changes are probably being driven by warming or cooling of the earth's oceans. Carbon dioxide is simply not a significant factor.[22] Why, then, should we destroy our industries and our economy to kowtow to a radical environmental agenda that is based on junk science?

OPTIMISTIC ABOUT AMERICA'S ENERGY FUTURE

A week before the 2008 election, I interviewed then-governor Sarah Palin of Alaska on my show. I said it then and I'll say it now: there is not another elected official in this country who has the résumé she does when it comes to tackling the nation's energy problems. As a candidate in 2008, she had a far greater record of executive accomplishment than John McCain, Barack Obama, and Joe Biden *combined*.

Sarah Palin pushed and signed into law a tough ethics bill, rooted out corruption in her own party, killed numerous wasteful spending projects (included many supported by Republicans), canceled the Gravina Island bridge pork-barrel project, promoted energy resource development, cut state spending, refunded money to the taxpayers, created a subcabinet advisory council on "climate change," shepherded the Alaska Gasline Inducement Act (a $40 billion pipeline to bring natural gas from the North Slope to the Lower Forty-Eight), sold off the Westwind II jet bought by the previous Republican administration, and more. And she did all that in just *two years* as governor!

I asked her what she would do as vice president to lessen America's dependence on foreign oil. She replied, "We had thirty years of failed energy policy that makes us rely on foreign sources of energy, on these volatile regimes that we're beholden to. We've been asking them to ramp up production of energy sources for us so that we can purchase from them. Some of these regimes don't like America, and they use energy as a weapon. They can cut off our supply at any time. Yet we circulate hundreds of billions of dollars every year into those countries.

"Meanwhile, we have the domestic solution here. Barack Obama and Joe Biden have said no to the domestic solutions that have been proposed. They've opposed offshore drilling. They oppose some of the alternative forms of energy that have been laid out. We need the 'all of the above' approach. Drillin' here—offshore, onshore. We need to develop clean coal technology. We cannot keep going down the path we've been on, relying on foreign sources of energy. We've got to become energy independent."

Well, here in the heartland, we have picked up Sarah Palin's challenge and we are leading the way to energy independence. Grassroots Americans are doing what Washington politicians won't do. We are securing America's energy future. And that's why I'm passionate and optimistic about America's energy future.

THE COMMONSENSE ACTION AGENDA

Here are some grassroots actions you can take, starting today:

✓ Become a tireless defender of the energy industry. Energy drives our economy, and we can't afford to allow America's energy future to be strangled by the myth of "green energy." We need to pursue an "all of the above" strategy, with a strong focus on fossil fuels and nuclear power. Windmills, solar panels, and corn ethanol have their place, but they can never provide the energy density, power density, cost, and scale required to replace hydrocarbons and nuclear energy.

✓ Become an energy expert. Read up on some of the new ways of extracting energy from the earth, such as fracking. In fact, I encourage you to come to North Dakota, visit the oil patch, and see a fracking rig with your own eyes. Come visit a coal mine—or the site of an old mine where the land has been reclaimed, and where trees, ponds, and streams have turned a former industrial site into a Garden of Eden. Then tell your friends and neighbors that you've seen with your own eyes that the people of the North Dakota energy industry are good stewards of the land.

✓ When you contact your legislators about energy issues, don't forget to talk to state and local representatives. Your governor and state legislature have a lot of control over the energy industry in your state. They need to hear that grassroots citizens are active, knowledgeable, and passionately pro-business and pro-energy. Enlist your friends and neighbors as citizen lobbyists for commonsense energy and environmental policies.

✓ Demand that all legislation affecting energy and environmental issues be based on sound, proven science, not junk science and emotionalism. Spread the word that the best scientific evidence shows that the earth is moving into a cooling phase—not "global warming." These cyclical changes in climate are normal, and they are not related to human-caused "greenhouse gases." Changes in the climate appear to be most strongly influenced by changes in the temperatures of the oceans.

5

PUTTING AMERICA BACK TO WORK

J im Arthaud is part of the energy boom and economic renaissance of western North Dakota. He owns Missouri Basin Well
Service, Inc., a Belfield, North Dakota, trucking company. He
reminds me a bit of Harold Hamm in that he started his company
with one truck and one driver—himself. From there, his company
grew and grew. I asked him how he got started in business.

"Our company started in 1979," he said, "and along the way, I had
help from a lot of people—my father, brother, brother-in-law, and
many others. Over time, the company grew to the point where we
now have seven hundred employees and a couple hundred trucks. We
do a lot of crude oil hauling for Continental Resources, Inc. We also
move a lot of salt water, freshwater, and sand for the frack jobs. We
dispose of freshwater from the wells and we move mud products for
the drilling companies. So we do a bit of everything.

"I know there's a recession going on around the country, but here
in North Dakota, business is booming. Our challenge is finding employees. We have our human resources group fanning out to job fairs
all around Montana, South Dakota, Minnesota, Indiana, Colorado,
everywhere.

"Another challenge is safety. Those Continental wells often start
out producing three thousand barrels a day, which is approximately
ten truckloads. For the frack jobs, we are hauling out ten to twenty

truckloads of water per day. So there's a tremendous amount of truck traffic on the roads, and that's a major safety concern for us. We instill defensive driving skills in our drivers, plus we have a twenty-person full-time safety staff. Their only job is to be out in the field, twenty-four/seven, making sure our drivers get home safely at night.

"As the infrastructure in the oil patch matures, some truck traffic will be replaced by pipelines and railroads. But as long as we have new drilling going on, there will be a need for tankers to transport water and crude oil. It's a major industrial project. So it's exciting to be a part of this oil boom. It's satisfying to see the people who work for you earn a good living with good benefits. Providing housing is a challenge, but we are working on that challenge, too. The state government works with us to find solutions to the infrastructure problems. Everybody on both the private side and the government side understands that these are good problems to have, and we're working together.

"There are a lot of success stories coming out of this oil boom," Arthaud concluded, "and everything that's happening out here is good for America." Jim Arthaud is one grassroots businessman who is helping to put America back to work.

THE FAILURE OF OBAMANOMICS

My friend Eugene Graner heads up Heartland Investor Services, Inc., a commodities brokerage firm in Bismarck. He's a businessman and a grassroots American who has taken the time to study economics. He is one of the most knowledgeable people I know about how our government's actions impact the business climate, investment, employment, and the creation of wealth. During one of our chats on *The Common Sense Club,* he explained exactly why $1 trillion of government "stimulus" spending ended up killing jobs and deepening the recession.

"The stimulus failed," he said. "President Obama promised that if we passed the 2009 stimulus bill, we would hold job losses at eight percent. But after all that 'stimulus' was injected into the economy, the unemployment rate continued climbing and hovered at close to ten percent."

But that didn't begin to tell the whole story. "Not only did the un-employment rate keep rising, but those who were still employed be-came *less* employed on a weekly basis. Government statistics show that weekly employment hours dropped after the stimulus bill passed. By September 2009, weekly employed people were working only thirty-three hours a week on average. Many employed people were actually *under*employed, making less money per week." So even those who still had jobs were being hurt by the Obama economy.

I asked Eugene why the stimulus failed to produce jobs. "Because the people who wrote the stimulus bill don't understand free markets. They operated from an anticapitalism mind-set, which says that free enterprise is the problem and big government has the solution. If the people in the Obama administration understood how free enterprise works, they would understand exactly why the stimulus failed. The reason we have job losses in spite of the stimulus is very simple. The stimulus bill doesn't do anything to help the people who actually cre-ate the jobs in this country.

"Many people think that large corporations like IBM and 3M cre-ate the jobs in America. But in a large corporation, you have a CEO who is beholden to his shareholders and his board of directors, and he's not going to stick his neck out in a bad economy and expand the business. Whether in a good economy or a bad economy, the engine of job creation continues to be small business. And here's a shocking statistic that most people are unaware of: historically, when this coun-try comes out of recessions, fifty percent of all job creation not only comes from small business, but from *small businesses that have been in existence for only five years or less*. Now, think about that. Why would relatively young start-up businesses point the way out of a recession?

"It's because most small businesses are typically one to three part-ners who are willing to take a risk because they feel optimistic about their chances in the local marketplace. These small businesses are nimble and less risk-averse than some big national or multinational corporation.

"But President Obama comes along and wants the 'rich' to pay 'their fair share.' He seems to think that small business owners are millionaires. But small business owners are the people who sit across from you at the diner. They're the people who go to your church. They're the people who show up at the charity events in your local community. They have stored up some wealth by being prudent with their money and occasionally investing in a business that does well and creates wealth.

"President Obama's message to these job creators is, 'If you succeed, if you make more than two hundred and fifty thousand dollars per year, your government will punish your success and redistribute your wealth.' So these entrepreneurs look at the business climate under the Obama administration, and they say, 'Why should I risk what I have accumulated? If I risk and fail, I could lose everything. If I risk and succeed, the government will swoop in and take a bigger share of my rewards.' So this small-businessman needs to think twice before he starts up a new business and hires employees. He's got a lot of variables to consider.

"First: 'What are my costs to hire new employees?' Because of Obamacare and other factors, all of these factors are unknown—and constantly changing. All the small-businessman knows for sure is that his costs are going up.

"Second: 'What are my energy and regulatory costs going to be?' Because of proposed cap-and-trade legislation, these costs could go sky-high. He thinks, 'I'd have to build a new office building, which would have to meet all the new regulatory requirements of the Obama government. So I have another layer of unknown costs.'

"Third: 'Will I be able to capitalize this new venture?' The businessman has some capital of his own, but he will need to borrow in order to start up this new business. With all the new banking restrictions and the paranoia in the financial industry, banks aren't lending. So this small-businessman is kept at bay because of an inability to obtain capital.

"You add all of these factors together, and it just doesn't pencil out. And the businessman thinks, 'Even if I could make it over those three hurdles and make this business successful, what is my reward? President Obama is going to increase my taxes. Not only will I jump into the next tax bracket, but I will also be penalized with an extra five percent surtax on top of my income tax because now I'm supposedly rich! Forget it. I don't need these headaches for the meager re-wards of success.' And that's exactly why the business environment is stagnant despite a trillion dollars of supposed 'stimulus.'

"The engine of job creation, especially coming out of recession, is small business, principally the start-ups, businesses five years old or younger. If the Obama administration was serious about creating jobs, it should get out of the way of small business—cut taxes, lighten the regulatory burden, and let entrepreneurs keep the rewards of risk taking and success. But that goes against everything the central eco-nomic planners in the White House believe in.

"The people who wrote the stimulus bill removed every last trace of free market capitalism from the bill. The money didn't go to brick-and-mortar construction, highways, bridges, and actual projects that create jobs. It went to political patronage, special interests, unions, and government boondoggles. Then they rushed the bill through the Congress so fast that no one had a chance to read it. It was drafted in secret and passed in the dark of night. And you know what was really ironic? The Democrats said, 'This is an *emergency*! We've got to pass the bill *now*! No time to read the bill, just *vote*!' So they passed it, and it was all ready for President Obama's signature—but instead of signing the bill, Obama took off on vacation. And there sat the bill. Candidate Obama had promised that all bills would be posted on the Internet for five days before voting—but President Obama and the Democrats broke that campaign promise right out of the chute!"

Wise words from my friend Eugene Graner. The policies of Barack Obama are killing jobs and destroying wealth in America. If only the voters had taken a closer look at the president's tissue-thin résumé be-fore hiring him as our nation's CEO.

Peter Ferrara is senior policy adviser on Social Security and Medi-care at the Institute for Policy Innovation, and worked for President Reagan and President George H. W. Bush. In July 2010, Peter and I had a conversation on my show about Obama's job-killing economic policies. "President Obama was in Racine, Wisconsin, saying, in ef-fect, 'Hey, I saved you from a second Great Depression,' " Peter said. "But if you look at the result of his policies, you see that he was *cre-ating* a second Great Depression. The average recession since World

War II lasted about ten months, according to the National Bureau of Economic Research. And the longest recession since World War II lasted about sixteen months. The current recession started in December 2007. [As of August 2010], this recession will go into its thirty-second month. It will have lasted *twice* as long as the longest previous recession since World War II.

"And what are we hearing in the news? Not talk of recovery. Economists are warning of a double-dip recession—*another* recession as we are trying to climb out of this one. The economy today is playing out just like the Great Depression. One of the reasons that's happening is that President Obama is pursuing the same policies as we had in the 1930s. This Keynesian stimulus program is the same thing FDR tried almost eighty years ago, and the result was that the Great Depression lasted for a decade."

"In that same speech you mentioned," I said, "President Obama made this claim: 'Now, every economist who has looked at [the effect of the stimulus plan] has said that the recovery did its job. It put a brake on the collapse of the economy. We avoided a Great Depression.'[1] Now, it's simply absurd to say that *every economist* who studied the stimulus bill said it worked. That is a flat-out lie. In fact, on the very day that President Obama made those remarks, Allan H. Meltzer, a professor of economics at Carnegie Mellon University, wrote an article that opened with the statement 'The administration's stimulus program has failed.'[2]

"I don't understand why Barack Obama says things that are so obviously untrue, and which can only undermine his credibility. He easily could have said 'many economists,' but no, he had to make the claim that *all* economists unanimously gave their stamp of approval to his stimulus program. You don't have to be an economist to know that if the economy is still shedding jobs some thirty-plus months after the official start of the recession, then your trillion-dollar stimulus plan clearly *did not* work."

"It's a massive failure, money down the drain," Peter said. "Why can't small businesses get any loans? Because the federal government is sucking up all the capital and spending it to create government jobs. President Obama doesn't understand that, because he doesn't understand how jobs are created . . . and therein lies a danger. Think about it: Does President Obama have any advisers who serve in the role of naysayer? Does anyone around him offer any alternative views or contrasting opinions? Is there anyone around him who will give him a reality check?

"And he's not just enclosed in that bubble of White House yes-men, but he's also enclosed in the left-wing media bubble. He reads his own press releases from the *New York Times* telling him how wonderful he is. So we are being led by a man who does not live in the real world. He does not accurately perceive reality. There's no one there to tell him 'Mr. President, it's not working.' "

"That fits my theory about what's wrong with this administration," I said. "Hardly anyone in his cabinet has any real-world business experience. Most administrations draw heavily from the corporate world, but most of Obama's advisers come from universities or think tanks. They are a bunch of academics who live in a world of theory, not reality."

Incidentally, investment banker Michael Cembalest wrote a piece for *Forbes,* "Obama's Business Blind Spot," which contrasted the business experience of the Obama cabinet against the business experience of all 432 cabinet members of every administration since 1900. Cembalest created a chart that showed that *fewer than 10 percent* of Obama's cabinet appointees had private sector business experience, which he defined as having "started a company or [run] one, with first-hand experience in hiring and firing, domestic and international competition, red tape, recessions, wars and technological change." By contrast, Presidents Eisenhower and Reagan and Presidents Bush I and II had recruited 50 to 60 percent of their cabinet appointees from the private sector business world.[3]

The fact-checking website PolitiFact quibbles with Cembalest's criteria, claiming that more of Obama's cabinet should be credited with private sector experience, including a former head of a Bell Laboratories research lab, three former attorneys, and a former consultant[4]—but I agree with Cembalest that research, legal, and consulting backgrounds do not equip someone to understand the problems of those who run companies and hire and fire employees. Cembalest's findings support my theory about what is wrong with the Obama administration.

President Obama's cabinet members lack an understanding of, and experience in, the free market—and they display a clear antibusiness bias. That's why we see the kinds of policy blunders we see today. It's Amateur Hour out there. My friend Tim Pawlenty, the then governor of Minnesota, warned repeatedly during the 2008 presidential campaign, "Barack Obama has not run or done anything. What experience does he have to lead the United States of America?" Unfortunately, Tim's warning fell on deaf ears.

As I went on to say to Peter Ferrara, "Anyone with any business sense would say 'Here's what the economy needs, Mr. President. Businesspeople need certainty. What are taxes going to be? What are health care costs going to be? Are we going to enact cap-and-tax and raise the cost of everything? People can't make business decisions in the face of such uncertainty. No wonder unemployment remains high. Who would hire anybody in this uncertain environment? If you have no private sector experience, if you've never signed the front of a payroll check, if you've signed only the back of a government check, you can't understand the problems of the businessperson."

"President Obama's entire life," Peter said, "has been devoted to an extreme left-wing political philosophy, including left-wing economics. He can't repeat the successful Reagan record because that's not what it's all about. He's devoted his entire life to a certain worldview. He's been a closet Marxist all his life. Now he's reached the pinnacle—he's the president of the United States. Is he going to turn his back on his lifelong beliefs? Is he suddenly going to practice Reaganomics? He could never do that. He's committed to the opposite course—and it's destroying our country.

"If there is one thing worse than the uncertainty generated by Obama's policies, it's the certainty of what he is actually trying to do. We have an economy headed for a double-dip recession, and the Obama administration has scheduled tax increases across the board— capital gains tax rates up sixty percent, dividend tax rates up two hundred percent, top individual income tax rates going up, every federal income tax rate of importance is being hiked in the teeth of a recession. What is that going to do to the economy?

"Just by the normal cycle of things, if President Obama had simply left well enough alone—no stimulus, no Obamacare, no Wall Street reform bill—the economy should have come back to life by the fall of 2009. History shows that a recession doesn't last longer than sixteen months at most, so if his administration hadn't thrown a wrench into the machinery, President Obama would be running victory laps by now. He'd be saying 'Look at me! Look at the Obama recovery!' But he had to inflict his leftist economic theories on us, and now we're all suffering the consequences."

"The worst of it," I said, "is that Barack Obama doesn't learn from his mistakes—he *doubles down* on his mistakes. Now he's going around making the case that government *hasn't done enough,* and we need to *do more* of what clearly doesn't work. It's as if he's determined to strangle this economy."

"Look at everything he's doing," Peter said, "and it's raising the cost of doing business. The tax rate is going up, regulation is going up, and now he wants to do cap and trade and maybe a value-added tax. And the net result of these proposals is to drive up the cost of doing business, drive up the cost of energy, drive up the cost of health care—all of which serve only to freeze investment and innovation and hiring."

I then asked Peter if he saw any light at the end of this tunnel.

"Yes," he replied. "It's called 'the November election.' "

Peter Ferrara was right about the 2010 congressional election. I pray he's right again in November 2012.

THE SMARTEST GUY IN THE ROOM

Mark Halperin is a political analyst for *Time* magazine and MSNBC, and was the coauthor (with John Heilemann) of *Game Change*. In the fall of 2010, Halperin rendered this stunning verdict:

With the exception of core Obama administration loyalists, most politically engaged elites have reached the same conclusion: The

White House is in over its head, isolated, insular, arrogant and clueless about how to get along with or persuade members of Congress, the media, the business community or working-class voters. . . .

There is a growing perception that Obama's decisions are causing harm—that businesses are being hurt by the Administration's legislation and that economic recovery is stalling because of the uncertainty surrounding energy policy, health care, deficits, housing, immigration and spending.

And that sentiment is spreading.[5]

A leader needs self-confidence—but when a leader becomes so drunk with confidence that he becomes "isolated, insular, arrogant and clueless," his leadership becomes dysfunctional. Once, during the 2008 primaries, candidate Obama spoke with reporter Richard Wolffe aboard his campaign plane. Wolffe recalled that Barack Obama "had no doubts about his desire to change the direction of the country. 'You know, I actually believe my own bullshit,' he told me with a big smile."[6] He certainly does . . . and he expects all of us to believe it, too.

After the G-20 economic summit in Toronto in June 2010, Obama said, "A durable recovery must also include fiscal responsibility."[7] He said it with a straight face after having saddled the American economy with weapons-grade deficits and debt. That is his modus operandi—to say one thing in his public speeches, then turn right around and do the opposite with his policies. That's why, with this president, and with Democrats in general, you have to focus on what they *do* instead of what they say.

Writing in *Forbes,* Dinesh D'Souza, the author of *The Roots of Obama's Rage,* remarks about Barack Obama's weird decisions and baffling actions as president of the United States:

The President's actions are so bizarre that they mystify his critics and supporters alike. Consider this headline from the Aug. 18, 2009 issue of the *Wall Street Journal*: "Obama Underwrites Offshore Drilling." . . . The Administration supports offshore drilling—but drilling off the shores of Brazil. With Obama's backing, the U.S. Export-Import Bank offered $2 billion in loans and guarantees to Brazil's state-owned oil company Petrobras. . . . He is funding Brazilian exploration so that the oil can stay in Brazil. . . .

The oddities go on and on. . . . The President continues to push for stimulus even though hundreds of billions of dollars in such funds seem to have done little. The unemployment rate when Obama took office in January 2009 was 7.7%; now it is 9.5%. Yet he wants to spend even more and is determined to foist the entire bill on Americans making $250,000 a year or more. The rich, Obama insists, aren't paying their "fair share." This by itself seems odd given that . . . the top 10% pays 70% of the taxes; the bottom 40% pays close to nothing.[8]

Barack Obama clearly doesn't understand how the economy works, how wealth is created, or how jobs are generated. In March 2009, ABC's Jake Tapper reported that President Obama had begun dispensing investment advice to the American people:

President Obama told Americans to take a look at investing in the stock market . . . a remarkable utterance for an American president, especially as the Dow Jones Industrial Average proceeds on its course southward.

"What you're now seeing is . . . profit and earning ratios are starting to get to the point where buying stocks is a potentially good deal if you've got a long-term perspective on it," the president said on a day that trading continued to hover under 7,000.

The president predicted that Americans' consumer confidence would improve as they see the stimulus bill "taking root."[9]

Frankly, it's a little unnerving to discover that our nation's chief executive officer doesn't know that *P/E ratio* means "price-to-earnings ratio," not "profit and earnings ratio." Predictably, the same old media that loved to mock George W. Bush for terms like "nucular" and "misunderestimated" made almost no mention of Obama's gaffe. Mr. Obama is not qualified to run a popcorn stand, much less preside

over the largest economy in the world. Yet there he is, sitting in the
Oval Office, pushing the buttons and yanking the levers of our economy, relentlessly determined to impose his failed economic theories
on us all.

Contrast Barack Obama with Ronald Reagan, who (after being
dubbed an "amiable dunce" by Clark Clifford) rescued the American economy and demolished Soviet communism. What were Ronald
Reagan's qualifications to preside over the U.S. economy? Well, for
starters, Reagan was one of the few American presidents who actually majored in economics, having graduated from Eureka College in
Illinois with a bachelor of arts in sociology and economics. His son
Michael Reagan once told me that Ronald Reagan's personal library
had a section devoted to the works of free market economists, from
Milton Friedman to the "Austrian school" economists such as Ludwig von Mises and Friedrich Hayek. Reagan read Hayek's classic
The Road to Serfdom several times. No wonder the "amiable dunce"
achieved so much.

Now, in saying that Barack Obama doesn't have a clue about how
to run the economy, I'm not saying that he's ignorant or stupid. Oh
no. When it comes to getting what he wants in the political realm,
Barack Obama is brilliant—and he knows it. In fact, I believe his
most dangerous character flaw is his arrogance. After the release of
Bob Woodward's book *Obama's Wars* in September 2010, Bill O'Reilly
asked Woodward point-blank, "So, Obama thinks he's the smartest
guy in the room?" And Woodward replied without hesitating, "Yes.
That's exactly right." [10]

As Ronald Reagan observed in "A Time for Choosing," his 1964
speech on behalf of Barry Goldwater, "The trouble with our liberal
friends is not that they're ignorant; it's just that they know so much
that isn't so." [11]

Barack Obama really does think he's the smartest guy in any room
he walks into. He knows all there is to know about the economy—
especially that part about "spreading the wealth around." He knows
all there is to know about running the banking industry and the au-
tomotive industry and every other industry in America. And because
he thinks he knows everything about running a business, his policies

have destroyed thousands of businesses that have taken lifetimes to build.

We see his know-it-all approach in a series of grotesque statements he made about the health care industry during the Obamacare debate. For example, President Obama told a press conference, "You come in and you've got a bad sore throat, or your child has a bad sore throat or has repeated sore throats. The doctor may look at the reimbursement system and say to himself, 'You know what? I make a lot more money if I take this kid's tonsils out.' " What an astounding statement—I've known many doctors, and I've never known one who would even think of putting profit above patient care. Fact is, the doctor who diagnoses the sore throat would, if necessary, refer you to a surgeon for a tonsillectomy, so this is a foolish statement on the face of it.[12]

Obama also said, "If there's a blue pill and a red pill and the blue pill is half the price of the red pill and works just as well, why not pay half price for the thing that's going to make you well?"[13] No doubt, that's exactly the simplistic approach we can expect from Obamacare. Never mind that the blue pill may have dangerous side effects in some individuals that the red pill doesn't. Never mind that the blue pill works for only 90 percent of the population, and you happen to be in the 10 percent—if Dr. Obama says you're getting the blue pill, then shut up and take your medicine.

Most shocking of all, Obama actually accuses doctors of performing unnecessary amputations. At a staged town hall meeting in Portsmouth, New Hampshire, in August 2009, the president said, "If a family care physician works with his or her patient to help them lose weight, modify diet, monitors whether they're taking their medications in a timely fashion, they might get reimbursed a pittance. But if that same diabetic ends up getting their foot amputated, that's $30,000, $40,000, $50,000—immediately the surgeon is reimbursed. Well, why not make sure that we're also reimbursing the care that prevents the amputation, right? That will save us money."[14] Again, this is a shockingly foolish statement. A family care physician is not the same physician who wields the scalpel—or the saw. And as for that fee of "$30,000, $40,000, $50,000," the reality is that Medicare pays an average of $541 to $708 for a foot amputation. The crass profit motive that President Obama imputes to the medical profession just isn't there.[15]

It's hard to believe, but our president *really does* view the medical profession as a bunch of knife-happy Hippocratic oafs who are in it only for a buck. Hearing such bizarre statements from this president, a rational person is tempted to respond "Idiot!" But Barack Obama is not an idiot. He just knows so much that isn't so.

THE OBAMA KAKISTOCRACY

In 1865, poet James Russell Lowell learned of the end of the Civil War and exclaimed, "There is something magnificent in having a country to love!" He thought that the end of slavery and the end of the Civil War would bring peace and harmony to the Union. But a decade later, after watching years of political squabbling and division, he became discouraged with the state of affairs in America. In 1876, he wrote a letter to his friend Joel Benton, saying, "These fellows have no notion of what love of country means. . . . What fills me with doubts and dismay is the degradation of the moral tone. . . . Is ours a 'government of the people, by the people, for the people,' or a Kakistocracy, rather for the benefit of knaves at the cost of fools?"[16]

What, you ask, is a kakistocracy? The word comes from two Greek words, *kakistos* ("worst") and *kratia* ("government"). It literally means "government by those who are the worst or least-qualified." If James Russell Lowell thought he was living under a kakistocracy in 1876, when Ulysses S. Grant was president, what would he think of America today? And if he thought the level of political discourse in America was morally degraded back then, what if he could see Keith Olbermann or Joy Behar on TV today? What if he could see the way the ruling class and the chattering class treat the patriotic Americans of the tea party movement? I can't help thinking he would be convinced that we fought a revolution and a civil war for nothing.

These are worrisome times, here in the Obama kakistocracy. We wonder how long America can last without any grown-ups at the controls. We hear a president mouthing platitudes about "fiscal responsibility" while day after day he explodes the deficit sky-high. Over at the Treasury Department, they are printing Monopoly money like there's no tomorrow. And most of us over here on the right side of the aisle remember the history lessons we learned in school—about another time when a government racked up mountains of debt, then printed up bales of paper money to cover it.

But late German-American law professor Friedrich Kessler didn't just read about those times—he lived through them. He recalled with horror the days of post–World War I Germany, the Weimar Republic. "It was horrible! Horrible!" he once said. "Like lightning had struck. No one was prepared. You cannot imagine the rapidity with which the whole thing happened. The shelves in the grocery store were empty. There was nothing you could buy with your paper money." [17]

The Weimar Republic was established in Germany in 1919, and takes its name from the city of Weimar, where the republic's constitution was adopted. During its fourteen-year existence, the Weimar Republic was plagued with a bad economy and political extremism on both the left and right. The years 1921 through 1923 were marked by a level of hyperinflation that eventually reached *35,000 percent per month*. Bank notes became so worthless that they were used as wallpaper or as kindling for wood-fired stoves.[18] Credit markets froze. The nationwide panic that hyperinflation caused in Germany undoubtedly helped bring Adolf Hitler to power in 1933. The Weimar Republic's constitution was not repealed when Hitler came to power; it was simply ignored.

Could it happen here? You bet your bottom dollar it could. The national debt is accumulating at an incomprehensible rate. The presses are printing Federal Reserve notes night and day. The Fed is increasing the money supply and buying up government bonds in a bid to stabilize their value and lower long-term interest rates—a practice known as "quantitative easing" (easing pressure on banks by creating an expanded quantity of money). The risk is that if too much money is created and banks still aren't lending and putting that money into the economy to spur demand, quantitative easing can trigger uncontrollable hyperinflation—even worse inflation than in the Jimmy Carter years.

Barack Obama's economic policies are speeding us toward a currency calamity. If you and I don't stand up now and *demand* an end to this insanity, we'll all look back with regret and echo the lament of Friedrich Kessler.

So what should we demand of our leaders? What specific action do our leaders in the White House and the Congress need to take in order to prevent the United States of America from becoming the next Weimar Republic? The answer is surprisingly simple: *Go back to what works.*

And that's Reaganomics, of course.

SIX CRISES

Michael Reagan, the elder son of the late president, has been a frequent guest on my show. He recently did something I'm surprised no one has ever done before. In his book *The New Reagan Revolution,* he went back through the six great economic crises of the twentieth and twenty-first centuries and examined how the government responded to each crisis. It became astonishingly clear exactly which government policies resolved those crises and produced a long-term economic boom—and which policies made those crises *worse*. Here's what Michael found:

First crisis: the "Forgotten Depression" of January 1920. In the final year of the Woodrow Wilson presidency, the economy took a sudden dive. The GNP dropped 17 percent and the unemployment rate zoomed from 4 percent to nearly 12 percent. Just over a year later, Warren G. Harding took office and he immediately cut the tax rates for all income brackets and cut spending to balance the budget. In other words, he applied the principles of Reaganomics long before the world ever heard of Ronald Reagan. "Harding was not following an economic theory," wrote Michael Reagan. "He was following common sense. He treated the federal budget as you would treat the family budget: When times are tough, cut spending and stay out of debt."

Results came almost immediately. The recovery began just six months after Harding took office. By 1922, unemployment had dropped to 6.7 percent; by 1923, to 2.4 percent. Harding was succeeded in office by Calvin Coolidge, who maintained Harding's policies of low taxes, balanced budgets, and limited government. Thus began what came to be known as the Roaring Twenties—a decade of bound-less prosperity, price stability, and optimism throughout the country.

Second crisis: the Great Depression of the 1930s. The stock market crash of 1929—the event that precipitated the Great Depression—took place eight months after Herbert Hoover took office. Hoover responded by raising taxes (boosting the top marginal rate from 25 percent to 63 percent) and imposing tough protectionist policies (the Smoot-Hawley Tariff Act fulfilled a Hoover campaign promise), which worsened the Depression. Hoover boosted government spend-ing by 47 percent during his term, driving the nation deep into debt.

When Hoover's successor, Franklin D. Roosevelt, took office, un-employment stood at 25 percent. Roosevelt doubled down on Hoover's tax-and-spend policies, applying the theory known as Keynesianism (after British economist John Maynard Keynes). The Keynes-FDR approach involved manipulating the economy through monetary and fiscal policy, deficit financing, and big-government public works pro-grams. Despite spending billions on massive New Deal make-work programs, the unemployment rate never went below 14 percent dur-ing the 1930s.

Michael Reagan writes, "From 1937 to 1939, the stock market lost almost half its value, car sales fell by one-third, and business failures increased by one-half. From 1932 to 1939, the U.S. racked up more debt than in all the preceding 150 years of America's existence. By early 1939, as the Great Depression was in its tenth year, unemploy-ment again climbed past the 20 percent mark." [19]

Over the years, people have credited FDR with getting America through the Great Depression—but historians have only recently begun to realize that the New Deal actually *prolonged* the Depression. FDR raised personal and corporate income tax rates, estate taxes, and excise taxes. During a time of unparalleled high unemployment, FDR increased the cost of employing people.

In May 1939, Secretary of the Treasury Henry Morgenthau told the House Ways and Means Committee, "We have tried spending money. We are spending more than we have ever spent before and it does not work. . . . I want to see this country prosperous. I want to see people get a job. I want to see people get enough to eat. We have never made good on our promises. . . . I say after eight years of this administration we have just as much unemployment as when we started. . . . And an enormous debt to boot!"

The common myth is that World War II pulled America out of the Great Depression. The truth is that the war simply yanked 12 million men out of the workforce and into uniform, ending the unemployment problem. Other symptoms of a struggling economy—depressed levels of private investment and personal consumption, plus low stock prices—continued throughout the war years. Roosevelt, and his successor, Harry Truman, wanted to impose an even bigger and more expensive Second New Deal on the country after the war—but Congress said, "No deal!" Instead, the Congress cut taxes and reduced spending—again, a commonsense "Reaganomics" approach. The result was a boom of prosperity that propelled the nation from the late 1940s through the 1950s.

Third crisis: the recession of 1960 and 1961. It really wasn't a "crisis"—this recession was actually fairly mild, with unemployment cresting at 7.1 percent. But the new president, John F. Kennedy, wanted the economy to keep pace with the growing manpower supply. So, in December 1962, JFK spoke to the Economic Club of New York and proposed a bold idea: "It is a paradoxical truth," he said, "that tax rates are too high today and tax revenues are too low and the soundest way to raise the revenues in the long run is to cut the rates now. . . . The purpose of cutting taxes now is not to incur a budget deficit, but to achieve the more prosperous, expanding economy which can bring a budget surplus." Of course, you recognize that idea: JFK was preaching Reaganomics.

Though Kennedy didn't live to see his ideas implemented, Lyndon Johnson signed his tax cuts into law in 1964. The result: The economy experienced a sharp upswing, a 5 percent expansion. The GNP surged from $628 billion to $672 billion, auto production rose by 22 percent, steel production by 6 percent, corporate profits by 21 percent, and personal income by 7 percent. Unemployment fell to an eight-year low of 4.2 percent. The Kennedy-Johnson tax rate cuts resulted in sustained economic expansion from 1961 to 1969.

Fourth crisis: the recession of the 1970s. Technically, this recession began in November 1973 (under Richard Nixon) and ended in March 1975 (under Gerald Ford)—more than sixteen months. According to economists, real GDP had slowly begun to rise—yet, inexplicably, both unemployment and inflation remained high throughout the rest of the decade. So while the recession had ended for the economists, most Americans were still suffering. After the election of 1976, the Ford economy became the Carter economy. President Carter was simply out of his depth and unequipped to deal with a crisis of "stagflation"—slow economic growth, high unemployment, and rampant inflation. The "spend your way out of a recession" approach failed in the 1970s, just as it had failed during the Great Depression.

Fifth crisis: the Carter Recession of 1980. By the time of the 1980 election, the nation was once again in a full-blown recession, according to all the indicators. The nation had suffered through years of double-digit interest rates, inflation rates, and unemployment rates, plus long lines at the gas pumps. Ronald Reagan defeated Carter in a landslide, prompting *Newsweek* to announce, "When Ronald Reagan steps into the White House . . . he will inherit the most dangerous economic crisis since Franklin Roosevelt took office 48 years ago." Reagan immediately changed the nation's economic course, slashing tax rates and domestic spending. The top marginal income tax rate dropped from 70 percent to 28 percent during his presidency. The results were astonishing, as Michael Reagan observes:

> Tax cuts generated 4 million jobs in 1983 alone and 16 million jobs over the course of Ronald Reagan's presidency. Unemployment among African-Americans dropped dramatically, from 19.5 percent in 1983 to 11.4 percent in 1989. . . .
>
> The inflation rate fell from 13.5 percent in 1980 . . . to 3.2 percent in 1983. . . .
>
> And here's the kicker: *The Reagan tax cuts nearly doubled federal revenue.* After his 25 percent across-the-board tax rate cuts went into effect, receipts from both individual and corporate income taxes rose dramatically. According to the White House Office of Management and Budget, revenue from individual income taxes went from $244.1 billion in 1980 to $445.7 billion in 1989, an

increase of over 82 percent. Revenue from corporate income taxes went from $64.6 billion to $103.3 billion, a 60 percent jump.

This was the fulfillment of the "paradoxical truth" which John F. Kennedy spoke of in his 1962 speech: "Cutting taxes now . . . can bring a budget surplus." Both JFK and Ronald Reagan predicted that *lower tax rates* would generate *more* revenue. This "paradoxical truth" worked exactly as predicted.[20]

Even though the Reagan tax cuts brought a tidal wave of new revenue into the Treasury, budget deficits under Ronald Reagan also increased. Why? Because House Speaker Tip O'Neill and the Democratic Congress outspent the Reagan revenue increase. While revenue from individual income taxes grew by 6.9 percent from 1980 to 1989, federal spending grew by 7.6 percent during those same years. Ronald Reagan was able only to slow down the growth of federal spending. Lacking a line-item veto, he didn't have the power to reduce the size and cost of government as he would have liked. As Michael Reagan concluded, "Ronald Reagan submitted nine budgets during his presidency—and the free-spending Democrats in Congress outspent all but one of them."

The sixth crisis: the Obama Recession. It began in December 2007 under George W. Bush, triggered by the collapse of the housing bubble, which resulted from Democratic Party policies, going back to the Community Reinvestment Act under Carter and Clinton. When Barack Obama took office, he threw a trillion dollars of stimulus and bailout money at the recession, promising to keep unemployment below 8 percent. The Obama stimulus not only failed to make a splash, it didn't even make a ripple. Unemployment nudged up to the 10 percent mark, and the economy continues to sputter and gasp to this day. Meanwhile, the Treasury Department keeps printing up crisp new currency, and the specter of the Weimar Republic looms up ahead.

Let's tabulate the results of the six economic crises that Michael Reagan laid out for us. Crises one, three, and five were all resolved with the same basic approach: cut taxes, cut spending, reduce government regulation, and set the free market free. We call this approach "Reaganomics" today, though for Presidents Harding, Coolidge,

Kennedy, and Reagan, it was simply a matter of common sense. The Reaganomics approach resulted in a near-decade-long economic boom whenever it was tried—the Roaring Twenties, the Kennedy-Johnson Sixties, the Reagan Eighties.

But what about crises two, four, and six? In each case, the government tried to "stimulate" the economy with massive government spending programs, resulting in huge deficits and debt. Not once did "stimulus" spending produce an economic cure. The result of these giant government spending programs was always economic stagnation, if not outright collapse: the Great Depression, the "stagflation" of the 1970s, the Obama Recession.

We now know what works every time, and what *never* works. You and I need to start preaching the good news of Reaganomics to our friends and neighbors, our children and grandchildren, and our leaders in Washington. We need to shout it from the rooftops. It's time for America to stop taxing and spending our way to oblivion. It's time to get back to Reaganomics. It works every time it's tried.

TAX THE RICH?

In Oliver Stone's 1987 movie, *Wall Street,* financier and corporate raider Gordon Gekko says, "Somebody wins, somebody loses. Money isn't lost or made. It's simply transferred."[21] Now, that's just dumb. Think about it: What is the total wealth of the world? I've heard estimates ranging from $70 trillion to $500 trillion. Whatever the number may be, if Gordon Gekko is correct, if wealth is neither lost nor made, then *where did the wealth of the world come from?* Has it always been here since the Big Bang? Of course not.

Wealth is constantly being created, every day. You and I and all of the productive people in this world are the creators of the wealth of the world. As the eighteenth-century Scottish philosopher Adam Smith observed, whenever we combine our ingenuity, our labor, our materials and property, and our technology in such a way that we can sell that product at a profit, then *we have created wealth*—a store of value that never existed in the world before.

Why is this important to understand? Because liberals look at wealth in a totally different and unrealistic way. Liberals see wealth as a pie. If a rich person takes a big slice of pie, then that means there is less pie for everyone else. According to liberals, rich people become rich by robbing the poor and taking their pie. But as George Gilder observed in *Wealth and Poverty* (1981), "The idea that all wealth is acquired through stealing is popular in prisons and at Harvard."[22]

Apparently, this notion is also popular in Obama circles. The Reverend Jeremiah Wright, President Obama's former pastor and mentor, put it this way in an interview on PBS: "People don't realize that to be rich, you've got to keep somebody else poor."[23] And the president's wife, Michelle Obama, said, "In order to get things like universal health care and a revamped education system, then someone is going to have to give up a piece of their pie so that someone else can have more."[24]

This idea that the rich take more than their fair share of the pie is the source of the liberal belief that rich people should be taxed at punitive rates. That is why, prior to the Reagan tax revolt of the 1980s, the rich were subject to confiscatory marginal tax rates as high as 91 percent. And that is why candidate Barack Obama told Joe the Plumber (aka Samuel Joseph Wurzelbacher) during a 2008 campaign stop in Ohio, "I think when you spread the wealth around, it's good for everybody."

What Barack Obama and his fellow liberals don't seem to understand is that there is already a perfectly fair and effective way of spreading the wealth around. It's called the free market system, where people with capital to invest put that capital at risk and start a business. That business may fail—or it may make millions or even billions.

If the business succeeds, if the person who took that risk becomes fabulously wealthy, does it mean that he or she has become rich at the expense of the poor? Absolutely not. That person has created wealth that never existed before. No one has been impoverished because of that person's success. Instead, the successful businessperson has improved the lives of many other people—investors, stockholders, suppliers, employees, and customers. In fact, by creating so much wealth and so many new jobs, that businessperson has stimulated the economy and brought more revenue into the United States Treasury.

Howard Schultz made millions when he turned a few Starbucks coffee shops into an espresso empire. TV host Oprah Winfrey became fabulously wealthy in the entertainment industry. Microsoft's Bill Gates, Apple's Steve Jobs, eBay's Meg Whitman, Facebook's Mark Zuckerberg, and Google's Larry Page became billionaires in the tech sector. My friend Ron Offutt became a billionaire raising potatoes and selling John Deere tractors. Another friend of mine, Harold Hamm, grew up in poverty but became a billionaire in the oil business. All of these people amassed incredible fortunes—not by taking from the poor, but by creating wealth and making life better for us all. Their ingenuity and hard work added value to our lives and grew the American economy.

When the rich get richer, the poor get richer as well. That's the meaning behind the phrase, coined by John F. Kennedy, "A rising tide lifts all boats." The Reagan Eighties proved it, and it's high time we did it again.

If we want to create jobs in America, if we want to bring this economy roaring back to life, then we have to do what Ronald Reagan did. We have to cut tax rates across the board—including taxes for the rich. That's not easy, because the liberal-progressive propaganda merchants have done a good job of selling the notion of "class envy" to the American people. Through movies, TV shows, and the nightly news, the left has sold America on the idea that rich people are evil and need to be punished for their success.

So you and I need to do a better job of defending success in America. We need to teach our children and tell our friends and neighbors the truth about successful people—that their success truly makes life better for *all* of us. We need to educate the people around us to understand that the best way to spread the benefits of success to everyone in our society, including the middle class and the poor, is to reduce tax rates for everyone, including the rich.

But it won't be easy—not with the way President Obama and his fellow Democrats continue to try to divide America and pit the poor against the rich in an endless war of class envy. For example, during a campaign event for Senator Patty Murray in Seattle, our president stated, "You remember our slogan during the campaign, 'Yes, we can'? Their slogan is 'No, we can't.' . . . That's really inspiring. . . . Their basic philosophy goes something like this: We're going to cut taxes for millionaires and billionaires, folks who don't need it, weren't even asking for it. . . . So if you can't find a job or you can't afford college or don't have health insurance, tough luck—you are on your own. . . . Now, I think you may have noticed that their philosophy didn't work out too well. It's not like we didn't test it, right? . . . It gave us record deficits and ultimately led to the worst economic crisis since the Great Depression."[25]

He's talking about the eight years of George W. Bush—but the fact is that the Bush years were, for the most part, very good years for the economy. President Bush inherited a recession, then 9/11 occurred eight months into his presidency. He called for two rounds of tax rate reductions (including cuts in capital gains and dividends taxes) in 2002 and 2003, and the impact on the economy was undeniable. The economy averaged nearly 4 percent growth over the next three years, and unemployment was cut to 4.4 percent by October 2006. Real wages grew in spite of increases in food and energy costs. Tax revenues grew dramatically. Up until the recession of 2007–2008, the Bush economy was one of the strongest on record.[26]

And who deserves the blame for that recession? You and I both know who belongs in the rogues' gallery that gave us the Community Reinvestment Act, the out-of-control antics of Countrywide, Fannie Mae, and Freddie Mac, and the ACORN intimidation of banks. We know who's to blame for the mortgage crisis and the financial meltdown: Jimmy Carter, Bill Clinton, Barney Frank, Christopher Dodd, Kent Conrad, Pelosi and Reid (especially after the Democratic takeover of Congress in 2006), and yes, Barack Obama.

President Obama scoffs at the philosophy of limited government, limited spending, and across-the-board tax cuts for all. But we tested that philosophy—and it worked brilliantly under George W. Bush. And before that, it worked under Harding and Coolidge, and under Kennedy and Johnson. Above all, we tested that philosophy under Ronald Reagan—and we experienced *ninety-two consecutive months* of economic growth, which *doubled* the size of the American economy.[27]

FOUR JOB KILLERS

In order to put America back to work, we need to look out for four job killers that are already undermining the American job market:

Job Killer Number One: Illegal immigration.

One of the biggest issues affecting jobs in America is our lack of border security. We know why the Democrats want open borders and amnesty for illegal immigrants. Their goal is to get as many illegal immigrants into America, pass so-called comprehensive immigration reform legislation (which is a code phrase for amnesty), convert these illegal immigrants into U.S. citizens, and voilà—the Democratic Party instantly has millions of new voters!

It's a mystery to me why African-Americans, Latino-Americans, and rank-and-file union members go along with the Democratic Party in its stance on mass illegal immigration. I understand why union leaders want to legalize illegals—the millions of illegal immigrants currently in America represent more union membership, more union dues, more power for the union bosses, and potentially more votes for Democrats.

But illegal immigration harms almost everyone else in America, including legal immigrants and minorities. Illegal immigration depresses wages—just ask American citizens who used to work in the construction industry—and it deprives citizens of jobs and affordable housing. All of this is in addition to the gang violence and drug cartels that illegal immigration brings inside our borders. The best interests of Latino-Americans, African-Americans, and *all* Americans are truly best served by an immigration policy of "high fences and wide gates." That's just common sense.

Job Killer Number Two: Unemployment insurance.

The *New York Times* finally figured out what most commonsense Americans have known for years: If you keep extending unemployment benefits, you also extend the length of time people stay unemployed. *Times* business reporter Liz Alderman wrote:

> For years, Denmark was held out as a model to countries with high unemployment and as a progressive touchstone to liberals in the United States. . . . But now Denmark . . . is facing its own strains. . . .
>
> Struggling to keep its budget under control after the finan-

cial crisis, the government in June cut into its benefits system, the world's most generous, by limiting unemployment payments to two years instead of four. . . . Officials are also redoubling longstanding efforts to move Danes more quickly out of the safety net.

"The cold fact is that the longer you are out of a job, the more difficult it is to get a job," Claus Hjort Frederiksen, the Danish finance minister, said during an interview. "Four years of unemployment is a luxury we can no longer allow ourselves."[28]

Four years of unemployment benefits?! But wait—in the 1990s, the Danes actually received *five years* of unemployment benefits. The government of Denmark charted exactly when Danish workers found work. When benefits ran out, there was a huge spike of people finding work at the end of the fifth year. Later, after the Danes cut benefits to four years, that same spike appeared at the end of the fourth year. In other words, Danish officials discovered what any common-sense conservative could have told them: When you pay people not to work, they figure, "Why work?" But when their benefits are about to run out, they somehow become surprisingly resourceful—and they miraculously find a job.

That's why, in June 2010, the government of Denmark cut unemployment benefits once more, this time from four years to two years. The Danish finance minister, Claus Hjort Frederiksen, says that the government has learned a lesson: "You need to have a period of unemployment that is as short as possible."[29]

A revealing study was conducted by two labor economists, Stepan Jurajda and Frederick J. Tannery, in Pittsburgh in the 1980s. From 1980 to 1985, unemployment rates in Pittsburgh reached as high as 16 percent. Jurajda and Tannery found that very few people found jobs two to three weeks before their unemployment benefits ran out. But *just one week* before unemployment benefits ended, there was a *huge* spike in the numbers of people finding work. The percentage of people finding jobs jumped from an average of 4 percent to *29 percent* during that final week (10 percent returned to their old jobs; 19 percent found new jobs).[30] Clearly, many people can and do find work—when they are motivated to do so. What you subsidize, you get more of—so if you subsidize unemployment, you will get more unemployment.

A 2008 Princeton study, conducted by Alan B. Krueger and Andreas Mueller, showed that those who are unemployed sleep almost an hour later on weekdays than working people, spend more time watching TV, and report feeling less happiness, more sadness, and a diminished sense of well-being.[31] There's nothing wrong with providing a safety net for people who are down on their luck. But if you let people stay in that safety net too long, they soon begin to treat it as a hammock. As a result, you enable people to remain unproductive, unfulfilled, and unhappy. You rob them of their dignity, their ability to improve their own lives, and their ability to contribute productively to our society.

America, do the unemployed a favor. Instead of extending their benefits, cut those benefits shorter. Let's put America back to work.

Job Killer Number Three: Green jobs.

In recent years, the left has been touting new "clean technology" industries and "green jobs" as the perfect win-win solution to all our problems. While helping to "save the planet" from global warming, a "green revolution" of wind, solar, and biofuels will supposedly free us from dependence on foreign oil and create millions of new jobs, ushering in a utopia of clean skies, abundant energy, and limitless prosperity.

The Obama administration even hired a self-professed communist named Van Jones to head up the green job effort in the White House.[32] Glenn Beck outed Jones as a Marxist and a wacko who once signed a "9/11-was-an-inside-job" petition, so Jones left the White House.[33] But the White House push for green jobs goes on.

As James Manyika of the McKinsey Global Institute points out, "The bottom line is that these 'clean' industries are too small to create the millions of jobs that are needed right away." In fact, the green technology sector makes up only 0.6 percent of the workforce in America today, and that sector is unlikely to grow very quickly. A McKinsey study points out that the green jobs sector today is much like the semiconductor industry of the 1990s, which was supposed to produce an explosion of high-tech jobs. Instead, the semiconductor industry produced a lot of assembly-line jobs for robots. The green sector is just not a labor-intensive industry, so don't expect a lot of jobs to replace the ones that have been lost during the Obama recession.

The McKinsey report urges government to stop betting billions on wind turbines, solar panel technology, and other exotic energy sources. Instead, government should encourage businesses and homeowners to take commonsense steps to improve energy efficiency, such as improving insulation and replacing energy-inefficient air-conditioning units.[34] The idea that we can produce an economic boom and millions of jobs by dotting the landscape with windmills is sheer fantasy.

Meanwhile, two of the highest-polluting nations in the world, China and India, demand that the United States reduce its "carbon footprint." Is it because China and India are so concerned about global warming and saving the planet? Of course not. The rest of the world knows that if the United States commits itself to a course of trading existing jobs for mythical green jobs, we will lose our competitive edge—and all the jobs we lose here in America will open up in China and India.

As the *Wall Street Journal* noted, the Obama administration embraces the fanciful notion that "cap and trade can generate five million 'green jobs.' If you throw enough tax subsidies at something, you're bound to get some new jobs. But if the money for those subsidies comes from higher energy taxes—and a cap and trade regime would amount to as much $1.2 trillion of new taxes—millions of jobs in carbon-using industry are also going to be lost. . . . Climate-change legislation means green unemployment."[35]

So the green jobs program is a job killer. And it's worse than that—the green jobs agenda is designed to take our freedom away. My friend Phil Kerpen of Americans for Prosperity places the green jobs issue in its proper perspective. "The ideology that underlies the green jobs push," he told me, "has much in common with the authoritarianism of the twentieth century—communism, fascism, socialism, and so on. The green jobs agenda would be imposed on us by social engineers, central planners, and czars who would be in charge of our economy. They would say, 'The market isn't investing in the right types of technologies. We need to take money away from these "dirty" jobs and give them to these "clean" jobs.' That mentality underlies every other failed attempt at central economic planning, including communism."

Phil offers a simple and colorful analogy. "Think of the green jobs agenda as a watermelon. From the outside, a watermelon is a big green fruit. But cut it open, and you see that the green portion of a watermelon is just the thin outer layer of the rind. Inside, it's a bright red all the way to the core. The green jobs agenda is only green on the outside. Inside it's as red as the old Soviet flag. All the utopian promises of the green agenda mask the deep red central economic planning of communism."

Phil Kerpen is exactly right. The only way to maintain a clean environment, achieve energy independence, and create jobs by the millions is *not* through a green jobs agenda, but by keeping the free market free.

Job Killer Number Four: Stimulus.

Barack Obama's $787 billion stimulus bill, which was supposedly intended to grow the economy and create jobs, is actually a job killer. The Texas Public Policy Foundation commissioned a research firm, Arduin, Laffer & Moore Econometrics, to conduct a study on the impact of stimulus spending on jobs in Texas. The researchers conclude:

> Federal government spending comes with costs; it should not be accepted as the free-lunch it is frequently considered to be. Every dollar the government spends must first be removed from the pocket of the private sector—through higher taxes today, or higher borrowing today implying higher taxes tomorrow. Either way, government spending crowds out private sector spending, diminishing the private economy's rate of growth. . . .
>
> [The Obama stimulus bill] will reduce the growth in real net business output by 2.5%, which translates to a reduction of 1.7 million jobs nationally—of which between 131,400 and 171,900 jobs will be lost in Texas.[36]

Eugene Graner of Heartland Investor Services talked about the financial burden the Obama stimulus bill placed on every American family. "This idea of taking a $787 billion stimulus package and jamming it into the economy, thinking you're going to get an instant economic boom—that just isn't going to get it.

"People don't realize how much this is costing us. Assuming there are 100 million households in the United States, let's break this thing down. If the government spends $1 billion, your household has just been charged $10. If we spend $100 billion, your household has just been billed $1000. If we spend $1 trillion, your household has been billed $10,000. That's not how you produce jobs. This so-called stimulus actually creates a drag on the economy—and people don't even realize it."

A LESSON FROM THE SULTAN OF SPUDS

President Obama promised that his $787 billion stimulus package would put America back to work. The stimulus not only failed, but it drove America deeper into debt. All this wasteful, pointless, ineffectual spending is nothing less than fiscal child abuse and generational theft.

But here in the heartland, it's a different story. North Dakota is one of only four states with a budget surplus. Our unemployment and foreclosure rates—two crucial benchmarks of the economy—are among the lowest in the country. Why? Because grassroots entrepreneurs and business leaders, large and small, are doing the job President Obama and the Democrats have stubbornly refused to do. Let me tell you about one of those business leaders.

In Island Park, just south of downtown Fargo, stands a gleaming office building with an American flag flying proudly in front—the corporate headquarters of a man known as the Sultan of Spuds: Ron Offutt. Ron is a fourth-generation potato farmer—and a lot more. He is a grassroots patriot who is putting America back to work.

As a young man, Ron had a lot of ambition and a strong work ethic. In the early 1960s, he worked his way through Concordia College in Moorhead, Minnesota, majoring in business administration.

He earned money by laundering the uniforms for fellow members of the football team. Graduating in 1964, he joined his father's two-hundred-acre farming operation as a full partner. He credits his mentor, Concordia professor Hiram Drache, for teaching him the fundamentals of a business career and helping advance him quickly along his learning curve.

Ron quickly expanded the family business, renting land, buying land, forming partnerships, and planting thousands of additional acres of potatoes. The key to his success, he says, is his ability to delegate authority and trust parts of his growing empire to managers, agronomic technicians, and field workers.

In 1968, a local John Deere dealership in Casselton, North Dakota, went up for sale. Ron convinced his father to let him mortgage the Offutt family farm and purchase the dealership. At the time, it was a huge risk. Ron had never been involved in such an equipment retailing business, but he saw a big advantage in being a Deere distributor and obtaining farm equipment directly from the manufacturer, in addition to selling to the public. That one dealership eventually became RDO Equipment, Inc., the largest John Deere distributorship in America, listed on the New York Stock Exchange, and operating fifty-four Deere dealerships, two heavy truck dealerships, and employing more than two thousand people in nine states.

But even more phenomenal is his role as the Sultan of Spuds, the ruler of a potato empire. In the early 1970s, McDonald's franchises were sprouting up nationwide. Ron Offutt knew how to grow exactly the kind of potato McDonald's needed for its highly popular french fries. The potatoes had to be large and nicely rounded, not knobby and irregular. Ron knew that thousands of gorgeous acres of western Minnesota sand lands were idle and available—and with proper irrigation, those lands would grow the perfect french fry potato.

So, in 1974, Ron Offutt tripled the size of his operation. He purchased a processing plant, then built even larger processing plants, so that he not only owns the farming operation but the processing operation as well. Today, this Fargo-based entrepreneur operates a multi-state, sixty-thousand-acre potato-farming empire. His company supplies the majority of the potatoes consumed in America—roughly 1.8 billion pounds of potatoes every year, which are sold to McDonald's, Frito-Lay, and frozen food processors such as Ore-Ida.

"If you take a raw potato and turn it into a frozen french fry," he once said, "you've 'value-added' that product." To put it another way, when Ron processes a potato into a french fry, *he creates wealth*.

In addition to being the nation's largest John Deere dealer and owning the nation's largest potato-farming operation, Ron Offutt also owns the nation's largest dairy herd, located in Washington State. And he uses his wealth to serve his community. He is involved in many charitable activities, but let me just mention two.

Ron has set up a fund that gives bridge loans to family farmers to get them through temporary tough times. In his early career, he saw many family farmers go under due to a run of bad luck or lack of capital—farmers who could have succeeded if they had received a helping hand. So Ron Offutt now lends that helping hand.

He also endowed his alma mater, Concordia College, with the largest single gift in the history of the institution. Though Ron didn't ask for anything in return, the school gratefully named its Offutt School of Business in his honor.[37]

Ron Offutt is one of the richest people in North Dakota—and you and I should be glad he is. His hard work and risk taking have improved the lives of everyone in America who has ever eaten a french fry. No one in America is poorer because Ron is rich. He has employed, promoted, and mentored thousands of people over the years, including many who have left his company to start businesses of their own.

Down through the years, whether in a Jimmy Carter economy or a Ronald Reagan economy, a George W. Bush economy or Barack Obama economy, Ron Offutt has been putting America to work. And I, for one, am grateful for Ron and for all the risk takers, the entrepreneurs, the self-employed, the managers, the hourly laborers—all the unsung heroes who get up every morning, do their jobs, create new wealth, and build a bright new future for themselves and their families.

These are the people who put America to work each day.

THE COMMONSENSE ACTION AGENDA

Here are some grassroots actions you can take, starting today:

✓ Become an economics student. Read the great books of free market econom-
ics. You may think it's all too hard to understand—but once you start reading,
I guarantee you'll find it fascinating. Here are a few titles to get you started:
The Road to Serfdom by Friedrich Hayek; *Capitalism and Freedom* by Milton
Friedman; *Free to Choose* by Milton Friedman; *Economics in One Lesson* by
Henry Hazlitt; *Basic Economics: A Common Sense Guide to the Economy* by
Thomas Sowell.

✓ Become an economics teacher. No, you don't have to stand in front of a class-
room. Instead, become a teacher in your everyday life, in the lunchroom and
around the water cooler at work, in emails and blogs and on your Facebook
page, and in your home. Teach your kids the principles of free market economics. Tell your friends and neighbors the historical truth: Keynesian stimulus
schemes fail every time they are tried—and Reaganomics always produces
spectacular results.

✓ Talk to friends, neighbors, family members, and coworkers about the creation
of wealth. Help people understand that the economy is not a "pie." Rich people don't get rich by making other people poor. In fact, when people create
wealth, everybody benefits, both rich and poor. The only way to truly "spread
the wealth around" is not through punitive tax rates and income redistribution. We "spread the wealth around" through the free market system, by giving
entrepreneurs the freedom to put their capital at risk and reap the rewards of
success. That's how Ronald Reagan did it in the 1980s, and that's the only
way we can ever revive our troubled economy. When you teach people around
you how the free economy really works, you help produce a new generation of
enlightened *conservative* voters.

6

SUPPORTING THE MILITARY

One Thursday, July 26, 2007, I got a call from Trey Bohn of the White House Media Affairs office, inviting me to come to the White House the following Wednesday. I would join a number of radio talk show hosts from around the country for a Q&A session with President George W. Bush.

I fumbled the phone in shock. "Why me?"

"President Bush is aware of all your good work on the radio, covering the War on Terror, and specifically a project you're involved in called 'Share the Story.' He appreciates your support for the troops."

Share the Story was a series of events we had held for our North Dakota and Minnesota troops and their families. The idea was conceived by my friends Mark Pfeifle, General William Caldwell, and Lieutenant Colonel Shawn Stroud (you'll hear more about these three special individuals later). A satellite uplink enabled soldiers and their families to see each other, ask questions, and express their love and support across the miles. It had been a long deployment for most of the soldiers, so these were emotional, heartwarming events involving personnel from every branch, including the Guard and Reserve. The media covered these events, and the public could gain a different picture of the war than the distorted images coming from the mainstream media.

At one of these events, a girl said to her soldier-father in Iraq,

"Dad, everybody in my school thinks the war is wrong. What do I tell them?" So he told his daughter about all the good things that were happening in Iraq, the schools and water-treatment projects that we had built, the fact that the Iraqi people could now vote for their leaders, and the fact that violence was declining throughout the country.

I was humbled to learn that President Bush was aware of Share the Story and our efforts to support the mission in Iraq. The summer of 2007 was a crucial time in the Iraq War. President Bush had announced the troop surge strategy at the beginning of the year. By the spring, as the surge had begun to take hold, the media and Democratic politicians were already pronouncing it a failure. On April 19, Senate majority leader Harry Reid bluntly declared from the Senate floor, "This war is lost. . . . The surge is not accomplishing anything."[1]

So when Trey Bohn called to invite me to the White House, I saw it as a golden opportunity to hear the Leader of the Free World talk about the global War on Terror and the status of military operations in Iraq. The meeting would be off the record, meaning I could share with my listeners a sense of what the president said to us, as long as I didn't quote him directly.

I juggled my schedule, told my listeners only that I was going on "special assignment," and flew to Washington National Airport. Arriving at the hotel, I picked up a message from Lieutenant General William B. Caldwell, who was then chief spokesman for the Multi-National Force—Iraq. He was in D.C. for meetings at the Pentagon, so we met at his hotel.

It was a good visit. General Caldwell was a communications genius who would cut through the fog of bureaucracy and make guests available to my show to explain the realities of the War on Terror. Because of General Caldwell, my listeners got to hear and talk to leaders like Secretary of Defense Donald Rumsfeld, Chairman of the Joint Chiefs General Richard B. Myers, Myers's successor, General Peter Pace, and many other key players in the War on Terror. General Caldwell gave me a commemorative military coin that I treasure to this day.

"Keep doing what you're doing, Scott," the general implored. "It's really tough to cut through all the chatter in the media and get the truth out about the war. The job you do on the radio is vitally important. We have to communicate the successes of our troops to the American people."

"LET IT REFLECT THE LIGHT"

I arrived at the White House at 9:45 the next morning, August 1, eager to find out which of my colleagues would be joining me in meeting with President Bush. Neal Boortz and I were the first to arrive. We were soon joined by Glenn Beck, Mark Levin, Hugh Hewitt, Bill Bennett, Michael Medved, Lars Larson, Janet Parshall, and Laura Ingraham. The radio talk show fraternity is small and close-knit, and I was glad to be in the company of so many good friends. We entered the White House via the West Wing entrance, passing a Marine guard whose presence traditionally signals that the commander in chief is in.

We entered the West Wing lobby, which is a gallery of priceless art. Glenn Beck introduced himself to me, then took me around and gave me a guided tour of all the artwork in the room. Glenn is a passionate student of history, and he explained the story behind each picture. The painting that fascinated me the most was *The Outlier,* Frederic Remington's last painting, completed shortly before his death in 1909. Remington was legally blind at the time, yet he had the vision to compose a haunting scene of a Native American warrior on a horse on a grassy plain. The image reminded me of the Badlands of North Dakota. The warrior's eyes were shut, expressing how Remington himself must have felt as his vision and his life were fading away.

As we waited, I also chatted with Bill Bennett, who was secretary of education in the Reagan White House. I asked him to tell me his favorite moment from his White House days, and he recalled that contentious era when the media and D.C. elites were demanding his head because of his public jousting with the teachers' unions and the bureaucracy.

"In the middle of this controversy," he said, "we had a cabinet meeting. President Reagan took out a bunch of news clippings and began reading them, one by one. The clippings quoted all my most controversial statements about the teachers' unions. As the president read each clipping, I could feel the other cabinet members leaning away from me, waiting for him to lower the boom.

"Finally, the president paused, looked around the table, tilted his head in that way he had, and said, 'Well, we know what Bennett is up to. Now, what are the rest of you doing to change this town?' "

I laughed. That was such a gracious gesture to Bill Bennett during a tough time, and it was so typically . . . Reagan.

At 10:40, a White House staffer escorted us to the Roosevelt Room, named for both Theodore Roosevelt and FDR. It's a windowless room, lit by a false skylight and decorated with paintings and mementos of both presidents, including Teddy's 1906 Nobel Peace Prize, the first Nobel won by an American. Because of Teddy's North Dakota connections, it's my favorite room in the West Wing. Candy dishes and water glasses bore the presidential seal. There was a name plate at every seat around the conference table—except in front of the high-backed chair at the middle of the table. That was the president's place. I was pleased to find my place next to his. My colleagues wanted to know whom I'd bribed.

While we waited, Karl Rove came by and greeted us. A few minutes later, Tony Snow—a good friend and fellow radio pro, and a man I dearly miss—also stepped in for a chat. Finally, the door opened behind us and we heard that familiar Texas drawl. "Hey," said the president of the United States, "why don't y'all come on in here?"

We turned and there he was, grinning and gesturing through the open doorway. We got up and he led us across the hallway that separates the Roosevelt Room from the Oval Office. I was the first to enter the inner sanctum, and Mr. Bush put out his hand and said, "How's the North Dakotan today? Great to see you again."

President Bush began by giving us a tour of the Oval Office. He pointed out a portrait of Abraham Lincoln. "That's a place of honor," he said, "traditionally reserved as a place where each president can hang a portrait of his most admired predecessor. Of course, Bush '41 will always be number one in my heart, but I draw a lot of strength from that portrait of Lincoln. I remember the trials he faced as president, and that six hundred thousand Americans died on his watch. He suffered a lot of personal anguish. His eleven-year-old son died early in his first term, and his wife was a very troubled woman. Yet Lincoln persevered. He saved the republic."

After a few moments, the president pointed to a place for me to sit, immediately to the left of his chair. We all took our places on the sofas and chairs that were set apart from the president's famed Resolute desk. And there I was, amazed to be elbow-to-elbow with the most powerful man in the world.

I had been in the Oval Office a couple of times before, back in the Clinton years. This time, the room had a distinctly different atmosphere than it had before. It seemed brighter and more airy somehow, though I couldn't put my finger on what was different.

Chief of staff Josh Bolten, senior adviser Karl Rove, communications director Ed Gillespie, press secretary Tony Snow, and Office of Strategic Initiatives director Peter Wehner joined us. The White House photographer snapped photos as we exchanged small talk. After the photographer left, all eyes turned to the president.

Mr. Bush welcomed us and told us he wanted to share some thoughts about Iraq and the War on Terror—then we could ask him anything we'd like. He said (and I'm paraphrasing here), "I called you into the Oval Office because this is the place where I make the majority of my decisions as president. I make these decisions based on my core conviction that the United States of America is a force for good in the world, and that we must lead and confront evil wherever it is."

He spoke about the reality of good and evil, light and darkness, in the world. He pointed to the Oval Office carpet with the Presidential Seal, and said, "When they asked me what color of carpet I wanted in the Oval Office, I said, 'Let it reflect the light, so that the light will guide my decision-making—the light of good versus the darkness of evil.' "

When he said that, I realized what was different about the Oval Office: the carpet. During the Clinton years, the carpet had been a deep royal blue, which gave the room a stately but somber feel. This carpet was light-colored, and pale rays streamed outward from the Presidential Seal, filling the office with brightness.

Mr. Bush talked about the cold-blooded brutality of the enemy— and as he spoke, he made me—a graying, out-of-shape talk show host—want to put on a uniform and rush to the battlefield. I wished that every American could sit with the president and hear him describe his ironclad resolve to win the War on Terror. He walked us through example after example of American successes on the battlefield, and described the advances we were making toward transforming Iraq into a working democracy.

President Bush also mentioned the role played by my good friend Mark Pfeifle, a Wishek, North Dakota, native. As deputy national security adviser to the president, Mark was the key coordinator of White House efforts to promote the 2007 surge strategy, which involved increasing American troop strength in Iraq to protect the population, secure the neighborhoods, clear out the insurgents, and stabilize the country. During the darkest days of early 2007, when opponents of the surge called it a failure and even some Republican senators were about to peel off, Mark Pfeifle applied North Dakota common sense. Working closely with Commanding General David Petraeus and U.S. Ambassador to Iraq Ryan Crocker, Mark arranged for think tank officials, journalists, and members of Congress from both parties to tour Iraq and see with their own eyes the dramatic changes that had taken place because of the surge.

The most touching moment of our Oval Office visit came when somebody asked, "Mr. President, what did you think of the O'Hanlon and Pollack piece in the *New York Times*?" An op-ed piece had appeared in the *Times* two days earlier. It was written by two public policy experts (and harsh Bush critics), Michael O'Hanlon and Kenneth Pollack of the left-leaning Brookings Institution. The piece, titled "A War We Just Might Win," began:

> Viewed from Iraq, where we just spent eight days meeting with American and Iraqi military and civilian personnel, the political debate in Washington is surreal. The Bush administration has over four years lost essentially all credibility. Yet now the administration's critics, in part as a result, seem unaware of the significant changes taking place.

> Here is the most important thing Americans need to understand: We are finally getting somewhere in Iraq, at least in military terms.

As two analysts who have harshly criticized the Bush administration's miserable handling of Iraq, we were surprised by the gains we saw and the potential to produce not necessarily "victory" but a sustainable stability that both we and the Iraqis could live with. . . .

The soldiers and marines told us they feel that they now have a superb commander in Gen. David Petraeus; they are confident in his strategy, they see real results, and they feel now they have the numbers needed to make a real difference. [2]

O'Hanlon and Pollack went on to describe in detail many of the huge advances that had been made not only militarily, but in winning the hearts and minds of the Iraqi people. When one of my colleagues asked Mr. Bush what he thought of that piece in the *Times,* the president paused for a long time.

Then he said, "I slept with it."

There was genuine emotion in his voice as he said those words. It was one of those rare moments when you could look into the man's soul and truly see the enormous burden he felt for the people he had sent into harm's way, combined with an absolute certainty of the rightness of the war. President Bush knew about all the good things that were happening in Iraq. But finally some of his harshest critics were beginning to report the good news as well. It was like a pillow to his head at night.

That was one of the most unforgettable moments I have ever experienced. In all the years of the War on Terror, amid all the character assassination and smears he had withstood from his opponents, George W. Bush had never defended himself. He had simply ignored the chattering class. But here was an opinion piece, written by two longtime critics—and they were saying that we just might be winning the War on Terror.

My heart swelled with pride knowing that my friend (and fellow North Dakotan) Mark Pfeifle had played a role in getting O'Hanlon and Pollack into Iraq. Because of Mark's efforts, two Bush critics were reporting firsthand on the positive changes we were bringing to that country—and the credibility of their report could not be challenged.

As a result, the American people were beginning to learn the truth about the success of the surge.

President Bush proceeded to take us inside the reports he was receiving every day from the ground. He went through all of the metrics and benchmarks, and he told us that we were dismantling Al Qaeda with sheer brute force. For every American soldier we lost (and yes, losing one is too many), we were killing hundreds of insurgents and terrorists. He summed up his presentation with these few blunt words: "We're kicking Al Qaeda's ass."

Looking around at my colleagues, I could see the same thought was on everyone's mind: *If the American people could hear what we're hearing from the lips of George W. Bush, public opinion on the war would swing his way in a heartbeat.*

So I spoke up and said, "Mr. President, isn't there some way that you could go before the American people and express what you have just told us—from the statistics to the anecdotal evidence—so that the people could see the success of this mission?"

He turned to me and said, "Scott, I asked General Pete Pace the same question." (General Peter Pace was then the chairman of the Joint Chiefs of Staff.) "He told me, 'Sir, with all due respect, if a soldier is on the battlefield, and he's got the enemy in his rifle sights, I don't want him to pull the trigger because he wants your statistics to look good in a press conference.' "

In other words, the president was saying, "Look, I might be taking some hits politically, but I'm doing the right thing. We are basing all of our decisions on what is right on the ground—not what's best for my poll numbers. I refuse to let politics affect what is happening on the ground. I'm fighting to win the War on Terror, not a popularity contest."

At that point, I thought, "Our nation is in good hands. This guy is brilliant—and totally principled. His answer makes perfect sense."

Politically, George W. Bush was getting his head handed to him. But he didn't care. He wasn't taking military advice from Nancy Pelosi or Harry Reid. He took his military advice from leaders on the ground and from the chairman of the Joint Chiefs. And because of that advice, he would not come out and tell the American people, "We are winning, and here's how we are doing it." He certainly hoped that all of us, the talk show hosts in that room, would go out and make that case, and that is why he called us to the Oval Office. But he was convinced, based on the advice he had received, that he could not personally make that case without adversely affecting the war effort.

A TEACHING MOMENT

At that point, Glenn Beck leaned forward and said, "Mr. President, with all respect, I urge you to reconsider your position. The War on Terror is too important, and you need to engage the American people and regain their support for the war. Tell them what you've just told us. Address the nation from the Oval Office with a bank of flat-screen TVs behind you, so you can get out from your desk and point and say 'Look at what we did in Baghdad and in Al Anbar.' You need an MTV kind of presentation!"

There was a very long pause.

"Glenn," the president said at last, "I'm more of a CMT guy than an MTV guy." That said it all. The president was going to conduct this war his way.

I think all of us in that room wished that President Bush would come out swinging immediately and turn public opinion around. But all in good time, it happened anyway—even without an Oval Office speech and a bank of flat-screens. The O'Hanlon and Pollack op-ed piece was just the first crack in the dam. Eventually, a whole torrent of good news came pouring out of Iraq. The truth about our mission in Iraq prevailed in the natural course of events, and President Bush never had to compromise his principles to make the case.

That was a teaching moment for all of us in that room. President Bush was telling us, in effect, "You guys don't walk in my shoes. You can help this effort by carrying the message to your audience. But I have to conduct this war in my own way." George W. Bush was a great president, and he is a great human being. I believe history will judge him kindly.

As I left the White House, I reflected on the extraordinary privilege I'd just had. Again, I wondered, "Why me?" President Bush didn't invite me because I'm anyone special. He invited me to the White House because of *you*—and because of thousands of grassroots Americans just like you. He chose me because I talk to you every day. He knew that I would tell the truth about America's achievements in the War on Terror, and he knew that you would support our troops and you would pray for him.

You, the grass roots of this nation, sent me to the Oval Office to represent you, to be your eyes and ears in the halls of our government. That makes me very proud—and very humble. Thank you for that opportunity.

SUPPORT THE MISSION

During a European tour in the spring of 2009, President Obama was asked by a journalist in France if he believed in American exceptionalism. Obama replied, "I believe in American exceptionalism, just as I suspect that the Brits believe in British exceptionalism and the Greeks believe in Greek exceptionalism."[3] Which, of course, means that President Obama doesn't believe in American exceptionalism at all. If *every* nation is exceptional, then *no* nation is exceptional.

Sometime later, Dick Cheney came on my show and talked about American exceptionalism. "This is a president," he said, "who doesn't have the same perception of our role in the world that I think most Americans have. America is an exceptional nation. We are the world's foremost democracy. We have sacrificed hundreds of thousands of American lives to bring freedom and democracy to people all over the world—World War I, World War II, Korea, and on and on. That is why America is an exceptional nation."

No other nation on earth has sacrificed more blood and treasure for the cause of freedom around the world. And it's one thing when our soldiers go out and fight wars to defend America against attack. But our soldiers are even more exceptional than that. They go out and fight to defend *other* nations against attack. They go out and fight to bring freedom and democracy to the people of *other* nations halfway around the world—to places like France and Poland and Italy, South Korea and South Vietnam, Kuwait and Iraq. I would say that is pretty exceptional. If only President Obama understood that.

But we, as grassroots Americans, can set an example for our president to learn from. We can show our men and women in uniform that we appreciate how exceptional they really are, and how exceptional America is because of their sacrifice.

On Veterans Day in 2010, I spoke by satellite phone with Lieutenant Colonel Shawn Stroud, a North Dakota native who was then in Afghanistan. He had previously served a long tour in Iraq before being assigned to NATO Training Mission Afghanistan. There he works with soldiers from twenty-nine countries to train leaders in the Afghan National Security Forces, so that they can one day take over the task of defending their country against the Taliban enemy.

I asked Colonel Stroud, "What's the best thing grassroots folks at home can do to support our troops?"

His answer: *support their mission*. "I'll tell you, Scott," he said, "what encourages us is knowing that the American people stand firmly behind us and that they show unwavering support not only for those of us who wear the uniform but for those we leave behind, our families."

The mainstream media has reported mostly bad news from Afghanistan, but Lieutenant Colonel Stroud wants us to know that there is a lot of good news to report. "I've had the opportunity to see the entire country of Afghanistan," he told me. "I've been to seven provinces. Afghanistan is an incredible country with some extreme terrain. But I must tell you, the Afghan people are making progress. They have hope now. They have opportunities they've never had before.

"We're seeing a growing capacity of the Afghan National Army and the Afghan National Police. We've conducted operations that were led by the Afghan National Army, with our coalition forces in support. That's a huge step, because the Afghan National Security Forces have to take the lead before we can withdraw. We can't fight our way out of this war. We've got to train our way out of this war. We've got to train the Afghan National Security Forces to stand on their own.

"Training the Afghan forces is totally different from training the Iraqi forces. Illiteracy was not an issue in Iraq, but it's a huge issue here in Afghanistan. Only fifteen percent of the Afghan recruits we train are literate, meaning they are able to read and write at even a first-grade level. The rest cannot write their own names or count their fingers and toes. In Iraq, we could give recruits a written manual on how to do maintenance on a vehicle or a weapon. Here, everything is show-and-tell.

"By the end of 2011, Scott, we will have trained over one hundred thousand Afghans in basic literacy. When they earn their certificate of literacy in basic training, we give them a pen. They keep that pen in their shirt pocket as a status symbol. It's the equivalent of a police officer's badge in the United States. That pen says, 'I can read and write. I'm significant in society.'

"Overall, the security situation has significantly improved. Every day, we see more and more senior Taliban leaders either killed or captured. Ultimately, it's about protecting the people. In both Iraq and Afghanistan, the enemy will target civilians with spectacular attacks. They will try to inflict as much damage, fear, and intimidation as possible.

"Yesterday, a girls' school in one of the provinces down south was burned. Along with it, the enemy burned four hundred and fifty Korans. Not only does the enemy try to intimidate the Afghan people, but they have no respect even for their own religion. The people see it overwhelmingly now, and recent polling shows that more than seventy-five percent of the people have a favorable view of serving in the police and the army. That's up from sixty percent just five months ago. This shows that the Taliban's attempt to inflict harm has cost them popularity with the Afghan people. That's a hopeful sign.

"I get a chance to drive around, and one of the most heartwarming things for me is when I leave the compound and drive past a nearby school. It's heartwarming, Scott, to go by at around three o'clock and see the children coming out, both boys and girls, and the boys wear white shirts with ties. The kids carry backpacks and run with their friends. I see that, and I think, 'That's why we're here.'

"That's why I appreciate everyone back home who supports this mission. We need to finish what we started so these little boys and girls will grow up with a chance for an education and a better life.

There's an oppressive group of men who want to keep them in poverty and ignorance. The 9/11 attacks were launched from this land with the help of the Taliban, and we have to finish this job to make sure that never happens again."

HONORING OUR VETERANS

Author C. S. Lewis (*The Chronicles of Narnia*) knew the horrors of World War I. He left school and volunteered in the British Army, arriving at the front lines in France on his nineteenth birthday. He experienced the terror of trench warfare, and saw many of his comrades killed or horribly wounded before he himself was injured by an artillery blast on April 15, 1918.

In his book *The Weight of Glory,* Lewis described the life of a soldier: "All that we fear from all the times of adversity, severally, is collected together in the life of a soldier on active service. Like sickness, it threatens pain and death. Like poverty, it threatens ill lodgings, cold, heat, thirst, and hunger. Like slavery, it threatens toil, humiliation, injustice, and arbitrary rule. Like exile, it separates you from all you love. Like the galleys, it imprisons you at close quarters with uncongenial companions. It threatens *every* temporal evil—every evil except dishonor and final perdition, and those who bear it like it no better than you would like it."[4]

I'm sure you have thanked many veterans for their service. You've prayed for our soldiers on the field. You've supported their mission. But I wonder if those of us who have not served ever truly think about what it means to be a soldier on active service—the long stretches of boredom, the intense moments of terror, the makeshift housing, the extremes of cold and heat, the regimented lifestyle, the hard work, the separation from family, the experiences of inhumanity, horror, and death. No wonder returning soldiers are so reluctant to talk about their experiences in war. Could anyone who has never walked a mile in their boots ever understand?

Even if we can't fully understand what our soldiers have endured and witnessed, we can help them and honor them for their service. Former Minnesota governor Tim Pawlenty recently appeared on *The Common Sense Club* to talk about honoring the American veteran.

"Honoring our veterans is not just about speeches and words," the governor said. "We have to honor them with our deeds. As citizens, we need to make sure that our politicians and our policies are backing our men and women in uniform and our veterans. So lobby your legislature or congressman about veterans' benefits.

"Why is America a great country? There are many reasons, but one of the most important is that we are free. And you can't remain free unless you're secure. The men and women of our military are the final guarantors of our security in this country. All of the values and traditions of honoring our military and our veterans are just one generation from extinction. If we don't pass it on to our kids, it will be lost. So in our schools, in our families around the dinner table, and in the community, it's important that we raise these values up and teach them to our children."

I said, "Governor, I have a proposal to suggest. Maybe instead of letting schools out on Veterans Day, we could keep kids in school and hold special classes and assemblies where students could learn how our veterans defended our nation in past wars. Maybe they could spend time talking to veterans and asking them questions. Wouldn't that be better than giving kids the day off to play video games?"

"That's a great idea, Scott," Governor Pawlenty said. "I think the schools have a role to play in reminding us all of what our veterans mean to this country. And there are things we can all do for our veterans on an individual level. If you see a veteran in a restaurant, go over and shake that person's hand, or better yet, pick up the tab, buy them a meal. Here in Minnesota, you can get a 'Support Our Troops' license plate. There's an extra charge for those plates, and the extra money goes into a fund to help veterans. And we can give money to an organization that helps veterans or members of the military." (One of the best organizations, by the way, is the Disabled American Veterans Charitable Service Trust, which has a low administrative overhead and delivers ninety-four cents of every donated dollar to serve disabled vets.)

"Another thing we can do," Governor Pawlenty added, "is show up and cheer and applaud at Memorial Day and Veterans Day ceremonies, or deployment and coming-home ceremonies. Beyond that, you can become a member of the military by being willing to join, by raising your hand and taking that oath. We can all do something. We all say we support our troops, but let's make sure we operationalize that and let it not just be empty words. Let's do our part to honor the troops every day."

Governor Pawlenty has traveled to Iraq, Afghanistan, and other places around the world to visit our men and women in uniform. One of his toughest duties is to attend funerals for our fallen soldiers. "I see families that are both proud and heartbroken," he said. "You see the outpouring of love and affection from the community. I remember one funeral, for example, in Northome, Minnesota. It was winter and the whole town came out for a memorial service in the gymnasium for Staff Sergeant Dale Panchot."

Dale Panchot joined the Army Reserve at age seventeen, then left college to enlist. He served nine years, and in his last phone call to his parents a few days before his death, he told them that he had just reenlisted for three more years. He was an avid hunter and fisherman and a committed Christian who was baptized and confirmed at Hope Lutheran Church in Northome. He was a third-generation soldier, proud to follow in the tradition of his father and grandfather.

On November 17, 2003, in the early stages of Operation Iraqi Freedom, twenty-six-year-old Sergeant Panchot was a squad leader assigned to B Company, 1st Battalion, 8th Infantry Regiment, 3rd Brigade Combat Team. At about 7:30 A.M., while Panchot was on patrol in a Bradley fighting vehicle in Iraq's deadly Sunni Triangle, the vehicle was ambushed. Attackers fired rocket-propelled grenades and automatic weapons. Bullets penetrated the left side of the vehicle, hitting and mortally wounding Sergeant Panchot.

At the memorial service, Governor Pawlenty stood before the flag-draped casket and said, "I don't know how this could be any sadder. We sit here and think of the many things Dale will never get to do. We think of all the dreams he had and that his family had for him. . . . But if the dead could speak, they would tell us there are some things worth fighting for and some things worth dying for."

The governor told me, "That was just one memory among many of the incredible sacrifice these folks have made. Our soldiers and their families are courageous, they are strong, they are patriotic. It's an incredible act of generosity to say, 'I'll do this for my country, I'll give it everything I have, and if need be, I will lay down my life for this country.' There are no words that can adequately express our appreciation for these men and women. But we need to do our best to try to express it."

One grassroots American who is finding ways to express appreciation and honor for our men and women in uniform is my friend Pat Traynor. Pat and his wife, Jamie, have three sons and live in Fargo. Coming from a legal background, Pat distinguished himself in the early 1990s by instituting major reforms at the North Dakota Workers Compensation Bureau, helping to turn a $240 million unfunded liability into a $350 million surplus. Today he is president of the Dakota Medical Foundation and ImpactGiveback.org, a foundation that funnels charitable giving to many worthy causes, including the Support Our Veterans Fund.

"There are many needs that aren't covered by federal programs," Pat Traynor told me. "For example, if you need to make adaptations to your house because of an amputation or other combat-related disability, the Support Our Veterans Fund provides that help. The Dakota Medical Foundation provides the organizational structure so that we already have the administration, audits, and everything covered, so we can leverage our impact. This way, donated funds can flow straight to the families without losing ten or twenty percent to overhead.

"There are about sixty thousand veterans across our state. We all know someone who has served or has a loved one who has served. These needs strike at the core of our population. So this is one small thing that we can all do to help our friends and neighbors who have served this country. On Veterans Day, which is the eleventh day of the eleventh month, we ask people to make donations to the fund in multiples of eleven dollars. One hundred percent of every donation goes to help veterans, who can apply for these benefits through the Department of Veterans Affairs. During that Veterans Day drive, Dakota Medical Foundation matches the first five thousand dollars in donations, so that an eleven-dollar donation becomes a twenty-two-dollar donation, which is a great way to maximize everybody's charitable dollar."

Wouldn't it be great to see programs like this sprout up all across the country? Think of the veterans who have served their country, only to find out that their service-related needs are not covered by the existing programs. It's as if their country is saying, "Thanks for your service, but now you're on your own."

Soldiers and their families face a host of problems that are much better solved at the grassroots, community-based level than by a government program. Soldiers often come home from the battlefront with invisible wounds of anger, anxiety, depression, and post-traumatic stress disorder (PTSD). Returning troops are committing suicide at record-high rates. Many returnees feel isolated. It's hard for them to open up and trust people who haven't been through the same experiences they have.

So what can you do to support the returning troops at the grassroots level? If you are a veteran yourself, you can be the person other soldiers turn to and talk to. You can start a group for soldiers and veterans struggling with emotional issues or PTSD. And what if you're not a veteran? Then you can host a soldiers' support group by opening your home and providing refreshments. Then leave for an hour or two so that those warriors can talk freely about their experiences. Find a meaningful and active way to let veterans know they are not alone, and that their neighbors care about them and honor them.

REMEMBER THE FALLEN

Life can get to be a treadmill. I happen to enjoy the treadmill that is my daily radio show. I have the good fortune of doing something I thoroughly enjoy every day. I come to the studio, roll up my sleeves, sit down behind the Chrome Microphone of Common Sense, and go to work. I talk about the great events of the day, the issues that have me fired up, and I thrive on bringing a little sunshine to the dark corners of our government. But every once in a while, a story comes along that puts all of life into perspective. It forces me and my listeners to pause and think about what really matters.

I have that experience every time I hear about the death of one of

our brave soldiers in combat in a distant place like Iraq or Afghanistan. I had that experience, for example, in May 2006 when I heard
about the loss of Specialist Michael Hermanson of Fargo, who served
with Company A of the Minot-based 164th Engineer Combat Battalion. Michael was on patrol, helping to clear roadside bombs about
fifty miles north of Baghdad, when his vehicle was hit by a rocket-
propelled grenade. He was twenty-one years old.

I knew Mike's parents, Layne and Lottie Hermanson. I was honored and humbled when they came on the show to talk about their
fallen son, just days after he was deployed to Heaven. We talked
about the special guy Mike was, how you hardly ever saw him without a big smile on his face. He was an athlete, and he loved playing
basketball. He was also an artist and a deep thinker. Like most young
men who have grown up in Scouting, he had sterling character, an
optimistic can-do attitude, and an air of self-reliance and confidence.
Everyone who knew him liked and respected Mike Hermanson.

I was similarly impacted by the death of Staff Sergeant Andrew
Paul Nelson, age twenty-two, of Moorhead, Minnesota. He was killed
while on patrol outside Tikrit, Iraq, on August 29, 2007. He served
with the 82nd Airborne Division. It was his third tour of duty in Iraq
and he had also served a tour in Afghanistan. He was planning to
leave the army in the spring and study for an engineering degree.

Andrew attended Shanley High School in Fargo, where he was
captain of the cross-country team and played football. A member of
Boy Scout Troop 644, he earned Scouting's highest honor, the Eagle
Scout Award. Known for his ever-present grin and outstanding leadership ability, Andrew was a hero and role model to other Scouts.
He enjoyed the outdoors, running, scuba diving, music (classical and
country), video games, and playing pinochle. There was no generation gap where Andrew was concerned, and he related easily to both
children and older folks, even volunteering time to visit the elderly
at local nursing homes. And he was no stranger to grief; his father
passed away in 1999 when Andrew was fourteen.

Staff Sergeant Andrew Paul Nelson had earned numerous military decorations, including the Bronze Star, Purple Heart, Army
Commendation Medal, four Army Achievement Medals, the Iraq

Campaign Medal, the Global War on Terrorism Expeditionary and Service Medal, and the Combat Infantryman Badge. He loved his country, and he loved helping the Iraqi people. Two years after his death, I was honored to have Andrew's mother, Suzanne Nelson, as a guest on my show to talk about her son.

"I think of him every day," she said. "It doesn't get any easier except for the support I find from family members and others who have lost a son."

I asked her about Andrew's decision to enlist.

"He decided at age seventeen that he wanted to enlist," she said. "He called me when I was at work and said, 'Mom, I need you to come to the recruiting office.' I went down there, and he'd already filled out the paperwork. I said, 'Andrew, I thought you were just going to get more information.' He said, 'Mom, I had already decided. Now I just need you to sign the permission form.'

"I asked the recruiter, 'Can't we wait?' He said, 'We can wait, but he wants to do this. Other young men like him don't always know what they want to do when they go to college. Andrew will have four years of service ahead of him, and they won't be wasted years. He'll be serving his country and serving other people.' That made sense to me. Andrew was very focused and he knew exactly what he wanted to do.

"I felt concern for Andrew while he was on duty. I never asked him specifically what his job was. I knew he worked with mortars, so I had some idea what sort of weapon he was using. But I always thought he was in the Green Zone in Baghdad. I found out later that he was in the back of a Humvee, driving around in some of the more dangerous parts of Iraq. We didn't have access to email very often, and I know now that it's because he was in high-security work."

I asked Suzanne Nelson about a plan to honor her son with a fitting memorial.

She said, "We're creating a running track in Townsite Park in Moorhead, near St. Joseph's Elementary School, where Andrew attended. He was a track and cross-country runner, so we suggested that a track be developed in the park and named in Andrew's honor. The park board adopted the idea, and the city will also put in a basketball court and foursquare court." With Suzanne Nelson spear-heading the fund-raising drive, the Fargo-Moorhead community raised the forty thousand dollars needed to create the running track. It will be completed around the time this book is published.

Another story that forced me to stop and think about what's truly important in life is the story of U.S. Army Specialist Keenan Cooper. This nineteen-year-old native of Wahpeton, North Dakota, lost his life on July 5, 2010. He was in Afghanistan, traveling in a convoy with the 82nd Airborne, when a roadside bomb went off, killing Keenan and four other soldiers. He was scheduled to rotate home after a year-long tour to marry his sweetheart, April Travis, in October.

Shortly after Keenan's death, I had this young man's pastor, Mike Adams of the Faith Evangelical Free Church in Wahpeton, as a guest on my show. Pastor Mike had first met Keenan Cooper as an eight-year-old in his church. Keenan was the oldest of David and Heather Cooper's five children, and the Cooper family had asked Pastor Mike to be their spokesman.

"Keenan is truly the best this country has to offer," Pastor Mike said. "He was a young man of great faith who loved life, who spoke straightforwardly, who respected everyone, and addressed everyone as 'sir' or 'ma'am.' He came from a wonderful family and had a great sense of humor. He was a hunter, a fisherman, and he loved this land. Keenan's dad told me that from the time he was in the fourth grade, he was headed for the army. He was the kind of guy who would think things through, make a decision, and that's how it would be. In Keenan's mind, there was never a doubt whatsoever.

"At the time of his death, Keenan was making plans for life after the army. He was interested in becoming a history teacher. Of course, our military has had many soldiers doing multiple deployments. Keenan faced the prospect of another deployment back to Afghani-stan, and he would have been good to go. He would do whatever his country asked of him. That's just the way he was.

"When word came that Keenan had been killed, the whole family was in shock. April was in shock. Initially, you just can't believe it. You wait for someone to call and say, 'We identified the wrong sol-dier. It was all a mistake.' But soon it starts to sink in. And that's when all of us, as a community, need to surround the family with love and support. The Bible says to weep with those who weep. And the grief doesn't go away in the first few weeks or months. After time passes, after the media attention is gone, your real friends are still there for you. Weeks and months later, a true friend says, 'Maybe this is a good time to call the family and ask, How are you doing? We're praying for you.' "

Why is the United States of America still the greatest country on the face of the earth? Because of young Americans like Staff Sergeant Dale Panchot, Staff Sergeant Andrew Paul Nelson, Specialist Michael Hermanson, and Specialist Keenan Cooper. The greatness of our nation is embedded in the hearts of people who are willing to put their lives on the line to defend freedom. They understand, right to the depths of their souls, that what Ronald Reagan said is true: "One's country is worth dying for, and democracy is worth dying for, because it's the most deeply honorable form of government ever devised by man."

There is a poem, often attributed simply to "Anonymous," that was actually written by army veteran Charles M. Province, founder of the George S. Patton, Jr. Historical Society and the author of such books as *The Unknown Patton* and *Patton's Third Army*. The poem is titled "It Is the Soldier," and it reads:

> *It is the Soldier, not the minister*
> *Who has given us freedom of religion.*
> *It is the Soldier, not the reporter*
> *Who has given us freedom of the press.*
> *It is the Soldier, not the poet*
> *Who has given us freedom of speech.*
> *It is the Soldier, not the campus organizer*
> *Who has given us freedom to protest.*
> *It is the Soldier, not the lawyer*
> *Who has given us the right to a fair trial.*
> *It is the Soldier, not the politician*
> *Who has given us the right to vote.*
> *It is the Soldier who salutes the flag,*
> *Who serves beneath the flag,*

And whose coffin is draped by the flag,
Who allows the protester to burn the flag.[5]

These lines sum up the feelings of every American who truly honors the sacrifice of the American soldier. When I visited the Oval Office in 2007, I caught a momentary glimpse of the burden President George W. Bush has carried for the people he sent into harm's way. Those who were closest to him, like Deputy Chief of Staff Karl Rove, saw President Bush dealing with that burden on a daily basis. Karl told me he sometimes accompanied President Bush to meetings with families of the fallen soldiers. He particularly remembers going to Fort Campbell, Kentucky, when the 101st Airborne returned home from Iraq.

"I believe there were fifty-five families President Bush met with that day," Karl told me. "He'd meet with each family individually and talk to them. More important, he would listen to them. George W. Bush is a very good listener. Some of the family members wept openly, and President Bush was incredibly strong throughout. He was their chaplain in chief.

"Watching this scene, I would choke back tears. I'd literally have to find an exit and go outside, gasping for air, because the emotions were so overwhelming.

"At the end of the evening, President Bush was spent. But he said he drew strength from the courage and faith of those families."

I gained a similar insight into the soul of George W. Bush when I had Dan Bartlett, former counselor to President Bush, as a guest on *The Common Sense Club.* Dan served in the Bush White House from 2002 to 2007.

"Dan," I said, "I want to talk to you about President Bush's interactions with the families of the fallen soldiers. This is one of the untold stories from the Bush administration and the War on Terror. I'm sure you had your marching orders not to allow the media into these deeply personal moments."

"That's true," Bartlett said. "As someone involved with communication, I always wanted the public to be able to see this aspect of the president. President Bush was meeting with families who were very much in the grieving stage, having lost a loved one, and he went to provide comfort to them—yet it was the president who received strength and comfort from these families. There were times when family members expressed anger over the loss of a son or daughter, and that's understandable. But at least ninety-five percent of the time, family members would look President Bush straight in the eye and say, 'Finish the job, Mr. President. Don't let this death be in vain. My son, my daughter, was there out of love for this country. Let's finish the job, Mr. President. Fight on.'

"The strength and courage of those families were an enormous encouragement to him. I remember the last big policy decision I was involved in before I left the White House in July 2007. It was about the troop surge in Iraq, and President Bush knew his decision would be unpopular with many people on both sides of the aisle. His encounters with these families strengthened his resolve. He said, 'If they can be as strong as they are in their hour of grief, I can demonstrate the strength as president to do what I think is right—even if we are not supported by the majority of the American people.'

"Over the years, he met with more than five hundred families. We'd usually go to a major metropolitan area on presidential business, and we would quietly put some advance word out to military bases, veterans posts, and hospitals in the area. The meetings would be arranged and scheduled discreetly, without notice to the media. We set it up so that the president could meet with the families before he left town, and there would be no publicity, which was the way President Bush wanted it."

I said, "President Bush is a man whose emotions are very close to the surface."

"That's true," Bartlett said. "He would spend a good fifteen minutes or more with each family, and all of these meetings would last several hours. At the end of that time, he would be absolutely exhausted, physically and emotionally. Yet he'd be strengthened spiritually."

I said, "Our listeners often mention a sense of frustration that President Bush did not do more to defend his own record."

"I understand that," Dan Bartlett replied. "I often felt that frustration myself. I can't tell you how many times President Bush sat in the Oval Office, dealing with the fallout of a tough decision. And there'd be someone like Jimmy Carter criticizing and piling on. But George W. Bush followed the dignified example set by his father, and when he left office, he said, in effect, 'I'm not going to be a former president who clings to the power I used to have. I'm not going to second-guess my successor.' In recent months, George W. Bush is seeing his popularity on the ascent. So I think his judgment has been proved right."

Freedom is not free. Our rights and our freedoms were purchased at a cost—and we owe a debt of gratitude and honor to those brave men and women who have paid the price of our freedom. As someone once said, "This flag may fade, but these colors don't run." The greatness of America will remain as long as we have Americans like these representing our flag.

HONOR FLIGHTS AND FREEDOM FEET

"War is an ugly thing, but not the ugliest of things," wrote British philosopher John Stuart Mill. "The decayed and degraded state of moral and patriotic feeling which thinks nothing worth a war, is worse.... A man who has nothing which he is willing to fight for, nothing which he cares more about than he does about his personal safety, is a miserable creature, who has no chance of being free, unless made and kept so by the exertions of better men than himself."[6]

There is an entire generation of soldiers who fit that description, who have earned the right to be called "better men." They have even been called "the Greatest Generation." They are the soldiers who fought a war in Europe and a war in the Pacific—a two-theater war that threatened America's existence—and the existence of civilization itself. During World War II, more than 12 million Americans were drafted or recruited into the military. It was a time of total war, the most widespread and deadly conflict in human history, killing between 50 and 70 million people between 1939 and 1945. The Americans who fought in that war literally saved the human race from enslavement.

Here in the heartland, we are honoring the World War II generation with a series of "Honor Flights." Over the years, my friend Kevin Cramer and I, along with other volunteers in North Dakota and Minnesota, have helped to organize chartered flights to take World War II–era veterans to Washington, D.C., to visit the beautiful National World War II Memorial, located between the Washington Monument and the Lincoln Memorial. These flights are life-changing events, and we've had four Honor Flights depart from Fargo, two from Grand Forks, and four from Bismarck (with a fifth in the planning stages).

The idea was suggested to us by a staff member at the radio station, Tracy Briggs. She came to me and my boss, Mark Prather, saying she had watched *CBS News Sunday Morning* and that host Charles Osgood had told the story of Jeff Miller, founder of the HonorAir Program in North Carolina, and Earl Morse, who started the Honor Flight Network in Ohio.

Morse, a physician assistant with a Department of Veterans Affairs clinic, once asked a World War II vet he was caring for, "Have you ever thought of visiting the World War II Memorial in Washington, D.C.?" The veteran said, "I don't have the money, and I don't have a way to get there." Morse, a licensed pilot, offered to fly the man there at no cost—and the aging veteran was so choked with emotion that he couldn't speak. That's when Morse realized how much it would mean to World War II vets to visit that memorial—and that's when the idea of the Honor Flights was born.

Tracy shared this story with Mark Prather and me, and she said, "We should do this." And it snowballed from there. I shared the idea with Kevin Cramer, and he became passionate about taking this idea to the next level. The Honor Flights we flew out of Fargo were the first in the nation to charter 747 jumbo jets, and Kevin's "Roughrider Honor Flights" from Bismarck were the first to use 757s.

I was honored to be invited by the pilot to sit in the cockpit jump seat for one flight. At every air traffic control handoff, the controllers would say, "747 DC to Fargo, who are you hauling?" And the pilot would proudly respond, "Heroes, a plane full of the Greatest

Generation—World War II heroes." It gave me goose bumps every time I heard it.

I recently had Kevin on the show to talk about the flights. "Watching these veterans as they visit a monument in their honor," Kevin said, "is one of the most rewarding experiences imaginable. Their lives are changed right before your eyes as they walk through this beautiful tribute to their service. It has changed my life to see the emotion on their faces and hear the emotion in their voices. They get together with fellow veterans and talk about their memories, including the friends they left behind."

"Kevin," I said, "I'll never understand why it took us so long to honor the Greatest Generation. But now it's happening, and in the twilight of their lives, these old warriors are having an awesome experience."

It's no small effort to get an honor flight off the ground. It costs around two hundred thousand dollars to charter a 747, so the generosity of our corporate citizens and grassroots private citizens was crucial. There were nearly seventy thousand men and women from our area who served in World War II—and as I write these words, only six thousand or so are still living. We lose a few more every day. So time is running out to show these men and women that we appreciate their service.

The former vice president Dick Cheney told me that Wyoming is doing its part to honor World War II veterans as well. The people of Wyoming flew more than a hundred veterans to Washington to see the memorial, and Cheney was there to greet them. "It's always a special occasion," he said, "and a great way to say thank you to those guys. It's also a great way to remind everybody of what a fantastic job they did when indeed the very existence of the nation was threatened.

"When President Ford passed away in July 2006, his state funeral was here in Washington, and he had planned the whole thing. He even planned the route of the hearse carrying his coffin from Andrews Air Force Base to the Capitol, where he would lie in state. And he arranged for the hearse to pass by the World War II Memorial and pause for a few moments—the late president's tribute to those who served in that war." (President Ford himself served aboard a carrier in the Pacific Theater of World War II.)

Many World War II vets never got the "welcome home" they deserved. On one honor flight I took part in, I talked with a World War II vet and asked him to compare his experience with the welcome that returning troops from Iraq and Afghanistan were getting.

"When I came back from the war," he told me, "I took the train to Fargo and arrived at three in the morning. My brother was there to meet me. He drove me to our farm near Wahpeton and I got to bed at a little after four. Before I left for the war, chores had always begun at five-thirty. Sure enough, five-thirty rolled around, and my 'welcome home' was when my dad kicked my bed and said, 'Get your butt out there and do the chores.' It was like I'd never left."

That was the kind of welcome a lot of soldiers from the Greatest Generation got. They'd come home on the train and resume their lives as if nothing had happened. So Maria and I take our kids to the airport and we welcome our soldiers home from Iraq and Afghanistan—and we also welcome our Honor Flight soldiers. We give them the welcome they should have gotten in 1945.

There are many ways to honor our soldiers and veterans. It doesn't have to involve chartering a jumbo jet. It can be something as simple as a creative grassroots idea called Freedom Feet. I recently had Wendy Gerlach on *The Common Sense Club* to talk about a great patriotic product for our "women in camouflage." Wendy is a distributor for Lemongrass Spa products, a line of all-natural personal care products. She credits a fellow Lemongrass Spa consultant, Stephanie Van Ness of Iowa, for the Freedom Feet idea.

"Stephanie's husband is in the service," Wendy said, "and he was just finishing an eighteen-month deployment. As he was coming home, a lady who was Stephanie's dearest friend was leaving on deployment. So after three sleepless nights, Stephanie came up with this idea to partner with folks to get foot spa kits sent to Iraq and Afghanistan to pamper our women in uniform.

"The Freedom Feet kit comes in a red-and-white-striped gift box and contains a four-ounce cucumber foot soak, a four-ounce scrub, and a four-ounce cucumber foot crème. Cucumber is wonderful for reducing swelling, and you can imagine how swollen your feet might be after marching all day in those boots. So this is a way for women on deployment to slip away from the war zone for a few minutes, and enjoy some relaxation and pampering.

"Imagine how refreshing it would be for these women, after long hot days serving our country in these desert regions, where the temperatures climb as high as a hundred and twenty degrees or more, to just unwind, slip their boots off, and slide into a foot soak. These women have given up on their Stateside life to devote a year or two or more to make this tremendous sacrifice for their country. What are we willing to sacrifice for the people who are fighting for our freedoms?

"Women in the military leave everything behind—children, husbands, jobs. The men do, too, but it touches women in a different way. So these women lose an awful lot when they leave home. One sergeant reported that it was the first time he had seen all the women in his squad smile. And a female soldier in Iraq wrote, 'I just received my Freedom Feet care package today and it almost brought me to tears.' We've gotten hundreds of letters back from women soldiers, and it is so encouraging."

It costs twenty-four dollars to sponsor a Freedom Feet kit, including shipping and tax. To learn more about sponsoring a Freedom Feet kit, visit Wendy's website at http://www.ourlemongrassspa.com/selah/ and become part of a "lemongrass-roots" effort to improve the lives of our feminine defenders of freedom.

And while you're at it, why not engage your own grassroots creativity? Let your mind roam. Can you imagine some new, inventive way of meeting the needs of our soldiers overseas? Talk to returning veterans. Ask them what they missed most while overseas. Then think of some inventive ways to involve your whole community or the entire country in meeting that need. That would be a very grassroots thing to do.

RUSTY OUART'S BRAIN FREEZE

After 9/11, my pal Rusty Ouart wanted to do something to serve his country. When I interviewed Rusty and his wife, Marilyn, on my show, he recalled, "I thought of all of the innocent people on those airplanes and in those buildings. Scott, you reminded me every day of what a privilege it is to be an American. I want my kids to have the same blessings and freedoms I had growing up in America. That's why I made a decision to join the North Dakota National Guard."

Rusty Ouart put his life and family business on hold and went down to the recruiter's office. "They told me I had to trim down to meet the weight requirements," Rusty recalled. "They said, 'Drop the weight, then come back.' They didn't think I would do it. But I was committed, so I lost approximately seventy pounds, then I returned and said, 'Okay, here's my commitment to you.' I was forty-two years old, which is over the age limit, but the recruiter got my age waiver pushed through. All my references were good, so I had no problem. I have many years of law enforcement experience, and I'm sure that helped. I went in as an MP with the 191st Military Police Company."

"Rusty is a man of his word," Marilyn Ouart added, "and when he wants to do something, he does it."

During Rusty's Guard training, he broke a toe on his left foot. "We were indoors," he recalled, "doing hand-to-hand training on the mat. Somehow while we were grappling, I snapped my right toe, and it was pointing off at a ninety-degree angle. I just kept going through the training. They told me I needed medical attention, but I said, 'It'll be okay, I'll just tape it.' This was on a Friday, so I drove home, taped up the toe, and came back for the rest of the drill weekend. I did what needed to be done and I never missed a day of drill.

"Time went by, and the toe didn't heal right, and I ended up having an operation. When my unit was getting ready to move out, there were complications and the doctor said, 'We can't allow you to deploy.' I said, 'What are the options?' He said—just kidding—'Well, we can cut it off. It would heal faster that way.' I said, 'Okay, take it off. I've *got* to ship out with my unit.' They laughed, but I was serious.

By this time, I'd been training with my brothers in arms for two years, and I wasn't going to be left behind because of a toe. So I convinced them to amputate my toe. I joined my unit three days after the doctors removed my stitches, and they sent us to Fort Sill, Oklahoma."

While at Fort Sill, Rusty was doing early morning guard duty when he stubbed his toes in the dark, reinjuring the site where his toe had been amputated. "I stitched it myself with a sewing kit," he told me. "I didn't want them to remove me from basic. They kind of got mad when they found out that I was sewing my own foot back together, but I just figured I had to do whatever it takes."

Rusty Ouart and his unit arrived in Iraq for the 2007–2009 tour of duty. He was stationed at a supply base nicknamed "Mortaritaville" because of the frequent mortar and rocket attacks there. Rusty provided security for Iraqi informants—which made him a target for terrorists.

While Rusty was walking the base perimeter, an attacker lobbed an IED over the wall. The explosive device, made from a propane canister, exploded and knocked Rusty facedown in the dirt, leaving him temporarily unconscious. When he came to, he didn't remember what had happened. Brain scans later showed he had suffered a traumatic brain injury.

Marilyn recalled, "Rusty had written home, telling me happy Mother's Day, and he mentioned that he'd been forty feet from an explosion that left him covered with debris. Well, that was alarming, but he seemed okay. Sometimes we'd talk over the webcam, and he was experiencing symptoms. We later found out that these symptoms fit a diagnosis of TBI or traumatic brain injury, but we didn't know it then. He had headaches, and he'd explain them away—'Well, it's a hundred and twenty degrees, and headaches are normal in this heat.' But what about the vomiting? Same thing, it's the heat. And the dizziness? Same thing.

"We just didn't associate these symptoms with traumatic brain injury. He started noticing a metallic taste in his mouth—but he shrugged it off as the result of all the mortar rounds coming into the base. It was all the metal and smoke in the air. Meanwhile, his brain injury was going untreated. When the base was hit with mortar fire, everyone hit the ground hard. Rusty would drop down, wearing his nine-millimeter on his chest, with no head protection, constantly jarring his brain. It wasn't until he actually passed out and was having trouble speaking that they finally realized there was something seriously wrong with this soldier. Rusty was very determined to stay with his unit, and he stopped calling home to tell me what was going on."

Rusty said, "My sergeant finally forced me to call home. He *threw* the phone at me and said, 'You *will* call your wife.' I didn't want to call."

After Rusty blacked out in a Humvee, it was clear that something was wrong with him. But instead of treating Rusty for a traumatic brain injury, military doctors gave him a psychiatric diagnosis of "conversion disorder." In other words, the doctors said that Rusty's physical impairments were caused by *anxiety,* not a brain injury.

"My problem," said Rusty, "is that the mortar hit I had suffered was not witnessed by any other personnel. So, as far as the army was concerned, it didn't happen. And the army to this day doesn't recognize my injuries."

Traumatic brain injury is, unfortunately, the story of all too many of our vets. While I have an unending respect for our United States Armed Forces, the military is a bureaucracy. A bureaucracy, by its very nature, is not equipped to recognize the sea change that is going on with all of these brain injuries. The wars in Iraq and Afghanistan are not like previous wars, and the prevalence of improvised explosive devices in these conflicts creates a different pattern of injuries.

In 2009, Salon.com ran a series of articles on this problem, and uncovered other cases similar to Rusty Ouart's. For example, writers Michael de Yoanna and Mark Benjamin write about a soldier they call "Sgt. X" who had sought treatment at Fort Carson, Colorado, for a brain injury and post-traumatic stress disorder (PTSD), which they call "the signature injuries of the Iraq war." Sgt. X suffers from memory loss and must take his wife with him to his appointments with psychologist Douglas McNinch, because he is unable to remember what the doctor tells him.

On one occasion, Sgt. X taped his conversation with McNinch.

The doctor said, "I will tell you something confidentially that I would have to deny if it were ever public. Not only myself, but all the clinicians up here are being pressured to not diagnose PTSD" but to diagnose "anxiety disorder" instead. "Unfortunately," McNinch added, "yours has not been the only case. . . . [Doctors] are under a lot of pressure to not diagnose PTSD. It's not fair. I think it's a horrible way to treat soldiers." McNinch said that he had argued with his superiors, trying to get the army to acknowledge the large number of brain injury cases that were being misdiagnosed, but when he asked his superiors how the army planned to treat so many brain injury cases, they replied, "We are just counting people. We don't plan on treating them."[7]

Even if the military did identify and diagnose TBI cases, there is no infrastructure for treating them. Rusty and Marilyn Ouart had to research the problem on their own, locate a physician who is familiar with TBI, and pay out of their own pockets for Rusty's treatment. Fortunately, they did find a physician, Dr. Paul Harch, who specializes in TBI. Dr. Harch, whose practice is in New Orleans, conducted a SPECT (single-photon emission computerized tomography) scan and found obvious evidence of "diffuse abnormalities and multiple significant areas of injury."

Rusty has undergone two courses of hyperbaric oxygen therapy treatments (nicknamed "the brain freeze program"). The therapy has performed miracles for him. In fact, the hyperbaric treatments proved that Rusty had shrapnel wounds, even though the army claimed he wasn't injured. During treatment, bruises showed up on Rusty's body—the oxygen caused the metallic impurities embedded in Rusty's skin to bring out those bruises.

In early 2010, I asked Bob Berg and Melissa Seitz to come on my show and talk about an event they were coordinating to help the Ouart family—"The Rusty Ouart Brain Freeze Benefit."

They raffled off a bright red 1988 Corvette in Rusty's honor—a "Vette for a Vet." There was a silent auction, a live auction, a pork chop feed, a 5K run in the Fargo-Moorhead area, and two guest speakers. One was former New York City fire chief Dan Daly, a heroic first responder on 9/11 who is now a motivational speaker; Rusty and Chief Daly became friends when they met at a Veterans Day event in New York City. The other is Dan Greathouse, author of *Doc, I Want My Brain Back;* Dan is a TBI patient who has benefited from hyperbaric oxygen therapy. Rusty's friends and neighbors also donated cash and frequent flyer miles to get him to New Orleans and back.

As I write these words, the army still refuses to acknowledge Rusty's traumatic brain injury. The army has literally tried to bribe him by offering him a payout equivalent to a death benefit—but the army bureaucracy refuses to change his diagnosis. So Rusty won't take the money. He could certainly use the money—especially after his house burned down. But the principle means more to him than the money. He refuses to give up.

Is this how America should treat its wounded war veterans? To me, this is absolutely unforgivable. This is a stain on the honor of the army. The Department of Veterans Affairs has (belatedly) acknowledged that Rusty does in fact have a brain injury. The VA doctors still won't acknowledge the effectiveness of hyperbaric oxygen treatment, but perhaps this book will help to right this wrong.

Talk show host Ellen Ratner is a liberal, a longtime friend, and a great lady. She's been on the air with me almost every day since 1995—proof that two people can disagree about almost everything politically and still be good friends. Not long ago, Ellen heard Rusty's story, and she told him, "Rusty, you need a good attorney who can help you get justice from the U.S. Army. You find the best attorney in the world, then send me the bill."

That's what America is really all about. Ultimately, it's not about right versus left. It's about neighbors helping neighbors—and patriotic citizens helping their wounded warriors. God bless Rusty Ouart—and God bless Ellen Ratner.

Today Rusty is helping other wounded warriors who suffer neglect from the military medical system. He's driven by the same love of country that once moved him to join the Guard and sacrifice everything to serve his country. No American soldier should ever be treated as Rusty was. He is one grassroots patriot serving others like himself.

"Our soldiers are North Dakota's best export," Rusty told me. "We're exporting our most precious commodity all over the world—the best of the best. Let's give them the support they deserve."

THE COMMONSENSE ACTION AGENDA

Here are some grassroots actions you can take, starting today:

✓ Do your homework. Read up on America's wars and the price that American servicemen and -women have paid to keep our country free. If there is a veteran in your family, study the conflict he or she served in. Then, when you talk to that veteran, you can ask meaningful questions that draw out more than one-syllable answers. Doing your homework is a way to show you care.

✓ Host a reunion for a veteran and his buddies from the service. Display the flag and other patriotic symbols. Make it a festive and memorable occasion.

✓ Make a scrapbook or trophy case of your family member's service memorabilia—photos, metals, discharge papers, souvenirs, uniform, and other mementos.

✓ When you see a member of the armed forces at a restaurant, thank him for his service—then pick up his tab or buy him a drink.

✓ Fly the flag on patriotic holidays—Independence Day, Flag Day, Memorial Day, and Veterans Day. When you honor the flag, you honor the cause the veterans fought for.

✓ Take your family to visit national cemeteries and honor those who died in service to their country. Even if you have no personal connection to a soldier buried there, you'll feel emotionally and spiritually moved just to be in the presence of America's fallen heroes. It's a great way to teach your children respect and gratitude for those who paid the ultimate price to purchase their freedom.

✓ Reach out to Gold Star widows and families in your community. We can never repay those who have given their lives in service to their country. But we can honor them by caring for the families they leave behind—parents, wives or husbands, and children. Make sure these families know that America remembers, and America cares.

✓ Go to your local VA hospital and ask about their volunteer program. Many veterans are alone, without family or friends to visit them. VA hospitals invite volunteers to spend time talking to veterans and relieving their loneliness and boredom. If you truly appreciate the service of veterans, take time to visit them in the hospital and tell them face-to-face.

7

FIGHTING TERROR

In October 2006, shortly before the midterm elections, I was scheduled to go to Washington, D.C., and interview Vice President Dick Cheney. So I told my listeners, "I want to be your voice. What questions would you like me to ask the vice president?" People phoned and emailed their questions to me.

One listener emailed, "Please tell Vice President Cheney this: with all the controversy swirling around enhanced interrogation techniques and the mindless drivel about so-called torture, the people here in the heartland want America to stand firm. Scott, tell Dick Cheney that if it takes dunking a terrorist in water, the folks here in North Dakota call that a no-brainer."

So I went to the White House and I was ushered into the vice president's West Wing office. I had introduced him at an event in East Grand Forks, Minnesota, and I had interviewed him on the air a couple of times before, but this was a first—interviewing the vice president of the United States in his White House office.

We talked for a while about how the Bush administration had kept America safe from attack ever since 9/11. "There have been several attempts, obviously, to try and launch attacks here in the United States," Cheney said. "The ones launched against us have all been intercepted, disrupted. They've all failed. And that's not an accident. It's because the president made some sound decisions, and we put in place some very important programs that let us collect intelligence against the enemy, to find out what they're up to, and then use that intelligence to defend the nation. . . . It has been a great success."

"So," I said, "with those accomplishments, why is there a debate as we head two weeks into an election about whether or not we're safer?"

"A lot of folks, obviously, don't want to focus on the threat," he replied. "To spend all your days worrying about that next attack is something that's difficult for people to adjust to. And I think there are some folks out there who say, well, [the 9/11 attack] was just a one-off affair. It will never happen again.

"Those of us who bear some responsibility for the security of the nation, on the other hand, look at it and say, next time, they could, in fact, have far deadlier weapons than they did last time, that the ultimate threat is a group of terrorists in one of our cities with a nuclear weapon, and that would cause more casualties than we lost in all the wars we've fought in the two-hundred-and-thirty-year history of the republic. So it is a huge problem, and periodically, I think people are reminded of it. But as long as things are going along swimmingly, and there hasn't been another attack, it's hard, I suppose, for us to get credit for what hasn't happened in a sense."

We talked some more about the terrorist threat and the coming election, and then I brought up the comments from my listeners. I said, "I've had people call and say, 'Please, let the vice president know that if it takes dunking a terrorist in water, we're all for it, if it saves American lives.' Again, this debate seems a little silly given the threat we face, would you agree?"

"I do agree," the vice president replied. "And I think the terrorist threat, for example, with respect to our ability to interrogate high-value detainees like Khalid Sheikh Mohammed, that's been a very important tool that we've had to be able to secure the nation. Khalid Sheikh Mohammed provided us with enormously valuable information about how many there are, about how they plan, what their training processes are and so forth—we've learned a lot. We need to be able to continue that."

Moments later, I asked, "Would you agree that a dunk in water is a no-brainer if it can save lives?"

"It's a no-brainer for me," Mr. Cheney said, "but for a while there, I was criticized as being the vice president 'for torture.' We don't torture. That's not what we're involved in. We live up to our obligations in international treaties that we're party to and so forth. But the fact is, you can have a fairly robust interrogation program without torture, and we need to be able to do that. And thanks to the leadership of the president now, and the action of the Congress, we have that authority, and we are able to continue to program." [1]

It took a couple of days for the mainstream media to pick up on the Hennen-Cheney interview—but when they did, all hell broke loose. The Associated Press said, "Vice President Dick Cheney embraced the suggestion that a 'dunk in water' might be useful to get terrorist suspects to talk" and added that "Cheney's words amounted to an endorsement of a torture technique known as water boarding." [2]

President Bush was quizzed about Cheney's comments during a White House photo op with NATO secretary-general Jaap de Hoop Scheffer. "This country doesn't torture," the president replied. "We're not going to torture. We will interrogate people we pick up off the battlefield to determine whether or not they've got information that will be helpful to protect the country." [3]

Vice President Cheney held an impromptu press conference aboard Air Force Two during a trip to Missouri and South Carolina. "I did not talk about specific techniques and won't," he told reporters. "I didn't say anything about waterboarding. . . . He"—meaning me, Scott Hennen—"didn't even use that phrase." [4]

But the worst of it for me was watching my friend Tony Snow, the White House press secretary, walk into the briefing room and withstand an absolute feeding frenzy from the piranhas in the White House press corps. I was in Fargo, sitting in my office at Radio WDAY, watching the briefing on live TV. I literally wanted to hide under my desk. Reporters kept saying my name over and over again. "Tony," they'd say, "let me read from the transcript. . . ." And they would go over that interview line by line, word by word, syllable by syllable, trying to maneuver Tony into acknowledging that the vice president of the United States had advocated torture.

As all this was going on, I thought, "Tony Snow is a good friend, I love the guy so much, and I admire Vice President Cheney so much—and now they're going to hate me! They have to be thinking, 'Thanks a lot, Hennen! Couldn't you have waited until after the midterm elections?'"

Finally, the press briefing ended and Tony walked away from the podium. I picked up the phone and called Tony's White House office. Tony's assistant, Ed Buckley, answered the phone (Ed and I now sit on the board of the Tony Snow Foundation). I asked to speak to Tony, and within moments, Tony was on the phone. "Scott Hennen," he said, sounding chipper and upbeat. "I was just thinking about you!"

"Tony," I said, "I'm so sorry."

"Don't be. You have nothing to apologize for."

"I saw the pounding they gave you. I feel terrible that this happened just before the midterm elections."

Tony brushed it off. "Trust me, this isn't going to matter one bit to the midterms. It's just the media being the media. Don't worry about it."

Well, that was Tony Snow. Gracious to a fault.

Not everyone was so gracious. I got hate mail from all over the country, and even from as far away as Switzerland. Some of the hate mail came from conservatives who were angry that I had lured Vice President Cheney into "admitting torture." Some came from liberals calling Dick Cheney and me all kinds of names because we supposedly advocated torture. I even heard that Glenn Beck was mad at me because I had landed a much-sought-after interview with the vice president—then I used that opportunity to set off a media firestorm.

I figured Dick Cheney would never do another interview with me. I was wrong. He's been a guest on my show many times since. In fact, he was a surprise guest speaker at CPAC in February 2010—nobody knew he was coming—and to whom did he come over and grant an impromptu interview? None other than the very same talk show host who got him waterboarded by the media.

The most important lesson I learned from this experience is *not* that I need to be more careful about what questions I ask. The lesson is this: I am privileged to sit behind the Chrome Microphone of Common Sense every day because I am the voice of my audience. The question I asked Vice President Cheney was not a question I came up with. It was sent to me by the audience. I don't remember who sent it, but I know it came from the grass roots.

If I ever forget whom I represent on these airwaves, I hope you'll call me, pull me up short, and set me straight. I speak for you. I speak for the grass roots.

CHANGING ALL THE RULES

I had called it "dunking a terrorist in water," but of course we were really talking about "enhanced interrogation" in general and waterboarding in particular. The position of our government, from President Bush and Vice President Cheney on down, is that the United States of America does not commit acts of torture. In that very interview, Dick Cheney said very clearly, "We don't torture. That's not what we're involved in. We live up to our obligations in international treaties that we're party to."

In the mind of the former president and vice president, we do engage in "enhanced interrogation" techniques—and one of those techniques is waterboarding. So the issue comes down to one all-important question: is waterboarding torture? It's a question that divided even some Republicans.

John McCain is a friend of mine. I honor him for his service, and for the way he conducted himself and sacrificed for this country as a prisoner of war in the Hanoi Hilton. But I do fault him for this: he magnified the difficulties President George W. Bush faced in prosecuting the War on Terror when he accused the Bush administration of committing acts of torture. The division between John McCain and George W. Bush over waterboarding was destructive and unnecessary. It hindered President Bush's war effort and it hindered John McCain's campaign for president.

I'll never understand why McCain and the president didn't sit down in a room together for a few hours and hash this whole issue out. But it never happened.

When you look at the history of man's inhumanity over the centuries, you discover that we human beings have an absolute genius for
inflicting pain on one another, from crucifixion to crushing to ston-
ing to burning at the stake to—well, you get the picture. The point
is that torture, as it is historically understood, generally involves inflicting not only pain and suffering but lasting (even fatal) damage to
the human body. Reasonable people can differ as to whether waterboarding should be considered torture. Waterboarding inflicts panic
and an intense feeling of drowning—a terrifying experience that can
leave psychological scars. On the other hand, waterboarding causes
no physical harm, no dismemberment, no flayed skin, no broken
bones.

People subjected to waterboarding generally break within fifteen
seconds; in fact, few last longer than four or five seconds. Many people assume that you could simply hold your breath and withstand the
process for a minute or so, but it doesn't work that way. In waterboarding, the captive is immobilized on his back with his feet raised
higher than his head. A water-soaked towel covers the mouth and
nose, then water is poured over the captive's face.

Because the individual is head-downward, water floods the breathing passages. The captive tries to breathe—but can't. He is *certain*
he's drowning. Panic is instantaneous. The brain senses approaching
death. The heart races. The individual struggles to escape—and that's
when interrogators remove the soaked towel and resume the interrogation. Let's not sugarcoat it: The captive is highly motivated to talk
because he is terrified. It is a psychologically brutal and nightmarish
experience. That's why it works.

Obviously, there's a lot more to waterboarding than "dunking a
terrorist in water," as I put it. But waterboarding is nothing like the
real torture that was inflicted on our soldiers by, say, the Viet Cong. A
person who has gone through waterboarding can still raise his arms
above his shoulders. John McCain can't. A person who has been waterboarded has no broken ribs, broken teeth, or dislocated shoulders.
John McCain had them all. Some of his fellow prisoners were tortured to death.

Navy SEALs and Army Special Forces have waterboarded trainees to prepare them for rough interrogation if captured. Also, a number of media personalities have volunteered to undergo waterboarding in order to report on its effects. *Vanity Fair* writer Christopher Hitchens, *Playboy* reporter Mike Guy, and Fox News reporter Steve Harrigan have all been waterboarded.

Hitchens described himself as a fifty-nine-year-old "wheezing, paunchy scribbler" when he was voluntarily waterboarded in 2008. Was he psychologically affected by the experience? Absolutely. "I have since woken up trying to push the bedcovers off my face," he says, "and if I do anything that makes me short of breath I find myself clawing at the air with a horrible sensation of smothering and claustrophobia. No doubt this will pass." The experience led him to conclude that "if waterboarding does not constitute torture, then there is no such thing as torture." Even so, Hitchens still makes a distinction between waterboarding and more grisly forms of torture practiced by America's enemies. He writes:

> A man who has been waterboarded may well emerge from the experience a bit shaky, but he is in a mood to surrender the relevant information and is unmarked and undamaged and indeed ready for another bout in quite a short time. When contrasted to actual torture, waterboarding is more like foreplay. No thumbscrew, no pincers, no electrodes, no rack. Can one say this of those who have been captured by the tormentors and murderers of (say) Daniel Pearl?[5]

Like Hitchens, Mike Guy of *Playboy* also expressed an ambivalence about whether waterboarding is truly torture—even after undergoing the terror of the experience. "It's pretty intense," he said. "Maybe that is torture." He added, laughing, "I spend a lot of money on psychotherapy." His hooded interrogator replied, "Be prepared to spend more." Guy laughed again—nervously.[6]

Steve Harrigan of Fox News was waterboarded three times, each time with a different technique. Harrigan did not offer an opinion as to whether he had been tortured. But he did say, "They took me to the brink where I was ready to submit and tell them anything. And then just minutes later I was standing by the side of that pool feeling fine. So, as far as torture goes, at least in this controlled experiment, to me it seemed like a pretty efficient mechanism to get someone to talk and then still have them alive and healthy within minutes."[7]

The bigger question is, does it work? ABC News correspondent Brian Ross believes coercive interrogation techniques not only work, but have saved lives. His reliable sources informed him that coerced interrogation methods produced breaks in at least fourteen cases.

"In the case of Khalid Sheikh Mohammed," Ross said, "the information was very valuable, particularly names and addresses of people who were involved with al Qaeda in this country and in Europe. . . . [Waterboarding foiled] one particular plot, which would involve an airline attack on the tallest building in Los Angeles, known as the Library Tower."[8]

So the question I have to ask myself is this: if we can waterboard reporters, and if we can waterboard trainees in our own military, then why shouldn't we waterboard a terrorist who has killed thousands of Americans?

The CIA has used waterboarding on only three individuals— Khalid Sheikh Mohammed (who masterminded 9/11 and personally beheaded *Wall Street Journal* reporter Daniel Pearl), and top Al Qaeda operatives Abu Zubaydah and Abd al-Rahim al-Nashiri.[9] The Bush administration, Vice President Cheney, and then-director of the CIA George Tenet all agree that the capture and "enhanced interrogation" of Al Qaeda leaders foiled more than twenty plots against targets on American soil, including buildings, nuclear power plants, tunnels, and dams.[10]

So, given all that we know about Al Qaeda's past crimes and future intentions, if it takes dunking a terrorist in water to save American lives, isn't this a no-brainer? And wasn't Dick Cheney's answer *exactly* what most Americans want to hear from their government?

In May 2009, a few months into President Obama's first year in office, former vice president Cheney was again a guest on *The Common Sense Club*. The Obama administration had recently carried out a selective release of Justice Department memos on the question of whether "enhanced interrogation" techniques are proper. The

Obama administration talked about prosecuting White House law-yers who advised the Bush administration on those interrogations—and there was even speculation about prosecuting President Bush and Vice President Cheney as "war criminals." With those events as back-ground, I asked Dick Cheney if he thought the Obama administra-tion was overreaching and harming national security.

"I watch what he [President Obama] is doing," Cheney replied, "especially in the national security area, which is sort of my first in-terest. This whole question of detainees and interrogation of de-tainees and the Terrorist Surveillance Program and so forth, closing Guantánamo—I don't think the vast majority of Americans sup-port what he wants to do. I think in fact most Americans are pleased, when they think about it, that we were able to go nearly eight years without another major attack on the United States. They think we handled that pretty well. We were not a perfect administration—none ever is—but I think what we did in the counterterrorist area was extremely effective.

"I think Obama needs to be careful because he appears to want to cancel out some of those most important policies. Then you get into this whole thing of closing Guantánamo and of course the bottom line there is: what are you going to do with all these terrorists that are in Guantánamo? . . .

"There are two documents in particular that I personally have read and know about that are still classified in the National Archives. I've asked that they be declassified. I made that request over a month ago on March thirty-first. What those documents show is the success, especially, of the interrogation program . . . that let us track down members of Al Qaeda and disrupt their plans and plots to strike the United States. It's all there in black and white. . . . It demonstrates conclusively the worth of those programs. I've asked the administra-tion to declassify them and so far they have not."

I asked Dick Cheney about Barack Obama's claim that he had read the memos and believed we could have gotten information from Kha-lid Sheikh Mohammed and his fellow terrorists without resorting to enhanced techniques.

"That assumes that we didn't try other ways, and in fact we did," the former vice president replied. "We resorted, for example, to waterboarding . . . with only three individuals. In those cases, it was only after we'd gone through all the other steps of the process. The way the whole program was set up was very careful to use other methods and only to resort to the enhanced techniques in those special circumstances."

From September 11, 2001, through the end of the Bush administration, there was not a single terrorist attack on U.S. soil. The Obama administration came in and promptly changed all the rules, ceased waging a War on Terror, and even changed the terminology, dropping the terms *terror* and *terrorism* from its lexicon in favor of *man-caused disasters*. Is it just a coincidence that the terror attacks against America quickly resumed?

On November 5, 2009, Army Major Nidal Malik Hasan went on a shooting spree at Fort Hood, Texas, killing thirteen unarmed soldiers and wounding thirty others. On December 25, 2009, a twenty-three-year-old Nigerian, Umar Farouk Abdulmutallab, tried to detonate plastic explosives concealed in his underwear aboard Northwest Airlines Flight 253 on approach to Detroit, Michigan. The attempt, foiled by a Dutch passenger, would have killed at least 290 people if it had succeeded. And on May 1, 2010, Faisal Shahzad, a thirty-year-old Pakistan-born Muslim, attempted to detonate a car bomb in New York's busy Times Square. The bomb ignited but failed to explode. Anwar al-Awlaki, an American-born Al Qaeda recruiter, has been tied to all three attacks, which took place during the first two years of the Obama administration.

AN ACT OF WAR

Fort Hood, near Killeen, Texas, is the most populous U.S. military installation in the world. When Nidal Malik Hasan entered the Soldier Readiness Center, he was armed with two pistols and his pockets bulged with ammo. Hasan is reported to have shouted "Allahu Akbar!" ("Allah is great!") as he fired on everyone in sight, including one pregnant soldier who later died.

As one wounded soldier ran out of the building, Hasan gave chase. When Hasan emerged from the building, two civilian police officers,

Sergeant Kimberly Munley and Sergeant Mark Todd, exchanged fire
with Hasan. Munley went down, shot three times (she survived), and
Hasan was felled by shots from both officers. The gunman's wounds
left him paralyzed.

In the days after the attack, we learned that Hasan was a follower
of Anwar al-Awlaki—a radical imam with ties to the 9/11 hijackers.
U.S. intelligence agencies had actually monitored email correspon-
dence between Hasan and al-Awlaki *before* the Fort Hood attack.[11]
In fact, Nidal Malik Hasan had been giving off warning signals for
months before the attack, but the "politically correct" military bureaucracy chose to ignore them. In fact, the morning after the Fort
Hood shooting, I went on the air and said, "We've always known
that political correctness was harmful. Yesterday, political correctness
turned deadly."

A trained psychiatrist, Hasan had attended med school at the
Uniformed Services University of the Health Sciences in Bethesda,
Maryland. There, Hasan was a source of frequent disciplinary
problems—yet his army superiors inexplicably promoted him to the
rank of major. One of Hasan's classmates recalled, "We asked him
pointedly, 'Nidal, do you consider Shari'a law to transcend the Constitution of the United States?' And he said, 'Yes.' We asked him if
homicidal bombers were rewarded for their acts with 72 virgins in
heaven and he responded, 'I've done the research—yes.' Those are
comments he made in front of the class. . . . I was astounded and
went to multiple faculty and asked why he was even in the Army. . . .
Political correctness squelched any opportunity to confront him."[12]

After the Fort Hood attack, General George W. Casey, Jr., Chief of
Staff of the Army, sent a mass email to soldiers expressing his concern
about a potential "backlash against our Muslim Soldiers and civilians.
We need to be vigilant to ensure this does not occur." Then he hit
all the Sunday morning talk shows, and his message was the same on
each show. As he said on NBC's *Meet the Press,* "Our diversity, not
only in our Army, but in our country, is a strength. And as horrific
as this tragedy was, if our diversity becomes a casualty, I think that's
worse."[13]

Can you believe that? The chief of staff of the U.S. Army actually said that a theoretical loss of politically correct "diversity" in the army would be *worse* than the real and tragic slaughter of thirteen soldiers and the horrific wounding of thirty others. Quite frankly, anyone who would make such a statement has no business being in charge of the U.S. Army. How could any military commander place a higher premium on "diversity" than on the lives of the brave men and women under his command?

It's an insult to the honor and professionalism of our men and women in uniform to treat them as if they are hair-triggered for an anti-Muslim backlash. And it's a crime to place a higher priority on multiculturalism than on the safety and security of our troops. The army had a chance to remove a bad soldier, a dangerous radical, from its ranks. Instead, the army *promoted* Nidal Malik Hasan! General Casey's statements prove that, even after the deadly Fort Hood attack, the army still doesn't get it.

I love and honor our men and women in uniform. And because of my admiration for those who sacrifice everything to defend this country, I have to say that there is something seriously wrong with the military bureaucracy. Political correctness exposes our fighting men and women to a deadly danger within their ranks. In fact, it exposes our entire nation to more terrorist threats. We need a military leadership that doesn't fear being labeled "politically incorrect" by Islamic pressure groups or the mainstream media. We need leaders who will put the best interests of our soldiers first.

A few days after the Fort Hood attack, I again had Dick Cheney as a guest on *The Common Sense Club*. I said, "Mr. Vice President, I want to ask you about what happened at Fort Hood. A lot of our listeners are offended by this. They are offended by the lectures about not rushing to judgment, about not taking part in a backlash, about the verbal gymnastics, the Teleprompter tap-dance to avoid calling this an act of terrorism—terrorism at the hand of an Islamic radical, Nidal Hasan. Were you offended, and should President Obama call this terrorism?"

"I think it clearly is an act of terrorism," said Cheney. "I don't know any other way to define it. This is a guy who has apparently been motivated by some of the same sentiments and philosophies that were behind 9/11. The man takes a weapon and kills thirteen of our soldiers and wounds many, many more. If that isn't an act of terror, I don't know what it is."

"Why was this guy still in the military?" I asked. "Who do you think blew it?"

"I don't know. I think we will find out eventually. Apparently there were emails back and forth between him and the radical Islamist leader in Yemen [Anwar al-Awlaki]. I haven't seen any of those, obviously, other than what is in the newspaper, but I think we've got a lot of digging to do to find out exactly what happened, and make certain that we know who is responsible—and how we can avoid it in the future. . . .

"There are a couple of key points here, Scott. Before 9/11, we treated terrorists as criminals and we treated terrorism as a law enforcement problem. So if somebody tries to blow up the World Trade Center in New York in 1993, we arrest him, put him on trial, then put him in prison. Case closed.

"What 9/11 did was it changed the way we look at this. All of a sudden we had sixteen acres of downtown Manhattan destroyed. We have people jumping out of windows eighty stories up to avoid being burned to death. We had the Pentagon being badly struck. We probably would've had the White House hit if it hadn't been for the brave passengers of Flight Ninety-Three. They took that plane down. We had three thousand dead Americans that day.

"That is not a law enforcement problem. That is an act of war. And you need to treat it as an act of war. Once you make the decision that it is an act of war, then you marshal all of your national assets and national means to go after the bad guys, to go after those who supplied them with weapons, and training, and to go after those who provided sanctuary and safe harbor, and you pursue a much more aggressive strategy. Which we did—and which paid off in preventing any further attacks against the homeland for eight years."

A GRASSROOTS WAR ON TERROR

On October 5, 2008, subscribers to the Fargo-Moorhead daily *Forum* found a free DVD inserted in their morning newspaper. The DVD was called *Obsession: Radical Islam's War Against the West,* produced by the Clarion Group. Within days, a controversy broke out and opponents of the DVD claimed that the *Forum* was distributing "Islamophobic propaganda."

I was invited, as the talk show host on Fargo's AM 1100 The Flag, to take part in a panel discussion on the controversy, to be held on the campus of North Dakota State University (NDSU) in Fargo. Other members of the panel were Matthew Von Pinnon, editor of the *Forum;* Dr. Ahmed Afzaal, professor of Islamic religion and history at Concordia College in Moorhead, Minnesota (a private liberal arts college of the Evangelical Lutheran Church in America); and Dr. Jarret Brachman, professor of terrorism at NDSU and former director of research at the U.S. Military Academy's Combating Terrorism Center at West Point.

In the course of Dr. Afzaal's remarks, he indicted not only the DVD, but American culture. The DVD claimed that radical Muslims are "obsessed with world domination"—to which he replied, "And [Americans] are not?" To the charge that radical Muslims are "religious fanatics," he replied, "And [Americans] are not?" To the claim that radical Muslims are terrorists, he replied, "Well, who are [Americans]? Peace-loving people? What is shock and awe? Another word for terrorizing."

He never refuted the claims in the DVD. He simply charged America with being just as guilty as Al Qaeda. He didn't deny the claim that radical Muslims have a genocidal hatred toward the Jews. Instead, he asked, "Who invented genocide? Where did the Holocaust happen? Did radical Islam create Naziism—or the West? . . . Naziism is a Western phenomenon."

When Dr. Afzaal had finished, it was my turn—and my blood was boiling. I said, "Did I hear what I think I heard? Did the previous speaker just suggest that there is a moral equivalence between the United States of America and people like Osama bin Laden and Al Qaeda—people who propagate a twisted view of an otherwise peaceful religion? Because that makes my stomach turn. The last time I checked, it costs a lot of money to go to Concordia College. And if that's what's being taught to our kids, then we're in a lot of trouble."

I pointed out that the United States military had crossed an ocean to put an end to Nazi genocide—at a great cost in American lives. "All this country has ever done," I said, "is stand for freedom. We've never asked anything in return. A lot of American blood was spilled. You talk about shock and awe? I'll tell you about shock and awe. The shock is to hear something like that come out of someone who is teaching our children."

Dr. Afzaal had indicted America for "shock and awe" in the Iraq War. Yet he conveniently forgot about the thousands of American servicemen and -women who paid the ultimate sacrifice defending Muslims in Lebanon, Kuwait, Somalia, Iraq, Kosovo, Bosnia, and Macedonia. He forgot that American-led NATO forces had ended ethnic cleansing against Muslims in Kosovo in 1999.

"Are we at war?" I said. "Yes. Don't take my word for it. Take Osama bin Laden's word for it. He issued a fatwa and declared war against the United States in 1996. This to me is not complicated. What's in that DVD is factual information. And quite honestly, the news media in this country has done a horrible job of reporting what is happening. But this DVD has reported it. It shows children—toddlers—saying, 'I hope Bush dies in flames and I want to go to [former Israeli defense leader and prime minister] Ariel Sharon and kill him with a gun. I want to tell Bush he's a pig and I hope he dies.' These are kids saying these things on Arab TV."

I pointed out that the DVD does not incite hatred or violence against Muslims. In fact, it differentiates between peaceful, mainstream, *moderate* Islam on the one hand, and the radical jihadists on the other.

"Look," I said, "I have good friends of the Muslim faith. What Al Qaeda does sickens them. They see terrorism as an offense to a peaceful religion. I have a friend who is a Muslim woman from Iraq—a widow with seven children. How did she lose her husband? When they lived in Iraq, her husband said, 'What Saddam Hussein is doing is wrong. And I'm going to help the United States.' And when he helped the United States, the jihadists murdered him. Our soldiers brought this man's widow and children to the States so they would have a better future. So there is absolutely no moral equivalence between Al Qaeda and the United States of America."

Some in the audience applauded. A few got up and walked out. During the back-and-forth discussion between the panel members and the audience, one man in the audience pointed to me and said, "The radio man is full of hatred." He didn't specify who I was guilty of hating. I admit that my comments regarding Osama bin Laden, Saddam Hussein, and Adolf Hitler were probably not too charitable, but I made it clear that I love freedom-loving people of *all* faiths. And I certainly have no hatred for Dr. Afzaal. Disagreement, yes. Hatred, no. There's nothing hateful about challenging the absurd claim that America is the moral equivalent of Al Qaeda.

There will always be those who try to intimidate us into silence. If you speak out against radical Islam, they will accuse you of hatred against all Muslims. Radicals know that Americans want to be seen as decent, tolerant people—so radical extremists love to fling these ridiculous accusations around to intimidate us and silence us. We mustn't be afraid of standing for the truth. We need to proclaim the fact that America is great because America is good.

The views of Dr. Afzaal represent a kind of political correctness gone mad that can be cured only with common sense and plain speaking. Every day, decent, goodhearted Americans prove him wrong by extending open arms and a helping hand to Muslim immigrants like my Iraqi friend and her seven fatherless children. Americans don't hate Muslims.

But unlike Dr. Afzaal, grassroots Americans know the difference between good and evil. And we don't hesitate to confront those radical voices that call good "evil" and evil "good."

ONE MILLION VOICES AGAINST TERRORISM

It's called Fuerzas Armadas Revolucionarias de Colombia—the Revolutionary Armed Forces of Colombia. The people of Colombia know it by its acronym, FARC. It claims to be a "peasant army," representing the aspirations and human rights of the exploited poor of Colombia against their rich oppressors. FARC's ideology is Marxist-Leninist. Its method of operation is paramilitary violence. Its main sources of funding are kidnapping for ransom and the illegal drug trade.

Since its founding in 1964, FARC has terrorized the people and battled the government of Colombia. Recently, one man decided to wage war against FARC—not with bullets, but with the peaceful grassroots cyberweapons of the Internet. On January 4, 2008, Oscar Morales Guevara launched a grassroots word-of-mouth campaign on the social networking site Facebook. He called the campaign "One Million Voices Against FARC." It became one of the most effective antiterrorism efforts ever devised.

Oscar Morales has no background in counterterrorism. He's simply a grassroots Colombian citizen, an engineer from Barranquilla, who was motivated to take a stand after hearing story after story of FARC brutality. One story that particularly angered him was the plight of a woman who was kidnapped by the terrorist group. While in captivity, she gave birth to a baby boy. The woman was eventually ransomed and released, but FARC cruelly demanded a separate ransom for the child. It eventually turned out that FARC had already abandoned the child two years earlier at a foster care facility.[14]

Determined to put an end to these abuses against the Colombian people, Oscar Morales decided to begin with Facebook. In his wildest dreams, he never imagined the response he would get. He created a Facebook page called "One Million Voices Against FARC," then he contacted friends and invited them to join. The theme of his Facebook group was simple:

No More!
No More Kidnapping!
No More Lies!
No More Murder!
No More FARC![15]

The secret of the website's success is that every friend you make on Facebook has dozens or hundreds of friends, and they have *more* friends, and those friends have still *more* friends. So just twelve hours after Oscar Morales formed his group, it boasted 1,500 members. One day later, it had grown to four thousand members. And after a week, it had gained no fewer than *one hundred thousand members*.

There was so much energy being expressed over Facebook that it simply had to find an outlet in the real world. Oscar recalled, "We needed to take the momentum from the Internet to the streets." So he and his fellow Facebook friends planned a nationwide protest throughout Colombia to take place on February 4, 2008. He soon discovered that there were Colombians in cities all around the world— and they wanted to take part in the protest. So, with Facebook as a meeting place, they began coordinating events in such far-flung places as Buenos Aires, New York, Toronto, Barcelona, London, Brisbane, Dubai, The Hague, and Tel Aviv. What began as a Facebook page became a global grassroots movement.

Soon, other Internet-based tools were added to the group's communications arsenal—Skype, Gmail, blogging, and various instant messaging platforms. Because these tools are free, there were hardly any costs involved. Oscar and his fellow organizers used the power of the Internet to transmit images as well as words, including photos of a Colombian town that was almost completely destroyed by a FARC retaliation raid.

Oscar Morales became sought after by members of the media, who were fascinated by this fast-growing grassroots movement. The faces of this movement were young and eager and full of optimism. The message of No More FARC was translated into a multitude of languages for a global audience.

When February 4 arrived, more than 4 million people took to the streets of the cities and villages of Colombia. An estimated 1.5 million people turned out in Bogotá alone. Millions more—estimates range as high as 12 million people—demonstrated in cities around the world.

One famous Colombian woman was unable to join the protests, but she heard the speeches and chanting demonstrators over the radio. Her name: Íngrid Betancourt. She had been kidnapped by FARC in February 2002 while running for president of Colombia as a Green Party candidate. After six years in captivity, her spirits were buoyed as she listened to the crowds chanting, "No more FARC! No more

FARC!" (She and fourteen other hostages were rescued just a few months later.)

What did Oscar Morales and "One Million Voices Against FARC" accomplish? Quite a bit. The power of FARC was violent intimidation. Seeing millions of Colombians take to the streets in protest demoralized FARC. The Marxist group, which had once enjoyed popular support, was now rejected by the people. As a result, more than three thousand FARC terrorists quit the group during 2008 alone.

Oscar Morales Guevara went on to found the One Million Voices Foundation to keep the grassroots momentum alive.[16] He was also appointed by former president George W. Bush as head of the Human Freedom Initiative at the Bush Institute on the campus of Southern Methodist University in Dallas. I recently had the honor of meeting Oscar when I took the Common Sense Club to Dallas. Ambassador James Glassman, the founding executive director of the Bush Institute (and former undersecretary of state for public diplomacy in the Bush administration), first met Oscar in Colombia while with the State Department, and he persuaded Oscar to come to the Bush Institute as a visiting fellow. Jim Glassman introduced us, and Oscar shared with me what he is doing today.

"I've been sharing everything we've been learning over the years," Oscar said, "on how to use technology to involve people in today's grassroots activism. There are many countries that are in trouble, big trouble, with terrorism or oppressive governments. They have had these troubles in Cuba for years, and we're seeing freedom under threat in Venezuela, Iran, Syria, Libya, and many other countries of the world. Wherever people are facing threats to freedom and democracy, young people are using Facebook and the Internet in every possible way to stand up and defend their society from terror and dictatorship."

I noted that, here in the States, we take the social media for granted. We go on Facebook just to connect with friends and share photos and so forth. But Oscar had shown the world how to use Facebook and the Internet as a grassroots tool to leverage social change.

"People definitely take these Internet tools for granted," Oscar said, "but we all just need to look in our own backyard to see that people around the world are suffering. Our mission in the Human Freedom Program is to provide not only knowledge but to share best practices, to share everything we can—our experience, the tools, and the strategies needed to bring about democratic change in their societies."

"Oscar mentioned sharing best practices," Ambassador Jim Glassman added, explaining that the concept of best practices simply refers to accomplishing a task using the means that are the most efficient (requiring the least amount of expense and effort) and most effective (capable of achieving the best results). Oscar's One Million Voices movement has proven that the new media, from talk radio to the Internet and social networking, provide the best practices for producing social change at the grassroots level.

"Last year," Jim said, "we had a conference at SMU on cyberdissent, the use of online tools in promoting freedom. We had people here from Iran, Venezuela, Cuba, China, Russia, Syria, and similar countries. Oscar was there to help them and teach them best practices. We want to encourage people in these oppressed nations—even in a closed society like North Korea—to use cybertools and other means to promote freedom. President Bush is a huge believer in the freedom agenda, and he believes that when people are free, they will make the right choices."

Oscar agreed. "We firmly believe that the future is in the hands of the citizens. People can ask for help from organizations and NGOs [nongovernmental organizations] and governments, but it's in the hands of citizens after all. These struggles and changes must lead to freedom, to letting the people choose their own destiny."

THE UNTAPPED POTENTIAL OF SOFT POWER

"Oscar," I said, "you are a part of history. One Million Voices Against FARC is the largest antiterrorist demonstration ever held. Where would you like to see this movement go next?"

"We are in the process of educating Colombians to not let go," Oscar replied. "We need to stand by our values and be firm in defending our country from terrorism. What we achieved with One Million

Voices Against FARC is that the citizens themselves discovered their own power. The citizenry of an entire country rose up and said with one voice, 'No more! We won't let our country be taken over by you guys!' So now we are empowering people in our neighborhoods to do the same against all threats against life and freedom.

"The people are fighting for their lives. People around the world are being killed daily by terrorism. In many places, governments support terrorist networks. We see these problems in South America, in the Middle East, in Asia. We need to pool our grassroots efforts and work together. We need to mentor one another to defend what we believe. We are doing this from the heart, because we firmly believe that this is the right thing to do."

Ambassador Glassman calls this approach "Public Diplomacy 2.0." It means using the new media technologies to promote an open competition of ideas. When informed people are given a true choice between freedom and radical Marxist ideologies, freedom always wins—just as freedom is winning in Colombia.

Clearly, the challenges are great. Terror groups, such as Al Qaeda, are already using Internet technology for recruiting, indoctrinating, and training terrorists. But hate-filled terrorist propaganda is no match for the ideals of liberty and democracy in an open marketplace of ideas. Glassman calls Public Diplomacy 2.0 a form of "soft power." Hard power is the ability to achieve goals through coercion, force, or financial means. Soft power is the ability to achieve goals by attracting people to your cause. The goal of Public Diplomacy 2.0, as Ambassador Glassman explained it to me, is not so much to promote specific ideas, but to promote the open expression and competition of ideas. He believes (as George W. Bush believes) that when ideas are freely expressed and freely debated, the best ideas always win.

One Million Voices Against FARC demonstrates the previously untapped potential of soft power. Of course, soft power can't always replace hard power. We still need the hard power of government and the military to do the heavy lifting in fighting the War on Terror. But soft power has a major role to play in influencing public opinion and government policy.

Oscar Morales Guevara is a warrior and a pillar of human freedom.

And you and I are warriors as well. Let's take a lesson from the grass-roots example of One Million Voices Against FARC. Let's use the new media, including social media, to its full advantage. Raise your voice. Express your ideas, your values, your beliefs, your passions—then invite others to join you. Watch your little group of friends grow into a community, then watch your community become a movement.

Then, when the time is right, take your grassroots movement to the streets. It's time to strike fear in the hearts of the terrorists. Just as Oscar discovered, you'll never know how much power you have at your fingertips until you use it.

THE COMMONSENSE ACTION AGENDA

Here are some grassroots actions you can take, starting today:

✓ You can help to defund global terrorism. Anne Korin, codirector of the Institute for the Analysis of Global Security, said in 2008, "This year, the United States and other countries will send OPEC countries more money than the United States taxpayers send our own Department of Defense."[17] As long as our money is going to OPEC, we are funding global jihad and weakening our own freedom. Every time you write or call your representatives to demand more domestic energy production, every time you tell a friend or neighbor about America's need to "drill here, drill now," you help loosen OPEC's grip on America's energy supply—and you strike a blow against terrorism.

✓ America continues to be a target of global terrorism. The terrorist goal is to strike the American homeland—and strike terror into the heart of every American citizen. You and I are on the front line of the terror wars, just as the average citizens in the World Trade Center, the Pentagon, and in those four airliners on 9/11 were on the front lines. We need to be observant, because the terrorists still want to destroy us. Many terrorist plots have been foiled by observant grassroots citizens who reported their suspicions to authorities. Call 911 if you notice these or other warning signs:

1. People and vehicles that visit the same location multiple times, but that do not seem to belong—especially people who seemed to be surveilling, photographing, or video recording.
2. People who seemed to take an interest in security measures at key buildings and facilities.
3. People who seem furtive and ill-at-ease. Some may stare at you, others may avoid your gaze. They don't seem to fit in.
4. People wearing bulky clothing in warm weather.
5. Abandoned vehicles or stockpiled materials near potential target facilities.
6. Unusual odors, fumes, or residues that might be related to explosives or bomb making.

✓ Don't let friends and neighbors forget what happened to America on 9/11. A terrorist's greatest ally is our complacency. It's only a matter of time until the next attempt at a massive attack on American soil.

I recently heard about people who memorialize 9/11 on a daily basis by setting the alarms on their watches or cell phones to go off at 10:03 A.M. every day. Why that particular time? Because United Airlines Flight 93 crashed in a field near Shanksville, Pennsylvania, at 10:03 A.M. on September 11, 2001. It crashed because the grassroots passengers aboard that flight revolted against the Al Qaeda hijackers who had taken over the plane. The passengers fought the hijackers and prevented them from crashing the plane into its intended target—probably the White House or the Capitol building.

Grassroots Americans gave their lives to thwart a terrorist attack against the United States of America. So some Americans memorialize that act of grassroots resistance to terrorism by setting their alarms as a daily reminder to pray for their nation. It's a way of keeping the memory of 9/11 alive and remaining alert to the terrorist threat we all face.

8

HOLDING THE MEDIA ACCOUNTABLE

On September 8, 2004, during President George W. Bush's campaign for reelection, CBS News anchor Dan Rather reported a story critical of the president's Texas Air National Guard service in the early 1970s. The story, aired on *60 Minutes,* was largely based on documents supposedly typed up in 1973 by the president's former commanding officer. CBS News placed images of the documents on its website.

An enterprising blogger, Charles Johnson of Little Green Footballs, downloaded the documents from the CBS website and did what the *60 Minutes* staff should have done: he retyped the documents with Microsoft Word using the computer's default settings. When he superimposed the retyped versions over the alleged 1973 documents from the CBS website, they were absolutely identical. Those documents could not have been produced on a 1970s-era typewriter. They were forgeries—and obvious, clumsy forgeries at that.

Johnson posted his analysis on the Internet just hours after the *60 Minutes* segment aired. A grassroots, work-at-home blogger exposed the fraudulent basis of a story aired by one of the preeminent TV newsmen in America—and helped hasten Rather's departure from the network.[1]

How was Dan Rather fooled? The answer is simple: when Rather received the documents from a Texas man named Bill Burkett, he failed to treat them with the skepticism they deserved. Dan Rather is still in denial today. During a 2007 appearance on *Larry King Live,* he insisted, "Nobody to this day has shown that these documents were fraudulent. . . . The truth of the story stands up to this day."[2]

The founding fathers gave us the First Amendment to guarantee that the news media would always be free to give Americans accurate, unfiltered information about their government. The problem is that the *old* media refuses to use its First Amendment freedom to give us the truth. Instead, the old media gives us spin, bias, one-sided reporting—and the occasional out-and-out fraud.

Well, if the news media has no use for the First Amendment anymore, We the People will use it to hold the news media accountable. We're using the *new* media to expose the truth ourselves. All across America, grassroots patriots are fact-checking, blogging, emailing, Facebooking, instant-messaging, writing letters to the editor, calling talk shows, and raising a ruckus whenever the news media lies or tries to bury the stories that are important to us all.

We are citizen journalists, and we are holding the media accountable.

A WIDE-OPEN MARKETPLACE OF IDEAS

My pal Rob Port of Minot, North Dakota, is a blogger and proprietor of the Say Anything blog at sayanythingblog.com. Rob's blog truly lives up to its name. He blogs mostly about politics, but also on anything and everything from the North Dakota lifestyle to global macroeconomics. And Rob invites his readers to "say anything" as well. The site features a freewheeling Readerblog section where anyone can post their views, as well as a lively and uncensored comments section. Say Anything is a totally democratic town hall meeting where viewpoints collide on a daily basis.

Say Anything is currently number 79 on the list of most influential political blogs on the news and blog search engine Wikio.com, and has been twice nominated for the Weblog Awards (Bloggies) as Best Conservative Blog for 2005 and 2007. Though Rob's personal viewpoint is libertarian-conservative, he keeps Say Anything "fair and balanced" by making room for numerous liberal bloggers on his site.

Rob's commentaries have become so popular that his posts are regularly picked up by mainstream media outlets, including *USA Today,* Reuters, and the *Houston Chronicle.* He also sits in as my guest host on *The Common Sense Club* from time to time.

In many ways, Rob reminds me of Thomas Paine, the revolutionary pamphleteer and a founding father of the United States. Paine emigrated from his birthplace in England to the American colonies in 1774. He is best known for his pro-independence pamphlet *Common Sense* (1776) and a series of pamphlets known as *The American Crisis* (1776–83). His influence was so central to the revolutionary cause that John Adams said, "Without the pen of the author of 'Common Sense,' the sword of Washington would have been raised in vain."[3]

What qualified Thomas Paine to become the voice of the American Revolution? He had limited education, had spent much of his adult life as a tax collector or a corset maker, and had failed in business in England. He arrived in America at age thirty-seven without a penny to his name. But a friendship with Benjamin Franklin, combined with a bold personality and a skill for compelling language, launched Paine to the forefront of the Revolution.

Like Rob Port, grassroots pamphleteer Thomas Paine maintained both a commitment to the freedom of the press and a healthy skepticism about the honesty and integrity of the mainstream press. Paine once wrote in an essay, "Liberty of the Press" (1806), that "the manners of a nation . . . can be better ascertained from the character of its press than from any other public circumstance. If its press is licentious, its manners are not good. Nobody believes a common liar, or a common defamer."[4]

I see Rob Port and his fellow conservative bloggers as heirs to the legacy of Thomas Paine. For that matter, I see myself and my fellow conservative talk show hosts as twenty-first-century pamphleteers as well. We broadcast the revolutionary message of individual freedom and liberation from oppressive taxation. We daily remind our readers and listeners—and the mainstream media—of what a limited, constitutional government is supposed to look like. We report the truth about the grassroots revolution known as the tea party movement. We tell the truth that the media tries to bury.

I vividly remember the early months of 2009 when Rob and I were the only media voices reporting on grassroots uprisings known as tea parties. The "lamestream media" (as former CBS newsman Bernard Goldberg has dubbed the mainstream media axis) went out of its way to ignore these events and hide them from the viewing public. But so what? The public has figured out that they can't get the straight scoop from the old media anymore. So here in the heartland and all across America, grassroots citizens are increasingly tuning in to voices like Rob Port, Scott Hennen, Fox News, Rush Limbaugh, Sean Hannity, Mark Levin, Glenn Beck, et al., to find out what's *really* going on in the world.

How did Rob Port build up the Say Anything blog into one of the most influential sites on the Internet? I put that question to Rob, and here's what he told me:

"I got started writing Say Anything back in March 2003, right around the invasion of Iraq. At the time, blogging wasn't part of our national political lexicon yet. I remember when we bloggers would all get excited when some mainstream media publication would run an article about these 'blogger' weirdos who were writing things on the Internet. At the time I started, we were called 'war bloggers' because that's what we wrote about. Iraq was the dominant political issue of the day, and we wrote about the war, providing coverage and perspectives that Americans weren't getting from traditional media sources. There were some bloggers, like Michael Yon, who were actually in the war zone. It was an amazing time.

"After that, of course, was the 2004 presidential election, which is when blogging *really* took off. It exploded around the time some bloggers caught Dan Rather trying to pass off forged memos about President Bush's service in the National Guard. I think that's when it hit people that this blogging thing just might catch on.

"For my part, I just plugged away. I was an original member of the Pajamas Media network—though I left when PJM moved toward becoming a more traditional media portal. I've always been both advantaged and disadvantaged living in North Dakota. One disadvantage is that I'm a long, long way from the media and political centers in the country, so I'm unable to join the cliques that many bloggers enjoy.

But one advantage is that I'm pretty much the only serious blogger with any sort of an audience in North Dakota. I get to be a sort of big fish in a small pond.

"North Dakotans don't have a lot of options when it comes to news and opinions about regional and local issues, so over the past five years or so I've tried to make that a big part of my focus. I still do national issues, of course, but I try to do a lot of local stuff as well and that's really helped me expand my audience."

Rob reminded me that he used to email his blogs and podcasts to me. I liked what he had to say, and his podcasts convinced me that he had a good presence behind the microphone. I had him into the studio a few times as a guest, then one day I decided to let him fill in for me as a guest host.

"That was a big break," Rob recalls. "And I discovered that live radio is a lot different from podcasting. The mike fright got to me, and I was throwing up just minutes before going on the air the first time. But once I got going, it was fun. Talk radio is as addictive as heroin. Scott, you opened a lot of doors for me, giving me a lot of exposure on the air, and that has expanded my audience in a big way.

"It still floors me that a guy writing from his couch in Minot, North Dakota, can be ranked in the top one hundred conservative websites in the country. But that's the amazing thing about the Internet. Anybody can write anything online and reach a potential audience in the millions. The Internet is the greatest tool a grassroots citizen could ever have.

"People used to get their news from some Walter Cronkite type on television or from a daily newspaper. These days, people get their information from a mixed bag of reporters and opinionators in all sorts of mediums. This means that a lot of chaff gets mixed in with the wheat, but I'd rather have Americans decide for themselves what is and is not true than some media gatekeeper. The reason we have the First Amendment is to make possible a wide-open marketplace of ideas."

The founding fathers would be proud of Rob Port. He's using the power of the First Amendment exactly as it was intended. And he's beating the newspapers at their own game. Rob's Say Anything blog is viewed by more people than read the websites of the *Bismarck Tribune,* the *Grand Forks Herald,* or the *Minot Daily News*—and he's nipping at the heels of the *Fargo Forum.*

What about you? Do you think you have what it takes to become the next citizen journalist like Rob Port? If you have a place to sit, a laptop computer, and an Internet connection, plus the ability to write the kind of snappy, attention-getting prose that is Rob Port's stock-in-trade, then what are you waiting for? Start typing!

"WE TOOK SIDES, STRAIGHT AND SIMPLE"

On the seventh anniversary of the 9/11 terror attacks, Alaska governor and vice presidential candidate Sarah Palin stood before hundreds of soldiers at Fort Wainwright, Alaska, as they prepared to ship out to Iraq. In her speech, she bade them Godspeed and commended them for courageously answering their nation's call to fight "the enemies who planned and carried out and rejoiced in the death of thousands of Americans" on 9/11. One of the soldiers being deployed to Iraq was Governor Palin's own son, Track.

Later that day, after the military transport planes had departed, Sarah Palin sat down in the living room of her Wasilla home. Surrounded by bright lights and TV cameras, she faced her first network interview. Across from her sat ABC newsman Charles Gibson, frowning at her over his glasses, which he had pushed down his nose. In the brusque, impatient tone of a journalist in search of a "gotcha" moment, he lobbed question after question. The Alaska governor fielded them all without a hint of nervousness.

Finally, Gibson asked, "Do you agree with the Bush doctrine?"

"In what respect, Charlie?"

"The Bush—Well, what do you—what do you interpret it to be?"

"His worldview?"

"No, the Bush doctrine, enunciated September 2002, before the Iraq War."

"I believe that what President Bush has attempted to do," Palin began, "is rid this world of Islamic extremism. . . ."

She went on for a few more sentences. Finally, Gibson interrupted and proceeded to give her a lecture, adopting the air of a professor correcting an undergrad who had just given a totally harebrained answer in class.

"The Bush doctrine, as I understand it," he said, "is that we have the right of anticipatory self-defense, that we have the right to a preemptive strike against any other country that we think is going to attack us."[5]

Though Gibson was clearly trying to embarrass Sarah Palin, he got it wrong. As Charles Krauthammer observed in the *Washington Post,* there is no one definition of the Bush Doctrine. Krauthammer writes:

> In fact, there have been four distinct meanings, each one succeeding another over the eight years of this administration—and the one Charlie Gibson cited is not the one in common usage today. . . . I know something about the subject because, as the Wikipedia entry on the Bush doctrine notes, I was the first to use the term . . . [in] the June 4, 2001, issue of the *Weekly Standard.* . . .
>
> [The] current definition of the Bush doctrine . . . [is] the idea that the fundamental mission of American foreign policy is to spread democracy throughout the world. It was most dramatically enunciated in Bush's second inaugural address: "The survival of liberty in our land increasingly depends on the success of liberty in other lands. The best hope for peace in our world is the expansion of freedom in all the world."[6]

Gibson was wrong—but he had achieved what he set out to do: "Gotcha!" All across the mainstream media, the headline was that Sarah Palin didn't know what the Bush Doctrine was. For example, the *New York Times* reported, "Ms. Palin most visibly stumbled when she was asked by Mr. Gibson if she agreed with the Bush doctrine. Ms. Palin did not seem to know what he was talking about."[7]

Journalist Carl Cannon of the online newspaper PoliticsDaily.com offers this assessment of the old media's treatment of candidate Sarah Palin: "The mainstream media is undergoing its demise, drip by drip, day by day. . . . In the 2008 election, we took sides, straight and simple, particularly with regard to the vice presidential race. I don't know that we played a decisive role in that campaign, and I'm not saying the better side lost. What I am saying is that we simply didn't hold Joe Biden to the same standard as Sarah Palin, and for me, the real loser in this sordid tale is my chosen profession."[8]

Cannon went on to list some of the deranged misinformation and spiteful opinion that were published about Sarah Palin in the mainstream media. Some examples: Palin is a book burner who tried to ban the classics from the Wasilla Public Library (never happened). She wants to replace the teaching of evolution with creationism in public schools (totally untrue). Palin slashed Alaska's special-education budget by almost two-thirds (fact: she *tripled* state spending for kids with special needs). She belongs to a political party that favors Alaska's secession from the union (absurd and false). The Palin baby, Trig, was actually born to Sarah's daughter Bristol—Sarah faked being pregnant (weird—and laughably untrue).[9] There are three important lessons to take away from the vicious way the mainstream media has treated Sarah Palin and the Palin family.

First, liberals are using the new media, too. The skewed liberal-progressive worldview is all over Facebook, YouTube, and the swamp of liberal blog sites—the Huffington Post, Daily Kos, Mediaite, Truthdig, Gawker, and the rest. So we need to make sure that the truth about constitutional government, free market economics, pro-life values, and a strong defense are forcefully represented in the marketplace of ideas. We know that conservative principles are grounded in the bedrock of the Declaration of Independence and the United States Constitution. We know that conservative principles pulled America out of its nosedive following the Carter years, and sent America soaring throughout the Reagan years and beyond. We know that conservative principles work—and you and I have to make sure that those principles receive a fair hearing. We're confident that if conservative truth competes on an equal footing with the false and failed ideology of the left, the truth will win.

Second, always take the high road. The vicious attacks against Sarah Palin show us exactly how low the liberal-progressives are willing to go. The attacks against Palin herself are one thing—but the brutal slanders against her children are another. This is the work of people without any conscience. If you are blogging, podcasting, or just talking to your friends and neighbors over the back fence, make sure that you never sink to the level of hateful, vicious sleaze that fills the Web pages of, say, Daily Kos. The left will always take the low road. Those of us who truly love and honor our country will always rise above that.

Third, always tell the truth. The lies of the left are as numerous as grains of sand. They lied about Reagan. They lied about Bush. They lied about the war in Iraq. They lied about Sarah Palin. They lied about the tea party movement. Every day, they lie about you and me, about our values, our character, our principles, and the history of America. Why do they lie? Because they have to. They don't have the truth on their side.

Our job is easier because we don't have to lie. We don't have to invent fanciful tales about Barack Obama. We don't have to attack his children (and what decent human being would ever want to?). The unvarnished truth is disturbing enough: his radical past, his associations with terrorists and extremists (like Bill Ayers and Bernardine Dohrn), his policies in office (which are bankrupting the nation and dismantling the free market economy), and his extreme ideas.

For example, we don't have to make up the fact that, as a constitutional law professor at the University of Chicago Law School, Barack Obama taught that the U.S. Constitution is a "flawed" document. On September 6, 2001, he was an in-studio guest on Chicago public radio WBEZ-FM and said of the Constitution, "I think it is an imperfect document, and I think it is a document that reflects some deep flaws in American culture, the Colonial culture nascent at that time. . . . I think we can say that the Constitution reflected an enormous blind spot in this culture that carries on until this day, and that the Framers had that same blind spot."[10] Yet it is this same "flawed" document that, on January 20, 2009, Barack Obama swore an oath to "preserve, protect, and defend."

We don't have to make up stories about Barack Obama, Joe Biden, Nancy Pelosi, Harry Reid, Kent Conrad, Byron Dorgan, or Earl Pomeroy. The truth, which is right out in the open for all to see, is condemnation enough. So always tell the truth. Never pass on an unconfirmed rumor as fact. Do your homework, check your sources, footnote your claims, and you'll never have to publish an embarrass-ing retraction. As we daily hold the mainstream media accountable for its lies, our best weapon is the truth.

SOCIALIZED GROUPTHINK

Bernard Goldberg has been a frequent guest on my show. He spent almost three decades as an on-camera correspondent for CBS News, and has won ten Emmy Awards. In his book *Bias: A CBS Insider Exposes How the Media Distort the News,* Bernie writes, "News, after all, isn't just a collection of facts. It's also how reporters and editors see those facts, how they interpret them, and most important, what facts they think are newsworthy to begin with."[11]

Goldberg notes that many liberal reporters pretend to be totally objective, and he cites Dan Rather's February 8, 1995, appearance on Tom Snyder's late-night TV talk show. "It's one of the great politi-cal myths, about press bias," Rather said. "Most reporters don't know whether they're Republican or Democrat, and vote every which way."[12] Yes, Dan Rather actually said that. I'll give you a moment to stop laughing.

Goldberg went on to cite a survey of journalists conducted after the 1992 presidential election. The survey found that fully *89 percent* of journalists had voted for Democrat Bill Clinton—more than twice the 43 percent of the general population that went for Clinton. "This is incredible when you think about it," Bernie concluded. "There's hardly a candidate in the entire United States of America who car-ries his or her district with 89 percent of the vote. This is way beyond mere landslide numbers."[13] So when Dan Rather says that most re-porters "vote every which way," you have to wonder—is he lying or merely deluded?

If we want to be charitable to the media, we can chalk up media bias to a "herd mentality." Everyone in the New York–Washington media axis lives within a bubble, and the only people they know, the only people they ever talk to, are other liberal media elites within that same bubble. They are like Pauline Kael, the drama critic for the *New Yorker,* who is said to have reacted in shock after Richard Nixon's

1972 defeat of George McGovern, "How can that be? No one *I* know voted for Nixon." [14]

If everyone you know has the same far-left worldview that you have, then that worldview doesn't seem far left to you. It seems normal. It seems middle-of-the-road. If everyone around you believes that George W. Bush is a Nazi, that global warming is going to kill us all, that tea partiers are all nut jobs and racists, and that Fox News and talk radio ought to be silenced, then these ideas seem perfectly reasonable to you. As a journalist, all of your reporting will be filtered through that worldview.

But in July 2010, the political website the Daily Caller disclosed the smoking gun—absolute proof that there is more to media bias than a mere "herd mentality." There is a *media conspiracy* to control what the public is allowed to know and how the public is allowed to think. The evidence is a series of emails exchanged among a number of big-name journalists and prominent journalism professors who were members of an electronic mailing list known as Journolist. The Daily Caller reported that Journolist members included some of the most famous writers from such elite U.S. and British news organizations as *"Time,* Politico, the Huffington Post, the *Baltimore Sun,* the *Guardian,* Salon and *The New Republic."*

After John McCain chose Sarah Palin as his running mate, Journolisters immediately began strategizing against her. The Daily Caller reported:

> Chris Hayes, Washington editor of *The Nation,* asked his Journolist colleagues to step up the anti-Palin vitriol, writing, "Keep the ideas coming! Have to go on TV to talk about this in a few min and need all the help I can get." After someone suggested that it was sexist to pick Palin—because she is not a Harvard grad and believes in choosing life—a *Mother Jones* reporter wrote, "That's excellent! If enough people—people on this list?—write that the pick is sexist, you'll have the networks debating it for days. And that negates the SINGLE thing Palin brings to the ticket." . . . Even *Time*'s Joe Klein . . . thanked Journolist for his first Palin piece: "Here's my

attempt to incorporate the accumulated wisdom of this august list-serve community."[15]

Members of the group discussed strategies for influencing the coverage of major political stories, controlling the kinds of questions asked in presidential debates, and smearing conservative journalists as racists. During the 2008 controversy over Barack Obama's radical pastor Jeremiah Wright, one Journolister, Spencer Ackerman (who was fired by the *New Republic*[16] and now blogs for *Wired*), urged fellow journalists to go on the attack against the conservative media. He wrote:

> It's not necessary to jump to Wright-qua-Wright's defense. What is necessary is to raise the cost on the right of going after the left. In other words, find a rightwinger's [Ackerman omits a word here, possibly head or face] and smash it through a plate-glass window. Take a snapshot of the bleeding mess and send it out in a Christmas card to let the right know that it needs to live in a state of constant fear. Obviously I mean this rhetorically.
>
> And I think this threads the needle. If the right forces us all to either defend Wright or tear him down, no matter what we choose, we lose the game they've put upon us. Instead, take one of them— Fred Barnes, Karl Rove, who cares—and call them racists. Ask: why do they have such a deep-seated problem with a black politician who unites the country? What lurks behind those problems? This makes *them* sputter with rage.[17]

One public radio producer on Journolist, Sarah Spitz of NPR affiliate KCRW in Santa Monica, California, said that if she saw Rush Limbaugh collapsing from a heart attack, she'd refuse to call 911. In fact, she said she'd "laugh loudly like a maniac and watch his eyes bug out" as he died in agony, adding, "I never knew I had this much hate in me. But he deserves it."[18]

The Journolisters were also quick to embrace the portrayal of the tea party protesters as "teabaggers" and Nazis. Ryan Donmoyer of Bloomberg News asked, "Is anyone starting to see parallels here between the teabaggers and their tactics and the rise of the Brown-shirts?" And freelance writer Richard Yeselson responded, "They want a deficit driven militarist/heterosexist/herrenvolk state. This is core of the Bush/Cheney base transmorgrified [*sic*] into an even more explicitly racialized/anti-cosmopolitan constituency. Why? Um, be-cause the president is a black guy named Barack Hussein Obama. But it's all the same old nuts in the same old bins with some new labels: the gun nuts, the anti tax nuts, the religious nuts, the homophobes, the anti-feminists, the anti-abortion lunatics, the racist/confederate crackpots, the anti-immigration whackos (who feel Bush betrayed them), the pathological government haters."[19]

After the Daily Caller blew the cover of Journolist, the online group disbanded, prompting this response from blogger Andrew Sullivan (who writes "The Daily Dish" for the *Atlantic*): "I'm glad Journolist is over. It should never have been begun. I know many of its members are good and decent and fair-minded writers. But social-ized groupthink is not the answer to what's wrong with the media. It's what's already wrong with the media."[20] Of course, we all know that the end of Journolist is not the end of "socialized groupthink" on the left—and doesn't even begin to make a dent in the problem of media bias.

Though old-school newsman Dan Rather denied the existence of media bias, many journalists today openly *embrace* media bias and claim that *bias is good*. Ken Silverstein, Washington bureau chief for *Harper's Magazine,* openly disparages journalism that strives for "bal-ance," because it "leads to utterly spineless reporting with no edge. The idea seems to be that journalists are allowed to go out to report, but when it comes time to write, we are expected to turn our brains off and repeat the spin from both sides. God forbid we should attempt to fairly assess what we see with our own eyes. 'Balanced' is not fair, it's just an easy way of avoiding real reporting . . . and shirking our responsibility to inform readers."[21]

Journalism professor Mitchell Stephens of New York University agrees. He calls reporters who strive for objectivity "fact-worshiping journalists," and celebrates today's new generation of journalists who "see through the pretense that news merely consists of collections of unbiased information. . . . More serious journalists are still going out and working to get the story right, but now the facts they collect have to be rehydrated, reconnected, placed back in context. Call it perspective; call it analysis. . . . The old twentieth-century line between fact and interpretation has become more difficult to draw (or pretend to draw)." [22]

Anticapitalist philosopher-activist Noam Chomsky actively promotes bias in the media as a tool for preserving the preferred far-left version of history. He observes:

> The New York Times is certainly the most important newspaper in the United States, and one could argue the most important newspaper in the world. The New York Times plays an enormous role in shaping the perception of the current world on the part of the politically active, educated classes. . . . The New York Times creates history.
>
> That is, history is what appears in The New York Times archives; the place where people will go to find out what happened is The New York Times. Therefore it's extremely important if history is going to be shaped in an appropriate way, that certain things appear, certain things not appear, certain questions be asked, other questions be ignored, and that issues be framed in a particular fashion. . . . In fact, if the system functions well, it ought to have a liberal bias, or at least appear to. [23]

Of course, historical events have already shown how media bias functions at the New York Times. Case in point: New York Times journalist Walter Duranty, Moscow bureau chief of the Times from 1922 through 1936. Duranty was awarded the Pulitzer Prize in 1932 for his reporting—or rather, his *misreporting*—of conditions in the Soviet Union under Joseph Stalin. His coverage of the Soviet dictator was so positive that Stalin granted him a rare exclusive interview in 1929. [24]

In 1932 and '33, Stalin deliberately engineered a famine in the Ukrainian Soviet Socialist Republic. That famine, now known as the Holodomor (Ukrainian for "plague of hunger"), is estimated to have killed as many as twelve million Ukrainians. As word began to trickle out about mass starvation in the Ukraine, Duranty went to work, filing stories for the *New York Times,* claiming that the rumors of famine were nothing but anticommunist propaganda.

As the United States entered the depths of the Great Depression, Duranty portrayed the Soviet Union as a workers' paradise.[25] He denied the existence of secret trials of dissidents, and of the prison camps known as gulags. Duranty's reputation and the reputation of the *Times* were so revered and trusted that no one thought to doubt his reports. Based largely on Duranty's description of life in the Soviet Union, Franklin Roosevelt officially recognized its government.[26]

British journalist Malcolm Muggeridge (who brought Mother Teresa to the attention of the world) saw through Duranty's deception as early as 1933. He secretly (and at great personal risk) journeyed to the Soviet Union and witnessed the Stalinist purges and atrocities with his own eyes. He came back to the West and reported in the *Manchester Guardian* on the scenes of starvation he had personally witnessed. He told about starving people being turned away by gun-toting guards from storehouses that bulged with grain. The media establishment sided with Duranty. Muggeridge was accused of lying and fired from his position at the *Guardian.*

While the Ukrainian people were systematically starved to death by the millions, Walter Duranty hid Stalin's crimes from the world. As Muggeridge bitterly observed, Duranty was the "greatest liar of any journalist I have ever met."[27] The Pulitzer Board has rejected calls to posthumously strip Duranty of his Pulitzer on the grounds that "there was not clear and convincing evidence of deliberate deception, the relevant standard in this case."[28]

If Noam Chomsky is right, if history truly is what appears in the *New York Times* archives, then history is all too often a pack of lies. Fortunately, Chomsky is wrong. The truth usually finds a way through the thicket of lies—especially if grassroots citizens keep a watchful eye on journalists and hold the media accountable for the truth.

The truth always prevails in a free marketplace of ideas.

"THE SOUND OF CRICKETS"

One of the biggest news stories of the past few years was practically ignored by the mainstream media: the New Black Panther Party voter-intimidation case. Two members of the New Black Panther Party, Minister King Samir Shabazz and Jerry Jackson, stood outside a Philadelphia polling place on Election Day 2008. Both were dressed in paramilitary berets and jackboots. Shabazz wielded a police-style club. They allegedly shouted antiwhite racial slurs at people who came to vote, some of whom left without voting. Republican poll watchers were called to the scene, one of whom recorded the incident with a video camera. That video was later posted to YouTube.

The Bush administration Justice Department charged Shabazz, Jackson, and the New Black Panther Party with voter intimidation. Months later, the Obama Justice Department, under Attorney General Eric Holder, reduced the charges against Shabazz and dismissed all charges against Jackson and the New Black Panthers. On May 14, 2010, Department of Justice attorney J. Christian Adams resigned his post as a Voting Section trial attorney, protesting the department's handling of the case. Testifying before the U.S. Civil Rights Commission, Adams stated, "I was told by Voting Section management that cases are not going to be brought against black defendants for the benefit of white victims."[29]

At a July 2010 town hall meeting, hosted by Democratic California congressman Brad Sherman, angry constituents showed up and demanded to know what Congressman Sherman planned to do about the Justice Department's refusal to prosecute the New Black Panther case. This was about two months after the Adams resignation. When constituents told Sherman about Adams's claims, the congressman was befuddled.

"I am extremely sure," he said, "that we do not have a policy in the Department of Justice of never prosecuting a black defendant if the victim is white. I'm sure it may say that somewhere on the Internet, but that doesn't mean it is true. And as to the Black Panther Party, I'm simply not aware of that case."[30] At that point, the audience booed loudly—and proceeded to inform Congressman Sherman of the facts of the case.

I have no doubt that Congressman Sherman's ignorance was every bit as deep as he professed. Many of his constituents had been closely following the New Black Panther case for more than a year, but the congressman was clueless because he never watched Fox News and never listened to talk radio. He was in the dark because *his* news source—the mainstream media—had spiked the story.

Newsweek, for example, had steadfastly refused to cover the case until clamoring readers forced the newsmagazine to address it in an editorial. "As voter-intimidation exercises go," said *Newsweek,* "it wasn't much. . . . It seemed like the sort of incident that happens at dozens of polling places every Election Day, then quietly recedes." The controversy over the case was merely being ginned up, claimed *Newsweek,* as "political theater" intended to hurt the Obama administration.[31]

In August 2010, I had J. Christian Adams as a guest on *The Common Sense Club.* It had been almost three months since he had resigned his well-paid position at the Justice Department in order to blow the whistle. I asked him, "How many interviews have you done with mainstream media sources about this case? The *Washington Post,* the *New York Times,* ABC, NBC, CBS, CNN, are they calling?"

"The sound of crickets," Adams said. "Nothing."

"That's unbelievable," I said. "Whistle-blowers are generally kind of the media darling. Here is the Justice Department in a case of voter intimidation that has been thrown out, and you have the Civil Rights Commission investigating. This is a big story. I don't know why you have been ignored by the mainstream media. Well—actually, I do know. It's more evidence of their incredible bias."

"And their incredible irrelevance," Adams agreed. "Talk radio is the beacon of liberty in this country. You can't get your news from the mainstream sources anymore. Everyone knows what's going on as far as the mainstream media. They are driving themselves into irrelevancy—and good riddance."

The broadcast networks and left-wing cable networks, such as CNN and MSNBC, are steadily declining in viewership. Newspaper circulation is plummeting. Where has the audience gone? Two places: Fox News Channel and talk radio.

Newspapers and broadcast/cable news outlets could get their audience back. All they would have to do is start covering the news, cover *all* of the news, cover it *fairly,* cover it without liberal bias, and stop insulting the values and the intelligence of their audience. Instead of trying to control what people think, permit a free flow of information and a free exchange of ideas.

But it will never happen. The old media will continue being the old media until it goes the way of the dinosaurs. And as J. Christian Adams said, good riddance. The day of the "lamestream" media has come and gone. When people truly want to know what is going on in the world, they go to the new media.

And by the way, it's time to stop using taxpayer money to fund entities like the Corporation for Public Broadcasting and the National Endowment for the Arts. Government should not spend taxpayer money to promote one-sided political opinions—and both the CPB and the NEA are bastions of far-left propaganda. The old Soviet Union had its propaganda arms, *Izvestia* and *Pravda,* but the United States of America should not be in the propaganda business. As Thomas Jefferson once said, "To compel a man to furnish contributions of money for the propagation of opinions which he disbelieves and abhors is sinful and tyrannical." [32]

And while we're holding the national media accountable, let's also keep an eye on the local media. Some of the worst examples of media bias and corruption have taken place at the local level. For example, our local media has regularly allowed members of the North Dakota congressional delegation to conduct their own "news" interviews. The senator or congressman will sit in front of a video camera and have one of his own staffers lob softball questions. He'll act as if he's being "grilled" by a reporter when it's actually a friendly interview with rehearsed questions and answers. The congressional office sends the tape to the TV station, and the station airs this piece of puffery as if it were news.

I remember when a National Guardsman was killed in Iraq, Kent

Conrad's office tipped off the newsrooms before the official notification went out. The instant the story officially broke, the TV stations aired videotape of Senator Conrad looking somber and expressing his condolences to the family. While some news organizations were still scrambling for the facts, Conrad was already exploiting a family's loss to make himself look caring and empathetic—even though he had opposed the fallen soldier's mission (he was one of only twenty-three senators to vote against the Iraq War Resolution of 2002). Using the death of a soldier as a means to grab the limelight is shameless—and it's equally shameless that the local news media goes along with this kind of "press release journalism."

When Senator Dorgan held a town hall meeting in Casselton, I did my show from the nearby Governors' Inn and promoted the event to my listeners. Later, as the town hall meeting was under way, I received a text message. Checking, I saw that it was a news alert from the *Fargo Forum* newspaper. It read something like "Voices raised at Dorgan town hall meeting." The next morning, the *Forum* and the *Grand Forks Herald* carried front-page stories about the Dorgan event and remarked about the fact that I had encouraged my listeners to come out to the town hall meeting:

> Buzz before [Senator Dorgan's] appearances prompted Dorgan's office to express concern to the city of Casselton. . . .
>
> Scott Hennen, the Fargo-based, right-wing radio host urged listeners to attend the meetings and make their voices heard. He also told *The Forum* that he encouraged people to "be respectful and ask questions."
>
> In addition, Hennen said media coverage of disruptions at other town hall meetings has been overblown, but that people are engaged in health care reform and other issues "at a level unlike anything I've seen in a long time."[33]

Now, is it just me—or do you detect a note of annoyance and concern over the fact that a "Fargo-based, right-wing radio host" ignited some "buzz" by urging his listeners to "make their voices heard"? I really do get a sense that the writer of this story thinks that encouraging North Dakotans to come out and get involved in their government is a dirty trick I played on Senator Dorgan!

For more than two decades, the North Dakota congressional delegation—Democrats all—have dictated to the local media how they should be covered, and the media eagerly went along with it. How pathetic! But the tea party movement and the new media have changed that. Through bloggers like Rob Port and through interactive talk radio like *The Common Sense Club,* the word has gone out about Dorgan, Conrad, and Pomeroy. The old pols can no longer hide behind their press releases.

That's the power of grassroots interactive media. We are cutting through the old media spin and we are putting the reins of the government back in the hands of the people.

A FULL-SPECTRUM COMMUNICATIONS APPROACH

Remember my friend Mark Pfeifle, who served in the White House as deputy national security adviser to President Bush? Let me tell you how I first met Mark.

In early 1997, I spoke to a communications class at the University of North Dakota, talking about the radio business. After the class, I stayed and talked to some of the students, including a senior who introduced himself as Mark Pfeifle from Wishek. He had grown up around the news business, and in his early twenties he'd even managed Radio KDRQ, a 500-watt station in Wishek. Mark was focused and mature, and I could tell he would accomplish great things in life.

A few weeks later, in April of that year, I was in my studio at radio station KCNN in Grand Forks, broadcasting flood information to my listeners. The Red River was overflowing its dikes and Grand Forks mayor Pat Owens ordered fifty thousand residents to evacuate.

Mark Pfeifle called and volunteered to take the late shift behind the microphone at night while gathering news and information during the day. I gratefully accepted Mark's help, and I credit him with enabling me to keep the information flowing to Grand Forks residents even after the floodwaters surrounded the KCNN studio building. Mark coordinated information from the Federal Emergency

Management Agency, gathered news in the streets, and enabled me to put out timely, accurate information when the floods triggered an electrical fire that destroyed eleven downtown buildings, including the newspaper office.

Our station won an Edward R. Murrow Award for its flood coverage, and Mark's work landed him a job in Washington, D.C. There his star rose quickly. Mark became deputy communications director for the Republican National Committee. After 9/11, he served as communications director at Ground Zero in Manhattan, where he conducted congressional delegations and press pools through the disaster site. Mark was later assigned to the White House, where he engineered the communication strategy for the global War on Terror.

So, in early 2009, as the Red River was rising once again, we needed not only sandbags and muscle power but a brilliant communications strategy to fight the flood. So I called Mark Pfeifle and told him what we needed. He flew home to the heartland, bringing a team of media experts with him, and immediately began applying his world-class communications savvy to the flood fight in the Red River Valley.

By this time, I was in Fargo, hosting *The Common Sense Club* on AM 1100 The Flag. Mark set up a command post at my studio, and together we used the power of the new media—interactive radio and the Internet—to keep North Dakotans and Minnesotans informed about rising floodwaters, the need for volunteers, and where to go to stay high and dry. Mark and our team quickly put the information out via YouTube, Facebook, and Twitter. We called this effort "The Flood Channel," and our team of volunteer announcers—including public service commissioner Kevin Cramer, former governor Ed Schafer, and U.S. Attorney Drew Wrigley—provided around-the-clock flood coverage.

We recruited student volunteers from the journalism school at North Dakota State University. I purchased digital flip cams so the students could file firsthand reports from disaster scenes all across the affected area. The students came back with amazing video, including dramatic scenes of families being rescued from rooftops by helicopters.

Jason Griep of State Farm Insurance picked up the tab to provide food for the volunteers at the dike-building sites. Though McDonald's had closed up shop due to the impending flood, they reopened their kitchens to make burgers and fries to feed the volunteers. Wal-Mart donated tools and waterproof clothing for sandbagging crews, and Verizon and Sprint donated phones for emergency workers. As a result, the costs of the flood fight and the Flood Channel were minimal—and the service to the community was incalculable. The Flood Channel website got hundreds of thousands of hits as people throughout the affected area checked in for up-to-the-minute reports. In the end, the people of Fargo-Moorhead filled and placed *nearly 2 million sandbags,* and the cities were spared the disaster that devastated Grand Forks in 1997.

Because of the Flood Channel effort, I received a *Talkers* magazine National Community Service Award. But I truly owe that award to the genius of my friend Mark Pfeifle and our team, and the heroic efforts of the citizens and business community. Mark and the rest of our Flood Channel leadership team (Jonathan Thompson, Matt Burns, James Davis, Chris Brooks, and my brother Chris Hennen) used the lessons we learned to create a disaster-response system that can be deployed in any disaster, from floods, earthquakes, fires, and tornadoes to terror attacks. We call it MiCAST (Mobile Information Crisis Action Support Team), and you can learn more about it at www.micast .org.

I learned that *The Common Sense Club* should not be just a radio show, but a multimedia experience. That's why I now have a website, a blog, a Twitter account, and a Facebook page. The radio show is merely the hub from which all of these Web-based interactive media spokes radiate.

I also have a couple of tech-savvy web geniuses—Ryan Kelly and Logan Little—who press the buttons, flip the switches, and make all of this wonderful social media stuff happen. I refer to Ryan and Logan as "millennials." They are young guys who understand today's culture and technological wizardry. They've taken on the challenge of turning *The Common Sense Club* into a force for freedom on the World Wide Web—and they are brilliant at what they do.

Also brilliant at what he does: my producer, my younger brother

Chris Hennen. He came to work at the radio station after graduating from high school. He started working the overnight shift, then would hang around to produce my 9 A.M. show, and eventually became my producer. He could be the executive producer at any television network, but he chooses to work with me and keep my show rocking. Chris keeps the radio show linked with Facebook and the rest of the new media.

A whole new world of grassroots media has opened up for us all. You can call local and national talk shows practically any time of the morning, afternoon, or night. You can blog. You can Facebook. You can YouTube. You can podcast. So plunge right in. Take hold of this twenty-first-century megaphone and let your voice be heard.

TELL YOUR STORY

My friend Chuck Tompkins founded Western Agency, Inc., in 1976 to serve the North Dakota farm and small-town insurance market. "I opened my business in a colossally adverse business climate," Chuck told me, referring to the stagflation of the Carter years. In 1979, the Soviet Union invaded Afghanistan, and President Carter imposed an embargo on grain exports to the U.S.S.R. The embargo had little effect on the Soviet Union, but it created a farm crisis in the United States.

"Crop insurance was a major part of my business," Chuck said. "When Jimmy Carter imposed the grain embargo, it collapsed the price of grain. It probably took more than twenty years for grain prices to recover. We saw prices so low that people wouldn't even buy insurance on the grain. Our farm economy was devastated, and so was our farm-related manufacturing. So the whole state was in trouble."

Chuck had to borrow fifty thousand dollars to stay in business. He figured (as many struggling business owners do), "Well, next year I'll make it back, and more." But the next year was just as bad, so he borrowed still more money—and his debt load nearly bankrupted him.

But Chuck learned from his mistakes. "You have to be able to look ahead. I've learned to watch for trouble brewing six months before it happens. If you're losing money, you've got to come up with a way to replace it. It's nice to be able to borrow money when you need it, but it's a lot smarter to increase your income and reduce your overhead if you can."

Today, Chuck Tompkins's Western Agency maintains eight offices around North Dakota and represents more than four thousand insured accounts and more than eight hundred farms. His company is worth an estimated $27 million.

In 2005, Chuck Tompkins published his first book, *The Insurance Wars*—a book of "war stories" about building a small business during tough economic times (www.theinsurancewars.com). It's a brutally honest book in which Chuck recounts his own mistakes along the way to becoming a multimillionaire. He told me he wishes he'd had a book like this when he started out in business. "When I got in trouble," he recalls, "I didn't have any place to go for information. I wrote this book to spare other people from making the mistakes I made."

One of the biggest mistakes people make when starting out in business is that they try to go it alone. "Anyone who goes into business for himself needs mentors," Chuck says. "One of my first mentors was a man named John Simonson. I was about twenty-six at the time, and I really admired this guy. He was an independent businessman who owned a string of convenience stores. He'd come through Minot and we'd have lunch.

"In those days, I did a fair amount of drinking with my buddies. John knew about my drinking, and one day he said, 'Chuck, you're going to have to decide if you want to be a good-time drunk or if you want to actually make something of yourself. You're a smart young man, but you're at kind of a crossroads, whether you know it or not.' Those words affected me deeply. It was the first time someone I really respected told me what I needed to hear. That one conversation changed my life."

Chuck learned to fly while in high school and he earned his pilot's license in 1968. Today he owns a Cessna 340 that he uses for business and pleasure—and to help fly political candidates during the campaign season. "John Hoeven is a good friend of mine," he said. "He was elected to three terms as governor before being elected to the Senate, and I was involved in his campaign. I also got involved in supporting Rick Berg, who was just elected to the House of Representatives.

"I helped a conservative Republican in his race against a Democrat who was a product liability attorney. Can you imagine, a trial attorney for insurance commissioner? Talk about the fox being in charge of the henhouse! We need tort reform in this country.

"I'll give you an example. If you're a farmer and you buy a round baler to make these big round hay bales, half of the price of that equipment is product liability insurance. Are round balers dangerous to operate? Not if you use a little common sense. These machines don't just chase a farmer around his field until they catch him and eat his arm. Farmers get injured when the baler bogs down and the farmer reaches into the running machine and gets his arm caught. Everyone who owns a round baler knows the danger of reaching into the machine, but some people do it anyway—then they sue the manufacturer when they lose an arm.

"We defeated the product liability attorney in the race for insurance commissioner, even though he outspent the Republican four-to-one. North Dakota is a grassroots state, and we ran a grassroots campaign. I talked to many of my friends, including my Democratic friends, and said, 'Fellas, this is not about Democrat or Republican. This is about survival economics.'

"I don't get political in my book. I wrote the book to help people and to share some of the lessons I learned the hard way. This is a tough economy, but I believe tremendous opportunities exist even in tough times. I think you've got to be bullish on America, while making sure you don't become overextended. If you work hard and work smart, the sky's the limit."

Chuck Tompkins has written a book about how to live the American Dream. He says his book isn't political—and it's not. But I'll tell you this: only a commonsense conservative could have written *The Insurance Wars*.

Barack Obama, Harry Reid, and Nancy Pelosi have all written books—but they could never write one like Chuck Tompkins. Not one of them has ever run a business. Not one of them is even qualified to run a business. They don't understand the American Dream. They think the American Dream is "spreading the wealth around"— soaking the rich and redistributing wealth to people who have done nothing to earn it. As Obama said in April 2010, "I mean, I do think at a certain point you've made enough money."[34] Who is Barack Obama to decide at what point you have made enough money?

The American Dream is the idea that if you work hard, play by the rules, and take advantage of the opportunities of this great land, there is no limit to where you can go and what you can achieve. Chuck Tompkins became a wealthy man by working hard and taking risks to build up his company. In the process he has improved the lives of his clients and the people who work for him. And he has written a book telling how he did it. It's a distinctly American book about how to achieve the American Dream.

By simply writing a book that tells his story, Chuck Tompkins is waging a grassroots war against media bias. He is using the printed page to push back against the liberal-progressive idea that there is something wrong with wealth and achievement. Chuck is telling his friends and neighbors: The American Dream is alive and well, even in Obama's America—but you have to fight for it. The American Dream won't be handed to you on a silver platter.

Chuck has told his story. Now, what's *your* story? Do you have a book in you that wants to get out? Do you have a blog or a Facebook page in you? It doesn't have to be about politics. Just tell your story and share your values. Let everyone around you know what it means to be an American.

Tell them what it means to be *free*.

THE COMMONSENSE ACTION AGENDA

Here are some grassroots actions you can take, starting today:

✓ Be a skeptical consumer of the news. Don't believe everything you read and hear from journalists. Many of them have an ax to grind, and the stories they report are routinely slanted. Many journalists today—even at the local level— are not merely reporting the news as it happens. They are trying to control what you know, what you think, and how you vote. Question and fact-check everything you see and hear in the news before you make up your mind.

✓ Hold the news media accountable. When you see slanted stories on the network or local news channels, or in a newspaper or newsmagazine, contact the editors and explain why you found their reporting to be biased and unfair. Call attention to that biased report in your blog or on Facebook. Let the news media know when you catch them in a lie.

✓ Keep the Thomas Paine tradition alive. Become a twenty-first-century pamphleteer like Rob Port. Broadcast your own grassroots conservative values through podcasts, YouTube videos, blogs, and social networking.

✓ In everything you write or say, be scrupulously honest. Provide links to all your sources so that readers can check your facts and see that you have done your homework. Avoid passing along unconfirmed rumors, especially those notoriously unreliable forwarded emails. Your best weapon is the truth.

9

DEFENDING LIFE

ow I miss Tony Snow.

I first became aware of Tony through his columns for *USA Today* in the early 1990s, when I was broadcasting on station KCNN. Tony's writing was pointed and well reasoned. A former speechwriter for George H. W. Bush, he knew his way around the Washington establishment. I booked Tony as a guest on my show, and he turned out to be every bit as witty and brainy on the air as he was in newsprint, and he became a semiregular.

One day, Tony called and said, "Scott, I need a favor. Could you send me the cassettes from all the times I've been on your program?"

"Sure, Tony. What do you need them for?"

"Trust me, I'll tell you someday."

So I sent him the cassettes. A few weeks passed, and I forgot all about it.

Then one day Tony called and said, "Thanks, Scott."

"Thanks for what?"

"For those cassettes. I sent them to Rush Limbaugh's people, and they played them for Rush, and Rush said, 'Okay, he's got it. Let's give the guy a shot.' They're letting me guest-host for Rush once in a while. So thanks for giving me my break in radio."

Tony Snow became Rush Limbaugh's first-choice guest host. Before long, Tony got a call from a fledgling cable news network, the

Fox News Channel, asking him to host a roundtable show called *Fox News Sunday*. Roger Ailes, president of Fox News and a close friend of Rush, had heard Tony and liked his style. Tony's star rose quickly. Soon he had his own show on Fox News Radio, beginning in late 2003.

But there was a shadow over Tony Snow's life. When he was seventeen, Tony had lost his thirty-eight-year-old mother to colon cancer. In February 2005, Tony himself was diagnosed with the disease. The surgeons removed a malignant tumor and he underwent six months of aggressive treatment. The doctors told him his cancer was in remission.

In April 2006, President George W. Bush tapped Tony Snow to replace Scott McClellan as White House press secretary. It was a smart choice. Tony was one of those rare individuals who could argue forcefully without being abrasive. He was tough yet unfailingly *nice*. Press secretaries tend to be bland and colorless; Tony brought charisma to the job. He served only a short time, but he was far and away the best press secretary in White House history. Everyone loved him, even his adversaries.

Eleven months into his White House job, a checkup showed that Tony's cancer had returned—and spread to his liver. He took a leave of absence for another round of treatments. After five weeks, he returned to the White House and received a standing ovation from the press corps.

Choking back tears, Tony talked about his ordeal. "Anybody who does not believe that thoughts and prayers made a difference, they're just wrong. . . . Faith, hope, and love are a big part of it. Not everybody will survive cancer, but on the other hand, you've got to realize you've got the gift of life, so make the most of it." [1]

Tony Snow never complained about having cancer. He fought it with dignity and determination—and with an unshakable faith in God.

"LOSE THE COLON"

I invited Tony Snow to speak to the North Dakota Chamber of Commerce in March 2008. As a favor to me, he flew out and we had lunch at Doolittles Restaurant in Fargo. We talked for a while about the radio business.

"Scott," he said, "I really screwed up when I laid out my radio studio. I didn't know what I was doing, so I built the crappiest studio in the world. I mean, there I am in the Fox News Channel complex, and I've got White House officials and senators and media stars coming through my studio all the time, and it's nothing but a hole in the wall. There's no place for a webcam, because the sight lines are terrible and the lighting is even worse. Let me show you what my dream studio would look like."

He took a pen and a paper napkin and together we sketched a design for the most gorgeous studio you could imagine—with *three* webcams and brilliant, well-placed lighting. (I later built Tony Snow's dream studio here in Fargo—the Tony Snow Memorial Studio.)

I asked Tony about his health. "What do the doctors say? Are you cancer-free?"

"Don't say that, Scott. You're never cancer-free. Once you've had cancer, it may be in remission, but you are never home free."

He told me how he was first diagnosed with the disease. "I was diagnosed with ulcerative colitis years ago," he said. "The doctors said it was 'precancerous' and they were watching the situation. I had a colonoscopy every year. But between one colonoscopy and the next, the cancer developed and spread pretty aggressively. The doctors never imagined it would happen that fast."

I got a cold chill. "I've got ulcerative colitis myself," I said. "It was diagnosed in 1997. Tony, if there was anything you could've done differently, what would it be?"

"Scott, if you ever see a warning sign, if they ever tell you they find a 'precancerous' lesion, lose the colon. Your colon doesn't matter. All that matters is that you love your wife, you love your kids, and they need to keep you around."

Four months later, in the early hours of July 12, 2008, Tony passed away at Georgetown University Hospital in Washington, D.C. He left behind the family he loved so much—his wife, Jill, and three children, Kendall, Robbie, and Kristi.

Tony's funeral was held at the beautiful Basilica of the National

Shrine of the Immaculate Conception in Washington, D.C. I attended with my friend and colleague Ellen Ratner. Rush Limbaugh was there, and we had a few moments to trade stories of our friend Tony Snow—including the story of how Tony landed his guest-hosting gig on Rush's show.

The memorial service was unforgettable, with George and Laura Bush attending, along with many other luminaries who had worked with Tony over the years—Roger Ailes, Charles Krauthammer, Byron York, Karl Rove, and many more. Brit Hume invited Ellen and me to sit in the Fox News section.

President Bush delivered a beautiful eulogy that sometimes brought tears to our eyes—and sometimes laughter. He reminded us of the time a reporter asked a question and Tony refused to answer it. When the reporter pressed him and asked, "Are you just going to evade the question?" Tony grinned and replied, "No, I'm going to laugh at it."

The president reminded us of a motto Tony Snow often gave during his heroic battle with cancer—"God doesn't promise tomorrow, but He does promise eternity." And he added, "Tony Snow has left the city of Washington for the City of God. May he find eternal rest in the arms of his Savior." Amen to that.

Tony Snow gave me some of the best advice I could ever receive. In fact, he may well have saved my life. In the fall of 2010, I went to the Mayo Clinic for a two-day consultation with a specialist. The doctors there are very thorough as they talk to you and listen to you. They carefully examined my history with ulcerative colitis, which first flared up in July 1997, shortly after the big flood in Grand Forks. I asked my doctor, "Was it stress-related? Is this my little gift from the flood?"

"We don't know," he replied. "We suspect that it may have to do with the use of antibiotics and not enough of the right kind of bacteria in your system, but we can't say for sure."

Bottom line, it's a condition many people have, and it's usually not a big deal—unless it erupts into cancer. I'd had a colonoscopy performed in Fargo in October 2009, and my doctors didn't see any cause for concern. In July, the doctors at the Mayo Clinic asked to see the results of that colonoscopy—and they saw what they suspected were precancerous cells. So they ordered another colonoscopy, which was performed at Mayo in August 2010. This time they were sure they detected precancerous cells. It wasn't cancer and might never become cancer—but the cells had an *increased potential* to become malignant.

"How long," I asked, "does it take for these cells to go from precancerous to cancerous?"

"We think it could be from two years to five years—if they become cancerous at all. But we don't know—and everybody is different."

I said, "Two colonoscopies eight months apart, and you've found precancerous cells—what would you do if you were me?"

"You were thinking of having the colon out, right?"

"Yes."

"Well, with each passing day, it becomes less of a choice and more of a necessity."

The doctors were telling me the same thing Tony Snow said four months before he passed away: lose the colon.

So I made a life-altering decision.

The process would entail three surgeries, each of which would put me out of commission and off the air for a week or more. I asked if I could wait until after the midterm elections on November 2. The doctors agreed, and we scheduled the first procedure for December 2010.

So, here I am, minus most of my colon, but with all my intestinal fortitude still intact. I still have the things that matter most. I'm still on the right side of the grass. And that means that I can still say that I'm the husband of Maria and the father of Alex, Hannah, and Haley. As a bonus, I can still talk to newsmakers and attend tea parties and do my level best to advance the conservative cause.

Life is what really matters.

SARAH AND BRISTOL, TRIG AND TRIPP

In October 2010, Bristol Palin, the eldest daughter of Todd and Sarah Palin, came to Fargo to speak at a fund-raiser for the Perry Center, a Christian pro-life ministry that offers housing, mentoring, and counseling for unmarried women with unplanned pregnancies. Bristol had just completed her third week on the top-rated ABC television series *Dancing with the Stars,* and I interviewed her for a live webcast on October 7.

It had been a hectic week for Bristol. She and her dance partner Mark Ballas had gotten some of their lowest judging scores and there was no way to know at that point that they would ultimately make it to the final week for a glittering third-place finish. In spite of all the pressure of performing every week on live TV, Bristol came across as poised, confident, and unspoiled. I had interviewed her parents a number of times, and Bristol has that same air of transparent honesty, an attitude that says, "Here I am, take it or leave it. I have nothing to hide, nothing to prove."

I asked her if she enjoyed a break from the hubbub of Hollywood and *Dancing with the Stars*. "Yeah," she said. "It's nice to be in North Dakota again. . . . I drove down with my folks in 2005 and we surprised my brother, who was at a hockey camp at the University of North Dakota."

I asked her how she became a spokesperson for abstinence. "I had talked about it with family and friends for a few months," she said, "and I decided I want to spread my message and share my testimony. . . . I'm one of the most qualified people to talk about abstinence. I live as a single mom. Every day of my life, I've had to sacrifice things for my son because I did have premarital sex. I feel I'm helping others out there, and it's something that I'm very passionate about. . . .

"I am blessed with a wonderful baby boy, but my life would have been a lot different if I'd made different decisions. My son Tripp was born under less-than-ideal circumstances. For me, sharing my message and telling girls that this isn't glamorous, I think it's a good message to have. . . . There are people in places like the Perry Center who are there to help young girls with the decisions they're going to have to make."

I asked Bristol about her efforts to improve her relationship with her son's father, Levi Johnston. "I tried to work it out for my son's benefit," she said. "It didn't work. I'm going to continue to be a single mom for Tripp, and I'm waiting for the right person to come into Tripp's life as a father figure." Of Sarah and Todd, she said, "My parents are awesome. They are a huge support system to me and I'm thankful to have them. They are guiding me constantly every day. . . . I'm so proud of my mom. I think she's awesome and she's doing wonderful things for our country."

"As a fan of your mom's," I said, "it annoys me when people say she's not qualified to be president. She's been a mayor, a governor, a business owner, and chairperson of the Alaska Oil and Gas Conservation Commission."

"I know she's qualified to do the job," Bristol said. "She knows what's right. She has common sense. She's the smartest woman I know—and she's a hoot, she's hilarious."

I asked Bristol about wild rumors that fly in the media about her family. "It rolls off my back," Bristol said. "Same as my mom. We all have very tough skin. It's an Alaska thing, for sure."

I said, "When I think about the pro-life message, and your brother Trig, who has Down syndrome, yet he's so special, so incredible, it breaks my heart when I hear the stories of Down syndrome babies who are aborted."

"It definitely breaks my heart," Bristol said. "I think nine out of ten babies with Down syndrome are aborted. If people only knew what a great blessing Trig is, and how much joy he brings to our lives, those babies would not be aborted. They are a blessing. And I couldn't ask for a better brother than Trig.

"My son Tripp is just a rowdy one-and-a-half-year-old. He'll be two in December. He's learning how to talk and he's running around a million miles an hour. He's a little ham, and he loves cameras and attention. . . . I hope he'll have a passion for hockey like my family does.

"I'm looking forward to going over to the Perry Center and meeting some of the girls, hearing their stories. People always ask me how do I do it without having a supportive spouse. It's a juggling act, and I'm blessed to have a supportive family system. So I just let the women know that the people at the Perry Center are there to give them the help they need. Yeah, it's going to be hard, and you're not going to sleep through the night ever again, but babies are a blessing."

I think one of the reasons Bristol and her famous mom stir up so much hostility among liberal-progressives is that they exemplify what it means to *choose life*. Sarah Palin chose life for her son Trig, a Down syndrome baby—the sort of child who is overwhelmingly targeted for abortion. And Bristol Palin chose life for her son Tripp, even though she is unmarried and faces special challenges because of that choice. These two courageous women are a living contradiction of the anti-life "choice" of abortion. Sarah and Bristol, Trig and Tripp, prove that the only moral choice is *life*.

40 DAYS FOR LIFE

There is only one abortion clinic in all of North Dakota—the mis-named "Red River Women's Clinic" in Fargo (I prefer to call it what it is—the Red River Abortion Mill). Every week, that one facility aborts the equivalent of a kindergarten class full of unborn children— about twenty-five unborn babies every week. I'm committed to seeing that facility close its doors. Because we're in the rare position of hav-ing just one abortion mill for the entire state, North Dakota could be the first domino to fall, triggering a pro-life chain reaction in other states.

I am proudly pro-life. Although it's important that we change the laws and roll back abortion-on-demand, I've always been more focused on changing hearts than changing laws. I want to persuade people that unborn life is *human* life that deserves protection. At the same time, I believe in supporting women with unplanned pregnan-cies, which is why I have endorsed great causes like the Perry Center, the FirstChoice Clinic in Fargo, and Saint Gianna's Maternity Home in Warsaw, North Dakota.

Colleen Samson of Park River, North Dakota, is a grassroots hero who defends unborn lives as head of the North Dakota organizing committee of the 40 Days for Life campaign. "It's a national effort," she explains. "We unite with eighty cities in more than thirty states, praying and fasting, holding peaceful prayer vigils, and reaching out to the community. We blanketed homes in the Fargo area with more than forty thousand flyers. We filled forty days and forty nights with nonstop prayer. As a result, three unborn lives were confirmed saved in Fargo, and there were two weeks in which not a single surgical abortion took place at the only abortion facility in North Dakota.

"Across the nation, scores of babies are being saved from abortion, and their moms and dads have been freed from the pain and guilt of abortion. We're seeing abortion facility workers leave the death industry and go to different jobs."

"Some people call this effort a 'protest,'" I said, "but it's not a protest at all, is it? The 40 Days for Life campaign is really a quiet movement of prayer for an end to abortion. You're not waiting for the politicians or the courts to end abortion. You are just saying, 'Let's put the power of prayer to work to end abortion in North Dakota.' It's a round-the-clock vigil at the one and only abortion facility in this region."

"People sign up for two-hour time slots to come to the abortion facility and pray," Colleen replied. "No protests, just prayer. There is one man from Dickinson, in the western part of the state, and he drives straight through the night so he can stand at the facility and pray for two hours—then he gets in his car and drives to work. There's no limit to what people will do when they know that these abortions are taking place."

I said, "We sometimes get so focused on the political differences we have with people over abortion that we forget to pray for them. We can pray for President Obama to have a change of heart. We can pray that abortion workers will experience a conversion of heart. We can pray that these innocent lives would be rescued. Little by little, our prayers make a difference—and lives are saved."

"It's true," Colleen said. "Again and again, women have come out of the abortion facility where our volunteers were praying, and they've said, 'I just couldn't do it. I saw you praying out here and I just couldn't go through it.'

"I heard about a mother and daughter in another state who were praying at an abortion facility. They were not able to get many volunteers to help them, so this mom and daughter were praying long hours at the abortion facility, just themselves. And they were getting discouraged. But then they received a letter from a Catholic priest who said, 'A baby has been brought to the church to be baptized, and the mother said it's because two women were on the sidewalk at the abortion facility, praying hour after hour.'

"I heard a woman tell her story about the day she was scheduled to have an abortion. She had the appointment, but she prayed that if God didn't want her to have the abortion that He would intervene. On her way to the abortion facility, her car broke down—so she didn't have the abortion. She kept the baby. It was an answer to her prayer and the prayers of all the people keeping vigil at the facility. And she came and joined our prayer vigil, and she brought her little boy who is almost a year old. She was weeping because her son brought her such joy, yet she had come close to aborting him.

"This woman is a living example of the power of prayer. She prays that everyone going inside will know we are praying for them, we love them, and we love the people who work inside that place. We're kind to them, we don't have conflicts with the women or the staff members. We know that these people are doing what they think is important, but we are praying for their hearts to be changed."

It's easy for me to talk into a microphone and tell people what I think about abortion. But it takes commitment, love, and faith to stand for two hours and simply pray. Yet prayer is a powerful form of grassroots activism. It's an action we can all take to make a huge difference for life.

One of the most dramatic success stories from the 40 Days for Life campaign took place in Bryan, Texas. In early October 2009, the director of Bryan's Planned Parenthood clinic, Abby Johnson, was preparing to help an abortionist perform an ultrasound-guided procedure. Johnson had worked at the clinic for eight years, and had been director for two years. The economic downturn had left Planned Parenthood cash-strapped, so the state headquarters was pressuring clinics to increase the number of abortions they performed. Abortions, performed on a cash-only basis, were a major revenue source for Planned Parenthood.

When Johnson joined Planned Parenthood, she thought that its goal was to reduce the demand for abortion through education and family planning. It was disillusioning to discover that the organization now wanted her to *increase* the number of abortions performed in Bryan. To do that, she had to skirt state regulations and offer "medication abortions" (using the drug RU-486) when no physician was on duty.

I spoke with Abby Johnson a few weeks after these events, and she explained what happened next. "For an ultrasound-guided abortion, someone has to actually hold the ultrasound probe on the woman's abdomen during the procedure. So I held the probe while the doctor inserted the cannula [suction tube]. Even though I had been at this facility for eight years, I had never actually seen an ultrasound procedure before, because they are not commonly done.

"It was a thirteen-week pregnancy. The mother was sedated, so she didn't know what was happening. I looked up at the screen and saw the full profile of the baby, a side view of the baby's body from the head to the feet. I saw the cannula go into the uterus and I saw the baby moving, actually fighting for its life. My heart was racing. I was thinking, 'Make it stop.' I couldn't believe what I was watching. I saw the baby just crumple—and that was it. I had never seen that done before. I had my hand on this woman's belly and I thought, 'There was life in there a few seconds ago. Now there's not. And I was a part of that.'

"After it was over, I kept thinking about my three-year-old daughter. I remembered when I was pregnant and I got to see the ultrasound and view my daughter for the first time. I was so happy and excited about it. But I had just seen a doctor destroy a life on an ultrasound screen. I asked myself, 'What am I doing?'

"That night, I told my husband what had happened. I was very upset, and I told him I didn't want to go back. But we were dependent on two incomes. I knew I had two weeks before the next surgical abortions were scheduled, so I told my husband, 'I've got two weeks to find another job.'

"I started looking for work, and the two weeks went by. I was sitting in my office with the door closed, crying. We were doing medication abortion procedures that day, and women were coming in and out of the clinic with their bags of RU-486 pills. I had no one to turn to, because my friends were affiliated with the pro-choice movement. I knew they wouldn't understand what was going on in my heart.

"I looked outside and noticed two people praying. I felt like God was telling me to go to them. I decided, even if I didn't have another job waiting for me, I couldn't do this anymore. So I resigned on the spot. Planned Parenthood offered me more money to stay, but it wasn't about money. It was about my change of heart."

Abby Johnson walked away from the abortion industry, and she's now a grassroots pro-life activist. In fact, she tells her story in a powerful book called *Unplanned*.

When I tell people I believe we can change hearts and redeem lives through prayer alone, I am often called a Pollyanna. People say, "Come on, Scott, the people who work in those abortion mills are so steeped in their ideology that they will never change."

But tell that to Abby Johnson.

Dr. Haywood Robinson of College Station, Texas, is another changed person, who gave up his lucrative practice, switched sides, and is now a pro-life activist. I had Dr. Robinson on *The Common Sense Club,* and he told me his story.

"I'm from South Central Los Angeles," he said, "and I trained and did residency in family practice at Martin Luther King Hospital in South Central L.A. I was trained to do abortions along with my training in family practice, obstetrics, and gynecology. But as you know, the Hippocratic Oath, which physicians are sworn to uphold, forbids the performing of abortions. Doctors are not to cause any harm. So there is a conflict between the oath and how medicine is actually practiced. I got involved in making money by moonlighting and performing abortions. It's a lucrative cash business.

"When you're first exposed to the abortion procedure, you begin that insidious process of becoming desensitized, and of dehumanizing the human being inside the womb. Once that process starts, you begin to think of abortion as a service you are performing. You rationalize and imagine that abortion is actually a good thing."

I asked Dr. Robinson, "When you looked at an ultrasound, did you ever have second thoughts?"

"Initially, I did," he replied. "But when you're in the company of older attending physicians, your instructors and your professors who are walking you through your training, you don't want to rock the boat. You tell yourself, 'Well, if Professor So-and-so is doing this, if everybody else is doing it, then I'm going to do it, too.' Now, there were a few people in our training program who said, 'No, I'm not going to kill those babies.' Because that's exactly what we were doing.

"It should tell us something that abortion is the only medical procedure in which a successful operation ends in the death of one of the patients. All other medical procedures improve health and save lives. Abortion is the only procedure that takes life. I knew all this, but unfortunately, none of the science I knew was enough to stop me, because my humanity was seared and I was desensitized.

"Those who work within the walls of those abortuaries—from the receptionist to the nurses to the nurse practitioners to the physicians—should stop and think: the blood of those preborn children is on your hands. You can't say, 'I'm not responsible, I'm just the receptionist.' When you make an appointment for a young woman to get an abortion, you play a role in that abortion procedure.

"I remember times when I would look at a woman who had come for an abortion, and I could tell she wasn't sure about the decision she had made. She was being pressured into the abortion by a parent or a boyfriend. If just one person—a nurse, a doctor, someone—had said, 'You don't have to do this,' it would have given her the courage to stop the process.

"Abortion is a business. It's big money. From the moment a young woman enters the abortion facility, she's surrounded by people who tell her, 'Don't worry, it won't hurt.' And some clinics give them sedation so they are not alert and cannot undo the decision they've made. You do the quick sell, you keep the process moving, because if you slow down the process at all, people have second thoughts. Abortion clinics make a lot of money, and the money drives the process."

"So," I said, "what was the epiphany for you? What changed your heart?"

"I had a Damascus Road experience," Dr. Robinson said. "When I became a Christian, one of the first things I realized was that I could no longer be involved in performing abortions. Before that, I'd been in a state of denial, thinking I was helping a woman in distress by killing the baby in her womb. I'd been thinking, 'This poor woman can't support her baby. The baby will be just another welfare baby, so look what I can do to help this mother and help society. And it really won't hurt the baby because it's too small to know anything or feel anything.'

"You do all of these mental rationalizations to silence your conscience. But when you have a profound conversion experience, God gives you a sense of conviction. That's what happened with me—but you don't even have to go through a conversion experience to see this truth. If you are intellectually honest, you can reason it out from a scientific and philosophical point of view. Scientifically, there's no question that life begins at conception. And philosophically, we can go to the Declaration of Independence, which says that every human being is endowed by the Creator with certain unalienable rights, including the right to life.

"The 40 Days for Life campaign is making a huge difference. Prayer is powerful. Babies are being saved. Hearts can change. I'm living proof."

My friend David Bereit, the founder and national director of 40 Days for Life, agrees. He told me about the changes he saw as a result of the nationwide campaign. In Greenland, New Hampshire, an abortion facility had to lay off employees because of a steep drop in business. A 40 Days for Life team holding vigil at an abortion clinic in Granite City, Illinois, was surprised when a nurse walked out of the clinic and hugged a woman from the team. "Thank you for praying for me," the nurse said. "This is my last day! I'm going off to do what real nurses should be doing." In Washington, D.C., volunteers prayed for a young couple who walked into a Planned Parenthood facility. An hour later, the couple emerged and said, "We changed our minds."

I had David Bereit on *The Common Sense Club* shortly before passage of the Obamacare bill. "The most recent polls show that seventy-one percent of Americans adamantly oppose taxpayer-funded abortions," he said. "But liberal legislators are trying to force you to pay for abortions through so-called health care reform. Does health care need reform? Certainly improvements need to be made. But is this a reason for the abortion industry to come in and hijack the process and make billions of dollars at taxpayer expense? Absolutely not.

"In July of 2008, candidate Obama spoke before the Planned Parenthood Action Fund, the lobbying arm of the largest abortion chain in the country, and he promised that his first act as president would be to pass the Freedom of Choice Act, a radical measure that would overturn every restriction on abortion and force taxpayer funding of abortion. This legislation was so extreme that, after Obama was elected, the abortion industry advised him, 'Don't go after this. It's so radical that it will be defeated and will hurt our industry.'

"So they came up with a secret document that was given to the administration with their plan for the abortion industry in his first one hundred days. Instead of implementing the Freedom of Choice Act as one sweeping piece of legislation, they placed its key provisions into the health care reform initiative. Obamacare is one of the cornerstones of what that Freedom of Choice Act would have represented—a massive taxpayer-subsidized abortion industry bailout.

"Under this takeover of one-sixth of our nation's economy, virtually every American would be forced into a health plan that would mandate abortion coverage. If abortion is not explicitly excluded from any health care reform proposal, abortion will be included by default."

And, of course, David Bereit was proven correct, as that's exactly what happened with the passage of Obamacare.

RATIONED HEALTH CARE

Dick Cheney has no pulse.

In July 2010, he underwent surgery to implant an electronic pump called a ventricular assist device, or VAD. The device is about the size of a flashlight battery and it pushes blood continuously instead of mimicking the *ka-thump ka-thump* of a beating heart. In fact, he has to wear a medical alert bracelet so that if he is ever treated by emergency room doctors, they will know it's *normal* for him to have no pulse.

Dick Cheney has suffered five heart attacks over the years, the first one when he was thirty-seven. These heart attacks have weakened his heart to the point where he is considered to be in a state of heart failure and a candidate for transplant. His VAD, a HeartMate II device, is not a cure for heart failure. It helps his heart, but does not replace it.

I have a photo in my office of Dick Cheney, former North Dakota governor Ed Schafer and his wife, Nancy, and me, grinning like a goofball. I keep that photo posted where I can see it, because it reminds me to pray for Dick Cheney. One day, shortly after I heard he was admitted to the Inova Fairfax Hospital in Virginia, I looked at that photo and just had an inkling that something was wrong. I believe that the Good Lord sometimes taps you on the shoulder and says, "You'd better pray a little harder today. You'd better pick up the phone or write an email today." And when He taps you, you'd better do something about it.

So I emailed Dick's daughter, Liz (who is an expert on national defense and a frequent guest on my show), and I asked about her dad. She emailed back, and though she didn't reveal any details, she said that my inkling was correct. Her dad was very ill—and she'd be grateful if my listeners and I would pray for him.

The next day, I asked my listeners to keep Vice President Cheney in their thoughts and prayers. I put the word out to the prayer chain of my church. I later learned that we came very close to losing this great man, that he was on his deathbed, and that installing a VAD was a sign of just how weakened his heart had become.

So it was a joyous day when I heard that Dick Cheney was released from the hospital. He came out looking gaunt, but smiling and waving.

I immediately overnighted a box of Chippers from Carol Widman's Candy Company. In the past, I always got handwritten thank-you notes from Dick when I sent him those world-famous chocolate-dipped potato chips, so I figured that if he needed any extra get-well incentive, Chippers would do the trick. I wrote on the card that all of us in the heartland were praying for him, and I invited him to bring Karl Rove out to North Dakota for some pheasant hunting.

Now, I'm told that the cost of a ventricular assist device for one year (including the device, hospitalization, and professional fees) is more than $222,000.[2] I would guess that Dick Cheney can probably afford his VAD. And if you have a reasonably good private health care plan, this lifesaving device will probably be covered.

But we have to ask ourselves: How many people will receive this kind of expensive lifesaving treatment under the Obamacare plan? Will government-controlled health care permit such expensive procedures to be offered patients with so-called end stage heart failure— or will the authorities determine that the cost outweighs the benefit? I believe it won't be long before bureaucrats say to patients, "We're sorry, but we don't think you're a candidate for a VAD. We're offering you end-of-life counseling instead."

Congressman Tom Price of the 6th District of Georgia is a citizen legislator and a physician. He's the kind of legislator the founding fathers envisioned when they wrote the Constitution—not a professional ruling-class politician, but a grassroots patriot with real-world experience. A surgeon, he ran an orthopedic clinic in Atlanta for twenty years and also served as a professor of orthopedic surgery at Emory University. He brings a wealth of insight to the health care debate that few other legislators can match. I had Tom Price as a guest on my show during the health care debate.

"The health care bill," he said, "will destroy five million jobs in this nation, and that's from the president's own chairman of the Council of Economic Advisers. This is just moving in the wrong direction. The American people know it. The final question is whether the Democrats, like Earl Pomeroy, will vote with their constituents or vote with their leadership."

I said, "Earl Pomeroy has already told us how he is going to vote." (And Pomeroy was later defeated because of his support for Obamacare.)

"Why would he represent his leadership instead of his constituents?" Tom said. "It's beyond me. . . . The wonderful folks of our greatest generation are going to be hurt by Obamacare because it slashes five hundred billion dollars from Medicare services. The only way to get those so-called savings is by rationing health care."

And, of course, when you ration health care, people die.

THE DEATH PANELS ARE HERE

Health care rationing was on Sarah Palin's mind when she coined the term *death panel*. On August 7, 2009, she wrote on her Facebook page:

> The Democrats promise that a government health care system will reduce the cost of health care, but as the economist Thomas Sowell has pointed out, government health care will not reduce the cost; it will simply refuse to pay the cost. And who will suffer the most when they ration care? The sick, the elderly, and the disabled, of course. The America I know and love is not one in which my parents or my baby with Down Syndrome will have to stand in front of Obama's "death panel" so his bureaucrats can decide, based on a subjective judgment of their "level of productivity in society," whether they are worthy of health care. Such a system is downright evil.[3]

Sarah Palin was bitterly criticized for that posting—and for the term *death panel*. The website PolitiFact awarded her its 2009 "Lie of the Year" designation. On August 13, Nobel-winning economist Paul Krugman wrote in the *New York Times:*

> Right now, the charge that's gaining the most traction is the claim that health care reform will create "death panels" (in Sarah Palin's words) that will shuffle the elderly and others off to an early grave. It's a complete fabrication, of course. The provision requiring that Medicare pay for voluntary end-of-life counseling was introduced by Senator Johnny Isakson, Republican—yes, Republican—of Georgia, who says that it's "nuts" to claim that it has anything to do with euthanasia. . . .
>
> Yet the smear continues to spread.[4]

The same day, another *New York Times* article derided the "stubborn yet false rumor that President Obama's health care proposals would create government-sponsored 'death panels' to decide which patients were worthy of living." The *Times* added, "There is nothing in any of the legislative proposals that would call for the creation of death panels or any other governmental body that would cut off care for the critically ill as a cost-cutting measure."[5]

But as Joseph Ashby of AmericanThinker.com points out, the health care bill does not need to authorize the creation of "death panels." In fact, Ashby says, death panels already exist. They were created not by the Obamacare bill, but by—are you ready for this?—the American Recovery and Reinvestment Act, otherwise known as the stimulus bill. The death panel provision in the stimulus bill is called the Federal Coordinating Council for Comparative Effectiveness Research, and it was the brainchild of former senator Tom Daschle.[6]

More than a year before Obamacare was passed, conservative health care activist Betsy McCaughey (a frequent guest on my show) warned that the stimulus bill contained disguised provisions that would impact the health of every American:

> One new bureaucracy . . . will monitor treatments to make sure your doctor is doing what the federal government deems appropriate and cost effective. . . . These provisions in the stimulus bill are virtually identical to what Daschle prescribed in his 2008 book, *Critical: What We Can Do About the Health-Care Crisis.* . . .
>
> The goal, Daschle's book explained, is to slow the development and use of new medications and technologies because they are driving up costs. He praises Europeans for being more willing to accept "hopeless diagnoses" and "forgo experimental treatments," and he chastises Americans for expecting too much from the health-care system. . . .
>
> The stimulus bill would . . . apply a cost-effectiveness standard set by the Federal Council . . . [which is] modeled after a U.K. board discussed in Daschle's book. This board approves or rejects treatments using a formula that divides the cost of the treatment by the number of years the patient is likely to benefit. Treatments for younger patients are more often approved than treatments for diseases that affect the elderly, such as osteoporosis. . . . If the Obama administration's economic stimulus bill passes the Senate in its current form, seniors in the U.S. will face similar rationing.[7]

Betsy McCaughey is right. The stimulus bill did set up the Federal Coordinating Council for Comparative Effectiveness Research, funding it to the tune of $1.1 billion. The council's special adviser for health policy is Dr. Ezekiel J. Emanuel,[8] brother of former Obama White House chief of staff Rahm Emanuel, leading architect of Obamacare, and a proponent of health care rationing. McCaughey notes that Dr. Emanuel "has written extensively about who should get medical care, who should decide, and whose life is worth saving. Dr. Emanuel is part of a school of thought that redefines a physician's duty, insisting that it includes working for the greater good of society instead of focusing only on a patient's needs."[9]

This is your death panel. It was established more than a year before passage of Obamacare. It was carefully constructed in stages, and construction began within days of Barack Obama's inauguration.

Another White House player who will have a major role in implementing the death panel functions of Obamacare is Barack Obama's regulatory czar Cass Sunstein, a legal scholar who taught at the University of Chicago Law School for nearly three decades (Barack Obama also taught there, from 1992 to 2004). Sunstein has written extensively about a concept called "quality-adjusted life years," or QALYs. As Joseph Ashby explains, QALYs are statistical formulas used to determine "whether a person's life is worth living." If, based on a statistical evaluation, "the government decides the life is not worth living, it is the individual's duty to die to free up welfare payments for the young and productive."[10]

President Obama himself has talked in cold statistical terms about the value of human life. During a televised White House health care town hall broadcast by ABC News, a woman named Jane Sturm told President Obama about her mother who, at age one hundred, was told by a doctor that she was too old to have a pacemaker implanted. The woman got a second opinion—and she got her pacemaker. Five years later, at age 105, the woman was still living. Ms. Sturm's point was that no one should be told, "You're too old for a lifesaving procedure. It's time for you to die."

Yet President Obama seemed to miss the point. "Look," he replied, "the first thing for all of us to understand is that we actually have some choices to make about how we want to deal with our own end-of-life care. . . . At least we can let doctors know and your mom know that, you know what? Maybe this isn't going to help. Maybe you're better off not having the surgery, but taking the painkiller."[11] In other words, these decisions are better left in the hands of a government death panel.

Some might say, "Don't HMOs already ration health care? What difference does it make if my health care is rationed by an HMO or by an Obamacare death panel?" Well, it makes a big difference.

HMOs do practice cost containment. They have gatekeeper doctors (internists and general practitioners) who control access to specialists. They have formularies of approved drugs; if you want a drug that is not on the formulary, you can still get it, though your copay might be very high. But HMOs do provide expensive lifesaving procedures like heart transplants and VADs—and HMOs cannot withhold lifesaving treatment and let a patient die.

Barack Obama has already told us that he is willing to give people painkillers and end-of-life counseling instead of lifesaving treatment—and he's got the legislation to prove it. It's in the Obamacare bill and the stimulus bill. The death panels are here.

Britain's health care system, which is one of the models for Obamacare, gives us a glimpse into how Obamacare death panels would work. Doctors told British cancer patient Linda O'Boyle that her chances of surviving colorectal cancer would be increased by a drug called cetuximab. Unfortunately for Linda, cetuximab was not on the formulary of Britain's health care rationing board, the National Institute for Health and Clinical Excellence (ironically called NICE). The British death panel did not consider cetuximab to be cost-effective and would not pay for it.

So Linda spent her own life savings to buy the drug. Unfortunately, this violates rules established by Britain's National Health Service. When the government found out she had gone outside the NHS system to buy cetuximab at her own expense, the bureaucrats cut off her treatment. Within a few months, Linda O'Boyle was dead—by death panel decree.[12]

According to socialized medicine proponent Peter Singer of

Princeton, the British government has set a price equal to about forty-nine thousand U.S. dollars as the maximum it will pay to extend a patient's life for one year. If your treatment exceeds that cost, then (as President Obama put it) you're better off taking the painkiller. That's why Great Britain has one of the lowest cancer-survival rates among Western countries, roughly 40 to 48 percent for men and 48 to 54 percent for women.[13]

President Obama has signaled his death panel intentions with his recess appointment of Dr. Donald Berwick as administrator of the Centers for Medicare & Medicaid Services. Berwick has said, "I am romantic about the [British] National Health Service; I love it." And he has also said, "The decision is not whether or not we will ration care—the decision is whether we will ration with our eyes open."

Those who deny that Obamacare means death panels have their eyes closed to reality.

DO WE HAVE THE STEEL TO REPEAL?

As a result of the tea party movement, people who were once politically apathetic have turned into engaged, involved activists. I remember one lady who questioned Senator Dorgan at a town hall in Casselton. She asked him about a provision in Obamacare that would require everyone to buy health insurance through so-called exchanges. Dorgan tried to brush off her comments, saying that's not what the bill actually said. So the woman reached into her bag and withdrew a printout of the legislation, which she had found on a federal website. She had it highlighted and she read it to him verbatim.

In one town hall meeting after another, Senators Conrad and Dorgan were challenged by people who had actually read the Obamacare bill—and who brought copies of the bill with them. The Internet has become a vital tool for grassroots activists, because it is now a simple matter to Google and print out any piece of legislation. The Internet also makes it easy to get crowds of people to show up for town hall meetings.

As blogger Rob Port recalls, "Our senators were shocked by the turnout. Most of these meetings weren't heavily publicized in advance. They were held in remote locations in the middle of workdays.

Yet these events were all standing room only. One reason so many people showed up was because I made an online map of the locations and put it on my website. That map got seventy-two thousand views."

The interactive medium of radio has been another big factor in bringing people out. The day of the Dorgan meeting in Casselton, I broadcast from the Governors' Inn and encouraged my listeners to attend. As a result, the meeting was packed to the rafters. When Senator Dorgan saw a standing-room-only crowd (including people with signs) at what was supposed to be a quiet little meeting, he turned and literally gave me a death stare.

Senator Dorgan was accustomed to controlling the news, controlling perceptions, and controlling events. Suddenly events were out of his control. The grassroots community was now in power.

After losing his bid for reelection in November 2010, Senator Dorgan told reporters that Rush Limbaugh and Scott Hennen were responsible for his defeat. I disagree. His *votes* brought about his defeat. All Rush and I did was publicize his voting record.

A few weeks before the White House health care summit in February 2010, my seven-year-old daughter Haley and I were at Wal-Mart, running an errand for my wife, Maria. We were in one of the aisles, loading items in the cart, when my cell phone rang. I checked my phone and saw that it was Congresswoman Michele Bachmann.

I turned to Haley and said, "Honey, I've got an important phone call, and I'm only going to be a few minutes. You can pick out one thing you want—just one. You've got a ten-dollar budget, okay?"

"Okay, Dad."

So I took the call and talked to Michele, pacing the aisles at Wal-Mart and watching Haley load up the shopping cart. While Haley emptied the shelves, Congresswoman Bachmann and I talked about the health care debate. I'm paraphrasing, but this is the gist of what she told me:

"Scott, this health care summit at Blair House [the official guesthouse of the president, across Pennsylvania Avenue from the White House] is going to be disastrous for our side. The Democrats have already decided they're going to pass the original legislation without any input from conservative Republicans. This summit is just a made-for-TV public relations stunt. Barack Obama wants to make a show of seeking bipartisan ideas, but you and I both know there isn't a single conservative, free market idea in the bill. We were shut out of the debate.

"The American people have rejected Obamacare in poll after poll. We are winning the public relations battle. If we boycott the summit, we can make the case that *both* parties need to start from scratch and work together in the best interests of the people. But if we walk into that summit, we lose our leverage. Barack Obama will say he has 'reached out' to Republicans, he has 'listened' and 'incorporated' Republican ideas into the bill—and then he'll jam the original bill through the Congress, which has been their intent all along. By going into that summit, the Republican leadership will *guarantee* passage of Obamacare. The Republicans will actually be helping the Democrats pass Obamacare."

That's a short summary of a long conversation. When I finally got off the phone and checked the time, I discovered I'd been talking to Michele for almost two hours. And I had promised Haley I'd be only a few minutes! I looked down and there was my seven-year-old looking up at me. "Dad," she said, "you were on the phone a *long* time."

"I'm sorry, honey." I looked at the shopping cart, loaded with goodies. "Look, let's negotiate. I said we would set a ten-dollar budget, but I didn't mean to be that long on the phone, so—"

"How 'bout thirty dollars?"

I said, "Twenty."

"Twenty-five."

I sighed. "Done." Haley's a *good* negotiator.

On February 25, members of both parties met with President Obama at Blair House for the health care summit. The Republican leaders reasoned, "We've got to go. We'll get our heads handed to us if we don't show up. The Democrats and the media will portray us as 'the party of no.' "

Just as Michele Bachmann predicted, it was a big dog-and-pony show. President Obama *said* he wanted to hear Republican ideas, but according to CNN, the Democrats used up 70 percent of the speaking time, leaving 30 percent for the Republicans. Barack Obama spoke almost as long as all the other Democrats combined.[14] Even so, the Republicans managed to score some good points.

Congressman Paul Ryan, for example, pressed the case that the grass roots had soundly rejected Obamacare—and the two political parties should start over and craft a bipartisan bill from scratch. "We are all representatives of the American people," Ryan said. "We all do town hall meetings. We all talk to our constituents. And I've got to tell you, the American people are engaged. And if you think they want a government takeover of health care, I would respectfully submit you're not listening to them."[15] Congressman Ryan's plea fell on deaf Democratic ears.

By and large, Michele Bachmann was proven correct. Prior to the summit, the Republicans were winning the argument. After the summit, the political momentum shifted in favor of Obamacare. Her contention was that Republicans were as much to blame for the passage of Obamacare as President Obama and the Democrats because the Republicans didn't stand up to Obamacare when the American people were with them. The Blair House summit is where we lost the health care battle.

Days before the Obamacare bill came to a vote, commentator Mark Steyn predicted that the Democrats would pass the bill, even if it cost them dearly. Sure enough, seven months later, the Democrats paid a heavy price at the midterm elections. But to Harry Reid, Nancy Pelosi, and Barack Obama, it was worth it. Steyn explains: "The governmentalization of health care is the fastest way to a permanent left-of-center political culture. It redefines the relationship between the citizen and the state in fundamental ways that make limited government all but impossible. . . . Right-of-center parties will once in a while be in office, but never in power, merely presiding over vast left-wing bureaucracies that cruise on regardless."

Conservatives, Steyn explains, do not understand the basic power dynamic. We think that if conservatives win an election, then conservatives are in charge. Not so. Once liberal-progressives install their big-government apparatus, whether it be the welfare state or the Department of Education or Obamacare, they can fill the bureaucracy with statists, social engineers, and socialists. Republicans may win elections and even win the White House—but the liberal-progressive bureaucracy goes on and on.

Steyn quotes my friend Andrew McCarthy: "Health care is a loser for the Left only if the Right has the steel to undo it. The Left is banking on an absence of steel. Why is that a bad bet?"

And that is our challenge as grassroots activists. You and I must be the steel in the spines of our elected representatives. We have to call our senators and representatives every day and ask them, "What are you doing today to make sure that Obamacare is repealed?" Because if we don't, we lose—and our children and grandchildren lose, too.

Steyn adds that no government on earth ever attempted centralized economic planning on the scale of Obamacare—the takeover of one-sixth of the American economy plus the confiscation of the health care choices for a society of more than 300 million people. It's the equivalent, says Steyn, of annexing an entire economy the size of Great Britain's or France's, or twice the size of India's economy. The only undertaking that is remotely similar, he adds, was the socialist experiment in the Soviet Union—"and we know how that worked out."

The Democrats claim that Obamacare "controls costs"—but, says Steyn, "it 'controls' costs by declining to acknowledge them, or pay them." And, of course, it controls costs by rationing—by setting up "death panels" to decide who gets surgery and who gets to take a painkiller and die. As Mark Steyn concludes, "Government health care is not about health care, it's about government." [16]

Democrats point to a January 2011 Congressional Budget Office report that claims that repealing Obamacare would increase the deficit by $230 billion. Now, how could that be? How could it *cost* money to shut down a government program?

Here's how the CBO arrives at that conclusion: Repeal of Obamacare would cut net spending by $540 billion during the period from 2012 through 2021. Over that same ten-year period, repeal of Obamacare would eliminate $770 billion in tax increases. Subtract $540 billion in spending from $770 billion in tax hikes and you get $230 million. There are at least two faulty assumptions in this scenario.

First, the CBO estimate assumes that the $770 billion tax increase would have no negative impact on the economy. Yet many of these tax increases are inflicted directly on employers, increasing the cost of employing workers. That's why Obamacare is a job killer and a drag on an already shaky economy. Historically, the very tax increases that are intended to generate revenue often inflict so much damage to the economy that they dry up revenue. Tax hikes are no way to balance a budget.

Second, the CBO estimate assumes that the $540 billion net cost of Obamacare is a realistic projection. But as Dean Clancy, legislative counsel and health care expert for FreedomWorks, points out, government health care schemes invariably underestimate cost projections. Clancy cites these examples:

- Britain's National Health Service cost 38 percent more than projected in its first year.
- Romneycare in Massachusetts cost 20 percent more than projected in its first full year.
- Medicare's kidney dialysis program, created in 1972, cost 2.3 times as much as projected in its first year.
- In 1965, Medicare was projected to cost $12 billion by 1990. Its actual 1990 cost: $110 billion—roughly nine times the original estimate. (The comparable figures for Medicare's first decade, 1966–75, are $2 billion and $14.8 billion, respectively—seven times the original estimate.)[17]

The notion that it would actually *cost* money to kill a government program is just another liberal delusion.

So the question is: do we have the steel to repeal and replace Obamacare? Almost immediately after Obamacare passed in the House by a vote of 219 to 212, Michele Bachmann introduced a bill to repeal Obamacare (legislatively known as "The Patient Protection and Affordable Care Act"). Her repeal bill is short and sweet:

A BILL

To repeal the Patient Protection and Affordable Care Act.

*Be it enacted by the Senate and House of Representatives of
the United States of America in Congress assembled,*

SECTION 1. REPEAL OF PPACA.

Effective as of the enactment of the Patient Protection
and Affordable Care Act, such Act is repealed, and the
provisions of law amended or repealed by such Act are
restored or revived as if such Act had not been enacted.[18]

Don't you love it? I think it would be a fitting end to that two-thousand-page Obamacare monstrosity if it were repealed by a bill consisting of less than seventy-five words! In an accompanying statement, Michele Bachmann also quoted these words of Thomas Jefferson, which speak directly to the threat posed by Obamacare:

Our country is too large to have all its affairs directed by a single government. Public servants at such a distance, and from under the eye of their constituents, must, from the circumstance of distance, be unable to administer and overlook all the details necessary for the good government of the citizens, and the same circumstance, by rendering detection impossible to their constituents, will invite the public agents to corruption, plunder and waste. . . . What an augmentation of the field for jobbing, speculation, plundering, office-building, and office-hunting would be produced by an assumption of all the State powers into the hands of the General Government.[19]

The essence of America, as the Declaration of Independence tells us, is "life, liberty, and the pursuit of happiness." Obamacare's death panels would deprive us of life. Its individual mandates would deprive us of liberty. And its crushing cost will deprive us and future generations of the pursuit of happiness.

Congressman Steve King of Iowa put it this way on my show:

"We've got to draw the line here. We must repeal one hundred percent of Obamacare. If we fail to do so, we will never get our freedom back in this country, and our vitality as a nation will be forever diminished. We'll never become that Shining City on a Hill that Ronald Reagan envisioned. It will be forever taken away from us."

WAR: THE ULTIMATE ECONOMIC STIMULUS?

In late 2010, Paul Krugman performed a gigantic flip-flop. Krugman is the Nobel-winning economist and *New York Times* columnist who had sneered at Sarah Palin's claim of "death panels" as "a complete fabrication." He had repeated these attacks in his columns, referring to "the death panel smear" (August 20, 2009, and February 25, 2010), death panel "lies" (August 30 and October 4, 2009), and "Sarah Palin—who . . . eagerly spread the death panel lie" (March 21, 2010).[20]

But in November 2010, Krugman appeared on ABC's *This Week with Christiane Amanpour* and predicted, "Some years down the pike, we're going to get the real solution [to our federal deficit crisis], which is going to be a combination of death panels and sales taxes. It's going to be that we're actually going to take Medicare under control, and we're going to have to get some additional revenue, probably from a VAT [value-added tax]."[21]

That's right. Krugman actually predicted that "death panels" will help us "take Medicare under control." He smirked when he said "death panels," but he was serious about using government health care rationing to contain costs. Krugman was not issuing a *warning* against "death panels." He *embraces* the notion of rationing health care to cut costs. And health care rationing kills people. So while Paul Krugman was accusing Sarah Palin of lying about "death panels," she was right all along.

But "death panels" are not the only "solutions" Paul Krugman offers to reduce the national debt. It gets worse. He also suggests—are you ready for this?—*war* as a form of economic stimulus.

Appearing at an economic forum in Washington, D.C., Krugman was asked when he foresaw America returning to full employment. His reply: "Basically never. There is nothing visible on the horizon that will make that happen." America's economic outlook is so bleak, he said, that "we're going to look at Japan's 'lost decade' as a success story" by contrast. Stimulus has failed. Therefore, only one thing can pull America out of its economic doldrums—another massive war on the scale of the "coordinated fiscal expansion known as World War II."[22]

This view comes from Paul Krugman's misreading of the history of the Great Depression and World War II. Krugman is a Keynesian, a disciple of John Maynard Keynes, and in his textbook *Economics,* he presents his students with this steaming pile of misinformation:

> The basic message many of the young economists who adopted Keynes's ideas in the 1930s took from his work was that economic recovery requires aggressive fiscal expansion—deficit spending on a large scale to create jobs. And that is what they eventually got, but it wasn't because politicians were persuaded. Instead, what happened was a war. . . .
>
> Deficit spending during the 1930s was on a modest scale. As the risk of war grew larger, the United States began a military buildup, and the budget moved deep into deficit. After the attack on Pearl Harbor on December 7, 1941, the country began deficit spending on an enormous scale: in fiscal 1943, which began in July 1942, the deficit was 30 percent of GDP. Today that would be a deficit of $3.5 trillion.
>
> And the economy recovered. World War II wasn't intended as a Keynesian fiscal policy, but it demonstrated that expansionary fiscal policy can, in fact, create jobs in the short run.[23]

Boiled down to its essence, Krugman's message is: *War brings prosperity.* According to this view, war is the ultimate economic stimulus. In wartime, the government spends like crazy, cranking out weaponry, putting soldiers into uniform, and transporting people and matériel halfway around the world. According to Keynesian theory, massive wartime spending jump-starts the economy. But is that true?

As we saw in chapter 4, the notion that World War II ended the Great Depression is a myth. Yes, World War II ended the *unemployment* problem of the Great Depression by sending 12 million workers off to war. But all the other symptoms of the depressed economy—low stock prices, low levels of personal investment, lagging personal consumption—remained constant during the war. The Great Depression was ended not by World War II, but by Congress. When President Harry Truman wanted to implement a Second New Deal, Congress rejected the FDR-Truman plan and adopted a common-sense approach (which we now call Reaganomics): cut taxes and cut spending. It was sound fiscal policy, not war, that produced the economic boom following World War II.

Paul Krugman's analysis ignores the facts of history. Still worse, his ideas are dangerously amoral. Suppose an American president saw this country tilting toward a second Great Depression, with unemployment topping 25 percent and stock prices scraping bottom—and suppose the president *believed* Paul Krugman's flawed version of history. Wouldn't that president be tempted to take the country to war in order to bring the country out of its depression? And don't you find it rather chilling that Krugman talks about mass killing as just another form of economic stimulus? I certainly do. The idea that war can bring about prosperity is dangerous and morally outrageous. War does not create wealth.

A pro-life conservative could never reach the kind of conclusion Paul Krugman proclaims so casually. Yes, there are times when war becomes a moral necessity. Sometimes an Adolf Hitler or a Saddam Hussein leaves you no moral option *but* war. Conservatives believe that war is sometimes necessary to end oppression or aggression. But only the amoral liberal-progressive mind-set of a Paul Krugman could dream up a war for prosperity.

THE TRUTH IN PLAIN ENGLISH

Take a drive through the center of Cooperstown, North Dakota. It may look like a quiet little western town as you pass by the Masonic Temple and the historic Griggs County Courthouse. But from the early 1960s through the late 1990s, tiny Cooperstown, population 1,053, had a ringside seat to the Cold War—and potentially to World War III. The town is just a few miles from two decommissioned launch sites that make up the Ronald Reagan Minuteman Missile State Historic Site—the Oscar-Zero Missile Alert Facility and the November-33 Launch Facility.

Today, visitors can go into the underground vaults and tunnels and see where the cold warriors of our air force once awaited orders to launch Armageddon. Oscar-Zero and November-33 were part of the 321st Missile Wing, a cluster of ICBM launch sites spread across a 6,500-square-mile region surrounding Grand Forks Air Force Base. These facilities, now named in honor of the greatest president of the twentieth century, remind us of Ronald Reagan's peace-through-strength strategy and of all he accomplished by ending the Cold War and collapsing the Soviet Union without firing a shot.

Ronald Reagan devoted his entire presidency to liberating oppressed people and shedding the light of freedom around the world. He saw America as the Shining City on a Hill, giving light and hope to the rest of the world. He didn't hesitate to call the Soviet Union an "evil empire." And when he saw people imprisoned behind the Berlin Wall, he went to Berlin, stood before that wall, and demanded, "Mr. Gorbachev, tear down this wall!" And the wall came down—because Ronald Reagan dared to demand it in plain, unambiguous English.

I recently had the privilege of talking to Peter Robinson, the speechwriter who worked with Ronald Reagan to craft that speech. Peter told me of the opposition President Reagan encountered on his way to toppling the Berlin Wall.

"It was a huge battle to keep the 'Tear down this wall' line in the speech," Peter told me. "I'm told it was the biggest battle over a speech in the entire eight years of the Reagan presidency. When Ronald Reagan gave a speech, it mattered. If cabinet members or White House advisers wanted to prevent a policy from going into effect, they knew they had to stop it before it got into one of Reagan's speeches. Once he delivered a speech, it became the policy. Words mattered to him.

"When I was assigned to draft the Berlin Wall speech, I flew to Berlin to do research. I went to the wall and saw for myself how ugly and frightening it was. I saw that the spot where the president would speak was one of the most dramatic settings in the world. After visiting the wall, I spoke to the ranking U.S. diplomat in Berlin, and he was full of ideas about what President Reagan should and should not say. He didn't want the President to bash communism. He said, 'You've got to be very careful what you say about the wall. People have gotten used to it after all these years.'

"That evening, I attended a dinner party with some Berliners. I told them, 'I've heard that you have all gotten used to this wall. I find it hard to understand how anyone could get used to the wall.' There was a moment of awkward silence, then one man pointed in the direction of the wall and said, with emotion in his voice, 'My sister lives just a few kilometers in that direction, but I have not seen her in more than twenty years. How do you think we feel about that wall?'

"Our hostess said, 'If this man Gorbachev is serious about his talk of *glasnost,* he can prove it by coming here and removing this wall!' Clearly, the diplomat was wrong. The people of Berlin hated the wall. They didn't talk about it unless you asked them—but they hated it every day.

"So I went back to Washington and drafted a speech around a demand to 'tear down this wall.' I turned in the speech, and it was delivered to the president on a Friday. He took it with him to Camp David and read it over the weekend. The president met with his speechwriters on Monday, and I explained, 'Mr. President, the speech will be heard not only in West Berlin but in East Berlin. In fact, people may be able to pick it up on their little radios throughout much of Eastern Europe. Is there anything you want to say to people on the other side of the Iron Curtain?'

"The president thought for a moment, then he said, 'Well, there's that passage about tearing down the wall. That's what I want to say to them, that the wall must come down.'

"But the State Department and the National Security Council objected to exactly that passage. Some said, 'You can't say, "Tear down this wall!" That line will raise false expectations!' Howard Baker, the chief of staff, said the line was unpresidential. The foreign policy folks said that it would put Gorbachev in too tight a spot. For the next three and a half weeks, they submitted memo after memo, draft after draft, and everybody tried to remove that line from the speech. But President Reagan stood his ground.

"A few days before President Reagan was supposed to deliver the speech, he sat down with his deputy chief of staff, Ken Duberstein, and they reviewed all the arguments. Finally, Reagan got that wonderful twinkle in his eye, and he said, 'Now, Ken, I'm the president, aren't I?' And Duberstein said, 'Yes, Mr. President, we're clear on that.' And Reagan said, 'Then the line stays in.'

"Even so, the State Department was cabling alternative drafts to President Reagan on the morning he was to deliver the speech. Ronald Reagan was one tough-minded man. He had total confidence in his beliefs. So he delivered those lines—'Mr. Gorbachev, open this gate! Mr. Gorbachev, tear down this wall!' As soon as President Reagan spoke those words, it was as if he could never have spoken anything else. That was the power of Ronald Reagan."

I asked Peter Robinson, "Shouldn't President Obama have been in Berlin for the twentieth anniversary of the fall of the Berlin Wall on November 9, 2009?"

"It was astounding that he wasn't there, just astounding. That was the end of the struggle that defined the second half of the twentieth century. It suggests to me a profound lack of historical understanding on the part of his administration."

Peter is right. President Obama doesn't understand what it meant for Ronald Reagan to go to that wall and give that speech. He doesn't understand what it meant when the gates were opened and the wall came down just twenty-nine months later. He doesn't understand the yearning of oppressed people to be free.

Ronald Reagan refused to coddle evil. Instead, he called an evil empire by its rightful name. Against the advice of almost all of his advisers, he went to Berlin and demanded that an evil wall be torn down. He formed a partnership with the greatest pope of the twentieth century, John Paul II, with British prime minister Margaret Thatcher, and with Eastern European dissidents Lech Walesa and Vaclav Havel, and together they brought down the Iron Curtain and shattered the Berlin Wall.

Most important of all, Ronald Reagan ended the Cold War by speaking the truth in plain, unambiguous English. He told the oppressed people of the world, "You are not alone. America stands with you. We will do whatever we can to help set you free."

Freedom is a matter of life and death. When Ronald Reagan demanded that the people of Eastern Europe be set free, he was taking a
stand for life, liberty, and the pursuit of happiness. Words matter, and
few words have done more to change the course of history than the
words of Ronald Reagan.

WHAT IT *REALLY* MEANS TO BE PRO-LIFE

On June 12, 2009, Iran held a presidential election in which President Mahmoud Ahmadinejad supposedly won 63 percent of the vote
against opposition leader Mir Hossein Moussavi. The Iranian people
knew the election was a farce. There were no voting booths; voters
filled in their ballots under the watchful eye of government officials.
All 40 million ballots had to be counted by hand, yet the government declared Ahmadinejad the winner just two hours after the polls
closed—which every voter knew was impossible. The election was an
insult to the intelligence of the Iranian people.

Civil unrest broke out across Iran—the most widespread antigovernment demonstrations in decades. Protesters took to the streets,
chanting, "Down with the dictator!" and "Give us our votes back!"
Iranian security forces flew helicopters over the protesters and
dumped hot water, mixed with caustic chemicals. They fired bullets and water cannons at the demonstrators, most of whom were
students.

On June 20, a twenty-six-year-old woman, Neda Agha-Soltan, was
shot in the chest while standing and observing the protests in Tehran.
The shooter was a rooftop assassin, a member of the Basij, a group of
thugs controlled by the Iranian mullahs. A video camera captured her
last moments as she lay on the ground, stared at the camera, and bled
from her mouth and nose. The video was posted to the Internet and
galvanized world opinion against the Iranian government.

At the beginning of the crisis in Iran, our president's response was
muted, to say the least. "It's not productive," he said, for the U.S. president to be seen as "meddling in Iranian elections." The Iranian government's "violence directed at peaceful protestors . . . is of concern to
me and it's of concern to the American people. That is not how gov-

ernments should interact with their people." Always eager to get on both sides of every issue, Mr. Obama warned the protesters not to go too far: "My hope is that the Iranian people will make the right steps in order for them to be able to express their voices."[24]

After he was criticized for his mealymouthed initial statement, President Obama decided to try again. In a June 19 interview with Harry Smith of CBS News, he said, "We stand with those who would look to peaceful resolution of conflict and we believe that the voices of people have to be heard. . . . The last thing that I want to do is to have the United States be a foil for those forces inside Iran who would love nothing better than to make this an argument about the United States."[25]

Ronald Reagan never worried about those who might want to use the United States of America as a "foil." He didn't worry about getting on both sides of the issue or finding just the right shade of nuance. He spoke plainly and bluntly to make sure that tyrants and dictators wouldn't mistake his meaning. But Barack Obama is no Ronald Reagan.

On June 23, during a White House press conference more than a week after the Iranian election, President Obama again tried to get it right. This time, he said that the United States was "appalled and outraged by the threats, the beatings, and imprisonments of the last few days. I strongly condemn these unjust actions, and I join with the American people in mourning each and every innocent life that is lost." Still, he couldn't resist walking that statement back a step, adding that "the United States respects the sovereignty of the Islamic Republic of Iran, and is not interfering with Iran's affairs."[26] It was not exactly a tear-down-this-wall moment.

Maybe I'm just a guy talking into a microphone, but this doesn't seem all that hard to me. Iran has been a thorn in America's side since the Jimmy Carter era. Now the Iranian people themselves have risen up to throw off the oppression of their own government. The people of Iran were literally trying to fix their own country *without* the United States having to invade Iran as we had invaded Iraq, *without* having to spill a drop of American blood, and *without* requiring intervention by Israel, which could spark region-wide war in the Middle East. This was a golden opportunity for the United States. A great leader like Ronald Reagan would have seized the moment and would have spoken the words that would embolden the Iranian people to seize their own destiny.

The grassroots citizens of Iran did something that was remarkably American—they staged a tea party—an Iranian tea party! They gathered en masse and spoke out against their government, just as we Americans do. As I watched the news coverage, I noticed something that none of the network reporters commented on: the protesters' signs were mostly written in English, not the Persian language of Iran. Why? *Because the protesters were calling out to us.* They were begging for our support.

But our president never spoke out in support of the Iranian people. Instead he encouraged both the Iranian government and the protesters to refrain from violence—and he excused his own weak response by saying he wouldn't let America become a "foil." As he made his excuses, all I could think of was Ronald Reagan before the Berlin Wall, and the blunt words, "Tear down this wall!"

Why was it so hard for President Obama to speak out for people who wanted to be free? Why was this so hard for him? We have seen videos of the demonstrations, of the woman who was shot to death before our eyes—videos that were smuggled out of Iran via Facebook and Twitter and YouTube because of the media blackout in Iran.

On June 23, 2009, ten days after the Iranian election, my longtime friend (and former Bush adviser) Mark Pfeifle came on the show and said that the leaders of new media—Twitter, Facebook, Flickr, YouTube—should all be nominated for a Nobel Peace Prize for the service they rendered in getting the stories of the protesters out to the world. In fact, Mark said, the techs at Twitter actually delayed a scheduled tune-up of their system in order to accommodate the extra Internet traffic coming out of Iran. Twitter seemed to understand what Barack Obama didn't: the crisis in Iran was a life-and-death emergency requiring an urgent response. On June 17 alone, Mark said, 221,000 tweets were sent about Iran and 3,000 Iran-related videos were uploaded to YouTube. "The social networking media took over at this time of crisis," Mark said, "and it gave voice to a lot of people the Iranian government wanted to silence."

The people of Iran called out to the world for help. Unfortunately, no one in the White House got the message. It was Tiananmen Square all over again. It was East Germany and Hungary in the 1950s, and Czechoslovakia in 1968. America, the strongest nation on earth, seemed impotent and uncertain—and the government of Iran was emboldened to brutally oppress its people.

Elections have consequences—sometimes global consequences. We elected a rank amateur to be the chief executive officer of the United States of America. That's why it's amateur hour at the White House whenever a crisis rears its ugly head. The leader of the free world has to consult with a pool of advisers to know what he thinks about any given issue—and he hasn't gotten it right yet.

What does it mean to be pro-life? I think it's more than just being anti-abortion. It means that you have consistent pro-life principles on every issue that affects human life—especially innocent human life. Pro-life people are committed to fighting against such scourges of our existence as cancer (which took the life of my friend Tony Snow), heart disease (which threatens the life of my friend Dick Cheney), and Alzheimer's disease (which took the life of our greatest president, Ronald Reagan). Pro-life people are committed to the repeal of Obamacare, with its rationing and "death panels." Pro-life people would never advocate war as economic stimulus. And when pro-life people see human beings shot down in cold blood for demanding freedom and democracy, they don't need to find just the right nuance. They speak out in plain, unmistakable English.

I love to visit the Ronald Reagan Presidential Foundation and Library. It sits atop a windswept hill in Simi Valley, California. There you can visit Air Force One, the modified Boeing 747 that flew President Reagan over 660,000 miles to forty-six states and twenty-six countries—including his trip to the Berlin Wall. You can see an actual section of the Berlin Wall, covered with peace graffiti. And you can visit Ronald Reagan's grave site. There, on the wall behind his grave, you'll find an inscription taken from words Reagan himself spoke when he opened the library in 1991:

> "I know in my heart that man is good,
> that what is right will always eventually triumph,
> and there is purpose and worth to each and every life."

I believe those words. I know you do as well. We agree with Ronald Reagan that there is purpose and worth to each and every life, to the life of an unborn child, to the life of a young woman shot to death in the streets of Tehran, to the life of those who face cancer or Alzheimer's disease.

Even in death, Ronald Reagan inspires us to defend life. We still have work to do. We still have lives to save. We still have a health care bill to repeal and replace. But we, as grassroots Americans, know that the right will eventually triumph if we pray, if we have faith, and if we work every day to make it so.

THE COMMONSENSE ACTION AGENDA

Here are some grassroots actions you can take, starting today:

✓ Defending life is a moral, ethical, and spiritual commitment. While we want to change the laws and roll back the tyranny of *Roe v. Wade,* our primary goal is to change hearts and minds. This means we commit ourselves to praying daily for an end to abortion. We pray for the unborn, for their parents, for the doctors and workers in the abortion facilities, and for legislators and judges who can ultimately make a difference for life at the state and federal level.

✓ Commit yourself to raising awareness of the pro-life cause wherever you have an influence—in your home, your community, your church, and your civic organizations.

✓ Talk to your children about pro-life values. Teach them the principles of abstinence. Let them know that if they stray from those principles, there will be consequences that they have to deal with. One of those consequences is that you will be disappointed in them—but you will still love them, and they can always come to you with their problems, even the problem of an unplanned pregnancy. Teach them that killing an unborn baby is not the solution to any problem. Encourage them to join a pro-life group at your school or church, and urge them to be involved in pro-life efforts such as 40 Days for Life.

✓ Be aware of the sex education programs in your children's school. Help make sure that abstinence is clearly presented as a positive choice.

✓ Encourage your pastor or priest to preach pro-life sermons—and thank them when they do. Even in my own Catholic community, I've heard stories of priests who preached a pro-life homily, only to receive complaints from CINOs (Catholics In Name Only). Make sure your minister or priest knows you stand with him and support his pro-life stance.

✓ Volunteer for prayer vigils at your local abortion clinic. Support local pro-life organizations and homes for unwed mothers.

✓ Look for good deals on baby clothes and maternity outfits, then donate them to homes for unwed mothers. Also, offer to babysit for single moms as a way of showing that you care not just about the unborn, but for the needs of unwed mothers.

✓ Be vocal. Write letters to the editor, letters to your elected representatives, and columns on your blog and Facebook page in support of the pro-life cause.

✓ Research the voting record and public stance of the politicians who seek your vote. Let them know that you support only pro-life political leaders.

✓ Remain vigilant and passionate about repealing Obamacare. Don't relax the pressure on your elected representatives. Don't assume that just because you are represented by a Republican, he or she is genuinely committed to repeal. Call your representative and ask, "What have you done this week to move us closer to repealing Obamacare?" Show up in person at your representative's local office and demand answers. Tell yourself, "The squeaky wheel gets repeal!" Don't let up until the battle is won.

10

KEEPING THE FAITH

I had just come from the MSNBC studios in Washington, D.C., where I had been locking horns (as usual) with Ed Schultz of *The Ed Show*. From the studio, I went to the Embassy of the Holy See on Massachusetts Avenue, near the U.S. Naval Observatory (which is the official residence of the vice president). My buddy John Dietrich had arranged a tour for me. John was once a student of Monsignor Richard E. Marchese, who serves as the secretary to the papal nuncio, the pope's official representative to the government of the United States.

As a lifelong Catholic, I was honored just to visit the embassy. The Holy See is the government of the Catholic Church, and the embassy is sovereign territory of the Holy See—so when I stepped across that threshold, it was the same as stepping into the Vatican itself. I couldn't help thinking, "Wouldn't it be amazing if I could meet the nuncio and shake his hand?" But I knew how unlikely that was. It takes weeks for even a senator or world leader to get an audience with him.

John and the monsignor guided me around and shared with me some of the history of the place. Then, to my astonishment, they took me into a study and introduced me to His Grace, the Apostolic Nuncio, Pietro Sambi. He was a white-haired man in his seventies with a warm smile. His English was accented but impeccable (I understand he also speaks French and Spanish, as well as his native Italian).

The monsignor introduced us, but the nuncio told me he knew who I was. "You," he said, "are the chairman of the Common Sense Club. I understand that you are able to call George Bush and Dick Cheney 'friend.' I have heard you have interviewed Vice President Cheney many times. Can we have a conversation?"

The nuncio already knew President Bush and Vice President Cheney—that was evident from the many photos of the three of them together that I had seen here and there throughout the embassy (there were also photos taken with President Obama). It was clear to me that the nuncio knew and admired Bush and Cheney. He spoke glowingly of the farewell speech Dick Cheney had delivered at JFK Airport at the end of Pope Benedict XVI's 2008 visit to America. Even though the nuncio knew Bush and Cheney well, he wanted me to tell him everything I could about the two men, especially any stories I could share.

His Grace is a fascinating man. He has served in Cameroon, Jerusalem and Palestine, Cuba, Algeria, Nicaragua, Belgium, India, Burundi, and Indonesia—and he is the titular archbishop of Belcastro in southern Italy. We sat down for an hour and had a phenomenal conversation—not about politics, but about the faith that he and I share, the faith that he is passionate about revitalizing across America. It was a conversation I'll remember to the end of my life.

More than any other subject, we talked about Mother Teresa. I have always admired Mother Teresa, and the nuncio knew her well. When I asked about her, his eyes lit up and he began telling stories. He recounted how he had helped obtain permission to enable Mother Teresa to go to China in 1985. He told me how Mother Teresa saw the face of Jesus in every human being she met, and he said that nearly all the problems of the world could be solved if every person on earth heeded her message and example. The theme of her life, he said, is that God loves us with an everlasting and unconditional love, and that is how we are to love one another.

I was impressed with the nuncio's hope and compassion for young people. He told me, "All the problems that ail this country—from abortion to the decline of values to the political and racial divisions of this nation—could be healed by the next generation if they will grow up differently from the previous generation. If parents would make time for their children, the next generation could change the world. The peace of the world begins with peace in the home."

As I listened to the nuncio's wisdom, I thought, "You know, he has a lot of insight into the generational and social problems here in America. He understands American youth and American families. And he understands that most of our social ills are truly spiritual problems at root."

Later, I asked my friend John if he had told the monsignor about me, but John said that the monsignor and the nuncio already knew who I was. So I haven't unlocked the mystery of how I came to have an hour-long audience with the papal nuncio, the man I think of as "the American pope."

But there's one thing I know for sure: our spiritual heritage is the key to saving America. If we want to restore America's goodness and preserve America's greatness for coming generations, we as grassroots Americans must *keep the faith*.

THE LAST BEST HOPE OF EARTH

Talk show host and author Dennis Prager is a Jewish conservative. In May 2010, he took part in a panel discussion at the University of Denver, along with fellow panelists Sarah Palin and Hugh Hewitt. In his remarks, Prager stated, "I believe the greatest threat facing America . . . is that we have not passed on what it means to be an American to this generation. . . . The average American who loves his country, and even has conservative values, cannot articulate what those values are."[1]

And what are those values that every American should know? Prager points out that our American values are conveniently engraved on all of our coins. If you ever want to know what makes America unique among all the nations of the world, simply take a coin out of your pocket and read it. There you will find three mottos: *E Pluribus Unum, In God We Trust,* and *Liberty.* No other country on earth has enshrined those three ideals, and it is those three ideals that make America not only exceptional, but unique.

Prager notes that the French had three mottos also: *Liberté, égalité, fraternité,* meaning *Liberty, equality, and brotherhood.* As Americans, Prager says, "We believe in equality of birth, but not equality of result. When it is understood what America stands for, when it is understood that there is a moral dimension to smaller government, it is not an economic question. It is a moral question. We give far more charity per capita than Europeans do. Why? Are we born better? No. The bigger the government, the worse the citizen. They are preoccupied in Europe with how much time off, where will they vacation, when will they retire. These are selfish questions. These are not altruistic questions. So the goodness that America created is jeopardized by our not knowing what we stand for. That is our greatest threat." [2] So what do we, as Americans, stand for?

First, we stand for *E Pluribus Unum.* This is Latin for "From the many, one." Americans emigrated from many lands and are made up of many races, but we have come together to form one culture, one people—the American people. Here in America, we don't care where you came from, we don't care about your ethnic origins. If you believe in the American ideal, if you have come here to build a better life for yourself and your family and to help keep America great, then you are one of us. You're an American.

Second, *In God We Trust.* America was founded on the idea that God is the source of our rights and the essence of our values. We do not insist that you worship as we do—or even that you worship at all. But as Americans we stand for the principle that our unalienable rights are endowed by our Creator and cannot be taken away. If you do not respect this principle, then you do not stand for one of the three essential ideals that make us Americans.

Third, *Liberty.* This is one of the three unalienable rights, along with the right to life and the right to the pursuit of happiness. As Dennis Prager notes, the French believe in liberty, and so do many other peoples and nations. But only America enshrines all three: *E Pluribus Unum, In God We Trust,* and *Liberty.*

Prager concluded, "Abraham Lincoln said that the United States is 'the last best hope of earth.' Or, as we often say, 'of mankind.' It will not be the last best hope for mankind if it becomes like Western Europe. Nobody has ever said Norway is the last best hope for mankind. . . . Nor have they ever said that . . . about France. It has only been said about the United States."[3]

Dennis Prager alluded to the words that Abraham Lincoln spoke in his annual message to Congress, on December 1, 1862, one month before signing the Emancipation Proclamation. He spoke about the urgent need to dismantle the old, tyrannical system of slavery, and to extend the unalienable rights of life, liberty, and the pursuit of happiness to every human being. Lincoln said:

> Fellow-citizens, we cannot escape history. . . . We—even we here—hold the power, and bear the responsibility. In giving freedom to the slave, we assure freedom to the free—honorable alike in what we give, and what we preserve. We shall nobly save, or meanly lose, the last best hope of earth. Other means may succeed; this could not fail. The way is plain, peaceful, generous, just—a way which, if followed, the world will forever applaud, and God must forever bless.[4]

We've reached another turning point in history. We hold the power. We bear the responsibility. And if we fail, we will lose the last best hope of earth.

On January 15, 1983, Ronald Reagan gave a speech at the White House commemorating the birthday of Dr. Martin Luther King, Jr. (later that year, he would sign a bill making Dr. King's birthday a federal holiday). In his speech, President Reagan said, "Freedom is not something to be secured in any one moment of time. We must struggle to preserve it every day. And freedom is never more than one generation away from extinction."[5]

E Pluribus Unum, In God We Trust, and *Liberty.* These three mottoes tell us what it means to be an American—and all three of these ideals are just one generation away from extinction. You and I have an obligation to teach our children, our friends, and our neighbors what it means to be an American—and what it means to be a united people, a free people, and a people who trust in God.

THE BLACK REGIMENT

Lutheran pastor John Peter Muhlenberg was thirty years old and a member of the Virginia House of Burgesses when he responded to General Washington's call for enlistees to the Continental Army. One Sunday morning in 1775, he preached a sermon from Ecclesiastes 3: "There is a season for everything, a time for every occupation under heaven . . . a time for war, a time for peace. . . ."[6] He concluded with a call to arms: "In the language of the Holy Writ, there is a time for all things. There is a time to preach and a time to fight." Then he removed his black clerical robe to show that he wore the uniform of a colonel in the 8th Virginia Regiment. That very afternoon, Colonel Muhlenberg led three hundred men to join the Continental Army. He served until the end of the war and was later elected to the United States Senate.[7]

Pastor Muhlenberg was one of the many grassroots preachers of the Revolutionary War era who came to be known as the Black Regiment—a name given them by a pro-British sympathizer, Peter Oliver, the chief justice of Massachusetts. Oliver complained bitterly about the Black Regiment for "unceasingly sounding the Yell of Rebellion in the Ears of an ignorant and deluded People."[8] The patriotic preachers of the Black Regiment galvanized their parishioners to resist tyranny and fight for independence.

Pastor Phillips Payson of Chelsea, Massachusetts, was another member of the Black Regiment. In April 1775, when the British were forced to retreat from Concord, a pair of supply wagons, loaded with food and rum and guarded by a dozen Redcoats, became separated from the main force. Payson led a small band of his parishioners to hunt down the wagons. They located the British stragglers in the village of Menotomy and set an ambush. Though Payson and his men were outnumbered, they killed one soldier, wounded several others, and took the entire convoy prisoner. Pastor Payson's group suffered no casualties.[9]

Another member of the Black Regiment was James Caldwell, pastor of the Elizabethtown Presbyterian Church in New Jersey. Known as "the Fighting Chaplain" and "the Rebel Priest," he preached every

Sunday with a pair of loaded pistols on the pulpit, next to his Bible. Caldwell served with the New Jersey Brigade and was hated by the British and loyalists. In June 1780, while Caldwell was serving with General Washington's troops, British forces overran and occupied Elizabethtown, including the parsonage of the Presbyterian Church. They made Caldwell's wife, children, and housekeeper provide food for the officers.

Soon the American forces—consisting of Continental Army soldiers, militia, and armed farmers—fought back and forced the British to retreat from Elizabethtown. Before they retreated, the Brits ransacked and burned the town. One of the retreating Redcoats saw Mrs. Caldwell through an open window and shot her in the chest, killing her as her children looked on in horror.

The British forces reached the town of Springfield, where the American forces had assembled to make a stand. Intense fighting broke out, and Parson Caldwell fought as fiercely as the rest. Eventually, the Americans ran low on wadding for their muskets. Parson Caldwell ran to a nearby church, loaded his arms with hymn books, then ran back to the firing line. He threw down the books, which contained many hymns composed by Isaac Watts. Caldwell tore out pages for wadding. "Now, put Watts into them, boys!" he shouted. "Give 'em Watts!" The outnumbered Americans rallied and forced the British to retreat.

More than a year later, on November 24, 1781, Parson Caldwell was assassinated on the docks of the Elizabethtown landing by a traitor within the American ranks. Both the parson and his wife became famous as martyrs of the Revolutionary War.[10]

In a June 28, 1813, letter to Thomas Jefferson, John Adams, the second president of the United States, reflected on the War for Independence and recalled that the army of patriots who won the war were either devoutly Christian people or educated in Christian principles:

There were among them Roman Catholics, English Episcopalians, Scotch and American Presbyterians, Methodists, Moravians, Anabaptists, German Lutherans, German Calvinists, Universalists, Arians, Priestleyans, Socinians, Independents, Congregationalists,

Horse Protestants, and House Protestants, Deists and Atheists, and
Protestants "*qui ne croyent rien*" [Protestants who believe nothing].
Very few, however, of several of these species; nevertheless, all educated in the general principles of Christianity, and the general principles of English and American liberty. . . .

Now I will avow, that I then believed and now believe that those
general principles of Christianity are as eternal and immutable as
the existence and attributes of God; and that those principles of liberty are as unalterable as human nature.[11]

Human liberty is a foundational principle in the Judeo-Christian
scriptures. For example, in Leviticus 25:10, God tells Moses, "You will
declare this fiftieth year to be sacred and proclaim the liberation of all
the country's inhabitants."[12]

And in Luke 4:18–19, Jesus applies an Old Testament prophecy
to Himself, declaring, "The spirit of the Lord is on me, for he has
anointed me to bring the good news to the afflicted. He has sent me to
proclaim liberty to captives, sight to the blind, to let the oppressed go
free, to proclaim a year of favour from the Lord."[13]

Why were people of faith—and especially the clergy—so vital to
the war effort during the Revolution? It's because the revolutionary
cause was not primarily about the Quartering Act or the Stamp Act,
but about profound principles of human rights and religious liberty.
That's why one of the slogans of the Revolution was "Resistance to tyrants is obedience to God." In the minds of the revolutionaries—and
especially the Black Regiment—resistance to British oppression was a
Christian duty.

The issues have changed. We no longer argue about such matters as
the Quartering Act or the Stamp Act. Today the threats to our rights
and our liberty come from TARP, the stimulus plan, cap and trade,
the nationalization of banks and car companies, and Obamacare. It's
tyranny to inflict unsustainable debt on our children. It's tyranny to
devastate the economy with out-of-control spending. It's tyranny for
our president and our Congress to cram Obamacare down our throats
when we have said, respectfully but firmly, "No!"

We have a spiritual obligation to oppose tyranny. Our faith demands it. Resistance to tyrants is obedience to God.

THE RIGHT TO PICK OUR POCKETS

At this point, you may be asking yourself, "Is Scott Hennen saying that America is—or ought to be—a theocracy?" Of course not. A theocracy is a government ruled by a single religious sect that claims to speak for God. The nation of Iran, ruled by mullahs and ayatollahs who claim to speak for Allah, is a theocracy. No American wants to live under a system like that.

Thomas Jefferson expressed a uniquely American tolerance for other points of view and other religions—and yes, a tolerance for atheists. In *Notes on the State of Virginia,* a book in which Thomas Jefferson sets forth his views on an ideal society, he wrote, "Our rulers can have authority over such natural rights only as we have submitted to them. The rights of conscience we never submitted, we could not submit. We are answerable for them to our God. The legitimate powers of government extend to such acts only as are injurious to others. But it does me no injury for my neighbor to say there are twenty gods, or no God. It neither picks my pocket nor breaks my leg."[14]

Now, that's an excellent philosophy for us all to adopt: Let's agree to tolerate all points of view that neither pick our pockets nor break our legs. That means we can accept people of other religions and people without any religion. The only things we *cannot* tolerate are people like Al Qaeda (who want to break our legs) and policies like Obamacare, Keynesian stimulus schemes, and other liberal boondoggles (which pick our pockets).

I have atheist and agnostic friends. We've had many lively and interesting discussions. I wish they had a faith in God as I do—but I wouldn't *force* my beliefs on anyone. Open, freewheeling discussions about God and faith are possible only where there is true First Amendment freedom of speech and religion. The last thing in the world I would want for my nonbelieving friends is for them to live under the tyranny of a theocracy—a government that would "break your leg" for holding the "wrong" religious views.

Now, there are some on the left who think there's an "unalienable right" for some Americans to pick the pockets of other Americans. That's what Senator Tom Harkin (D-Iowa) suggested when he said during the health care debate, "What this bill [Obamacare] does is we finally take that step . . . from health care as a privilege to health care as an inalienable right of every single American citizen." [15] Senator Harkin does not have the right to insert new "unalienable rights" into the Declaration of Independence. We are endowed by our Creator with rights to life, liberty, and the pursuit of happiness—but a right to health care at our neighbor's expense? Don't we have some personal responsibility for our own health care?

Because we live in a compassionate society, *everyone in America* gets health care. If you are injured in an automobile accident, or if you have a heart attack, an ambulance will pick you up and take you to the emergency room of the nearest hospital and you *will* get health care. It's not because you have an unalienable right to health care. It's because Americans are compassionate, decent, and moral people. We always take care of those who are in need, regardless of their ability to pay, and we don't leave our sick and wounded to die by the side of the road.

We have never had a health care problem in America. We have had an *insurance* problem in America. The problem has never been "Who gets health care?" but "Who gets the bill?" So the question I would put to Senator Harkin is this: does every American citizen have a right to pick the pocket of his fellow citizens to pay for his health insurance? Because that's really what Senator Harkin and his fellow Democrats have put in place through Obamacare.

I object to Tom Harkin, Barack Obama, Nancy Pelosi, Harry Reid, and Kent Conrad picking my pocket and my children's pockets, and driving America into bankruptcy in order to rewrite the Declaration of Independence. Americans have not been endowed by their Creator with the unalienable right to pick the pockets of their fellow citizens and future generations. It's wrong, it's tyranny, and we must resist it, because resistance to tyrants is obedience to God.

What the government gives, the government can take away. What God gives to us is rightfully ours forever, and no government has the right to take it away.

THE NEW BLACK REGIMENT

Bishop Samuel J. Aquila was appointed bishop of Fargo in 2001. The theme of his life is the command that Mary, the Mother of Jesus, gave to the servants at the wedding before Jesus turned water into wine: "Do whatever He tells you" (John 2:5). Bishop Aquila is a member of the twenty-first-century Black Regiment. In a peaceful, Christlike way, he resists tyranny, he obeys God, he does what his Master tells him.

During the 40 Days for Life campaign, you can find Bishop Aquila at the Red River Women's Clinic in Fargo, fasting and praying for the lives of the women, babies, and abortion workers inside that building. He always urges the priests of the diocese to join him in scheduling time to pray at the facility. His prayers and quiet presence are often enough to cause a woman to rethink her decision—and to leave the facility with her baby still alive within her womb. Though Bishop Aquila's witness for life is soft-spoken, he can be moved to indignation.

In April 2009, Father John I. Jenkins, president of Notre Dame University, invited President Obama to give the commencement address at the university and receive an honorary doctor of laws degree. This was in direct violation of the United States Catholic Bishops' instruction in 2004, "Catholics in Political Life," which said, "The Catholic community and Catholic institutions should not honor those who act in defiance of our fundamental moral principles. They should not be given awards, honors or platforms which would suggest support for their actions."

In 2002, as an Illinois state senator, Barack Obama cast a controversial vote opposing the Induced Birth Infant Liability Act, a measure to prevent the infanticide of babies who had survived late-term abortions. Jill Stanek, a registered nurse in obstetrics who has witnessed babies born alive after failed abortions, testified before the Illinois Senate's Health and Human Services Committee, chaired by Obama. She showed Obama photographs of viable babies who were left to die. "Those pictures didn't faze him at all," Stanek told Amanda Carpenter of *Human Events*. Instead, Obama told Stanek that the Induced

Birth Infant Liability Act would place a burden on a woman having an abortion, "and I can't support that."[16]

Clearly, President Obama is disqualified from receiving honors from Notre Dame University, in view of the Catholic Bishops' instruction. This isn't a matter of politics, but of morality and obedience to God. That's why, on April 5, 2009, Bishop Aquila wrote an open letter to Father Jenkins, which included these words:

> Inviting President Obama to award him a degree and to speak at a Catholic University implicitly extends legitimacy to his views on these issues in the minds of the average onlooker. . . . Your actions provide a forum for an advocate of abortion in a university which is committed to teaching the truths known to reason and science, and most of all to our faith in Jesus Christ and the teachings of His Church. This places commitment to these truths on an equal plane with a commitment to an intrinsic evil which destroys innocent human life. Your judgment in this matter is seriously flawed, with damaging consequences, for ". . . you are not on the side of God, but of men" (Matthew 16:23).[17]

Father Jenkins did not change his stance. President Obama gave the commencement address and received his honorary degree, in violation of the bishops' instruction. But Bishop Aquila of the Diocese of Fargo made a stand for unborn life, for resistance to tyranny, and for obedience to God. He did what any good soldier of the Black Regiment should do.

Another courageous grassroots member of today's Black Regiment is a pastor in Warroad, Minnesota, Reverend Gus Booth. I was honored to share a bully pulpit with Pastor Booth at a tea party celebrating Constitution Day, September 2009, in Thief River Falls, Minnesota.

In May 2008, in the thick of the presidential primary, Pastor Booth preached a sermon at Warroad Community Church. In that sermon, he named the presidential candidates who favored unrestricted abortion—Hillary Clinton and Barack Obama—as well as the candidate who is on record as consistently opposing abortion, John McCain.

But Pastor Booth didn't stop there. After preaching his sermon, he wrote a letter to the IRS, boldly announcing that he had violated a federal law against endorsing political candidates. Under that law, the Warroad Community Church stood to lose its tax-exempt status. Pastor Booth also sent a copy of the letter to Americans United for Separation of Church and State, an activist organization that tries to stamp out every trace of religion from the public square. In short, Reverend Gus Booth blew the whistle on himself.

Americans United took the bait. They filed a complaint against the church with the IRS. The group's executive director, Barry Lynn, said that when Pastor Booth "is standing in his tax-exempt pulpit as the top official of a tax-exempt religious organization, he must lay partisanship aside."[18] Such a statement is absurd, both constitutionally and religiously. No pastor should have to think of his pulpit as a "tax-exempt pulpit" from which he is required to dispense only government-approved sermons. Pastor Booth was not speaking as a partisan; he was dispensing moral counsel to his congregation, based on his own conscience and understanding of the scriptures.

Reverend Booth understands the clear meaning of the First Amendment, which begins, "Congress shall make no law respecting an establishment of religion, or prohibiting the free exercise thereof; or abridging the freedom of speech. . . ." A law that forbids pastors from informing their congregations about the candidates' positions on key moral issues such as abortion is in clear violation of the First Amendment. When the IRS uses the tax code to prohibit the free exercise of religion and freedom of speech, that's a direct violation of the intent of the First Amendment. So Pastor Booth drew a line in the sand—and put himself and his church on the line to protect unborn life.

It's a myth that churches can't address political issues from the pulpit because of "separation of church and state." In reality, the muzzling of churches goes back to a 1954 law known as the Johnson Amendment, named after then-senator Lyndon B. Johnson, a Democrat from Texas. LBJ sponsored the amendment that bears his name—but not out of deep respect for the doctrine of "separation of church and state." He proposed that law as a matter of political expediency. While running for reelection to the Senate, Johnson received heavy criticism from conservative preachers, so he sponsored the Johnson Amendment to silence his opponents. It was a flagrant abuse of power—but it passed and became part of the IRS code. Cal Thomas, who is a frequent guest on my show, calls the Johnson Amendment the " 'Berlin Wall' between church and state" and he offers this perspective:

> The law restricting political language from the pulpit is of rather recent vintage. Until 1954, election sermons could be heard on the first Sunday in November, or virtually any other time, without invoking the wrath of government. . . .
>
> If one takes the position that the political life of the country is a fit subject for sermonizing—whether the subject is poverty, abortion or low behavior in high office—then the First Amendment should certainly prevail over efforts to categorize, and thus restrict, free speech. The early colonial sermons were filled with righteous indignation and some indignation that was anything but righteous, but people were free to make up their own minds as to whether their pastor was speaking for God, or if he had more temporal concerns.[19]

The IRS has no business telling churches what they can and cannot say from the pulpit. Many moral issues are also political issues, and that is why the First Amendment was written—to protect the right of people of faith to speak out on the important moral issues that affect us all, including the issue of abortion.

As for Reverend Gus Booth, the Internal Revenue Service began an audit of his finances and his sermons in 2008—but in July 2009, the IRS announced it had closed its investigation of Booth and the Warroad Community Church. Was the reverend relieved? No! He was *disappointed,* because he wanted to fight it all the way to the Supreme Court, if necessary, in order to get the Johnson Amendment declared unconstitutional.[20] He may yet get his chance. The IRS says it may still reopen the matter.

Reverend Booth and his congregation are true grassroots heroes. I hope many more ministers of the Gospel rise up and join him in this cause.

Another member of today's Black Regiment is Mark Skogerboe, a Lutheran lay preacher, a tea party activist, and the author of *The Threefold Plan to Save America*. He's the spiritual voice of the tea party movement here in the heartland. When Mark gets up to speak, brace yourself! He'll turn any microphone into a pulpit, and any tea party gathering into a revival meeting.

The world needs more humble, dedicated servants like Mark Skogerboe—people who actually live out their beliefs with integrity. Most political issues, he says, are really moral issues. America's economic woes, high tax rates, mounting debt, and bailouts reflect a moral failing. It's immoral and sinful to borrow our way into debt, then pass the bill along to our children and grandchildren.

Mark urges tea partiers to remain humble, to reject bitterness or personal attacks on opponents, and to continually seek God through prayer and fasting. In fact, he will sometimes fast—taking no food for three or four days in a row while drinking only water—as he prays for spiritual renewal for himself, his family, his friends, and all of America. "We are losing our freedom, one court decision at a time," he once told me, "and we don't even realize it's happening. We need to return to the spiritual standards that guided the founding fathers— the Ten Commandments and the Word of God. Nothing great in America has ever happened without a spiritual revival."

The man who introduced me to Mark Skogerboe deserves an honorary commission in the new Black Regiment. His name is Jerry Breyer. My pal Jerry is not a preacher. He's a businessman in Grand Forks, North Dakota. He owns the Gold and Silver Exchange and Generous Jerry's Fireworks Stands. He's also a man of deep and humble faith, and he doesn't hesitate to share his faith with anyone, anywhere, anytime. He's active in the tea party movement because he's convinced that America must return to its founding principles, including faith in God, or this "last best hope of earth" is doomed.

Jerry's love of God and his love of country are bound up in his enthusiasm for fireworks. Nothing makes him happier than to see people celebrating America's birthday with fireworks from his stands.

And Jerry donates a significant portion of the proceeds from his fire-works sales to Christian causes. "It's a business," he once told me, "but it's a business that puts Jesus first."

All around the country, priests, ministers, and grassroots believers are responding when the Good Lord taps them on the shoulder. They are awakening to a call not only to *preach* the Gospel but to *live* it in sacrificial and risky ways. This new twenty-first-century Black Regiment understands that human liberty is a foundational principle in the scriptures—and that resistance to tyranny is still our moral duty today.

A WALL OF SEPARATION

On May 5, 2010—the eve of the National Day of Prayer—a group of fifteen junior high school students formed a circle near the United States Supreme Court building in Washington, D.C., and began to pray for our country. The students were all members of an American history class from Wickenburg Christian Academy in Arizona. Moments after they began praying, a court police officer came over to them, interrupted their prayer, and told them that what they were doing was against the law. If they wanted to pray, he said, they had to go elsewhere.

The teacher, Maureen Rigo, told Todd Starnes of Fox News Radio, "It was just supposed to be a time that we could pray quietly for the Supreme Court, for the decisions they need to make and for our congressmen. . . . We kind of feel like our government can use all the prayers it can get."

Rigo and her students moved to a place where they could pray without being interrupted by the police—the gutter. There they continued their prayer. It was, the teacher said, a learning experience. "We do a long study on the U.S. Constitution," she explained. "We talked about the rights that we have given to us in the First Amendment—the right to freedom of speech, the right to freedom of religion. We have the right to peaceful assembly. We have the right to due process of law. We feel like all of those things had been denied us there."

Ironically, those rights were denied them on the Supreme Court property itself, on the day before the National Day of Prayer.[21]

At a tea party in Bismarck a few days before Independence Day 2009, a man from the audience took the microphone and told about a trip he had recently made to Washington, D.C., with some friends. During their visit to the National Mall between the Washington Monument and the Lincoln Memorial, they began singing "Amazing Grace." Police officers stopped them and told them they were breaking the law.

"We cannot sing religious songs on the National Mall in Washington, D.C.," he concluded, "on our own property! In 2001, a group of us went to Moscow and visited Red Square. You know what would have happened to us if we had sung 'Amazing Grace' in Red Square? Nothing! But they made us stop singing in Washington. That's what's fundamentally wrong with this country. That's what we have to change. God bless America!"

In May 2010, after tornadoes devastated the small town of Ebenezer, Mississippi, church volunteers with the Salvation Army joined with Federal Emergency Management Agency (FEMA) workers to clean up debris. Two church workers, Angela Lott and Pamela Wedgeworth, were engaged in cleanup chores when they were approached by a FEMA videographer who asked them to do an on-camera interview.

Before the interview began, the videographer asked the two volunteers to change their T-shirts. Lott said the man told them, "We would like to ask you to change your shirt because we don't want anything faith-based," referring to the Salvation Army logos on their shirts. When the young women asked why they had to hide their affiliation with the Salvation Army, the man replied that removing faith-based logos is what they normally did.

The two women changed shirts and gave the interviews, but later wished they had stood their ground and kept their Salvation Army logos in full view. "It kind of hurt my feelings," Pamela Wedgeworth explained. "I made the comment, 'I think that's the reason we're all here, is by faith.' " FEMA apologized to the two church volunteers after the story received widespread news coverage.[22]

The $621 million United States Capitol Visitor Center (CVC) was designed to serve as a rest stop and information center for visitors to the Capitol complex. When Senator Jim DeMint of South Carolina took a preview tour, he noticed that there wasn't a single reference to America's religious heritage in any of the CVC's displays. There were politically correct references to Indian gaming casinos and environmentalism, but not a single reference to God, not even a photo of a church. A display on one wall proclaimed America's national motto to be *E Pluribus Unum*. While this is one of the three mottos found on our coins, our *official* national motto (established by an act of Congress in 1956) is *In God We Trust*.

A scale model of the Speaker's Rostrum in the House Chamber was perfect in every detail except one: it omitted the motto *In God We Trust* engraved in gold letters above the Speaker's chair. The display also featured photos of the Speaker's rostrum, but cropped in such a way that *In God We Trust* was not visible.

A display featuring the United States Constitution had also been altered. In the actual Constitution, there's a line above the signatures that reads: "Done in Convention by the Unanimous Consent of the States present the Seventeenth Day of September in the Year of our Lord one thousand seven hundred and Eighty seven. . . ." In the CVC display, the words "in the Year of our Lord" were removed.

There were other examples that showed that the Capitol Visitor Center had been *deliberately* scrubbed of every reference to God. Appearing on my show, Senator DeMint said he had witnessed what looked to be "a whitewash of our nation's faith heritage" at the CVC. Senator DeMint, along with Congressman Randy Forbes of Virginia, Rick Tyler of Renewing American Leadership, and others, pressured the government into correcting those inaccuracies and omissions so that the CVC would present a more complete image of America's religious heritage to Capitol visitors.[23]

Why does our government seem to exhibit so much hostility toward religion today? The opening lines of the First Amendment seem easy enough to understand: "Congress shall make no law respecting an establishment of religion, or prohibiting the free exercise thereof. . . ." This means simply that Congress shall not establish a state religion, such as the Church of England, and that the government may not prevent people from freely practicing their religion.

This means the government may not prevent students from praying on the grounds of the Supreme Court. The government may not keep people from singing "Amazing Grace" on the National Mall. It may not stop relief workers from wearing Salvation Army T-shirts while being interviewed on camera by FEMA. And it may not distort and obliterate America's religious history at the Capitol Visitor Center.

Even though the First Amendment protects religious expression, leftists and secularists, led by the American Civil Liberties Union (ACLU), keep trying to expunge all religious expression from the public square. They recite the slogan "separation of church and state" like a mantra, but hardly ever do they quote the actual words of the First Amendment. Why? Because the wording of the First Amendment *protects* the very religious expression they are trying to ban.

The phrase "separation of church and state" does not appear anywhere in the U.S. Constitution. Where, then, did that phrase come from? It came from a letter written in 1802 by President Thomas Jefferson to the Danbury Baptist Association of Connecticut. The Baptists were a religious minority and Jefferson wanted to assure the Danbury Baptists that the federal government would always protect the free exercise of their religion. So he wrote, "I contemplate with sovereign reverence that act of the whole American people which declared that their legislature should 'make no law respecting an establishment of religion, or prohibiting the free exercise thereof,' thus building a wall of separation between Church & State."[24]

When you look at that phrase in the context of Jefferson's letter to the Baptists, it is clear that the phrase "a wall of separation between Church & State" refers to a wall that protects religion from being suppressed or restricted by the government. The secularists of today, such as the ACLU and Americans United for Separation of Church and State, have reversed Thomas Jefferson's original intentions. They use the argument of "separation" to silence religion and erase all traces of it from the public square. Jefferson would be furious to know how his words have been twisted.

Let's defend the original intent of Thomas Jefferson and the United States Constitution. When you hear people parrot the phrase "separation of church and state," *challenge* them. Inform them that there's no such language anywhere in the Constitution. Enlighten them as to what the First Amendment actually says—and what it truly means. Defend your faith and your right to freely express your faith.

BLEEDING-HEART CONSERVATIVES

Jesus taught us to be compassionate and to give to the poor. "But when you give alms," He said, "your left hand must not know what your right is doing; your almsgiving must be secret, and your Father who sees all that is done in secret will reward you."[25] Most of the Christians I know are generous and compassionate to a fault. It's hard to catch them at it, because they obey the words of Jesus—they give in secret, and they don't let their left hand know what their right is doing.

Conservatives love to give. They love to help people in need. True, they resent having the government take money from them and squander it on big-government social programs. But they love to support people in need and charitable organizations that do good work. Wherever you find conservatives being generous and compassionate with their money, you find they are also generous and compassionate with their time. They volunteer at homeless shelters, homes for unwed mothers, adoption and foster care homes, tutoring and mentoring programs, urban ministry, short-term overseas missionary work, and much more.

Liberals will tell you that they have a corner on compassion. We all know the stereotype of "bleeding-heart liberals." But the facts tell us otherwise. According to a study conducted by the Gallup polling organization, conservatives are *far* more generous and compassionate than liberals. This may come as a shock to many liberals, but it is no surprise to me. As Arthur C. Brooks observed in an article for the *Wall Street Journal:*

> People who called themselves "conservative" or "very conservative" made up 42 percent of the population surveyed, but gave 56 percent of the total charitable donations. In contrast, "liberal" or "very liberal" respondents were 29 percent of those polled but gave just 7 percent of donations.

These disparities were not due to differences in income. People who said they were "very conservative" gave 4.5 percent of their income to charity, on average; "conservatives" gave 3.6 percent; "moderates" gave 3 percent; "liberals" gave 1.5 percent; and "very liberal" folks gave 1.2 percent.[26]

Isn't that amazing? The more conservative you are, the more generous you are. The more liberal you are, the more stingy you are. Fact is, we should start calling ourselves "bleeding-heart conservatives"!

The Gallup study also found (and again, this is no surprise to me) that conservatives volunteer more of their own time and energy to charity. And get this: red-blooded American conservatives actually donate more blood to the Red Cross than liberals do! Gallup also discovered that those who agree with the statement that "government has a responsibility to reduce income inequality" donated only 25 percent as much as those who disagree with that statement.[27] What does that tell you? It tells you why liberals are so stingy! Liberals believe in being generous only with *your* money, not their own. They want the government to pick *your* pocket and "spread the wealth around."

Conservatives and liberals both believe in something called *compassion,* but we define the word differently. Conservatives believe it's compassionate to *give*. Liberals believe it's compassionate to *take*.

MOUNTAIN-MOVING POWER

It could be said that Jimmy Carter cost my dad his radio station—and Barack Obama cost me mine.

My investment group and I acquired Radio WZFN (now WZFG) in Fargo-Moorhead in mid-2008, along with three other radio stations. We were casting around for a name for our new flagship station, and my wife, Maria, came up with the perfect name for a station with a conservative, patriotic talk format: "AM 1100 The Flag." We began broadcasting around the same time Barack Obama was running around the country, campaigning on how horrible everything was in America. Starting in January 2009, when Obama got into office, his failed policies devastated the economy even further. That was the environment in which we were trying to build our business—our timing could not have been worse.

As the economy faltered, advertising revenue dried up. Though the station had exceeded its sales goals through the fall of 2008, we hit a brick wall going into 2009. As America was accumulating more and more debt due to failed bailouts and stimulus schemes, our company was accumulating far more debt than we had anticipated, and we just couldn't get right-side-up quick enough. It was costing my investors a lot more money to keep the station running than it was originally supposed to.

All through 2009 and on into 2010, I experienced a lot of stress and worry about the financial situation at the station. I was feeling the heat from my investors and I feared I might lose everything I had built.

In February 2010, I did a National Pancake Day broadcast from the International House of Pancakes in Fargo. After the broadcast, a fellow came up, shook my hand, told me he was a regular listener and loved the show. He introduced himself as Clinton Sletten from Casselton, just west of Fargo, and he said he had an engine-rebuilding business.

We chatted for a few moments, and he told me he prayed for me, for my family, and for the work I was doing on the radio. Well, I was glad to hear that. I needed all the prayer I could get.

In the weeks that followed, Clinton would occasionally call with a word of encouragement and a few words of prayer. It seemed he always called when I needed a spiritual lift, and his prayers were always targeted on exactly what I was going through.

The financial stress and pressure from my investors was peaking during the summer of 2010. I knew my investors were running out of patience.

In July, we had our big Fargo Street Fair. That was when Wendy Gerlach, the Lemongrass Spa lady, had a booth in front of our radio station, raising funds to provide spa products for our women soldiers in Iraq. I was out on the street, shaking hands and smiling on the outside—

But inside, I was hurting.

Suddenly, there was Clinton. He came up to me out of the crowd and said, "Scott, how are you doing?"

"I'm hanging in there." Though I had a big grin on my face, I meant it, literally. I was barely hanging in there.

"I feel I need to pray for you," Clinton said.

"Well, bring it on, buddy," I said.

So right in the middle of the street, with hundreds of people milling around us, Clinton reached out and put his hand on my head. Then he said the most awesome prayer—a prayer for my health, for the radio station, for financial success, for continuing to speak out for those who need to be heard, and for our nation.

I've never been shy about sharing my faith on the air, but I'm not one to outwardly pray in public. But here we were with hundreds of people all around us, many of them stopping and staring—and I didn't care about any of that. Everything else was shut out, as if the world around me had stopped. I closed my eyes and focused on that beautiful prayer. I don't know how long Clinton prayed—two, three, four minutes?—but it was nothing less than awesome.

Clinton has been my prayer warrior ever since.

Going into the fall of 2010, the situation with my financial partners continued to worsen. The handwriting was on the wall. We were headed for a showdown.

I called my friend former governor Ed Schafer and asked if he and I could get together to talk. Ed had always been a good sounding board for me. Although I was about to lose the station, I still had a lot of options in front of me, including syndication. I was also involved in the political wars, and counting down to the big midterm election.

So I drove up to Ed and Nancy Schafer's lake home. I remember taking a call from Karl Rove as I was driving, and during that call, another call came in. I checked the number, but didn't recognize it. I finished talking to Karl just as I pulled up in front of Ed's lake home. Then I returned the call I didn't recognize—and it turned out to be Clinton.

"I can't believe you called me back," he said. "I know how busy you are."

"Well, Clinton," I said, "you're my prayer warrior. I just pulled up at Ed and Nancy Schafer's to talk about my future."

"Well, I want to pray for you," he said. And he did so over the phone. His prayer helped settle my mind as I went into the meeting with Ed.

In early September, Maria and I sat down with my partners and they informed me that they were taking back the station and pulling my show off the air. It was tough news to take, yet the moment I heard the news, I felt a sense of calm wash over me. It was as if the burden I had been carrying all those weeks was suddenly lifted. I asked my partners how they thought it would improve things at the radio station to have me off the air. They just said, "Well, we'll find out." I looked at Maria—and I could see that she was actually happy. Like me, she was relieved that all of the pressure had been lifted.

News reports on my departure insinuated that some sort of wrongdoing was involved. One news story began, "Exactly why longtime radio talk show host Scott Hennen was abruptly dismissed from the local radio station he helped build continues to be a mystery." [28]

Well, it wasn't much of a mystery. The economy had tanked—and so had advertising revenue. So my financial backers bought out my contract and took back the station I had built.

During the weeks of my exile from the air, there was a huge outpouring of support for me. Meanwhile, advertising revenue continued to drop. So the investors and their attorney called for a meeting with me and my attorney in hopes of getting me back on the air. In November 2010, I came back in a new role. I was no longer in management, but I was hosting *The Common Sense Club* in a new time slot.

My friend Clinton and his prayers, along with our own faith, were a big part of getting us through this chapter in our lives. I can't quote his prayers exactly, but certain phrases stand out. He once said, "Just because the economy is crumbling all around the nation, Lord, doesn't mean that Your economy is crumbling with it. The earth is the Lord's and the fullness thereof." And he asked God to supply my financial needs. The amazing thing is that he prayed for these needs even though I had never told him what I was going through. Clinton seems to have a pipeline to the One who knows everything.

He once told me, "I believe in my heart that God does set up divine appointments. It's amazing how God can bring people together. The Lord puts a burden on you to pray for somebody, and you know it's from God Himself. I believe prayer will move mountains. I don't take prayer lightly. I take it to extremes. I've seen prayer answered right before my very eyes. I believe in praying for finances. God enjoys the prosperity of His saints. But there are things more important than money. What is a family worth? What is a friend worth? Even if you don't have a lot of money, God wants us to prosper in the things that really matter."

Like my friend Clinton Sletten, I believe in prayer—and I believe in divine appointments. I know that Clinton from Casselton came into my life because God sent him.

A BETTER LIFE

I believe that even the "bad news" events in our lives are placed there for a reason. For example, I think God is using the presidency of Barack Obama as a wake-up call to this nation. The election of Barack Obama was bad news for grassroots conservatives. It meant the triumph of a far-left, redistributionist, big-government agenda. But what happened after Obama became president? He overreached! He forced his radical agenda down the throats of the American people—and the people choked on it.

The sleeping giant has awakened. People are beginning to say, "You know, maybe the politicians I've been sending to Washington, D.C., don't really represent my values. Maybe I need to take a closer look at these candidates and stop being fooled by their slick words. Maybe I need to take a hard look at what they do instead of being lulled by what they say—because their campaign promises and their actions don't match." Grassroots Americans are putting up a firewall against the big-government policies of this far-left administration. A lot of good is coming out of a bad situation.

And I agree with my friend Clinton when he says, "Prayer will move mountains." I have found that when you pray, you actually end up getting what you ask for. Not every time, not always on your own schedule, but in God's time, you get it. What a gift that is!

I believe in God from my head to my toes, and I pray that my kids will have the same faith that Maria and I share. Faith solves so much. If you have fallen away from your faith, from prayer, from reading the Bible, from attending your church, I'd encourage you to return to it. When the storms come in your life—and they will—you'll face them with a strength far beyond your own.

We send our kids to Catholic school, and I would encourage you as a parent to consider a faith-based school for your children, whatever your faith. Every year, Maria and I speak to prospective kindergarten parents at Fargo Catholic School. I tell them that when our children were baptized, we promised God that we would raise them in the faith. And I say that, of all the things you can give your children, faith is the one gift that will enable them to handle whatever life throws at them.

I've recently undergone surgery to remove my colon. Was I frightened at the prospect? Was my wife, Maria? Were my kids? No. We were concerned, but not frightened, because all of us in the Hennen family are convinced that everything happens for a reason, and that God is in control.

And please remember to pray for our nation. Pray for the economy. Pray for our leaders. Pray for President Obama. Pray for hearts and minds to change in America—and then believe that God can change those hearts and minds through prayer alone. Prayer is mountain-moving power.

The worries of this world don't have to weigh you down. "Unload all your burden on to him," wrote St. Peter, "since he is concerned about you." [29] I have found that if you follow the simple rules God has laid out in the Bible, life turns out well. If you place your trust in Him, then when this good life is over, you get to go on to *another* life, a life *after* life, and that is even *better*. I know this because I have a strong Catholic faith. You may have a different faith, and that's okay—we all choose our lane. What matters is that you walk with God, and He walks with you.

Because of my faith, I can look into my wife's eyes and say, "If I die tomorrow, Maria, I'll be fine. I'll know we had a lot of fun. And I know God will take care of you." Now, I don't want to die, of course. I want to go on living for Maria, Alex, Hannah, and Haley. But my faith tells me that, no matter what the future may bring, it will be just fine.

So, my grassroots conservative friend, keep praying, keep trusting, keep fighting for everything that's true and right and pure and admirable.

And above all, *keep the faith*.

THE COMMONSENSE ACTION AGENDA

Here are some grassroots actions you can take, starting today:

✓ Remember Dennis Prager's simple reminder of what it means to be an American. Anytime you need to explain what makes Americans different from the rest of the world, just take a coin from your pocket and read these three mottos: *E Pluribus Unum, In God We Trust,* and *Liberty.*

✓ Always remember—and remind the people around you—that the Bill of Rights does not "give" you your rights. You are *endowed by your Creator* with certain unalienable rights, and the Bill of Rights requires that the government protect and respect your God-given natural rights.

✓ Whenever you hear someone parrot the phrase "separation of church and state," take a polite but firm stand. Remind people that there is no such phrase anywhere in the Constitution. Instead, the First Amendment stands as a guarantee that the government is not to interfere in matters of religion. It also guarantees the right of the people to voice their religious views in the public square and to petition the government to act in a moral way. The First Amendment protects believers from the government, not the government from believers.

✓ Hold the government accountable when it tramples on your religious freedoms. Take a stand for praying and sharing your faith in the public square. Don't let the government infringe on your First Amendment right to freely exercise your religion in public. Tell your story to the newspapers, publish it on your blog and Facebook, and post it to YouTube.

✓ Practice compassion for the poor. Oppose higher taxes and higher government spending, which crowd out charitable giving. Organizations like the Salvation Army, Catholic Charities USA, local pro-life organizations, and 40 Days for Life will use your donations far more effectively than the welfare state will. Donate generously to organizations that show genuine compassion to people in need. Be a true "bleeding-heart conservative."

✓ Pray for your nation. Pray for your leaders regardless of what party or political philosophy they belong to. Pray for President Obama. Pray for a change of heart in our nation's capital. Pray for the repentance and salvation of America.

When Ronald Reagan was inaugurated president of the United States on a cold, rainy day in January 1981, he chose to be sworn in on the well-worn Bible that had once belonged to his mother, Nelle, and which was opened to 2 Chronicles 7:14: "If my people, which are called by my name, shall humble themselves, and pray, and seek my face, and turn from their wicked ways; then will I hear from heaven, and will forgive their sin, and will heal their land." In the margin next to that verse, Nelle Reagan had written, "A most wonderful verse for the healing of a nation." [30]

The skies were gray and threatening until Ronald Reagan put his hand on a Bible and took the oath. Suddenly, even miraculously, the clouds broke and the sun shone brightly on Ronald Reagan. [31] Those bright rays of sunshine symbolized the change that came over America at that moment. President Reagan dedicated his eight years in office to carrying out the words of 2 Chronicles 7:14. Those were indeed the most wonderful words for the healing of a nation.

Prayer is the most powerful grassroots action of all.

EPILOGUE

A CALL A DAY

The tea party movement loves Congresswoman Michele Bachmann—and the liberal-progressive movement *hates* her with a purple passion. Nancy Pelosi and the Democratic Party targeted Michele for defeat in 2010, spending more than $4 million to wage a massively negative campaign against her. The Democrats failed, and Michele collected 53 percent of the vote in a three-way race (her closest opponent garnered only 40 percent).

I am proud of Michele Bachmann—proud to be her friend and to have her representing the American people. She is a great American success story. Following her parents' divorce, Michele was raised by her mother, who worked at a bank in Anoka, Minnesota. Michele worked at several jobs to pay her own way through college, graduating from Winona State University with a B.A. in political science and English. She went on to earn juris doctor and master of laws degrees. She has raised five children and is a foster mom to twenty-three children.[1] No wonder Michele Bachmann has so much credibility with grassroots Americans.

In late 2009, I worked with Gary Emineth, chairman of the Republican Party in North Dakota, on an event designed to bridge the gap between the tea party and the GOP. Gary wanted to convince the tea party folks that they and the Republicans had a lot in common. He envisioned an event that would encompass the issues and concerns of both tea partiers and conservative Republicans. That event would eventually become known as Win Back Washington. I invited Michele Bachmann to take part, and she agreed.

Then I met with North Dakota governor (now senator) John Hoeven and his staff. I invited him to be on the platform as well—and I was surprised at his reaction when I mentioned Michele Bachmann. "You invited Michele Bachmann?" he said. "Be careful, Hennen! Have you seen her poll numbers? Her negatives are very high with independents!"

"That's because the Democrats and the mainstream media have been pounding away at her," I said. "But this isn't about Michele Bachmann. This is about respecting the people who think the world of her—and the people who are coming to Win Back Washington *love* Michele Bachmann. And with all respect, Governor Hoeven, you could learn a lot from those people."

Well, our discussion quickly degenerated into a shouting match. One thing was clear: John Hoeven didn't want to be at Win Back Washington. For one thing, he and his aides didn't like the format. It was designed to allow grassroots citizens to take the microphone and say anything they wanted—including criticism of their elected leaders. The plan was for those leaders (including Governor Hoeven) to sit at what we called a "listening post" in the front of the room. Those leaders would not speak, they would have no microphone. They were there to listen to the voice of the people.

John and his staffers hated the idea. Don Larson, the governor's campaign manager, said, "I can see it now! Somebody will grab the mike and tear into John—and that scene will be replayed endlessly on the news and on YouTube."

I said, "You should hope that happens! It will show the voters that John Hoeven is big enough to go face-to-face with people who disagree with him! Why are Dorgan, Conrad, and Pomeroy in political trouble? Because they won't listen to the people. They're hiding from the people. Don't repeat their mistakes."

Larson was adamant. "John has everything to lose and nothing to gain by going."

"That's where you're wrong," I said. "If John Hoeven isn't there, the story is going to be that he ducked the event. These are freedom-loving, God-fearing North Dakotans and Minnesotans—people just like you. Just come and hear what they have to say."

But John and his staff remained unconvinced.

"Look," I said, "if Governor Hoeven doesn't attend, my monologue on Monday's show is going to be entitled 'Missed Opportunity.' I'm going to talk about how you passed up the chance to show the people of this state that you're different from the Democrats."

What was Governor Hoeven so worried about? His conservative credentials were just fine. The people loved him. Sure, as governor, he had spent a lot of money—but our economy was growing and the state budget was in excellent shape thanks to John Hoeven's good governance. Unlike the federal government or bankrupt states like California, we don't deficit-spend in North Dakota. We live within our means.

Finally, I persuaded John to attend the Win Back Washington rally. As it turned out, he had nothing to fear. The conservative crowd was warm and friendly. When I introduced Governor Hoeven, the folks gave him a standing ovation—and deservedly so. He's a good man. His worries about being attacked by tea party conservatives were unfounded. Everyone was polite, and quite a few people praised John's successful tenure as governor.

We also invited Byron Dorgan, Kent Conrad, and Earl Pomeroy to come to the event—but they were AWOL. I think that spoke volumes to the audience. Perhaps if Earl Pomeroy had attended, he might have won reelection.

To John Hoeven's credit, he shook my hand after the event and said, "Thank you, Scott. You were right. It worked out great!"

We had more town hall and tea party events throughout the year, and I challenged every political leader in the state to come and listen to the people. Oh, they were mad at me! But the ones who came made an impression on the voters. Come to think of it, the ones who *didn't* show up made an impression, too.

There's a moral to this story, especially for politicians. If you want to get elected, you need to *listen* to the grass roots. You need to stop trying to control every event, and simply trust the hearts of the people who elected you. If you listen to your people, odds are they'll give you a chance to lead.

A GRASSROOTS REBELLION

Historian Ray Raphael is the author of such books as *A People's History of the American Revolution: How Common People Shaped the Fight for Independence* and *Founders: The People Who Brought You a Nation*. As a historian, he specializes in debunking historical myths. One of the great truths he has uncovered is the fact that the Revolution was not merely the result of the actions of a handful of famous individuals we know as "the founding fathers." The American Revolution was, first and foremost, a *grassroots rebellion*.

In 1774, two years before the Declaration of Independence was adopted in Philadelphia, thousands of grassroots farmers, shopkeepers, blacksmiths, and artisans rose up in rebellion all across Massachusetts—a rebellion known as the Worcester Revolution. More than 4,600 grassroots militiamen rousted all the British officials out of their homes and into the streets and drove them away. Like the tea party movement today, this was a leaderless movement. "The people elected representatives who served for one day only," writes Raphael, "the ultimate in term limits." The names of the Massachusetts militiamen who drove out the British were lost to history—but we know what they did. Those early grassroots patriots set the colony of Massachusetts free from British domination.

The following year, in 1775, British forces marched into Lexington and Concord—an event generally considered to be the official beginning of the American Revolution. But as Raphael points out, that was not the true beginning of the Revolution. The British went to Lexington and Concord *to put down a grassroots rebellion that had already taken place* all across Massachusetts the previous year. "The United States was founded not by isolated acts of heroism," he writes, "but by the concerted revolutionary activities of people who had learned the power of collaborative effort. 'Government has now devolved upon the people,' wrote one disgruntled Tory in 1774, 'and they seem to be for using it.' That's the story the myths conceal."

Raphael worries that when we teach American history only in terms of the acts of a few famous leaders, "we misrepresent, and even contradict, the spirit of the American Revolution. . . . Throughout the rebellious colonies, citizens organized themselves into an array of local committees, congresses, and militia units that unseated British authority and assumed the reins of government. These revolutionary efforts could serve as models for the collective, political participation of ordinary citizens. Stories that focus on these models would confirm the original meaning of American patriotism: Government must be based on the will of the people."[2]

The Great American Experiment has always been a grassroots movement. The early patriots didn't look to politicians to save their country. They rolled up their sleeves and did the hard work themselves. They "blogged" with pamphlets and sermons and heated arguments on the village green. They went to town hall meetings. They picked up their muskets and fought and died on the battlefields. They held the first tea party in Boston Harbor. They raised a ruckus and defeated the oppressor. They built America out of a dream and a desire for freedom.

This is not to diminish the greatness and the genius of those great men whom we revere as the "founding fathers"—men like Washington, Franklin, Adams, Jefferson, Madison, Hamilton, and the rest. But these leaders didn't act in isolation from the rest of their countrymen. They were part of the fabric of grassroots revolutionary fervor that gripped the thirteen colonies. The founding fathers were part of a founding generation of grassroots patriots whose names are no longer remembered, but who pledged their lives, their fortunes, and their sacred honor to this new nation.

Those early grassroots patriots believed in a citizen legislature, not an elite class of career politicians—and that's just what tea party patriots believe in today. I often say that we could pick out 535 better members of Congress from the phone book than most of the ones we have now—and that's no exaggeration. We need to remember that the power rests with us. Average, everyday Americans are changing this country by reminding our elected leaders to obey the Constitution.

There is an enormous storehouse of commonsense wisdom in average, everyday people. Even though we are disappointed and angry with *both* political parties, the *tea party* movement has resisted the temptation to become a *third party* movement. We've seen third parties before, and all they do is split the conservative vote and hand elections to the left on a silver platter. We are the working people, the blue-collar people, the farmers, the stay-at-home moms, and all the other people who roll up their sleeves and toil every day to provide for their families. And after putting in a full day's work, we take the time to paint a sign, go to a tea party, and fight for the future of our country.

The tea party must never become a political party. The tea party is what it is because there are no leaders, there are no entrance requirements, and everyone is welcome. The moment leaders rise up to take control and assert their personal agendas and egos and fight turf battles, the movement will go south—quick. We are united around the Constitution and principles of limited government—not personalities.

The secret sauce of our tea parties here in North Dakota and Minnesota is that they are not about politicians grabbing the microphone and telling the rest of us about their big ideas and grand agendas. Here in the heartland, we hand the microphone to ordinary folks. We tell the politicians to sit down and listen up. That's our tea party model.

Our message to politicians, regardless of party, is simple: "If you listen to us, if you trust the people, if you obey the Constitution, if you practice common sense when it comes to budgets, deficits, taxes, national defense, secure borders, and freedom, you have nothing to fear from us. We will support you. Are we going to agree with you on everything? No! But hey, welcome to America! Does everybody agree with everybody else in America? No! But one of the best ways to learn is by sitting down with people who disagree with you and finding out *why* they disagree."

Now, there are some people who will try to paint the entire tea party movement as a bunch of kooks and extremists. Even Bill O'Reilly of Fox News once said, "Some of these tea party people are nuts. They are. They're crazy. I mean, we sent Jesse Watters down there [to a tea party], and he puts the number at about 10 percent that are just loons, out of their mind. . . . No matter what group you're talking about, you'll find loons."[3]

I think I know the people he's talking about—the people with tea bags hanging from their hats, the people dressed like Paul Revere or Benjamin Franklin. But those people aren't "loons" or "crazy." They are just having a good time. They're the ones who put the "party" in tea party.

The tea party movement is one of the most maligned groups in American history. They are routinely smeared by a hostile media that portrays them as some kind of political freak show. When people ask me, "Who are these tea party people?" I reply, "They're real people. They're ordinary, salt-of-the-earth Americans. They're just like you and me. They have jobs and families. They work hard to put food on the table and pay their taxes. They sit next to you in church, they drive their kids to soccer practice and piano lessons, they stand next to you at the checkout line. They love their country."

Demonizing the tea party movement has become a fixation with the prattlers of the left. For example, in May 2010, Paul Krugman of the *New York Times* wrote, "News organizations have taken notice: suddenly, the takeover of the Republican Party by right-wing extremists has become a story." Who are these "right-wing extremists" Krugman is talking about? Why, the tea party folks, of course!

"The rise of the Tea Party," he explains, is "exactly what we should have expected in the wake of the economic crisis." As the economy shows improvement, he adds, "we can expect some of the air to go out of the Tea Party movement." Krugman even engages in that tired old canard that "it's about race, the shock of having a black man in the White House."[4] Well, Mr. Krugman couldn't be more wrong.

One of the few mainstream media sources that got it right about the tea party movement was the *Christian Science Monitor,* which wrote, "Most of those who have been to actual tea party protests report that it's largely a decentralized, middle-class movement focused chiefly on taxes, deficits, and the nature of representation in Washington. . . . 'We have traditionally been the people that pay the bills and vote on Election Day but have sat back and been involved in other things rather than politics,' activist Phillip Dennis told the *Texas Tribune*."[5]

The liberal-progressives want to marginalize us and portray us as kooks and extremists. But I have a question for the smear merchants of the left: Exactly what part of the tea party agenda do you consider "extreme"? Is it our demand that our government adhere to the Constitution? Is it our insistence that we not spend more money than we take in? Is it our advocacy of limited government, lower taxes, and greater freedom? Tell me, which of these tea party positions do you consider "extreme"? Because *that* is the essence of the tea party agenda.

I have made quite a few guest appearances on MSNBC's *The Ed Show,* hosted by Ed Schultz. Before he became a liberal talker on radio and TV, Ed was a Fargo sportscaster at my old station WDAY, and later at KFGO. So Ed and I go back a long way. On more than one occasion during my appearances on his MSNBC show, I'd say something like, "We need to follow the Constitution," or, "We need to listen to the people." And Ed would impatiently growl, "Those are just talking points! Hennen, you've got to lose those talking points!"

But you and I know that those aren't just talking points. Those are *principles*. I know they must sound like talking points to liberals, because we keep saying these things over and over again. We keep talking about obeying the Constitution and listening to the people. We kept saying it the whole time the Democrats were passing the stimulus bill and nationalizing banks and passing Obamacare. We said it and said it until we were blue in the face! Why? Because the Democrats weren't obeying the Constitution and weren't listening to the people! So we threw the bums out in 2010—and 2012 is just around the corner.

We grassroots conservatives stick to our principles as articles of faith, because our principles have been proven reliable down through history. We know that tax cuts and balanced budgets produce economic booms every time they're tried. We know that Keynesian stimulus schemes produce recessions and depressions every time they're tried. These are proven principles, not talking points.

A CALL TO ACTION

Have you ever thought of running for Congress? Or, if that seems too daunting, how about running for a seat on your state legislature, city council, or school board? America needs commonsense grassroots citizens who are willing to get involved in running our local, state, and federal governments. America needs more citizen legislators—people who bring real-world experience to the job, and who are driven less by ego and more by a desire to serve.

In the 2010 midterm election, I had a tough choice between the two candidates for Minnesota's 7th Congressional District. Should I support Lee Byberg, the grassroots Republican candidate? Or Collin Peterson, the conservative Democrat incumbent? Both Lee Byberg and Collin Peterson are friends of mine. Both are pro-lifers.

But the decision became obvious when I saw that Collin Peterson was willing to side with Nancy Pelosi and his party leadership, even at the expense of what was best for his constituents. I decided I had to support the Republican, Lee Byberg.

My friend Ellen Ratner strongly disagreed with me. She asked, "How can you do that to a friend?" I said, "Collin Peterson is putting his party ahead of friendships, ahead of what's best for the country. I have to put my country first." So I campaigned for Lee Byberg—and against Collin Peterson. I haven't talked to Collin since the campaign. I'm told he's upset with me over the decision I made. But I had to vote my conscience and my principles, in spite of my friendship with him.

Lee Byberg, the son of Christian missionaries who worked in Latin America and Norway, is an executive and consultant who lives in Willmar, Minnesota. In addition to his accomplishments as an accountant, economist, and manager for several corporations, Lee is a songwriter and publisher, having produced and performed a twelve-song CD called *Twice American*.

I spent time with Lee as he took his "Twice American Express" campaign bus around the district. His slogan, "Twice American," refers to the fact that he was born in the United States, but lived most of his early life abroad as a child of missionaries, then returned to the United States from Norway while in his twenties.

At campaign rallies he would say, "Here in America, we talk about the American Dream. And you wonder: In Russia, do they speak of a Russian dream? In Germany, is there a German dream? In Scandinavia, is there a Scandinavian dream? Yes, they have their dreams. But many of them dream about America."

Lee Byberg believes in limited government, and often quotes Thomas Jefferson: "The natural progress of things is for liberty to yield and government to gain ground." And then he would tell the crowd that his goal was to force government to yield so that liberty could gain ground. I'd love to hear Lee Byberg's Norwegian accent and American ideals echoing in the House chamber. Lee lost the 2010 election, but he has announced that he will run again in 2012.

And what about you? Are you willing to put your grassroots ideals on the line? You know how badly we need grassroots common sense in our Congress, in our statehouses, and in the local community. We need people with principles, not just campaign rhetoric. We need people with real-world experience, not just political ambition. We need grassroots legislators, not just political hacks.

Now, I'm not going to kid you and say it's easy to run for office. It takes a lot of hard work, sacrifice, and getting knocked around by the media and your opponent—and there's no guarantee of success at the end of the road. Just ask Lee Byberg. Running for office takes a strong work ethic, perseverance, a tough skin, and courage—the very same character traits it took to start a revolution and build this country.

If you put yourself out there as a grassroots citizen candidate, the left is going to come after you. Just ask Sarah Palin. Just ask Michele Bachmann. Just ask Lee Byberg.

Or ask Joe the Plumber—Samuel Joseph Wurzelbacher. He was in his own neighborhood, minding his own business, when Barack Obama came sauntering along, trawling for votes. Wurzelbacher went up to Obama, asked him a question about his tax policies, and Barack Obama gave him that famous answer, "I think when you spread the wealth around, it's good for everybody." Barack Obama had let it slip that he favored Marxist-style income redistribution.

When Obama's redistributionist remarks were roundly criticized, the liberal establishment flew into a rage and tried to destroy Joe the

Plumber. Democratic officials of the Ohio Department of Job and Family Services rummaged through his records, looking for any unpaid taxes, liens, child support, or other problems that could be used to discredit him.[6] A former Ohio state contractor sifted through computerized police records, looking for dirt on Wurzelbacher.[7] Journalists hounded him and gave him far more intensive scrutiny than Barack Obama ever got. And Joe the Plumber wasn't running for office—all he did was ask a question.

Many on the hard left are driven by an unreasoning hatred for grassroots tea party values—for people who just want limited government, who don't want their children to become slaves to the national debt, who believe in liberty and personal responsibility. The hatred of the left is hard for us understand—yet it's real and it's aimed at you and me.

Glenn Beck brought forth some stunning audio from a strategy session of a militant socialist conference in New York City in November 2010. In the audio, a speaker says, "We all want to raise people's consciousness but we also want to fight people, right? . . . We want to fight people who have signed up on the other side of the barricade, who are fighting us. We have to fight them. We're a militant organization when it comes to the fight against gay bigotry, the fights against racism and sexism. The labor movement has this old saying . . . 'If you can't open their minds, open their heads.' [*Audience laughter.*] I don't know if we want to take it quite that far in all the issues. I think that, you know, we have to be fighters. . . .

"And especially you can point to the tea party, right? I mean, this was a Democratic Party platform during the elections, to whip everybody up into the fear of the tea party. . . . And obviously the tea party is awful. The tea party sometimes does look like a white supremacist mob and, you know, the logic of the Democrats is sort of like, 'Well, this mob is coming. Are you really going to fight with us? At least we're against them. Vote for us.' That's the logic that has a strong appeal among the working class."[8]

The liberal-progressives hate us with an irrational fury that is beyond our comprehension. They portray us as a "white supremacist mob," when all we want to do is preserve the promise of America for

future generations. Their fear makes them extreme—and dangerous. "If you can't open their minds," they say, "open their heads." And
they are talking about you and me.

I'm not saying this to scare you. I'm saying this to *challenge* you.
This is a call to action. We're going to fight hate with love—love of
God, love of country, love of our fellow human being. We're going
to fight lies with truth. We're going to fight fear with courage. We'll
overcome evil with good. If we can't open their minds, we *won't* crack
open their heads. No, we'll pry open their hearts. We'll pray for them
and talk to them and help them see the greatness and the goodness of
this idea we call America.

I've recently been working with Ed Schafer on a grassroots effort called Fix the Tax (www.FixTheTax.com). We've been driving
around the state, from Fargo to Bismarck to Minot and back again,
talking to people and generating support for a lower tax on oil exploration and development. At one point in our travels, Ed leaned over
to me and said, "You know, Scott, in the coming weeks and months,
we're going to encounter a lot of people we respect but disagree with.
I know you sometimes tend to disagree a little too strongly and you
need to be careful with that."

What could I say? Ed knew me well. He knows that I'm a talk
show host, not a diplomat. But to persuade people to support Fix the
Tax, I needed to become more of a diplomat. Ed gave me good fa-
therly advice—and he also gave me a handwritten note he had made.
The note read, " 'We must love them both, those whose opinions we
share and those whose opinions we reject; for both have labored in the
search for the truth, and both have helped us in the finding of it.' St.
Thomas Aquinas."

An us-versus-them approach has served me well in the talk radio
world. It has served me well when I have debated liberal opponents.
But I'm learning that my ultimate goal is not to *defeat* my opponents,
but to *persuade* them and win them over to my cause.

I'm grateful to my friend and mentor Ed Schafer. He knows me
well, and he gave me some wise, constructive criticism that will help
me in the days and years to come. We need to always remember to
love and respect our opponents. Don't hate them. They are searching

for the truth just as we are. If we can maintain our civility, if we can be good listeners, if we can show them courtesy and respect, in time we'll win them over.

And that is how we'll change the world.

WE CAN RAISE A SHOUT

Many people say, "What difference can one person make? I'm just one voice. The United States government won't listen to me." My friend, you've no idea of the power you have. One person calling an elected representative can have an enormous impact.

A *Common Sense Club* caller once said, "Scott, I have an idea for a tea party slogan."

I said, "Let's have it."

He said, "A call a day will keep Congress at bay."

What a brilliant idea! I immediately adopted that suggestion and have repeated that slogan on my show countless times in the past few years. Your calls matter. Members of Congress will tell you that when they receive a call from a constituent, they listen up. Two calls? They think a movement is building. Three calls? Why, that's a mandate! Our leaders in the House and the Senate take it seriously when we call.

So I have a suggestion: get the phone numbers of your elected representatives, put them in your speed dialer, and whenever you have a few spare minutes—when you're waiting at the dentist office or standing in line at the supermarket checkout—make that call. Let your representatives know what you think of pending legislation. Ask where your representative stands on this or that issue. Anytime you make a call, you make a difference.

A call a day really does keep Congress at bay. To make those calls count, stay informed. Listen to *The Common Sense Club* every day, as well as Rush, Sean, Levin, and the rest. Check my webpage at scotthennen.com, and my commonsense commentary at blog.scott hennen.com. Follow me on Facebook and Twitter. We've set up something on my show that I call the "Call a Day Initiative." We give listeners an issue every day to call about. As a result, our representatives have been forced to personally answer calls from constituents.

One of my listeners, a lady named Heather, called me and said, "I phoned Senator Dorgan's office like you said, and I was amazed—the senator *personally* took my call! I talked to him about a lot of different issues. I told him I was watching to make sure that he kept his promise not to vote for taxpayer-funded abortions. I gave him my thoughts on cap and trade, and I told him that if President Obama signs that darn global warming treaty, then Senator Dorgan had better not vote to ratify it!

"I also told him that my husband had just left for Afghanistan—his seventh deployment. I said, 'My husband went to Afghanistan because he believes in the War on Terror. It's not just a political position with him. He's in the middle of it. He's on the front lines, fighting that war.'

"I'm glad you told me to call Senator Dorgan. I feel good about it, because I feel I cleared the air with him. He knows at least how *this* North Dakotan feels."

Every call is important. I've had listeners tell me about similar experiences with other senators and representatives from North Dakota and Minnesota. One listener told me that former congressman Earl Pomeroy actually gave him his private cell phone number! Until the rise of the grassroots tea party movement, our elected officials never had to worry about public opinion. Now, all of a sudden, they're *very* worried. They know people are watching. They know they'll be held accountable for the promises they've made—and the promises they've broken.

A friend of mine knows a man who was an aide for then-congressman Earl Pomeroy. The aide told him, "You wouldn't believe how bad things are! It's those tea party people! They call all the time, and their calls are running nine-to-one against our agenda! Our phones are melting down. We draw straws to see who's going to take the next call."

What does it mean? It means we're *winning*! During the health care debate, only 28 percent of North Dakotans supported Obamacare—yet all of North Dakota's elected representatives voted for it. So our representatives were put in the uncomfortable position of having to explain to their constituents why they snubbed the will of the people and voted with Pelosi and Reid. They were forced to listen to voices of the American people—and those voices were angry.

Here in the heartland, grassroots citizens are proving that one person armed with a cell phone can make a big difference. And many grassroots citizens, working together, can change the course of the nation. As Thomas Jefferson observed, "When the people fear the government, there is tyranny; when the government fears the people, there is liberty." [10]

When your representatives are wrong, let them know. And when they do something right, praise them—give 'em an "Attaboy!" Call your conservative representatives to tell them you support them, you're praying for them, and to keep fighting the good fight. Your encouragement will bolster their determination to keep defending the Constitution.

Letters, emails, and phone calls are good, but from time to time, why not show up at your congressman's regional office and share your views in person? Take a vacation in Washington, D.C., and visit the office of your senator or congressperson. Let your representatives know you are involved and you are watching.

Some people say, "I vote in every election. Isn't that enough? What else can I do?" It's important to be an informed voter, but voting alone may not be enough. What good does it do to vote for the candidate who says all the right things, but then does all the wrong things once he or she gets to Washington? And what good is voting when our votes are routinely stolen?

Minnesota, the state next door to me, certified Al Franken as the newest senator from that state. According to Democratic secretary of state Mark Ritchie and the state Canvassing Board, Franken won by a razor-thin margin of 312 votes. But did he? Did Al Franken actually receive more votes than the Republican incumbent, Norm Coleman? Very doubtful.

On election night, the vote count left Franken trailing by 215 votes. During the subsequent recount, Mark Ritchie and the Canvassing Board issued a series of strangely inconsistent rulings—yet all of Ritchie's rulings had one thing in common: they all favored Franken. After analyzing the results of the recount, the *Wall Street Journal* concluded, "We can't recall a similar recount involving optical scanning machines that has changed so many votes, and in which nearly every crucial decision worked to the advantage of the same candidate. The Coleman campaign clearly misjudged the politics here, and the apparent willingness of a partisan like Mr. Ritchie to help his preferred candidate, Mr. Franken."[11]

Later, a conservative watchdog organization, Minnesota Majority, conducted an eighteen-month study showing that *at least* 341 convicted felons in the Democrat-leaning Minneapolis–St. Paul area voted illegally in the Coleman-Franken writes. The actual number of felons who voted in the Twin Cities may have been more than 1,300, but Minnesota Majority researchers are using the smaller number because they don't want to claim a felon voted unless they can match first, middle, and last names, year of birth, and the community in which the individual resides.[12]

There's no question in my mind that Norm Coleman ought to be the rightful senator from Minnesota, and that Al Franken was elected by fraud. But once he has been certified, it's official and it can't be undone. All we can do is look to the future, learn our lessons, and make sure it doesn't happen again. We need to make sure that conservatives win future elections by such a wide margin that no amount of cheating can flip an election.

This means, of course, that we must vote. Without question, there are hundreds, if not thousands, of conservative Minnesota voters who stayed home on election night 2008. They could have taken a few minutes, gone down to the polls—and put the election outside the margin of cheating. They have no one to blame but themselves for having a refugee from a bad *Saturday Night Live* skit as their senator.

But voting is just the beginning. We have to get involved in the political process. We have to persuade and convert our friends and neighbors to conservative values and constitutional principles. We have to get involved in campaigns, donating time and money to the candidates and causes we say we believe in. That's how democracies work.

Samuel Adams, in an essay written under the pseudonym "Candidus" for the *Boston Gazette,* October 14, 1771, wrote: "The liberties of our country, the freedom of our civil constitution, are worth defending at all hazards; and it is our duty to defend them against all attacks. We have received them as a fair inheritance from our worthy ancestors. They purchased them for us with toil and danger and expense of treasure and blood, and transmitted them to us with care and diligence. It will bring an everlasting mark of infamy on the present generation, enlightened as it is, if we should suffer them to be wrested from us by violence without a struggle, or be cheated out of them by the artifices of false and designing men."[13]

These words have never been more urgently true than they are today.

You may have just one voice and one vote. But so does your next-door neighbor. So does the guy you talk to at the water cooler every day. So does the clerk you chat with at the store every week. Everybody has just one voice. But when we join our voices together at a tea party or at the ballot box, we can raise quite a shout.

And we can make our government listen.

I'LL MEET YOU AT THE TEA PARTY

I've had the privilege of meeting with President George W. Bush in the Oval Office on two occasions, once in August 2007, the year of the troop surge in Iraq, and the second time in January 2009, less than a week before he left office. During that second visit to the White House, I was ushered into the Roosevelt Room, along with a number of my talk radio colleagues, to wait for President Bush.

The meeting was originally to take place in the Roosevelt Room, so I took my notebook out of my briefcase, and set the briefcase on the floor beside my chair. Moments later, President Bush came in and invited us into the Oval Office, so I grabbed my notepad and left my briefcase in the Roosevelt Room.

We met with President Bush for about an hour and twenty minutes, and he reflected on the eight years of his presidency. At times he was forceful, at times wistful, but he seemed very much at peace with himself. The Bush era was coming to an end and Barack Obama's inaugural was just a few days away.

I've always been impressed by George W. Bush's respect for the office he held for eight years. Unlike certain former presidents, Mr. Bush steadfastly refuses to criticize his successor. During our Oval Office meeting, he maintained that policy—though he did make one off-the-record statement to the effect that Barack Obama would soon find out that his campaign rhetoric was about to come up against the hard realities of the office. With a wry smile, Mr. Bush added, "He'll learn."

Barack Obama had made a lot of promises along the campaign trail—withdrawal from Iraq, the closing of the Guantánamo detention facility within one year, no lobbyists in his administration, no recess appointments, and on and on. Once Barack Obama took office, he learned that it was a lot easier to make campaign promises than it is to keep them.

Now, that's not a criticism of Barack Obama. It's a statement about the tough challenges of that job. But several White House staffers seemed visibly nervous after President Bush made that observation—and I knew why. They were afraid that one of us "loose cannon" talk show hosts just might spin President Bush's innocent remarks into a jab at his successor—and that would be a PR nightmare just days before the Obama inauguration.

(In fact, sometime after our Oval Office meeting, fellow talk show host Lars Larson and I went down to the basement of the White House media center in the West Wing to do our respective radio shows. We were accompanied by two White House Media Affairs staffers, Trey Bohn and Jeanie Mamo. While Lars and I were doing our shows, Trey and Jeanie hovered near our broadcast booths, making sure we followed the "off the record" rules—no direct quotes of the president, paraphrases only. They seemed worried and apprehensive, but Lars and I kept our word.)

Near the end of our Oval Office meeting, President Bush said, "I've got a surprise for you." Then he asked Vice President Cheney to step in. This was during the time when there was sharp disagreement between the president and vice president over former Cheney aide I. Lewis "Scooter" Libby. Cheney wanted Libby to receive a full pardon for his perjury conviction in the Valerie Plame case, but Bush would commute only Libby's prison sentence, leaving his felony conviction in place. So when Cheney came in, I sensed a tension between the two men.

Still, we had a great visit. I got my photo snapped with my arms around the shoulders of Cheney and Bush. The vice president promised to give me his first post–White House interview (he kept his word, giving me an exclusive interview at CPAC in February 2009).

Eventually, my talk show host colleagues and I were ushered out of the Oval Office—and that's when I remembered that I had left my briefcase in the Roosevelt Room. So I crossed the hall and swung the door open—

And found four very surprised people waiting in the Roosevelt Room: Senator Majority Leader Harry Reid, Speaker of the House Nancy Pelosi, Senate Minority Leader Mitch McConnell, and House Minority Leader John Boehner.

"Scott Hennen!" said Boehner. "Are *you* the reason we've been waiting half an hour to see the president?"

Pelosi and Reid knew me—I had interviewed them before. They didn't say a word. They didn't have to. They were giving me *death stares*.

I'll never forget that moment as long as I live. The look on their faces was priceless. Those four leaders of the two great political parties had been sitting in the Roosevelt Room, cooling their heels, waiting for their exit interview with the president of the United States—

And they were kept waiting by Scott Hennen, a "right-wing wacko" talk show host. I savored the expression on Nancy Pelosi's face. She looked like she'd been sucking on a lemon.

That's an expression I hope to see again and again in the coming years on the faces of Nancy Pelosi, Harry Reid, Barack Obama, Kent Conrad, Barney Frank, and all the other liberal-progressives who have driven America to the very brink of collapse with their deficits and debt, their failed stimulus and ruinous social engineering. I want to see that sucking-lemons expression again when we roll back Obamacare, drive down taxes and spending, and start living up to the Constitution and the ideals of our founding fathers.

Wouldn't you love to see that?

Then join me! I'll meet you at the tea party, with all the other grassroots patriots. And remember, a call a day keeps the Congress at bay. Keep fighting for the truth. Keep praying for America. Keep spreading the word to your friends and neighbors.

God bless you, my friend. And God bless the United States of America.

ACKNOWLEDGMENTS

I owe a debt of gratitude to all the people who made this book possible.

My wife, Maria, persuaded me to accept this challenge when I didn't think it was humanly possible. I'm so glad she did! Maria and my children, Alex, Hannah, and Haley, support and encourage me in ways too numerous to mention.

My producer and brother, Chris Hennen, knew where in the archives the exact tape or MP3 file we needed could be found. His assistance was indispensable throughout the writing of this book.

Ivan Kronenfeld was the first to suggest this book. He and Nathalie Casthely of Koerner Kronenfeld Partners, LLC, developed the strategy for this project and opened the doors to the publishing world. They believed in me as an author long before I did.

My friend Mary Matalin encouraged me, counseled me, and led me to my publishing home at Simon & Schuster. "Thank you" doesn't begin to cover it.

My agent, Frank Weimann, expertly shepherded this book from conception to completion.

I'm grateful to my collaborator, Jim Denney, for all of his insights, skills, and hard work.

Thanks to my administrative assistant, Nicole Paulson, whose efficiency and attention to detail made the entire process go smoothly.

I also wish to acknowledge my editors at Simon & Schuster, especially Anthony Ziccardi, Ed Schlesinger, and copyeditor Tom Pitoniak, for believing I had something important to say, and for helping me to say it on the printed page.

Thanks to my dear friends, business mentors, and counselors-in-chief: my banker, Dan Carey; Gene Nicholas (a true North Dakota legend); my number-one oil industry tutor and brother, Mike "Bubba" Cantrell; and Ed Schafer—business leader, former governor, former secretary of agriculture, man of faith and integrity, and wise counselor. And thanks to another great mentor and father figure in my life, John Pierce of Concordia College.

My spiritual mentors: Father William Sherman, who truly grounded me in my faith during my eighteen years in Grand Forks; Father Brian Bachmeier, Father Paul Ducheshere, and Father Chad Wilhelm, all of the Diocese of Fargo; and our hometown pastor from St. Joe's in Montevideo, Father Henry Christiansen. These men have all been instrumental in helping me grow in my faith.

Special thanks to my buddy Harold Hamm, the blue-collar billionaire; Ron Offutt, the Sultan of Spuds; Mark Pfeifle, flood fight veteran and longtime friend; Chuck Tompkins, the insurance warrior; Rusty Ouart, the "brain freeze" warrior; Kevin Cramer, one of North Dakota's all-time great public servants, energy experts, and a solid conservative.

My longtime friend and fellow author Ellen Ratner, who is somewhere to the left of Lenin, has helped me hone my political chops. She is also one of the most generous, gracious, and giving people in the world.

Thanks to my personal prayer warrior, Clinton Sletten from Casselton, North Dakota; my tea party pal Leon Francis, who knows more Ronald Reagan quotations by heart than I do; Julie Sorensen from Moorhead; and my pal Ross Ueckert, the one-man walking tea party.

I gratefully acknowledge Michael Hermanson and so many other fallen warriors who sacrificed all to keep America free.

Finally, my thanks go to you, the reader, a grassroots American. You are following in the footsteps of the patriots who built this country. Keep defending, guarding, calling, talking, praying, and fighting the good fight to save America for generations to come.

America will remain free as long as her grass roots are strong.

NOTES

INTRODUCTION

1. Source: http://www.miseryindex.us/.
2. Ronald Reagan, "Farewell Address to the Nation," Oval Office, Washington, D.C., January 11, 1989, http://www.reagan.utexas.edu/archives/speeches/1989/011189i.htm.
3. Sandra Fabry, "61 percent of National Income Goes to Government," Heartland Institute, October 2009, http://www.heartland.org/publications/budget%20tax/article/25904/61_Percent_of_National_Income_Goes_to_Government.html.
4. Peter Archer, *The Quotable Intellectual: 1,417 Bon Mots, Ripostes, and Witticisms for Aspiring Academics, Armchair Philosophers and Anyone Else Who Wants to Sound Really Smart* (Avon, MA: Adams Media, 2010), 139.

1. GRASSROOTS PEOPLE JUST LIKE YOU

1. Paul Joseph Watson, "Paulson Was Behind Bailout Martial Law Threat," PrisonPlanet.com, November 20, 2008, http://www.prisonplanet.com/paulson-was-behind-bailout-martial-law-threat.html.
2. Matt Taibbi, "The Great American Bubble Machine," Rollingstone.com, July 13, 2009, http://www.rollingstone.com/politics/story/29127316/the_great_american_bubble_machine.
3. Watson, "Paulson Was Behind Bailout Martial Law Threat."

4. Rick Santelli, "Video: Rick Santelli's CNBC Rant," February 23, 2009, transcribed and abridged from embedded video, http://archives.chicagotribune.com/2009/feb/23/business/chi-santelli-cnbc-video.

5. Naftali Bendavid, "Blueprint Finds Support, Unease on Capitol Hill," *Wall Street Journal*, February 27, 2009, A10.

6. Rob Port, "Call In: Earl Pomeroy To Hold A Tele-Town Hall Tonight," SayAnythingBlog.com, November 1, 2010, http://sayanythingblog.com/entry/call-in-earl-pomeroy-to-hold-a-tele-town-hall-tonight/.

7. Katie Connolly, "Tea-Party Protests: Loud, Mad, and Dangerous (For Republicans)," *Newsweek*, March 21, 2010, http://www.newsweek.com/blogs/the-gaggle/2010/03/21/tea-party-protests-loud-mad-and-dangerous-for-republicans.html.

8. Casey Gane-McCalla, "Bill Clinton Likens Tea Party Anger To Timothy McVeigh," *Nation*, April 16, 2010, http://newsone.com/nation/casey-gane-mccalla/bill-clinton-likens-tea-party-anger-to-timothy-mcveigh/.

9. Jann S. Wenner, "Obama in Command: The Rolling Stone Interview," RollingStone.com, September 28, 2010, http://www.rollingstone.com/politics/news/17390/209395?RS_show_page=0#.

10. Andrew Zarowny, "Sheryl Crow Calls Tea Party Uneducated, Angry & Potentially Dangerous," RightPundits.com, June 30, 2010, http://www.rightpundits.com/?p=6517.

11. Kyle Drennen, "CBS's Harry Smith on Tea Party: 'Can Anger Govern?,'" Media Research Center, October 12, 2010, http://www.mrc.org/biasalert/2010/20101012042117.aspx.

12. Associated Press, "Michele Bachmann: Tea Party Caucus Not Movement Mouthpiece," *U.S. News & World Report*, July 21, 2010, http://politics.usnews.com/news/articles/2010/07/21/michele-bachmann-tea-party-caucus-not-movement-mouthpiece.html.

13. Peter Baker, "Education of a President," *New York Times Magazine*, October 12, 2010, http://www.nytimes.com/2010/10/17/magazine/17obama-t.html?_r=2&hp=&pagewanted=all.

14. NRO Staff, "Krauthammer's Take," The Corner, *National Review*, October 14, 2010, http://www.nationalreview.com/corner/249844/krauthammers-take-nro-staff.

15. Ray Raphael, "First American Revolution—The Worcester Revolution of 1774," City of Worcester, Massachusetts, http://www.worcesterma.gov/city-clerk/history/general/worcester-revolution.

16. David Hackett Fischer, *Paul Revere's Ride* (New York: Oxford University Press, 1994), 75–76, 89.

17. Alan Axelrod, *The Real History of the American Revolution: A New Look at the Past* (New York: Sterling, 2007), 84–85.

18. The Connecticut Society of the Sons of the American Revolution, "The Scarlet Standard No. 4: Liberty Defined . . . New England's Colonial Clergy," http://www.connecticutsar.org/articles/scarlet_no4 .htm; 2 Corinthians 3:17, New Jerusalem Bible, http://www.catholic .org/bible/.

19. Axelrod, *The Real History of the American Revolution;* James Grant Wilson and John Fiske, *Appleton's Cyclopædia of American Biography*, vol. 1 (New York: Appleton, 1891), 629, viewed at http://books.google .com/.

20. Ralph Waldo Emerson, "Concord Hymn," Sung at the Completion of the Battle Monument, April 19, 1836, http://www.bartleby.com/102/43 .html.

21. Connecticut Society of the Sons of the American Revolution, "The Scarlet Standard No. 4."

22. Brother John, "Dr. Thomas Young, Early American Deist," Christian DeistFellowship.com, February 17, 2009, http://www.christiandeist fellowship.com/dryoung.htm.

23. Axelrod, *The Real History of the American Revolution*, 84; Jennifer Hartwell-Jackson, "Sybil Ludington: a Revolutionary Hero," Traverse ForWomen.com, http://traverseforwomen.com/Herstory/SybilLuding ton.htm.

24. Wilson and Fiske, *Appleton's Cyclopædia of American Biography*, vol. 1, 261, viewed at http://books.google.com/.

25. National Women's Hall of Fame, "Women of the Hall: Mercy Otis Warren," GreatWomen.org, http://www.greatwomen.org/women .php?action=viewone&id=195; Library Company of Philadelphia, "Portraits of American Women Writers: Mercy Otis Warren," LibraryCompany.org, http://www.librarycompany.org/women/portraits/ warren.htm.

26. History Channel, "Joseph Plumb Martin," History.com, http://www .history.com/topics/joseph-plumb-martin.

2. GUARDING THE SPIRIT OF FREEDOM

1. Jason Linkins, " 'Tea Bagging' Rallies Ruthlessly Mocked On Maddow Show," Huffington Post, April 9, 2009, http://www.huffingtonpost .com/2009/04/09/rachel-maddow-ana-marie-c_n_185445.html.

2. Fox News Channel, "Cable Anchors, Guests Use Tea Parties as Platform for Frat House Humor," FoxNews.com, April 16, 2009, http:// www.foxnews.com/politics/2009/04/16/cable-anchors-guests-use-tea-parties -platform-frat-house-humor/.

3. Jonathan Alter, The Promise: President Obama, Year One (New York: Simon & Schuster, 2010), 129.

4. Amanda Carpenter, "Hot Button," Washington Times, April 17, 2009, http://www.washingtontimes.com/news/2009/apr/17/hot-button-9653 3248/.

5. Amanda Terkel, "Pelosi Is Not 'Deranged'—Swastikas and Comparisons to Hitler are On Display at Town Hall Protests," ThinkProgress.org, August 7, 2009, http://thinkprogress.org/2009/08/07/pelosi-swastikas/.

6. Noel Sheppard, "Garofalo: Tea Party Goers Are Racists Who Hate Black President," NewsBusters.org, April 16, 2009, http://newsbusters .org/blogs/noel-sheppard/2009/04/16/garofalo-tea-partiers-are-all-racists -who-hate-black-president.

7. CNN, "Carter Again Cites Racism as Factor in Obama's Treatment," CNN.com, September 15, 2009, http://articles.cnn.com/2009-09-15/ politics/carter.obama_1_president-jimmy-carter-president-obama -health-care-plan?_s=PM:POLITICS.

8. Jimmy Carter, "Carter: 1970s Saw a Tea Party-Like Wave," USA Today, September 29, 2010, http://www.usatoday.com/news/opinion/ forum/2010-09-29-column29_ST_N.htm.

9. Elizabeth Vargas, "The Note: Pelosi and the Tea Party 'Share Views,' " ABCNews.com, February 28, 2010, http://blogs.abcnews.com/thenote/ 2010/02/pelosi-and-the-tea-party-share-views.html.

10. Press Conference Transcript, "Sheriff Clarence W. Dupnik, Pima County, Arizona, Holds a Press Conference," Political Transcript Wire, January 9, 2011, http://findarticles.com/p/news-articles/political -transcript-wire/mi_8167/is_20110109/sheriff-clarence-dupnik-pima -county/ai_n56643229/?tag=content;col1.

11. Megyn Kelly, Interview with Sheriff Clarence Dupnik, America Live, Fox News Channel, transcribed and abridged from embedded video,

YouTube.com, January 9, 2011, http://www.youtube.com/watch?v=cvc
_7Fb5T5M.

12. James Kelly, "Jared Loughner Is a Product of Sheriff Dupnik's Office,"
Cholla Jumps, January 11, 2011, http://thechollajumps.wordpress.com/.

13. Suzy Khimm, "After Giffords Shooting, Rep. Grijalva Blames Rage-
Fueled Political Climate," *Mother Jones*, January 8, 2011, http://mother
jones.com/mojo/2011/01/grijalva-giffords-shooting-tea-party-palin.

14. Paul Krugman, "Climate of Hate," *New York Times*, January 9, 2011,
http://www.nytimes.com/2011/01/10/opinion/10krugman.html?ref=
politics.

15. Tommy Christopher, "Mark Penn Says Obama Needs 'Similar Event'
to Oklahoma City to Reconnect with Voters," Mediaite.com, November 5, 2010, http://www.mediaite.com/tv/mark-penn-says-obama
-needs-similar-event-to-oklahoma-city-to-reconnect-with-voters/.

16. Matthew Balan, "CNN's King Apologizes For Guest's 'Crosshairs'
Term," NewsBusters, January 19, 2011, http://newsbusters.org/blogs/
matthew-balan/2011/01/19/cnns-king-apologizes-guests-crosshairs-term.

17. Jared Loughner, "Introduction: Jared Loughner," transcribed and
abridged from embedded video, YouTube.com, December 15, 2010,
http://www.youtube.com/watch?v=nHoaZaLbqB4.

18. Colby Hall, "Jared Loughner's Friend Tells GMA: 'He Did Not Watch
TV, He Disliked The News,'" transcribed and abridged from
embedded video, Mediaite.com, January 12, 2011, http://www.mediaite
.com/tv/jared-laughners-friend-tells-gma-he-did-not-watch-tv-he-dis
liked-the-news/.

19. Ibid.

20. David A. Fahrenthold, "Jared Loughner's Behavior Recorded by
College Classmate in E-Mails," *Washington Post*, January 9, 2011, http://
voices.washingtonpost.com/44/2011/01/jared-loughners-behavior-recor
.html?hpid=topnews.

21. Nick Baumann, "Exclusive: Loughner Friend Explains Alleged
Gunman's Grudge Against Giffords," *Mother Jones*, January 10, 2011,
http://motherjones.com/politics/2011/01/jared-lee-loughner-friend-voice
mail-phone-message.

22. MSNBC, "Police Kill Discovery Building Gunmen," MSNBC.com,
September 1, 2010, http://www.msnbc.msn.com/id/38957020/ns/us_
news-crime_and_courts/.

23. Drew Zahn, "Look Who Else Put 'Bull's-Eye' on Giffords," World NetDaily, January 9, 2011, http://www.wnd.com/index.php?fa=PAGE .view&pageId=249273.

24. "Kos" (Daily Kos founder Markos Moulitsas), "2010 Will be Primary Season," Daily Kos, June 25, 2008, http://www.dailykos.com/story/2008 /6/25/1204/74882/511/541568.

25. Jay Nordlinger, "The Corner: Hypocrisy Unending," National Review Online, January 10, 2011, http://www.nationalreview.com/corner/ 256765/hypocrisy-unending-jay-nordlinger.

26. Van Jones, "Uncloak the Kochs," Common Cause, February 2, 2011, http://www.youtube.com/commoncauseethics.

27. Christian Hartsock, "White Political Ralliers Call for Lynching of Black Justice," transcribed and abridged from embedded video, Big Government, February 3, 2011, http://biggovernment.com/chartsock/ 2011/02/03/white-political-ralliers-call-for-lynching-of-black-justice -sorry-msm-no-tea-in-this-blend/.

28. Daniel Hannan, *The New Road to Serfdom: A Letter of Warning to America* (New York: HarperCollins, 2010), 161–62.

29. Note: Grace Custer refers to President Obama's comments on *The Tonight Show with Jay Leno,* when he said of his poor skills as a bowler, "It's like the Special Olympics or something," an obvious insult to people with physical and intellectual disabilities. Rob Port, "President Obama: 'I Bowl Like a Retard,'" SayAnythingBlog.com, March 20, 2009, http://sayanythingblog.com/entry/president_obama_i_bowl_like _a_retard/.

30. Benjamin Franklin, "The Rattle-Snake as a Symbol of America," Pennsylvania *Journal,* December 27, 1775, AmericanHeritage.com, http://www.americanheritage.com/articles/magazine/ah/1988/2/1988_2 _74.shtml.

31. See Psalms 75:7.

32. See Psalms 119:165.

3. PROMOTING SMALLER, SMARTER GOVERNMENT

1. P. J. O'Rourke, *Parliament of Whores: A Lone Humorist Attempts to Explain the Entire U.S. Government* (1991; reprint New York: Grove/ Atlantic, 2003), xxv–xxvi.

2. James Madison, "Alleged Danger From the Powers of the Union to the State Governments Considered," *The Federalist* No. 45, *Independent*

Journal, January 26, 1788, http://www.constitution.org/fed/federa45
.htm.

3. James O'Toole and Edward E. Lawler III, Executive Summary: *The New American Workplace*, Executive Book Summaries, December 2006, p. 3, http://www.cognitionnet.com/member/resources/summaries/ Personnel_HR/New_American_Workplace.pdf.

4. American Federation of State, County, and Municipal Employees, "Workplace Violence," AFSCME Issues, 2010, http://www.afscme.org/ issues/1293.cfm; Sam Hananel, Associated Press, "Private-sector union membership sinks," KnoxvilleBiz.com, January 22, 2010, http://www .knoxnews.com/news/2010/jan/22/private-sector-union-membership -sinks/.

5. Conn Carroll, "Morning Bell: Big Government's Government Union Firewall," Heritage.org, The Foundry blog, October 18, 2010, http:// blog.heritage.org/2010/10/18/morning-bell-big-governments-government -union-firewall/.

6. Representative Cynthia Lummis, R-Wyoming, "What the Federal Government Should Be Doing," C-SPAN, May 26, 2010, transcribed from embedded video, http://www.c-spanvideo.org/videoLibrary/clip .php?appid=598199680; the time frame Representative Lummis cited in her presentation before the House was "in the years since the majority party has switched hands and Democratic control of Congress has been in place," which would have begun with the installation of the 110th Congress on January 4, 2007.

7. Mark J. Perry, "The Two Americas: Public Sector vs. Private Sector," Wall Street Pit: Global Market Insight, February 9, 2010, http://wall streetpit.com/16385-the-two-americas-public-sector-vs-private-sector; Dennis Cauchon, "For Feds, More Get 6-Figure Salaries," *USA Today*, December 11, 2009, http://www.usatoday.com/news/washington/2009 -12-10-federal-pay-salaries_N.htm.

8. John Stossel, "The Battle for the Future," Fox News Channel, transcribed from broadcast aired October 23, 2010.

9. Star Parker, *Uncle Sam's Plantation: How Big Government Enslaves America's Poor and What We Can Do about It* (Nashville, TN: Thomas Nelson, 2005), 36–40.

10. Star Parker, "Why I'm Running for Congress," Townhall.com, April 12, 2010, http://townhall.com/columnists/StarParker/2010/04/12/why_ im_running_for_congress/page/full/.

11. J. Purver Richardson, *Life and Literature: Over Two Thousand Extracts from Ancient and Modern Writers* (Lynchburg, VA: Brown-Morrison, 1910), http://www.gutenberg.org/cache/epub/30373/pg30373.txt.

12. George W. Bush, *Decision Points* (New York: Crown, 2010), 447.

13. CNN Wire Staff, "Mullen: Debt is top national security threat," CNN .com, August 27, 2010, http://articles.cnn.com/2010-08-27/us/debt.security .mullen_1_pentagon-budget-national-debt-michael-mullen?_s=PM:US.

14. Army Sergeant 1st Class Michael J. Carden, American Forces Press Service, "National Debt Poses Security Threat, Mullen Says," JCS.mil, August 27, 2010, http://www.jcs.mil/newsarticle.aspx?ID=360.

15. James Pethokoukis, "Big Media Distorts Bush Economic Record," *U.S. News & World Report*, January 14, 2009, http://money.usnews.com/ money/blogs/capital-commerce/2009/1/14/media-distorts-bush-economic -record.html.

16. Bill Adair, "Obama's Promise to Go after Earmarks 'Line by Line,'" PolitiFact.com, March 3, 2009, http://www.politifact.com/truth-o-meter/ article/2009/mar/03/obamas-promise-go-after-earmarks-line-line/.

17. D. Sean Shurtleff and Pamela Villarreal, "Six Steps to Paying off the U.S. Government Debt," National Center for Policy Analysis, March 31, 2009, http://www.policyarchive.org/handle/10207/bitstreams/ 15990.pdf.

18. Doug Bandow, "Social Security's Coming Crash: The Certain End of Entitlement," Cato Institute, October 20, 2009, http://www.cato.org/ pub_display.php?pub_id=10688; Bruce Bartlett, "The 81% Tax Increase," *Forbes,* May 15, 2009, http://www.forbes.com/2009/05/14/ taxes-social-security-opinions-columnists-medicare.html.

19. Robert L. Borosage, "Here's How Progressives Can Ensure Obama's Success," OpEdNews.com, March 10, 2009, http://www.opednews.com/ articles/Here-s-How-Progressives-Ca-by-Robert-Borosage-090310-180 .html.

20. Michael Reagan, *The City on a Hill* (Nashville, TN: Thomas Nelson, 1997), 168–72.

21. Jeffrey Lord, "The War of the Presidents: Reagan Battles Obama in 2010," *American Spectator*, January 5, 2010, http://spectator.org/archives/ 2010/01/05/the-war-of-the-presidents-reag/1.

22. Dinesh D'Souza, *Ronald Reagan: How an Ordinary Man Became an Extraordinary Leader* (New York: Simon & Schuster, 1999), 116–17.

23. Dr. Marc K. Siegel, "Medicare's *Not* Fixed," *New York Post*, March 3, 2010, http://www.nypost.com/p/news/opinion/opedcolumnists/medicare _not_fixed_HxdiJCU1sIq20UB5jw7WwL.

24. Ross Douthat, "Tales of the Tea Party," *New York Times*, October 17, 2010, http://www.nytimes.com/2010/10/18/opinion/18douthat.html?_ r=1&scp=4&sq=tea%20party&st=cse.

25. William Voegeli, "Paul Ryan's Roadmap," Claremont Institute, September 19, 2010, http://www.claremont.org/publications/crb/id.1749/ article_detail.asp.

26. Ibid.

27. William A. Niskanen, Chairman, Cato Institute, "Repeal the Community Reinvestment Act," Testimony before the Subcommittee on Financial Institutions in Consumer Credit, Committee on Banking and Financial Services, United States Senate, March 8, 1995, http:// www.cato.org/testimony/ct-ni3-8.html.

28. Steven A. Holmes, "Fannie Mae Eases Credit to aid Mortgage Lending," *New York Times*, September 30, 1999, http://www.nytimes.com/1999/ 09/30/business/fannie-mae-eases-credit-to-aid-mortgage-lending.html; "About Fannie Mae," FannieMae.com, http://www.fanniemae.com/kb/ index?page=home&c=aboutus.

29. Jonathan Stempel, "Countrywide Dismisses Subprime Naysayers," Reuters.com, March 16, 2007, http://www.reuters.com/article/idUSN16 25465520070316?pageNumber=1.

30. Dan Golden, "Angelo's Many 'Friends,' " Portfolio.com, July 16, 2008, http://www.portfolio.com/news-markets/national-news/portfolio/2008/ 07/16/Countrywide-Deals-Exposed.

31. Common Sense Issues, "Kent Conrad Bailed Out," Commonsense NorthDakota.com, transcribed from embedded audio, http://www .commonsensenorthdakota.com/.

32. Abraham H. Miller, "The Financial Mess: How We Got Here," American Thinker, September 29, 2008, http://www.americanthinker .com/2008/09/the_financial_mess_how_we_got.html.

33. Bill Sammon, "Lawmaker Accused of Fannie Mae Conflict of Interest," FoxNews.com, October 3, 2008, http://www.foxnews.com/ story/0,2933,432501,00.html.

34. Sam Dealey, "Barney Frank's Fannie and Freddie Muddle," *U.S. News & World Report* Politics Opinion, September 10, 2008, http://politics.us

news.com/opinion/blogs/sam-dealey/2008/9/10/barney-franks-fannie
-and-freddie-muddle.html.

35. "The Fannie Mae Dice Roll Continues," editorial, *Wall Street Journal*,
November 11, 2009, http://online.wsj.com/article/SB1000142405274870
4402404574527440083580698.html.

36. Thomas Sowell, "Barney Not-So-Frank," *National Review*, October 21,
2010, http://www.nationalreview.com/articles/250467/barney-not-so
-frank-thomas-sowell.

37. "Review & Outlook: Barney the Underwriter," editorial, *Wall Street
Journal*, June 25, 2009, http://online.wsj.com/article/SB12458078445294
5093.html.

38. Sowell, "Barney Not-So-Frank."

39. Peter Schweizer, *Architects of Ruin: How Big Government Liberals
Wrecked the Global Economy* (New York: HarperCollins, 2009), 1–3.

40. Ameripac, "Obama-ACORN Root Causes of Mortgage Crisis?,"
DiscoverTheNetworks.org, September 30, 2008, http://www.discover
thenetworks.org/Articles/Obama%20ACORN%20Root%20Causes%
20of%20Mortgage.html; Ed Morrissey, "What Does a Community
Organizer Do? Pressure Banks to Make Bad Loans," HotAir.com,
September 29, 2008, http://hotair.com/archives/2008/09/29/what-does
-a-community-organizer-do-pressure-banks-to-make-bad-loans/.

41. Jesse A. Hamilton, "Dodd Listed As Top Recipient Of Lender's
Contributions," *Hartford Courant,* June 19, 2008, http://articles.courant
.com/2008-06-19/news/dodd0619.art_1_ceo-angelo-mozilo-s-vip-senate
-ethics-ethics-committee.

42. Lindsay Renick Mayer, "Fannie Mae and Freddie Mac invest in
Democrats," OpenSecretsBlog, July 16, 2008, http://www.opensecrets
.org/news/2008/07/top-senate-recipients-of-fanni.html.

43. James Pethokoukis, "Why Dodd Should Stay on the Banking Com
mittee," Reuters.com, September 2, 2009, http://blogs.reuters.com/
james-pethokoukis/tag/financial-regulatory-reform/page/10/.

44. Keith Hennessey, "A Decade of Spiraling Deficits," RealClearPolitics,
July 14, 2010, http://www.realclearpolitics.com/2010/07/14/a_decade_
of_spiraling_deficits_237550.html.

45. U.S. Congress Votes Database, "Members of Congress/Barack Obama/
Votes," *Washington Post*, http://projects.washingtonpost.com/congress/
members/o000167/votes/page4/; Tom Curry, "What Obama's Senate

Votes Reveal," MSNBC.com, February 21, 2008, http://www.msnbc .msn.com/id/23276453/.

46. Amir Sufi and Atif R. Mian, "The Effects of Fiscal Stimulus: Evidence from the 2009 'Cash for Clunkers' Program," Social Science Research Network, September 1, 2010, http://papers.ssrn.com/sol3/papers.cfm? abstract_id=1670759; David Kestenbaum, "Study: Cash for Clunkers Was a Wash," National Public Radio, September 3, 2010, http://www .npr.org/blogs/money/2010/09/02/129608251/cash-for-clunkers.

47. Adam Maji, "The Bad Economics of Cash for Clunkers," Examiner .com, August 4, 2009, http://www.examiner.com/libertarian-in-tucson/ the-bad-economics-of-cash-for-clunkers.

48. Peter Schiff, "Peter Schiff on Cash for Clunkers," YouTube.com, October 1, 2009, transcribed and abridged from embedded video, http:// www.youtube.com/watch?v=gwVpaB0JBx8.

49. John Stossel, "Myths, Lies and Straight Talk," *ABC News 20/20*, December 30, 2005, http://abcnews.go.com/2020/story?id=123606.

50. Mark Steyn, *America Alone: The End of the World As We Know It* (Washington, DC: Regnery, 2006), 44.

51. Ronald Reagan, "Remarks at a Reagan-Bush Rally in Warren, Michigan," October 10, 1984, http://www.reagan.utexas.edu/archives/ speeches/1984/101084d.htm (emphasis added).

52. Ronald Reagan, "Remarks at a Campaign Rally for Senator Mack Mattingly in Atlanta, Georgia," October 8, 1986, http://www.reagan .utexas.edu/archives/speeches/1986/100886b.htm (emphasis added).

53. Celeste Katz, "The Daily Politics—VPOTUS Joe Biden: Dems Will 'Keep The Senate And Win The House,' " *New York Daily News*, October 26, 2010, http://www.nydailynews.com/blogs/dailypolitics/2010 /10/vpotus-joe-biden-dems-will-kee.html.

54. Anne E. Kornblut and Michael A. Fletcher, "Obama Says Economic Crisis Comes First," *Washington Post*, February 10, 2009, http://www .washingtonpost.com/wp-dyn/content/article/2009/02/09/AR200902090 3430.html.

55. Christopher Byron, Frederick Ungeheuer, and Mary Cronin, "A Whiff of Panic," *Time*, Monday, October 12, 1981, http://www.time.com/time/ magazine/article/0,9171,924914-3,00.html.

4. SECURING OUR ENERGY FUTURE

1. T. Boone Pickens, "The Plan: America Is Addicted to Foreign Oil," PickensPlan.com, http://www.pickensplan.com/theplan/.

2. Robert Bryce, author of *Power Hungry: The Myths of Green Energy and the Real Fuels of the Future* (New York: PublicAffairs, 2010), 21.

3. Note: Hydrocarbons are organic compounds consisting entirely of hydrogen and carbon, and are found naturally occurring in crude oil. Hydrocarbons also take the form of gases such as propane, and liquids such as benzene and petroleum spirits. "Saturated hydrocarbons" are saturated with hydrogen and form the basis of petroleum fuels.

4. Barack Obama: "Shock Audio Unearthed: Obama Tells San Francisco He Will Bankrupt the Coal Industry," transcribed and abridged from embedded video, http://www.youtube.com/watch?v=Hdi4onAQBWQ.

5. Sierra Club, North Star Chapter, "Midwest Coal Rush: Welcome to the Big Stone II Age?," Minnesota.SierraClub.org, September 2009, http://minnesota.sierraclub.org/campaigns/air/coal/bigStoneFactsheet.html.

6. Cindy Bittinger, "The Business of America Is Business?," Calvin Coolidge Memorial Foundation, http://www.calvin-coolidge.org/html/the_business_of_america_is_bus.html.

7. James Melik, "Nuclear Power: Energy Solution or Evil Curse?," BBC, March 14, 2011, http://www.bbc.co.uk/news/business-12730473.

8. Ibid.

9. James MacPherson, "ND Oil Patch Could Double Production," *Minot Daily News*, January 3, 2011, http://www.minotdailynews.com/page/content.detail/id/550601/N-D--oil-patch-could-double-production.html?nav=5010.

10. Adam J. Lieberman and Simona C. Kwon, "The Greatest Unfounded Health Scares of Recent Times, Part I: DDT," National Policy Analysis No. 386, National Center for Public Policy Research, January 2002, http://www.nationalcenter.org/NPA386.html; John Pollock, "DDT: The Story of a Scandal That Has Killed Millions," *Sunday Times* (of London), May 1, 2004, http://www.timesonline.co.uk/tol/comment/columnists/guest_contributors/article847896.ece.

11. Apollo Alliance, "About," ApolloAlliance.org, http://apolloalliance.org/about/.

12. Keith Schneider, "Recovery Bill Is Breakthrough on Clean Energy, Good Jobs," Apollo News Service, February 17, 2009, http://apollo

alliance.org/feature-articles/at-last-federal-government-signs-up-for
-clean-energy-economy/.

13. Apollo Alliance, "Apollo Board Member Van Jones Accepts White
House Post," Apollo News Service, March 10, 2009, http://apollo
alliance.org/what%E2%80%99s-new/apollo-board-member-van-jones
-accepts-white-house-post/.

14. Phil Kerpen, "NY's Tax-Funded Ex-Terrorist," PhilKerpen.com,
September 9, 2009, http://www.philkerpen.com/?q=node/292.

15. Michael Shellenberger and Ted Nordhaus, "Cap and Charade: The
Green Jobs Myth," New Republic, October 14, 2010, http://www.tnr
.com/article/politics/78209/clean-energy-jobs-obama.

16. Barack Obama, "Remarks of President Barack Obama, Southern
California Edison Electric Vehicle Technical Center," Pomona,
California, March 19, 2009, http://www.energy.gov/7067.htm.

17. "The Green Jobs Myth," editorial, Investor's Business Daily, May 20,
2010, http://www.investors.com/NewsAndAnalysis/Article/534696/201
005201839/The-Green-Jobs-Myth.aspx.

18. Václav Klaus, "The Other Side of Global Warming Alarmism,"
Address at Chatham House, London, November 7, 2007, http://cepin
.cz/cze/article.php?ID=793.

19. Willie Soon, Robert Carter, and David Legates, "Disputing The
Skeptical Environmentalist," International Climate and Environmental
Change Assessment Project, October 29, 2010, http://www.icecap.us/
index.php/go/joes-blog.

20. Ross McKitrick, Ph.D., "A Critical Review of Global Surface
Temperature Data Products," July 26, 2010, 11, http://rossmckitrick
.weebly.com/uploads/4/8/0/8/4808045/surfacetempreview.pdf.

21. S. Fred Singer, ed., "Nature, Not Human Activity, Rules the Climate:
Summary for Policymakers of the Report of the Nongovernmental
International Panel on Climate Change," Heartland Institute, April
2008, 19, http://www.heartland.org/custom/semod_policybot/pdf/22835
.pdf.

22. Joseph D'Aleo, "US Temperatures and Climate Factors Since 1895,"
International Climate and Environmental Change Assessment Project,
http://icecap.us/images/uploads/US_Temperatures_and_Climate_Factors
_since_1895.pdf.

5. PUTTING AMERICA BACK TO WORK

1. Barack Obama, "Remarks by the President at a Town Hall Meeting on the Economy: White House Transcript of Obama's Remarks in Racine," June 30, 2010, WisPolitics.com, http://www.wispolitics.com/index.iml?Article=201738.

2. Allan H. Meltzer, "Why Obamanomics Has Failed," *Wall Street Journal*, June 30, 2010, http://online.wsj.com/article/SB10001424052748 704629804575325233508651458.html.

3. Michael Cembalest, "Obama's Business Blind Spot," *Forbes,* November 24, 2009, http://www.forbes.com/2009/11/24/michael-cembalest-obama -business-beltway-cabinet.html.

4. Louis Jacobson, "Beck Says Less Than 10 Percent of Obama Cabinet Has Worked in Private Sector," PolitiFact.com, December 2, 2009, http://www.politifact.com/truth-o-meter/statements/2009/dec/02/glenn -beck/beck-says-less-10-percent-obama-cabinet-members-ha/.

5. Mark Halperin, "Why Obama Is Losing the Political War," *Time*, October 11, 2010, http://www.time.com/time/politics/article/0,8599,202 4718,00.html.

6. Richard Wolffe, *Renegade: The Making of a President* (New York: Crown, 2009), 102–3.

7. Barack Obama, "News Conference in Toronto, Canada," June 27, 2010, Complete Obama Speech Archive, http://completeobamaspeech archive.com/?p=1132.

8. Dinesh D'Souza, "How Obama Thinks," *Forbes*, September 27, 2010, http://www.forbes.com/forbes/2010/0927/politics-socialism-capitalism -private-enterprises-obama-business-problem_print.html.

9. James Taranto, "Best of the Web Today: Obama's Katrina? The New President Seems Dangerously Out of Touch," *Wall Street Journal*, March 4, 2009, http://online.wsj.com/article/SB123617892941430079 .html.

10. Bill O'Reilly with guest Bob Woodward, "Barack Obama the War President," *The O'Reilly Factor*, September 28, 2010, http://www.fox news.com/on-air/oreilly/transcript/barack-obama-war-president.

11. Ronald Reagan, "A Time For Choosing," October 27, 1964, Public Papers of President Ronald W. Reagan, Ronald Reagan Presidential Library, http://www.reagan.utexas.edu/archives/reference/timechoosing .html.

12. Editorial, "Dr. Obama's tonsillectomy," *Wall Street Journal*, July 26, 2009, http://online.wsj.com/article/SB10001424052970204886304574308 472181248330.html.

13. Ibid.

14. President Barack Obama, "Remarks by the President in health insurance reform town hall," Portsmouth High School, Portsmouth, New Hampshire, August 11, 2009, WhiteHouse.gov, http://www.white house.gov/the_press_office/Remarks-by-the-President-at-Town-Hall -on-Health-Insurance-Reform-in-Portsmouth-New-Hampshire/.

15. Bret Baier, " 'Special Report' Panel on Polling of Americans on Health Care Reform," *Special Report with Bret Baier,* Fox News Channel, August 14, 2009, http://www.foxnews.com/story/0,2933,539526,00 .html.

16. Charles Austin Beard and Mary Ritter Beard, *History of the United States* (1921; reprint Hamburg, Germany: Classic Books, 2008), 395.

17. William Bonner and Addison Wiggin, *The New Empire of Debt: The Rise and Fall of an Epic Financial Bubble* (Hoboken, NJ: Wiley, 2009), 310–11.

18. Irvin B. Tucker, *Macroeconomics for Today* (Mason, OH: South-Western Cengage Learning, 2008), 187.

19. Michael Reagan, *The New Reagan Revolution* (New York: Thomas Dunne, 2011), 217.

20. Ibid., 228–29.

21. Internet Movie Database, "Memorable Quotes for *Wall Street* (1987)," http://www.imdb.com/title/tt0094291/quotes.

22. Jude Wanniski, "The Invisible Helping Hand," *New York*, February 2, 1981, 52.

23. Jeremiah Wright, "Interview: Rev. Jeremiah Wright," *Religion & Ethics*, Episode 1051, PBS, August 17, 2007, http://www.pbs.org/wnet/ religionandethics/week1051/interview4.html.

24. Michael Goldfarb, "Michelle Will Steal Your Pie," *Weekly Standard*, April 9, 2008, http://www.weeklystandard.com/weblogs/TWSFP/2008/ 04/michelle_will_steal_your_pie.asp.

25. Barack Obama, "Remarks by the President at Luncheon for Senator Patty Murray," Westin Seattle, Seattle, Washington, August 17, 2010, http://www.whitehouse.gov/the-press-office/2010/08/17/remarks-presi dent-luncheon-senator-patty-murray.

26. "The Bush Economy," editorial, *Wall Street Journal*, January 17, 2009, http://online.wsj.com/article/SB123215327787492291.html.

27. John Podhoretz, *Bush Country: How Dubya Became a Great President While Driving the Liberals Insane* (New York: Macmillan, 2004), 169.

28. Liz Alderman, "Denmark Starts to Trim Its Admired Safety Net," *New York Times*, August 16, 2010, http://www.nytimes.com/2010/08/17/business/global/17denmark.html?pagewanted=1&_r=1.

29. Liz Alderman, "Why Denmark Is Shrinking Its Social Safety Net," *New York Times*, August 16, 2010, http://economix.blogs.nytimes.com/2010/08/16/why-denmark-is-shrinking-its-social-safety-net/.

30. Casey B. Mulligan, "Economix: Do Jobless Benefits Discourage People From Finding Jobs?" *New York Times*, March 17, 2010, http://economix.blogs.nytimes.com/2010/03/17/do-jobless-benefits-discourage-people-from-finding-jobs/.

31. Alan B. Krueger (Princeton University) and Andreas Mueller (Stockholm University and Princeton University), "The Lot of the Unemployed: A Time Use Perspective," Discussion Paper No. 3490, May 2008, 1–2, http://ftp.iza.org/dp3490.pdf.

32. Eliza Strickland, "The New Face of Environmentalism," *East Bay Express*, November 2, 2005, http://www.eastbayexpress.com/gyrobase/the-new-face-of-environmentalism/Content?oid=1079539&showFullText=true.

33. Ben Smith and Nia-Malika Henderson, "Glenn Beck Up, Left Down, and Van Jones Defiant," Politico.com, September 8, 2009, http://www.politico.com/news/stories/0909/26813.html.

34. Rana Foroohar, "The Real Green Revolution," *Newsweek*, April 02, 2010, http://www.newsweek.com/2010/04/01/the-real-green-revolution.html.

35. "The 'Green Jobs' Myth," editorial, *Wall Street Journal*, December 10, 2008, http://online.wsj.com/article/SB122886086448792609.html.

36. Arduin, Laffer & Moore Econometrics, "The Economic Impact of Federal Spending on State Economic Performance: A Texas Perspective," Texas Public Policy Foundation, April 2009, http://www.texaspolicy.com/pdf/2009-04-federalspending-laffer-final.pdf.

37. Gene Rebeck, "2001 Minnesota Business Hall of Fame: Ron Offutt," *Twin Cities Business*, July 2001, http://www.tcbmag.com/halloffame/minnesotabusinesshalloffame/104281p1.aspx; Michelle Conlin, "The Sultan of Spuds," *Forbes*, May 19, 1997, http://www.forbes.com/

forbes/1997/0519/5910060a.html; Press Release, "RDO Leader Ron Offutt to Receive MSU Moorhead's 28th Annual L. B. Hartz Award," September 03, 2009, http://news.mnstate.edu/2009/09/rdo-leader-ron -offutt-to-receive-msu-moorhead%E2%80%99s-28th-annual-lb-hartz -award/; Robert Jerome Glennon, *Water Follies: Groundwater Pumping and the Fate of America's Fresh Waters* (Washington, DC: Island Press, 2002), 145–48.

6. SUPPORTING THE MILITARY

1. Harry Reid, "The Iraq War is Lost," Fox News Channel, April 19, 2007, transcribed and abridged from embedded video, http://www .youtube.com/watch?v=sYZEGot-xU4.
2. Michael O'Hanlon and Kenneth Pollack, "A War We Just Might Win," *New York Times*, July 30, 2007, http://www.nytimes.com/2007/ 07/30/opinion/30pollack.html.
3. James Kirchick, "Squanderer in Chief," *Los Angeles Times,* April 28, 2009, http://articles.latimes.com/2009/apr/28/opinion/oe-kirchick28.
4. C. S. Lewis, *The Weight of Glory and Other Addresses* (New York: HarperCollins, 2001), 89.
5. Charles M. Province, "It Is the Soldier," copyright 1970, 2010 by Charles M. Province, U.S. Army, www.pattonhq.com. Used by permission.
6. John Stuart Mill, "The Contest in America," *Harper's Magazine*, 1862, http://www.gutenberg.org/dirs/etext04/conam10h.htm.
7. Michael de Yoanna and Mark Benjamin, "Coming Home: The Army's Fatal Neglect—'I Am Under A Lot of Pressure to Not Diagnose PTSD,' " Salon.com, April 8, 2009, http://www.salon.com/news/special/ coming_home/2009/04/08/tape.

7. FIGHTING TERROR

1. Dick Cheney, "Interview of the Vice President by Scott Hennen, WDAY at Radio Day at the White House," Vice President's Office, Washington, D.C., October 24, 2006, http://georgewbush-whitehouse .archives.gov/news/releases/2006/10/20061024-7.html.
2. Associated Press, "Bush says U.S. doesn't torture after Cheney flap," MSNBC.com, October 28, 2006, http://www.msnbc.msn.com/id/1545 3452/.
3. Ibid.
4. Ibid.

5. Christopher Hitchens, "Believe Me, It's Torture," *Vanity Fair,* August 2008, http://www.vanityfair.com/politics/features/2008/08/hitchens 200808.

6. Mike Guy, "Lab Rat: Waterboarding," embedded video, Playboy.com, October 2009, http://www.playboy.com/articles/lab-rat-waterboarding/index.html.

7. Steve Harrigan, "Video: Steve Harrigan gets waterboarded on Fox," embedded video, Hotair.com, November 5, 2006, http://hotair.com/archives/2006/11/04/video-steve-harrigan-gets-waterboarded-on-fox/.

8. Rich Lowry, "Waterboarding Saved American Lives," National Review Online, September 25, 2006, http://www.nationalreview.com/corner/129134/waterboarding-saved-american-lives/rich-lowry.

9. Mark Thompson and Bobby Ghosh, "Did Waterboarding Prevent Terrorism Attacks?," *Time*, April 21, 2009, http://www.time.com/time/nation/article/0,8599,1892947,00.html.

10. BBC, "CIA Admits Waterboarding Inmates," February 5, 2008, http://news.bbc.co.uk/2/hi/americas/7229169.stm.

11. Philip Rucker, Carrie Johnson, and Ellen Nakashima, "Hasan E-Mails to Cleric Didn't Result in Inquiry," *Washington Post,* November 10, 2009, http://www.washingtonpost.com/wp-dyn/content/article/2009/11/09/AR2009110902061.html?sid=ST2009110903704.

12. Mark Thompson, "Fort Hood: Were Hasan's Warning Signs Ignored?," *Time*, November 18, 2009, http://www.time.com/time/nation/article/0,8599,1940011,00.html.

13. Jonah Knox, "Treason, Bradley Manning, and Army PC," August 24, 2010, http://www.aim.org/aim-column/treason-bradley-manning-and-army-pc/.

14. Brannon Cullum, "Oscar Morales and One Million Voices Against FARC," Movements.org, http://www.movements.org/case-study/entry/oscar-morales-and-one-million-voices-against-farc/.

15. Oscar Morales Guevara, "One Million Voices Against FARC," Facebook.com, http://www.facebook.com/pages/One-million-voices-against-FARC/10780185890#!/pages/One-million-voices-against-FARC/10780185890?v=info.

16. Cullum, "Oscar Morales and One Million Voices Against FARC."

17. Citizen Warrior, "Support an Open Fuel Standard," CitizenWarrior.com, November 3, 2008, http://www.citizenwarrior.com/2008/11/support-open-fuel-standard.html.

8. HOLDING THE MEDIA ACCOUNTABLE

1. Charles Johnson, "Bush Guard Documents: Forged," LittleGreen Footballs.com, September 9, 2004, http://littlegreenfootballs.com/article/12526_Bush_Guard_Documents-_Forged; Peter Johnson, "Rather's 'Memogate': We Told You So, Conservatives Say," *USA Today*, September 26, 2004, http://www.usatoday.com/life/columnist/mediamix/2004-09-26-media-mix_x.htm; David Folkenflik, "Q&A: The CBS 'Memogate' Mess," NPR.org, January 12, 2005, http://www.npr.org/templates/story/story.php?storyId=4279605.

2. Jeff Bercovici, "Dan Rather's 70 Million Little Pieces," Portfolio.com, September 21, 2007, http://www.portfolio.com/views/blogs/mixed-media/2007/09/21/dan-rathers-70-million-little-pieces/.

3. Jill Lepore, "The Sharpened Quill," *New Yorker*, October 16, 2006, http://www.newyorker.com/archive/2006/10/16/061016crbo_books.

4. Thomas Paine, *The Writings of Thomas Paine*, vol. 4 (London: Putnam, 1896), 475.

5. Charles Gibson, "Interview with Sarah Palin," ABC News, September 11, 2008, transcribed and abridged from embedded video, http://abcnews.go.com/video/playerIndex?id=5783816.

6. Charles Krauthammer, "Charlie Gibson's Gaffe," *Washington Post*, September 13, 2008, http://www.washingtonpost.com/wp-dyn/content/article/2008/09/12/AR2008091202457.html.

7. Jim Rutenberg, "In First Big Interview, Palin Says, 'I'm Ready,' " *New York Times*, September 11, 2008, http://www.nytimes.com/2008/09/12/us/politics/12palin.html?ref=politics.

8. Carl M. Cannon, "Sarah 'Barracuda' Palin and the Piranhas of the Press," PoliticsDaily.com, July 8, 2009, http://www.mrc.org/biasalert/2010/20101021024521.aspx.

9. Ibid.

10. David A. Patten, "Obama: Constitution is 'Deeply Flawed,' " News Max, October 27, 2008, http://newsmax.com/InsideCover/obama-constitution/2008/10/27/id/326165.

11. Bernard Goldberg, *Bias: A CBS Insider Exposes How the Media Distort the News* (Washington, DC: Regnery, 2002), 127.

12. Ibid., 124.

13. Ibid., 129.

14. Myrna Blyth, *Spin Sisters: How the Women of the Media Sell Unhappiness—and Liberalism* (New York: Macmillan, 2005), 282.

15. Daily Caller, "The DC Morning—July 22, 2010," DailyCaller.com, July 22, 2010, http://dailycaller.com/2010/07/22/the-dc-morning-july-22 -2010/.

16. Michael Calderone, "Off the Record," *New York Observer*, October 29, 2006, http://www.observer.com/node/39607#.

17. Jonathan Strong, "Documents Show Media Plotting to Kill Stories about Rev. Jeremiah Wright," DailyCaller.com, July 23, 2010, http:// dailycaller.com/2010/07/20/documents-show-media-plotting-to-kill -stories-about-rev-jeremiah-wright/3/#ixzz0uFCNE0W5.

18. Jonathan Strong, "Liberal journalists suggest government censor Fox News," DailyCaller.com, November 21, 2010, http://dailycaller.com/ 2010/07/21/liberal-journalists-suggest-government-shut-down-fox -news/.

19. Ibid.

20. Andrew Sullivan, "The Corruption of Journo-List," Daily Dish, *Atlantic,* July 20, 2010, http://andrewsullivan.theatlantic.com/the_ daily_dish/2010/07/the-corruption-of-Journolist.html.

21. Ken Silverstein, *Turkmeniscam: How Washington Lobbyists Fought to Flack for a Stalinist Dictatorship* (New York: Random House, 2008), 166.

22. Mitchell Stephens, "We're All Postmodern Now," *Columbia Journalism Review*, July 1, 2005, http://www.allbusiness.com/buying_exiting_ businesses/3484120-1.html.

23. Noam Chomsky, "Excerpts from Manufacturing Consent: Noam Chomsky Interviewed by Various Interviewers," *Manufacturing Consent: Noam Chomsky and the Media*, 1992, http://www.chomsky.info/ interviews/1992----02.htm.

24. Paul Jackson, "Stalin's Apologist: *New York Times* Scandal Sparks Memories of Far Worse One," *Calgary Sun*, May 20, 2003, http://www .orwelltoday.com/stalinliar.shtml.

25. Sally J. Taylor, *Stalin's Apologist: Walter Duranty, the New York Times's Man in Moscow* (New York: Oxford University Press, 1990), 48.

26. Jackson, "Stalin's Apologist."

27. Ibid.

28. Pulitzer Prize Board, "Statement on Walter Duranty's 1932 Prize," Columbia University, November 21, 2003, http://www.pulitzer.org/ durantypressrelease.

29. Peter Kirsanow, "Civil Rights Commissioners Rebut Thernstrom," National Review Online/The Corner, July 29, 2010, http://www

.nationalreview.com/corner/233743/civil-rights-commissioners-rebut
-thernstrom-peter-kirsanow.

30. Fox News Channel, "Congressman Says He Didn't Know Black Panther Case Because Media Didn't Cover It," FoxNews.com, July 14, 2010, transcribed and abridged from embedded video, http://www .foxnews.com/politics/2010/07/13/congressman-shouted-claiming-know -new-black-panther-case/.

31. "The New Black Panther Party Is the New ACORN," editorial, *Newsweek*, July 14, 2010, http://www.newsweek.com/2010/07/14/the -new-black-panther-party-is-the-new-acorn0.html.

32. Americans for Limited Government, "Defund Public Broadcasting: Petition to Members of the U.S. Congress," http://defundpublic broadcasting.org/.

33. Forum Staff, "Crowd Turns to Yelling and Screaming during Dorgan Town Hall Meeting in Casselton," *Grand Forks Herald*, August 12, 2009, http://www.grandforksherald.com/event/article/id/129750/.

34. Barack Obama, "Remarks by the President on Wall Street Reform," Oakley Lindsay Civic Center, Quincy, Illinois, April 28, 2010, http:// www.whitehouse.gov/the-press-office/remarks-president-wall-street -reform-quincy-illinois.

9. DEFENDING LIFE

1. Mark Knoller, "Happy to Have Snow in April," CBSNews.com, April 30, 2007, http://www.cbsnews.com/8301-500803_162-2742965-500803 .html.

2. Barbara Lock, M.D., "Thoratec's HeartMate II Improves Survival in End-Stage Heart Failure Patients," MedPie.com, November 18, 2009, http://www.medpie.com/health-technology/in-the-news/thoratecs-heart mate-ii-improves-survival-in-end-stage-heart-failure-patients.html.

3. Brendan Nyhan, "Why the 'Death Panel' Myth Wouldn't Die: Misinformation in the Health Care Reform Debate," *Forum*, vol. 8, no. 1, Article 5, 2010, 10, http://www-personal.umich.edu/~bnyhan/health -care-misinformation.pdf.

4. Paul Krugman, "Republican Death Trip," *New York Times*, August 13, 2009, http://www.nytimes.com/2009/08/14/opinion/14krugman.html.

5. Jim Rutenburg and Jackie Calmes, "False 'Death Panel' Rumor Has Some Familiar Roots," *New York Times*, August 13, 2009, http://www .nytimes.com/2009/08/14/health/policy/14panel.html?_r=1.

6. Joseph Ashby, " 'Death Panel' Is Not in the Bill . . . It Already Exists," American Thinker, August 15, 2009, http://www.americanthinker .com/2009/08/death_panel_is_not_in_the_bill.html.

7. Betsy McCaughey, "Ruin Your Health With the Obama Stimulus Plan," Bloomberg, February 9, 2009, http://www.bloomberg.com/apps/ news?pid=newsarchive&refer=columnist_mccaughey&sid=aLzfDxfb whzs.

8. Federal Coordinating Council for Comparative Effectiveness Research Membership, "Recovery Act Allocates $1.1 Billion for Comparative Effectiveness Research," U.S. Department of Health and Human Services, http://www.hhs.gov/recovery/programs/os/cerbios.html.

9. Betsy McCaughey, "Obama's Health Rationer-in-Chief," Wall Street Journal, August 27, 2009, http://online.wsj.com/article/SB100014240529 70203706604574374463280098676.html.

10. Ashby, " 'Death Panel' Is Not in the Bill . . . It Already Exists."

11. Editorial, "Obama's Health Future," Wall Street Journal, June 29, 2009, http://online.wsj.com/article/SB124597492337757443.html.

12. Conn Carroll, "Morning Bell: The Rationer-in-Chief," Heritage Foundation, July 7, 2010, http://blog.heritage.org/2010/07/07/morning -bell-the-rationer-in-chief/.

13. Ibid.

14. Charles Riley and Jeff Simon, "Democrats Dominated Speaking Time at Health Care Summit," CNN, February 25, 2010, http://political ticker.blogs.cnn.com/2010/02/25/democrats-dominated-speaking-time -at-health-care-summit/.

15. Paul D. Ryan, "Dissecting the Real Cost of ObamaCare," Remarks at President Obama's Blair House Summit on Health Care, February 25, 2010, Wall Street Journal, March 4, 2010, http://online.wsj.com/article/ SB10001424052748703807904575097394068626652.html.

16. Mark Steyn, "Obamacare Worth the Price to Democrats," Orange County Register, March 5, 2010, http://www.ocregister.com/articles/ health-237719-care-government.html.

17. Dean Clancy, "Five Reasons Why Repealing Obamacare Will Not Increase the Deficit," FoxNews.com, January 7, 2011, http://www .foxnews.com/opinion/2011/01/07/reasons-repealing-obamacare-increase -deficit/.

18. Michele Bachmann, "A Bill to Repeal the Patient Protection and Affordable Care Act," PhotoBucket.com, March 22, 2010, http://i306

.photobucket.com/albums/nn271/repmichelebachmann/Misc/Repeal HealthCareBill.jpg.

19. Michele Bachmann, "Legislation Introduced to Repeal Obamacare," Tipsheet, Townhall.com, March 22, 2010, http://townhall.com/tipsheet/MicheleBachmann/2010/03/22/legislation_introduced_to_repeal_obamacare.

20. Newsmax staff, "Krugman Smears 'Death Panel' Critics," Newsmax.com, November 14, 2010, http://www.newsmax.com/InsideCover/krugman-death-panels-palin/2010/11/14/id/377013?s=al&promo_code=BIDA-1.

21. Newsmax staff, "Krugman: Death Panels, VAT Will Fix Debt Crisis," Newsmax.com, November 14, 2010, http://www.newsmax.com/InsideCover/krugman-death-panels-vat/2010/11/14/id/377008?s=al&promo_code=B1AB-1.

22. Michael Hirsh, "Feldstein, Krugman Agree: Another War Would Help," *National Journal*, October 6, 2010, http://nationaljournal.com/njonline/ec_20101005_5357.php.

23. Paul Krugman and Robin Wells, "The Making of Modern Macroeconomics," in *Economics,* uncorrected preliminary edition (New York: Worth, 2009), 421.

24. Barack Obama, "Remarks by President Obama and President Lee Myung-Bak of the Republic of Korea in Joint Press Availability," White House, June 16, 2009, http://www.whitehouse.gov/the-press-office/remarks-president-obama-and-president-lee-republic-korea-joint-press-availability.

25. Barack Obama, "Transcript of the President's Answer to Harry Smith's Question on Iran," CBS News, June 19, 2009, http://www.whitehouse.gov/the-press-office/transcript-presidents-answer-harry-smiths-question-iran-cbs-6-19-09.

26. Barack Obama, "The President's Opening Remarks on Iran, with Persian Translation," White House Press Conference, June 23, 2009, http://www.whitehouse.gov/blog/2009/06/23/presidents-opening-remarks-iran-with-persian-translation.

10. KEEP THE FAITH

1. Dennis Prager, "Q & A at University of Denver," transcribed and abridged from embedded video, http://www.youtube.com/watch?v=XNUc8nuo7HI.

2. Ibid.

3. Ibid.

4. Abraham Lincoln, *Collected Works of Abraham Lincoln*, vol. 5 (New Brunswick, NJ: Rutgers University Press, 1953), 537.

5. Ronald Reagan, *Speaking My Mind: Selected Speeches* (New York: Simon & Schuster, 2004), 164.

6. Ecclesiastes 3:1,8 (New Jerusalem Bible), http://www.catholic.org/bible/.

7. William J. Federer, *America's God and Country: Encyclopedia of Quotations* (St. Louis: Amerisearch, 2000), 641–42.

8. Chuck Baldwin, "Resurrecting the Black Regiment," *New American*, September 4, 2009, http://www.thenewamerican.com/index.php/history/american/1789.

9. Benjamin Cutter and William Richard Cutter, *History of the Town of Arlington, Massachusetts* (Boston: David Clapp & Son, 1880), 63, viewed at http://books.google.com/.

10. Baldwin, "Resurrecting the Black Regiment"; Frank Leslie, *Frank Leslie's Pleasant Hours*, vol. 23 (New York: Frank Leslie, 1878), 328–30, viewed at http://books.google.com/; "James Caldwell: 'The Fighting Chaplain,' " *Leben: A Journal of Reformation Life*, November 17, 2010, http://www.leben.us/index.php/component/content/article/62-volume-4-issue-2/254-james-caldwell-the-fighting-chaplain.

11. Charles Francis Adams, ed., *The Works of John Adams, Second President Of The United States*, vol. 10 (Boston: Little, Brown, 1856), 45–46, viewed at http://books.google.com/.

12. Leviticus 25:10 (New Jerusalem Bible), http://www.catholic.org/bible/.

13. Luke 4:18–19 (New Jerusalem Bible), http://www.catholic.org/bible/.

14. Thomas Jefferson, "Query 17: Religion," *Notes on the State of Virginia*, 1782, 285, http://etext.virginia.edu/etcbin/toccer-new2?id=JefVirg.sgm&images=images/modeng&data=/texts/english/modeng/parsed&tag=public&part=17&division=div1.

15. Situation Room, program transcript section on Senate health care debate, CNN, December 23, 2009, http://archives.cnn.com/TRANSCRIPTS/0912/23/sitroom.01.html.

16. Amanda Carpenter, "Obama More Pro-Choice Than NARAL," *Human Events*, December 26, 2006, http://www.humanevents.com/article.php?id=18647.

17. Keith Fournier, "Bishop Samuel J. Aquila Rebukes Notre Dame President and Board," Catholic Online, April 9, 2009, http://www .catholic.org/politics/story.php?id=33085&wf=rsscol.

18. Andy Birkey, "IRS Postpones Case Against Pastor Who Endorsed McCain," Minnesota Independent, July 29, 2009, http://minnesotain dependent.com/40543/irs-postpones-case-against-pastor-who-endorsed -mccain.

19. Cal Thomas, "Bullying the Pulpit Distracts Faithful," Washington Examiner, October 3, 2008, http://washingtonexaminer.com/node/ 192046.

20. Steve Karnowski, Associated Press, "IRS Drops Inquiry Into Minnesota Church," Minneapolis–St. Paul Star Tribune, July 29, 2009, http://www.ecfa.org/Content/IRS-Drops-Investigation-of-Minnesota -Pastor-EP-News.

21. Todd Starnes, "Students Allegedly Ordered to Stop Praying Outside Supreme Court Building," FoxNews.com, July 15, 2010, http://www .foxnews.com/us/2010/07/15/students-ordered-stop-praying-outside -supreme-court-building/.

22. Michele Ruiz, "FEMA Apologizes to Volunteers over T-Shirt Flap," AOLNews, May 19, 2010, http://www.aolnews.com/nation/article/ fema-apologizes-to-volunteers-over-t-shirt-flap/19483615; Rob Port, "FEMA Worker Asks Disaster Volunteers To Take Off Their Salvation Army T-Shirts," SayAnythingBlog.com, May 19, 2010, http:// sayanythingblog.com/entry/fema-worker-asks-disaster-volunteers-to -take-off-their-salvation-army-t-shirts/.

23. Senator Jim DeMint, "DeMint CVC Amendment Accepted," July 7, 2009, http://demint.senate.gov/public/index.cfm?p=JimsBlog&Content Record_id=55ab8fdc-d8be-2353-d25b-9926959083ad&ContentType_ id=bf0907bb-57a8-4718-a10a-b2601f161302&Group_id=4cb9fcda-3270 -432c-a83f-bc5b9bd50258; Rick Tyler, "Capitol Visitor Center Report: Reconstructing American History," Renewing American Leadership, December 12, 2008, http://www.torenewamerica.com/images/stories/ pdf/Reconstructing%20American%20History.pdf.

24. Thomas Jefferson, "Jefferson's Letter to the Danbury Baptists: The Final Letter, as Sent," January 1, 1802, Library of Congress, http://www .loc.gov/loc/lcib/9806/danpre.html.

25. Matthew 6:3–4 (New Jerusalem Bible), http://www.catholic.org/bible/.

26. Arthur C. Brooks, "Conservatives Have Answered Obama's Call," *Wall Street Journal*, January 22, 2009, http://www.aei.org/article/29242.

27. George Will, "Conservatives Really Are More Compassionate," Town hall.com, March 27, 2008, http://finance.townhall.com/columnists/ GeorgeWill/2008/03/27/conservatives_really_are_more_compassionate ?page=full&comments=true.

28. Kristen M. Daum, "Hennen's Abrupt Departure Remains a Mystery," *Grand Forks Herald*, September 10, 2010, http://www.grandforksherald .com/event/article/id/175019/.

29. 1 Peter 5:7 (New Jerusalem Bible), http://www.catholic.org/bible/.

30. Paul Kengor, *God and Ronald Reagan: A Spiritual Life* (New York: HarperCollins, 2005), 158.

31. Becky Norton Dunlop, "A Leader to Believe In," Heritage Foundation, June 7, 2004, http://www.heritage.org/Research/Commentary/2004/06/ A-Leader-to-Believe-In.

EPILOGUE: A CALL A DAY

1. Washington Partners, LLC, "New Members of Congress," 2006, http:// www.nekia.org/files/New_Members_110th_Congress.pdf.

2. Ray Raphael, "Are U.S. History Textbooks Still Full of Lies and Half-Truths?," History News Network, September 20, 2004, http://hnn.us/ articles/7219.html.

3. Bill O'Reilly, "Talking Points: The Tea Party and Extremism," FoxNews.com, February 17, 2010, http://www.foxnews.com/story/ 0,2933,586325,00.html.

4. Paul Krugman, "Going to Extreme," *New York Times*, May 16, 2010, http://www.nytimes.com/2010/05/17/opinion/17krugman.html.

5. Patrik Jonsson, "Does 'Tea Party' Populism Verge Into Extremism?," *Christian Science Monitor*, February 17, 2010, http://www.csmonitor .com/USA/Politics/2010/0217/Does-tea-party-populism-verge-into -extremism.

6. Randy Ludlow, "Checks on 'Joe' More Expensive Than First Acknowledged," *Columbus Dispatch*, October 29, 2008, http://www.dis patch.com/live/content/local_news/stories/2008/10/29/joe30.html?sid= 101.

7. Randy Ludlow, "Former Police Association Contractor Charged with Snooping on 'Joe the Plumber,' " *Columbus Dispatch*, October 14, 2009,

http://www.dispatch.com/live/content/local_news/stories/2009/10/14/
plumber.html?sid=101.

8. Naked Emperor News, "Exclusive Audio: Militant Anti-Tea Party National Socialist Strategy Session Calling for Head-Cracking Revolution," TheBlaze, November 16, 2010, transcribed and abridged from embedded video, http://www.theblaze.com/stories/exclusive-audio -militant-anti-tea-party-national-socialist-strategy-session-calling-for -head-cracking-revolution/.

10. Andrew Napolitano, *Lies the Government Told You: Myth, Power, and Deception in American History* (Nashville, TN: Thomas Nelson, 2010), 316.

11. "Funny Business in Minnesota," editorial, *Wall Street Journal*, January 5, 2009, A12.

12. Ed Barnes, "Felons Voting Illegally May Have Put Franken Over the Top in Minnesota, Study Finds," FoxNews.com, July 12, 2010, http://www.foxnews.com/politics/2010/07/12/felons-voting-illegally-franken -minnesota-study-finds/.

13. Selim H. Peabody, ed., *American Patriotism: Speeches, Letters and Papers Illustrating the Foundation, Development and Preservation of the U.S.A.* (1881; reprint Whitefish, MT: Kessinger, 2005), 32.

INDEX